PEOPLE, MARKETS, G(

ECONOMIES AND SOCIETIES

Volume 8

C000077117

Almshouses in
Early Modern England

PEOPLE, MARKETS, GOODS:
ECONOMIES AND SOCIETIES IN HISTORY

ISSN: 2051-7467

Series editors
Barry Doyle – University of Huddersfield
Nigel Goose – University of Hertfordshire
Steve Hindle – The Huntington Library
Jane Humphries – University of Oxford
Willem M. Jongman – University of Groningen

The interactions of economy and society, people and goods, transactions and actions are at the root of most human behaviours. Economic and social historians are participants in the same conversation about how markets have developed historically and how they have been constituted by economic actors and agencies in various social, institutional and geographical contexts. New debates now underpin much research in economic and social, cultural, demographic, urban and political history. Their themes have enduring resonance – financial stability and instability, the costs of health and welfare, the implications of poverty and riches, flows of trade and the centrality of communications. This paperback series aims to attract historians interested in economics and economists with an interest in history by publishing high quality, cutting edge academic research in the broad field of economic and social history from the late medieval/early modern period to the present day. It encourages the interaction of qualitative and quantitative methods through both excellent monographs and collections offering path-breaking overviews of key research concerns. Taking as its benchmark international relevance and excellence it is open to scholars and subjects of any geographical areas from the case study to the multi-nation comparison.

PREVIOUSLY PUBLISHED TITLES IN THE SERIES ARE
LISTED AT THE END OF THE VOLUME

Almshouses in
Early Modern England

Charitable Housing in the
Mixed Economy of Welfare, 1550–1725

Angela Nicholls

THE BOYDELL PRESS

© Angela Nicholls 2017

All Rights Reserved. Except as permitted under current legislation
no part of this work may be photocopied, stored in a retrieval system,
published, performed in public, adapted, broadcast,
transmitted, recorded or reproduced in any form or by any means,
without the prior permission of the copyright owner

The right of Angela Nicholls to be identified as
the author of this work has been asserted in accordance with
sections 77 and 78 of the Copyright, Designs and Patents Act 1988

First published 2017
The Boydell Press, Woodbridge

ISBN 978-1-78327-178-8

The Boydell Press is an imprint of Boydell & Brewer Ltd
PO Box 9, Woodbridge, Suffolk IP12 3DF, UK
and of Boydell & Brewer Inc.
668 Mt Hope Avenue, Rochester, NY 14620–2731, USA
website: www.boydellandbrewer.com

A catalogue record for this book is available
from the British Library

The publisher has no responsibility for the continued existence or accuracy of URLs for
external or third-party internet websites referred to in this book, and does not guarantee
that any content on such websites is, or will remain, accurate or appropriate.

Typeset by BBR, Sheffield

Contents

List of Illustrations   vii
List of Tables   ix
Acknowledgements   x
List of Abbreviations   xii

Prologue   I

Introduction   3

1. Housing Policy   20

2. Chronology and Distribution of Almshouse Foundations   37

3. Almshouse Founders and Their Motivations   56
   Who were the donors?   57
   The role of religion   61
   Memorialisation   67
   Status, reputation and responsibility   71
   Religious identity   81
   Order and good governance – the Commonwealth and the
       Anglican Restoration   86
   Conclusion   89

4. Almshouse Residents and the Experience of Almshouse Life   90
   Rules of eligibility   91
   Age   103
   Gender   111
   Poverty   117
   Rules of behaviour   126
   Conclusion   136

5. The Material Benefits of an Almshouse Place   138
   Accommodation   139
   Stipends and material benefits   157

        The standard of living of almshouse residents   171
        Conclusion   184

6. Case Study: A Seventeenth-Century Welfare Republic – the Parish
        of Leamington Hastings and its Almshouse   188
        The founding of the almshouse   191
        Gaining control of the almshouse   195
        How the parish used the almshouse   199
        Who were the almspeople?   200
        The parish elite   207
        The Poors Plot Charity   210
        Parish housing   216
        Conclusion   221

Conclusion   224

Appendix 1: Almshouse Foundations by County, 1550–1870   237
Appendix 2: Size of Almshouses in Eight English Counties,
        1550–1725   239
Appendix 3: Almshouse Numbers and Places in Three Counties,
        1550–1800   240
Appendix 4: Minimum Subsistence Budget in 1690s Adjusted for
        Inflation   241

Bibliography   242
Index   261

Online Appendices

Appendix A: Almshouse Foundations in County Durham,
        Warwickshire and Kent   http://boybrew.co/2fgqQU5
Appendix B: Almshouse Foundations by Decade in Eight Counties,
        1550–1800   http://boybrew.co/2fjbuwk
Appendix C: Almshouse Stipends by Decade in Six Counties,
        1550–1700   http://boybrew.co/2eiEZvD

Illustrations

0.1 England, showing position of Durham, Warwickshire and Kent   16

2.1 Almshouse foundations by decade   43

2.2 Almshouse foundations by decade for eight counties   45

2.3 Annual amounts raised by poor rates per head of population   50

2.4 Warwickshire almshouse locations and hearth tax exemption   52

3.1 Plaque on John Waldron's almshouse, Tiverton, Devon
(photo: Angela Nicholls)   68

3.2 Gateway to Abbot's Hospital, Guildford High Street
(photo: Angela Nicholls)   69

3.3 Hare Almshouses (1603) at the gates of Stow Hall, Stow
Bardolph, Norfolk (photo: Angela Nicholls)   76

4.1 Great Linford almshouses and school house (1696), Milton
Keynes (photo: Angela Nicholls)   96

5.1 Chimney inserted inside hall at St Mary's Chichester
(photo: Angela Nicholls)   141

5.2 John Langstafe's plan of the Palace Green almshouses, Durham,
showing internal doors and no staircases   142

5.3 John and Ann Smith's almshouses at Longport, Canterbury
(photo: Angela Nicholls)   145

5.4 Almshouse stipends, 1550–1700   179

5.5 Almshouse stipends by county, 1550–1700   179

5.6 Almshouse stipends by decade, 1550–1700   179

5.7 Gramer's almshouses, Mancetter, Warwickshire, beside the
    parish church (photo: Angela Nicholls)   185

6.1 Humphrey Davis almshouse, Leamington Hastings
    (photo: Angela Nicholls)   192

7.1 Framlingham Poor House, Suffolk, built in 1729
    (photo: Angela Nicholls)   233

7.2 Sir John Banks's Almshouses, Maidstone
    (photo: Angela Nicholls)   234

Tables

0.1 Almshouse numbers in three counties, 1550–1725   17

2.1 Almshouses and places, 1550–1670   45

2.2 Almshouse places in relation to the elderly population in 1670   48

2.3 Hearth Tax Returns c.1670 for three counties   48

4.1 Age criteria for admission to almshouses, 1550–1725   104

4.2 Age criteria for post-Reformation almshouses only   105

4.3 Age criteria for almshouses founded between 1700 and 1725   107

4.4 Gender of almshouse occupants, 1550–1725   112

4.5 Gender of occupants of surviving pre-Reformation almshouses   112

4.6 Gender of occupants of almshouses founded 1700–1725   112

5.1 Accommodation in almshouses, 1550–1725   150

5.2 Traditional almsman's stipend (1d per day) increased in line with inflation   173

5.3 Budget per annum for single poor person without dependants   177

5.4 Suggested subsistence budget per annum for an almsperson   177

6.1 Expenditure on the poor in Leamington Hastings   215

Acknowledgements

There are very many people who have helped to bring this book into being. My greatest debt is to Steve Hindle, who not only provided the inspiration for the topic through a chance remark many years ago, but who went on to supervise my doctoral research, and has provided me with endless support, encouragement and practical assistance over the years. I feel privileged to have served my apprenticeship with so accomplished a master. I have also been fortunate in the many friends and colleagues, historians and non-historians alike, who make Warwick University a true community of scholars. In particular I am grateful to Beat Kümin, whose help has been immeasurable, and to Bernard Capp and Peter Marshall for their enthusiasm, support and advice. I also appreciate the help I received from the many historians who took the trouble to talk to me at an early stage of my research, and those who shared information with me when I had nothing myself to contribute. In particular, I want to thank Matthew Alexander, Ian Archer, Jeremy Boulton, John Broad, Gillian Crosby, Gillian Draper, Adrian Green, Margaret Harvey and Miri Rubin. I am especially grateful to Marjorie McIntosh for her interest and her generosity in giving me access to her data compiled over a lifetime's research.

I considered myself lucky to stumble across the Family and Community Historical Research Society's Almshouse Project while it was still ongoing, discovering so many people who shared my obsession with almshouses. My thanks are due to Nigel Goose and Anne Langley who led the project, and to Helen Caffrey, Sylvia Pinches, Jackie Grant, Christine Seal and the many other researchers who were happy to share with me their findings. While conducting my own research I was grateful to receive financial help from the Economic History Society, and assistance from many archivists and librarians who offered suggestions and local knowledge. Often they were valiantly providing a professional service against a background of demoralising cuts and closures.

I am extremely grateful for the patience and forbearance of my friends and family who have put up with my preoccupation for longer than is reasonable, and even pretended a kindly interest at times. I want to thank Dave Steele for his help with the photographs and maps; my sister Helen Donald for her encouragement and exemplary proofreading; and my daughter Tessa Nicholls for her practical support and help with the maths, as well as for her calm detachment and good sense.

Lastly, my oldest debts of gratitude are to my mother, Afril Donald, who first taught me to look around and be curious about what I saw; and to Judith Penrose and Professor H. S. Offler, two inspirational teachers of history. This book is dedicated to the memory of these three.

Abbreviations

CCA	Canterbury Cathedral Archives
CHC	Coventry History Centre
CKS	Kent History and Library Centre, Maidstone (formerly the Centre for Kentish Studies)
DCL	Durham Cathedral Library
DRO	Durham County Record Office
DULSC	Durham University Library Special Collections
FACHRS	Family and Community Historical Research Society
HCPP	House of Commons Parliamentary Papers
LRO	Lichfield Record Office
MALSC	Medway Archives and Local Studies Centre, Strood
NRO	Northumberland Record Office, Woodhorn
ODNB	*Oxford Dictionary of National Biography*
SANT	Society of Antiquaries of Newcastle upon Tyne
SBT	Shakespeare Birthplace Trust Record Office, Stratford-upon-Avon
TNA	The National Archives, Kew
WQS	Warwick Quarter Sessions (*Warwick County Records*, vols 1–7, ed. S. C. Ratcliff and H. C. Johnson; vol. 8, ed. H. C. Johnson; vol. 9, ed H. C. Johnson and N. J. Williams (Warwick, 1935–64))
WRO	Warwickshire County Record Office, Warwick

A Note on Pre-Decimal Currency

Pre-decimal currency is denoted in pounds, shillings and pence (£ s d), in which £1 (one pound sterling) = 20s (twenty shillings), and 1s (one shilling) = 12d (twelve pence).

Prologue

In the small Warwickshire village of Leamington Hastings stands an attractive seventeenth-century stone building with the following inscription:

> Humphry Davies Gent Fownder of this Almeshowse dyed aboute the 28th of December Anno Domini 1607 and gave his lands in Lemmington Burdinbury Marton and Ethorpe for the mainetenance of the said Almeshowse and eight poore people to be placed there for ever, which landes were deteyned from the said Almeshowse by the space of sixe and twentie yeares and were this present yeare 1633 by the helpe and assistance of Sir Thomas Trevor Knight one of his Ma[jes]ties Barons of the Exchequer and Lord of the Mannor of Lemmington aforesaid recovered for the said almeshowses at the prosecution of Mathew Over and Richard Walton John Mason and John Clerke & for the good of the poore of Lemmington aforesaid: Anno 1633.

The narrative conveyed in this lengthy inscription raises many questions, not least who was the benefactor Humphrey Davis (or Davies)? Why did he found this almshouse; who were the poor people who lived in it; and what benefits might they have received? One might also ask: who were the five men named as rescuing the almshouse and why did they become involved in the way that they did?

Almshouses like this one and others, some very much older, are a feature of many towns and villages across England. They are curious institutions, built by the rich to be lived in by the poor, tangible representations of philanthropy, and a visible demonstration of historic attitudes towards the poor. They have a long history: the oldest recorded almshouses pre-date the Conquest, with almshouses continuing to be founded through the centuries up to the present day.[1] The period after the Reformation and into the early years of the eighteenth century, in particular, saw a remarkable number of almshouses founded, as people from many different backgrounds used new wealth to revive and remodel an ancient form of provision to meet new

---

1 There are 1,700 almshouse charities in existence today, housing approximately 35,000 people: Almshouse Association website, http://www.almshouses.org (accessed 5 March 2016).

needs and aspirations. Post-Reformation almshouses are often considered to have been places of privilege for the respectable deserving poor, operating outside the structure of parish poor relief to which ordinary poor people were subjected, and doing little to assist the poorest and most needy. Yet in the early modern period, private charity was still a significant element in the relief of the poor, and many almshouses, like this one, played an important role in their local communities. This book explores the nature and extent of almshouse provision in early modern England within the context of overall approaches to the poor, and examines the contribution made by this form of charity within the developing welfare systems of the time.

Introduction

Almshouse: a house founded by charity, offering
accommodation for poor people.[1]

There is a very considerable body of research into the nature and scale of poverty in early modern society, and the responses to need which this prompted.[2] More recently, historians have been interested in the *experience* of poverty, in the lives of the poor themselves; in particular, how poor people managed, to use Olwen Hufton's evocative phrase, in an 'economy of makeshifts', and how they negotiated their way through local welfare and charity systems.[3] Nonetheless, poor people's housing seems to have remained a 'known unknown' until very recently.[4] Little evidence survives to indicate the material lives of poor people in general, and their living conditions and accommodation in particular. Few examples of poor people's housing have

1   Oxford English Dictionary, http://www.oxforddictionaries.com/definition/english/almshouse
?q=almshouse (accessed 17 October 2013).
2   To pick out only the most prominent examples: E. M. Leonard, *The Early History of English Poor Relief* (Cambridge, 1900); S. Webb and B. Webb, *English Local Government*, vol. 7: *English Poor Law History, Part I: The Old Poor Law* (London, 1927); P. Slack, ed., *Poverty in Early-Stuart Salisbury* (Devizes, 1975); P. Slack, *Poverty and Policy in Tudor and Stuart England* (London, 1988); S. Hindle, *On the Parish? The Micro-Politics of Poor Relief in Rural England c.1550–1750* (Oxford, 2004); M. K. McIntosh, *Poor Relief in England 1350–1600* (Cambridge, 2012).
3   O. Hufton, *The Poor of Eighteenth-Century France, 1750–1789* (Oxford, 1974); T. Hitchcock, P. King and P. Sharpe, eds, *Chronicling Poverty: The Voices and Strategies of the English Poor, 1640–1840* (Basingstoke, 1997); S. King and A. Tomkins, eds, *The Poor in England 1700–1850: An Economy of Makeshifts* (Manchester, 2003); T. Hitchcock, *Down and Out in Eighteenth-Century London* (London, 2004); S. Hindle, '"Without the cry of any neighbours": A Cumbrian Family and the Poor Law Authorities, c.1690–1730', *The Family in Early Modern England*, ed. H. Berry and E. Foyster (Cambridge, 2007), pp. 126–57; J. Healey, *The First Century of Welfare: Poverty and Poor Relief in Lancashire 1620–1730* (Woodbridge, 2014).
4   A recent collection of essays, *Accommodating Poverty*, conceived as a 'successor volume' to *Chronicling Poverty*, has attempted to address this omission. It includes chapters on rents and lodgings in London, poor people's dwellings in England and the colonies, parish housing, a parish workhouse, and a single contribution covering almshouses: J. McEwan and P. Sharpe, eds, *Accommodating Poverty: The Housing and Living Arrangements of the English Poor, c.1600–1850* (Basingstoke, 2011).

survived, and there are scarcely any contemporary descriptions or pictorial representations before the late eighteenth century. Until then, moreover, even commentators on the state of the poor rarely mentioned their houses.[5] Yet housing was a basic need and contemporary settlement disputes and habitation orders, together with the many prohibitions on the construction and subdivision of accommodation in a period of rising population, suggest that housing for the poor was, in fact, a major and contested issue in early modern England.[6]

The invisibility of poor people's housing, in the historical literature as much as in the landscape, is at odds with its importance. Apart from its significance in the material culture of the poor, housing is much more than a matter of the roof over one's head. It is a fixed place, locating the occupants in geographical and social space; providing a stake in the local community, or excluding the occupants on the margins; giving individuals and families a stage on which to play the role of householder, parent, or dependant; and confirming the occupants' status, or lack of it, within the local hierarchy. Providing housing for the poor is therefore not just about physical shelter, but is freighted with meaning. The most well-known and documented examples of houses for the poor in the early modern period are almshouses, yet they are not often considered integral to discussions of poor relief or poor people's housing. There are thus two main strands to the relevant historiography: that of poor relief, in which almshouses do not generally figure prominently; and that of almshouses, in which the historical context is sometimes lacking or only superficially addressed. It has been argued that historians should adopt a 'holistic approach to understanding the Old Poor Law', on the basis that charitable funds and statutory provision combined in practice to assist the poor in the early modern period, with parish poor relief the last resort until the late eighteenth century.[7] This book accordingly adopts an integrated approach, examining the place of almshouses within the early modern welfare economy: why they were founded, who they helped, what they provided, and how important they were as institutions of relief.

The extent of poverty in early modern England, and the concern it caused contemporaries, is well known, and the ways in which early modern society responded has provided a rich field for historians. Poverty was not a new

5   S. Lloyd, 'Cottage Conversations: Poverty and Manly Independence in Eighteenth-Century England', *Past and Present* 184 (2004), 69–108.
6   A. L. Beier, 'The Social Problems of an Elizabethan Country Town: Warwick, 1580–90', *Country Towns in Pre-Industrial England*, ed. P. Clark (Leicester, 1981), pp. 46–79; J. Broad, 'Housing the Rural Poor in Southern England, 1650–1850', *The Agricultural History Review* 48/2 (2000), 151–70; W. C. Baer, 'Housing the Poor and Mechanick Class in Seventeenth-Century London', *The London Journal* 25/2 (2000), 13–39.
7   J. Broad, 'Parish Economies of Welfare, 1650–1834', *The Historical Journal* 42/4 (1999), 985–1006 (pp. 985–7).

phenomenon in early modern times. There had always been an obligation on Christians to relieve the poor, and historians of the late medieval period have shown that this was not just a responsibility met by the church, but also by individuals and communities.[8] The early modern period, however, was characterised by an increase in the scale and extent of poverty, and increasing anxiety about how to deal with it as traditional responses proved ineffectual. The late medieval and early Tudor distinction between the deserving and undeserving poor, between the impotent and the idle, became complicated by the recognition of a third category created by demographic and economic changes – the labouring poor: those willing to work but unable to earn enough to sustain themselves and their families. The changing nature and extent of the problem resulted in a gradual move away from purely philanthropic and ad hoc individual and communal responses to a more systematised, bureaucratic response through statutory poor relief administered by the parish. The detail, extent and pace of these changes are discussed in an extensive literature.[9]

McIntosh, for instance, emphasises the early origins of many examples of local attempts at organised poor relief. She is clear, however, that the position in 1600 was undoubtedly very different from 1500, and argues that the reign of Edward VI was the critical period of change.[10] Slack detected a slow but inexorable shift from old forms of indiscriminate charity towards a more organised regime of endowed charity and public welfare.[11] In particular, the contribution made by parish poor relief undoubtedly rose during the seventeenth century. Tim Wales and others demonstrate that the amounts of poor relief being paid out under the Poor Law were mostly insufficient to sustain life on their own, clarifying the residual and supportive rather than central role of relief in the economic lives of the poor. Yet he also shows that in the Norfolk villages he studied, relief was likely to increase to become the sole source of income for a few people in the last years of their lives, and that the overall amounts of poor relief administered by these parishes had increased significantly in real terms by the end of the seventeenth century.[12]

---

8 E. Clark, 'Social Welfare and Mutual Aid in the Medieval Countryside', *Journal of British Studies* 33 (1994), 381–406; P. Horden, 'Small Beer? The Parish and the Poor and Sick in Later Medieval England', *The Parish in Late Medieval England*, ed. C. Burgess and E. Duffy (Donington, 2006), pp. 339–64; McIntosh, *Poor Relief in England*.

9 The key text is Slack, *Poverty and Policy*, but see also McIntosh, *Poor Relief in England*, for the early period; Hindle, *On the Parish?* for rural England; and S. King, *Poverty and Welfare in England 1700–1850: A Regional Perspective* (Manchester, 2000), which proposes that a regional division in approach and expectation had emerged by the eighteenth century.

10 McIntosh, *Poor Relief in England*, pp. 130–2.

11 Slack, *Poverty and Policy*, pp. 168–9.

12 T. Wales, 'Poverty, Poor Relief and the Life-Cycle: Some Evidence from Seventeenth-Century Norfolk', *Land, Kinship and Life-Cycle*, ed. R. M. Smith (Cambridge, 1984), pp. 351–404. Richard Smith also found that parish pensions, supplementing wages, increased with advancing age: R. M. Smith, 'Ageing and Well-Being in Early Modern England: Pension

The role of accommodation in the system of poor relief developing alongside private charity has until recently been a neglected area of research. The Tudor poor laws encouraged parishes to make provision for housing poor impotent people, and the many references in overseers' accounts and quarter sessions records to rent payments and habitation orders demonstrate how far this was implemented.[13] Although not a great deal is known about the kind of housing that was actually provided, John Broad has highlighted the extent of parish provision, and demonstrated the importance that was attached to housing for poor people.[14] He argues that in the seventeenth and eighteenth centuries ordinary people upheld the right of poor families to a home of their own, even after workhouses were becoming common and despite the desire of parish elites to exercise control over the underemployed poor. Although focused on the later period and not discussing the origins of parish housing, Broad includes at least one example which went back to a charitable bequest to the parish in the fifteenth century.[15] Many parishes had church houses from before the Reformation, which had been used to house priests or hold church ales, some of which later became used to house paupers.[16] Others acquired or had houses bequeathed to them for this use, sometimes referred to as parish almshouses, indicating the breadth of this spectrum of provision.[17]

The Oxford English Dictionary definition of an almshouse is 'a house founded by charity, offering accommodation for the poor'. The medieval term was more commonly 'hospital' (denoting hospitality), with 'almshouse' being little used before the fourteenth century.[18] Other medieval terms included 'God's House', *Domus Dei*, *maison dieu*, 'spital' or 'spittle house', 'bede

Trends and Gender Preferences Under the English Old Poor Law c.1650–1800', *Old Age from Antiquity to Post-Modernity*, ed. P. Johnson and P. Thane (London and New York, 1998), pp. 64–95 (pp. 78–9). Lynn Botelho, however, suggests from her material that there was discrimination against older people in the seventeenth century, receiving less in poor relief than younger people: L. A. Botelho, *Old Age and the English Poor Law, 1500–1700* (Woodbridge, 2004), pp. 111–12.

13 D. Marshall, *The English Poor in the Eighteenth Century: A Study in Social and Administrative History* (London, 1926), pp. 107–11; S. Hindle, *The Birthpangs of Welfare: Poor Relief and Parish Governance in Seventeenth-Century Warwickshire*, Dugdale Society Occasional Paper 40 (Stratford-upon-Avon, 2000); Hindle, *On the Parish?*

14 Broad, 'Housing'; J. Broad, 'The Parish Poor House in the Long Eighteenth Century', *Accommodating Poverty*, ed. McEwan and Sharpe, pp. 246–62. For a discussion of the accommodation provided in parish housing in rural Warwickshire from documentary evidence, see A. Nicholls, '"A convenient habitation fit for Christians to dwell in": Parish Housing for the Poor in Seventeenth-Century Rural Warwickshire', *Warwickshire History* 16/4 (2015/16), 156–69.

15 Broad, 'Housing', p. 163.

16 P. Cowley, *The Church Houses* (London, 1970); E. H. D. Williams, 'Church Houses in Somerset', *Vernacular Architecture* 23 (1992), 15–23.

17 McIntosh, *Poor Relief in England*, pp. 91, 111.

18 B. Howson, *Almshouses: A Social and Architectural History* (Stroud, 2008), p. 14. The restriction of the term hospital to an institution providing health care and treatment for those

house', 'college', or even, in a formulation unique to Lincolnshire, 'callis' (thought to derive from the Staple of Calais). Marjorie McIntosh and others draw a distinction between the functions of almshouses and hospitals in late medieval times. McIntosh describes hospitals as offering 'accommodation and simple bedside care' to the bedridden, sick and old, as distinct from almshouses which 'usually served the elderly poor, providing permanent free housing and sometimes food, clothing, fuel, or a weekly cash stipend'. However, as she recognises, 'neither category was clearly defined'.[19] Although McIntosh continues to distinguish these two types of institution in her discussion of late-sixteenth-century foundations, by this stage the distinction barely existed. In the early modern period the terms 'almshouse' and 'hospital' were used loosely and interchangeably to denote any accommodation that housed people receiving 'alms' or relief. This book adopts the same approach, including within its remit any form of charitable provision that contemporaries called an almshouse or hospital, and using the term 'almshouse' for both.[20] As a consequence, it encompasses a considerable range of accommodation and a variety of types of institution. Some foundations are difficult to distinguish from church or parish housing, particularly those poorer foundations effectively being run by parish elites, and it may be that even this distinction is an artificial one.

Much of the provision which towns and parishes had at their disposal to carry out their functions, such as assisting the poor, had its origin in charitable bequests. Many bequests were subsequently supported in fulfilling their objectives by a multitude of further donations through, for instance, the parish poor box or church rates. The almshouses founded by the guilds and livery companies might be built as a result of a single bequest, or by levies upon the membership in the form of voluntary, or even compulsory, taxation. The pre-Reformation Trinity Almshouses at Deptford, for example, were built and maintained by a compulsory levy on mariners.[21] The introduction of compulsory parish poor rates in the second half of the sixteenth century added yet another source of funding, which in some places was used interchangeably with charitable funds. The result was considerable overlap between private charity and public provision, a distinction itself which, according to McIntosh, would have 'puzzled Elizabethans'.[22] As an example,

with medical conditions only became usual with the development of these institutions during the eighteenth century: D. Owen, *English Philanthropy 1660–1960* (Oxford, 1965), p. 37.

19 McIntosh, *Poor Relief in England*, pp. 7, 61.

20 Hospitals for children, which we would now term orphanages, are included although not specifically addressed.

21 A. A. Ruddock, 'The Trinity House at Deptford in the Sixteenth Century', *English Historical Review* 65/257 (1950), 458–76 (pp. 465–6).

22 M. McIntosh, 'Networks of Care in Elizabethan English Towns: The Example of Hadleigh, Suffolk', *The Locus of Care: Families, Communities, Institutions and the Provision of Welfare in Antiquity*, ed. P. Horden and R. Smith (London, 1998), pp. 71–89 (p. 72).

albeit a particularly complicated one, the eighteen parish almshouses of St Martin-in-the-Fields, London, built between 1683 and 1686, consisted of six separate foundations, some endowed by named individuals, some by anonymous subscribers, and some built by the parish to replace earlier parish almshouses. The stipends for the almswomen derived from three separate sources including the parish rates; while some of the women had their pensions paid to them by the overseers, and others by the churchwardens.[23] In this example, distinguishing between public and private charity would seem singularly fruitless. It is only by including, as this study aims to do, the whole spectrum of almshouse provision, that a true understanding can be reached of how almshouses featured in their local economy of welfare.

There is a growing body of literature on almshouses, and the recent emergence of a lively field of research into almshouse provision. Individual almshouses, particularly those of ancient foundation, have often attracted local interest, and a few celebrated endowments have been covered by a detailed monograph.[24] Several general histories or surveys of almshouses have also been published, mainly focused on foundations with surviving buildings of architectural or aesthetic interest, and tending to the descriptive rather than the analytical with, at times, only a superficial interpretation of the historical context.[25] Some of these general works are arranged chronologically to describe the development of almshouses over time, but only the medieval period has, to date, warranted specific attention.[26] Post-Reformation foundations, despite their ubiquity, have not received similar consideration.

23 J. Boulton, 'The Almshouses and Almswomen of St Martin-in-the-Fields, 1614–1818', paper given at the Almshouses in Europe conference, Haarlem, the Netherlands, 7 September 2011.

24 P. Joyce, *Patronage and Poverty in Merchant Society: The History of Morden College, Blackheath 1695 to the Present* (Henley-on-Thames, 1982); S. Porter, *The London Charterhouse* (Stroud, 2009); N. Goose and L. Moden, *A History of Doughty's Hospital, Norwich, 1687–2009* (Hatfield, 2010). For an outstanding example of a detailed consideration of one period in an almshouse's life, see J. Goodall, *God's House at Ewelme: Life, Devotion and Architecture in a Fifteenth-Century Almshouse* (Aldershot, 2001).

25 See, for instance: W. H. Godfrey, *The English Almshouse, with Some Account of its Predecessor, the Medieval Hospital* (London, 1955); B. Bailey, *Almshouses* (London, 1988); B. Howson, *Houses of Noble Poverty: A History of the English Almshouse* (Sunbury-on-Thames, 1993); A. Hallett, *Almshouses* (Princes Risborough, 2004). Bailey's survey is the best general history, addressing the influence of the Black Death on charitable provision, and early-fifteenth-century attempts at reform. Nigel Goose's more recent contribution provides a brief but helpful overview of almshouses in their historical context: N. Goose, 'The English Almshouse and the Mixed Economy of Welfare: Medieval to Modern', *Local Historian* 40/1 (2010), 3–19.

26 R. M. Clay, *The Medieval Hospitals of England* (London, 1909); E. Prescott, *The English Medieval Hospital 1050–1640* (Melksham, 1992); N. Orme and M. Webster, *The English Hospital 1070–1570* (New Haven and London, 1995), which also includes a detailed study of the medieval hospitals of a single region, south-west England.

Some of the general histories, such as those as old as Clay (1909) and as recent as Bailey (1988), include an impressive amount of detail on the range and diversity of foundations, but are marred by an almost complete absence of footnotes. Clay, moreover, treats the medieval period as a single, undifferentiated time period, albeit one covering many centuries, which results in the loss of any historical frame of reference or sense of progression and development in the founding and running of medieval hospitals.

There are also an increasing number of county or regional surveys, which have the advantage of including most or all known institutions for their locality.[27] Local and regional studies often reveal interesting information on a far wider range of institutions than is generally known to have existed. For instance, Linda Crust's survey of Lincolnshire reveals that there was a large number of very small foundations in that county, often providing accommodation for no more than two, three or four almspeople. She notes, for example, that three dilapidated cottages at Willingham by Stow were called 'almshouses' into the twentieth century, although they had no known endowment; she comments: 'there must be many cases of such 'unofficial' almshouses (usually maintained by the parish) in Lincolnshire villages'.[28] Unendowed charitable foundations and parish or church housing, though less substantial and by their nature less likely to have survived, seem to have been more widespread than has generally been recognised, and may have made a real contribution to the welfare of the poor in early modern England. In which case our modern understanding of almshouses, as foundations with a permanent endowment and independent existence, may be unduly restrictive for the early modern period.[29] Our current knowledge, moreover, is heavily influenced by an emphasis in the literature on the wealthier foundations which are more likely to have surviving buildings and archives. These are not necessarily typical of the genre. The concentration on those establishments with architecturally interesting buildings, arcane rules and surviving documentation has tended to favour elite institutions which do not represent the great majority of almshouse foundations.[30] Howson, for instance, acknowledges the contribution of the many parish fraternities and guilds which ran almshouses

27 For example: E. O. Cockburn, *The Almshouses of Dorset* (Dorchester, 1970); L. Crust, *Lincolnshire Almshouses: Nine Centuries of Charitable Housing* (Sleaford, 2002); H. Caffrey, *Almshouses in the West Riding of Yorkshire 1600–1900* (King's Lynn, 2006); S. Watts, *Shropshire Almshouses* (Woonton Almeley, 2010); C. Smith, *The Almshouses of York* (York, 2010); E. A. Earl, *Nottinghamshire Almshouses, from Early Times to 1919* (self-published, 2011).
28 Crust, *Lincolnshire Almshouses*, pp. 27–44, 46.
29 Patricia Cullum addressed a similar problem in her study of fourteenth- and fifteenth-century *maisons dieu* in Yorkshire: P. Cullum, '"For Pore People Harberles": What Was the Function of the Maisondieu?', *Trade, Devotion and Governance: Papers in Late Medieval History*, ed. D. J. Clayton, R. G. Davies and P. McNiven (Stroud, 1994), pp. 36–54.
30 For a more balanced approach, see Caffrey, *Almshouses*.

as part of their local charitable provision, and their successors, the 'hundreds of small local charities ... scattered throughout the land'; but small local foundations are not those which interest him. By his own admission, his work 'covers mainly the largest and best-documented institutions'.[31]

Much of this literature has focused primarily on the architecture of surviving almshouse buildings.[32] For instance, Elizabeth Prescott used the architecture of medieval hospitals to trace changes and developments in their function, while Sidney Heath conceded that he chose his examples principally for their 'architectural or picturesque qualities'.[33] For many of these establishments, a main purpose of their spectacular buildings appears to have been the memorialisation of the founder; and this function usually takes precedence in the literature over any consideration of the actual accommodation provided for the almspeople. The grand architecture of such institutions, with their halls, chapels, audit rooms and quadrangles, may be interesting in itself, and certainly lends itself to discussion of the use of power and space, but it also gives a distorted portrayal of the generality of almshouses. More typical is the vernacular architecture of the ubiquitous rows of simple cottages which characterise the majority of almshouses, but which make little appearance in the literature. The nineteenth-century antiquarian and architect F. T. Dollman identified four traditional building types associated with medieval almshouses and hospitals, namely: the infirmary hall, with or without attached chapel; cruciform layout; and courtyard.[34] Howson uncritically follows the same categorisation for all almshouses, to the extent of declaring that 'the courtyard form was adopted as the most common type of development for almshouses during the next five hundred years or so'.[35] One has only to look around at the very many surviving almshouse buildings, the majority of which appear to be in the form of simple buildings or rows of cottages, to recognise that this is not true.[36]

Most writers, like Howson, assume that almshouses in all their forms are direct descendants of medieval hospitals.[37] Whether true or not, this may be of little help in understanding the nature of post-medieval hospitals. In the

---

31   Howson, *Almshouses*, pp. 11, 27–8.

32   For example, S. Heath, *Old English Houses of Alms: A Pictorial Record with Architectural and Historical Notes* (London, 1910); Godfrey, *English Almshouse*; Bailey, *Almshouses*; Howson, *Noble Poverty*.

33   Prescott, *English Medieval Hospital*, p. 4; Heath, *Old English Houses*, p. 12.

34   F. T. Dollman, *Examples of Ancient Domestic Architecture: Illustrating the Hospitals, Bede-Houses, Schools, Almshouses, Etc. Of the Middle Ages in England* (London, 1858).

35   Howson, *Noble Poverty*, p. 53.

36   Helen Caffrey's study of West Yorkshire almshouses finds no example of the 'collegiate' style previously assumed to be typical, and describes the simple row as the 'most numerous and enduring form'. Caffrey, *Almshouses*, pp. 21, 27.

37   For instance, Bailey, *Almshouses*, p. 16; Howson, *Noble Poverty*, p. 17; Hallett, *Almshouses*, p. 6; Caffrey, *Almshouses*, p. 8.

late medieval period there was already a considerable variety of foundations providing accommodation for the impotent poor. Some were attached to monastic institutions, or were themselves religious foundations; some were chantries where the almspeople's function was to pray for the soul of the benefactor; but many were entirely secular institutions founded by individuals for defined groups of poor, or by guilds for the benefit of their members. McIntosh, for instance, has discovered that of institutions founded after 1350, only 15% were assigned to monastic houses; increasingly, lay organisations such as town corporations, guilds or groups of lay feoffees, were instead used for administrative oversight.[38] The dissolution of the monasteries, chantries and religious fraternities at the Reformation resulted in the loss of many medieval hospitals. Those that survived were mainly the secular institutions or those which could be refounded in secular form. This discontinuity suggests that the origins of early modern almshouses may more properly lie not with the monastic institutions but with the mainly secular foundations, of which there are many survivors from the fifteenth century. It leaves unexplored other possible precursors in late medieval developments such as guilds and colleges, and also early housing provision by parishes and manors, for which there appear to be fleeting references but little documentation.

The questions also arise of why medieval almshouses survived at all, and why so many new institutions were founded in the early modern period, at a time when the implementation of statutory relief for the poor was becoming solidly embedded in the process of local government. Despite (or because of) contemporary anxieties about a decrease in charitable giving, private charity survived and in many cases flourished after the introduction of compulsory poor rates. Casual doles undoubtedly declined, but endowed charity, in particular, appears to have increased exponentially. W. K. Jordan's monumental works on English philanthropy between 1480 and 1660 reveal the extent of charitable giving in this period.[39] He took as his thesis the change in 'men's aspirations for their own age and for generations yet to come' from primarily religious preoccupations to more modern secular concerns.[40] He regarded almshouses as among those permanent, endowed charitable institutions through which merchant and gentry benefactors attempted to revolutionise the approach to poverty and need, describing them as 'carefully ordered institutions offering sanctuary to the socially and

38 McIntosh, *Poor Relief in England*, pp. 89–92.
39 Jordan recorded all testamentary charitable bequests between 1480 and 1660 in ten English counties, including London and Bristol: W. K. Jordan, *Philanthropy in England 1480–1660: A Study of the Changing Pattern of English Social Aspirations* (London, 1959); W. K. Jordan, *The Charities of London 1480–1660* (London, 1960); W. K. Jordan, *The Charities of Rural England 1480–1660* (London, 1961).
40 Jordan, *Philanthropy*, pp. 15–16.

economically derelict ... applauded by the best and most sensitive men of the era'.[41] Jordan's assumption of increasing secularisation has been the subject of well-worn criticisms.[42] Similarly, his figures for the remarkable increase in secular endowments he claimed for the early years of the seventeenth century have been severely challenged, most particularly for deliberately ignoring the effects of inflation and population growth.[43] But, as Slack points out, endowed charity, if it survives, is cumulative in effect, so it is possible to see a real growth in the seventeenth century in charitable provision such as almshouses.[44] This is relevant to any consideration of the impact of almshouse foundation on welfare provision. Despite the criticisms that have been levelled against Jordan's methodology and figures, it is perhaps surprising that there has been no subsequent attempt to build on his survey of foundations from the early modern period.

There have been relatively few scholarly studies since Jordan which include a comprehensive consideration of early modern almshouses and the role they played in contemporary approaches to the poor. The notable exception is McIntosh's work on poor relief, focusing on the period of transition from medieval to early modern society. Two of her most recent studies devote substantial sections to almshouses and hospitals (although only up to 1600).[45] McIntosh emphasises that they were an integral part of a comprehensive early system of relief. She argues that in those places where they existed, almshouses played a small but significant part in the care of the elderly poor, describing them as 'a touchstone of concern with life-cycle poverty'.[46] Few other historians of poor relief in the period have included almshouses, or have considered them to have made much of a contribution to the genuinely poor and needy.[47]

---

41   Jordan, *Philanthropy*, p. 41.
42   See, for instance, the critique in Hindle, *On the Parish?*, pp. 98–9.
43   For instance, D. C. Coleman, 'Review: W. K. Jordan, Philanthropy in England', *Economic History Review* (series 2) 13 (1960–61), 113–15.
44   Slack, *Poverty and Policy*, p. 163.
45   McIntosh, *Poor Relief in England*, pp. 186–224, and CUP Online Appendices 1 and 2. M. K. McIntosh, *Poor Relief and Community in Hadleigh, Suffolk 1547–1600* (Hatfield, 2013), pp. 175–6, includes mini biographies of twelve late-sixteenth-century residents of Hadleigh's almshouses. See also M. McIntosh, 'Local Responses to the Poor in Late Medieval and Tudor England', *Continuity and Change* 3/2 (1988), 209–45; M. McIntosh, *A Community Transformed: The Manor and Liberty of Havering, 1500–1620* (Cambridge, 1991); McIntosh, 'Networks of care'; M. McIntosh, 'Poverty, Charity and Coercion in Elizabethan England', *Journal of Interdisciplinary History* 35/3 (2005), 457–79.
46   McIntosh, 'Local Responses', p. 221.
47   Boulton and Schwarz, for instance, include a single paragraph on the 55–80 almswomen who occupied the St Martin-in-the-Fields parish almshouses, and state that there was little overlap between them and workhouse occupants: J. Boulton and L. Schwarz, '"The Comforts of a Private Fireside"? The Workhouse, the Elderly and the Poor Law in Georgian Westminster: St Martin-in-the-Fields, 1725–1824', *Accommodating Poverty*, ed. McEwan and Sharpe, pp. 221–45 (p. 235).

Slack's often-cited reference to almspeople as 'respectable, gowned, Trollopian worthies' is typically dismissive.[48] This stems partly from the emphasis, in much of the existing literature, on the wealthier, better-documented foundations whose residents were more likely to exemplify Slack's characteristics, but were not necessarily representative of the generality of almshouse occupants. More recent research identifying a wider range of provision including smaller, poorer almshouses may correct this perception in time. But it is also possible that a measure of unconscious discrimination has influenced the choices of historians in the past, with the deserving poor being considered less interesting than the deviant, respectable independence less valid a topic than incarceration, and old age as unattractive and unrewarding for historians as in life. Lately, the interest by a number of women historians in the study of old age, for example, is a hopeful indication of a shift in focus.[49]

This change is also reflected in a growing attention to the social significance of almshouses, and in the contribution they might have made to the lives of the poor, which is in contrast to the mainly antiquarian perspective of the past. This has led to a new emphasis on almshouse occupants and the experience of almshouse life. Alannah Tomkins, for instance, in one of the few studies of almshouse dwellers between 1650 and 1850, demonstrates the great variation in material benefits that different almshouses provided. She also attempts to understand the 'emotional freight' attached to an almshouse place, why admission should have been considered desirable despite the sometimes meagre material benefits received.[50] Similarly the Family and Community Historical Research Society's Almshouse Project, set up in 2007, is an example of the new interest in almshouses and their social significance.[51] Helen Caffrey's contribution on almshouse buildings, for instance, not only records differences in form and function but also attempts to understand the meaning conveyed through such architectural details.[52]

---

48   P. Slack, *From Reformation to Improvement: Public Welfare in Early Modern England* (Oxford, 1999), p. 25.
49   P. Thane, *Old Age in English History: Past Experiences, Present Issues* (Oxford, 2000); L. Botelho and P. Thane, *Women and Ageing in British Society Since 1500* (Harlow, 2001); Botelho, *Old Age*; S. Ottaway, *The Decline of Life: Old Age in Eighteenth Century England* (Cambridge, 2004); P. Thane, *The Long History of Old Age* (London, 2006).
50   A. Tomkins, 'Retirement from the Noise and Hurry of the World? The Experience of Almshouse Life', *Accommodating Poverty*, ed. McEwan and Sharpe, pp. 263–83.
51   The work of the Family and Community Historical Research Society (FACHRS), recently published, includes local and thematic essays, and provides a wealth of detail on diverse aspects of almshouse life such as almshouse gardens, residents' clothing and possessions, and their social status: N. Goose, H. Caffrey and A. Langley, eds, *The British Almshouse: New Perspectives on Philanthropy ca. 1400–1914* (Milton Keynes, 2016).
52   H. Caffrey, 'Almshouse Buildings: Form, Function and Meaning', *The British Almshouse*, ed. Goose, Caffrey and Langley, pp. 22–45.

The origins of this book lie in this new approach to the study of almshouses. The recognition that there were wide variations in the wealth and status of both founders and the institutions they endowed challenges received opinion on almshouses and the place they occupied within the 'welfare economy' of their communities. Similarly, the different experiences of almshouse life among this defined category of poor people enriches our understanding of the material lives of the poor, and sets this within the wider historio-graphical interest of recent decades in the experience of poverty in early modern England. Contemporary attitudes to the poor generally, the nature and availability of alternative forms of welfare provision, and their potential impact on the character and desirability of almshouse provision, are essential parts of this context. There is, of course, also a European context, in which almshouses and poor relief appear to have taken forms that varied in many ways from their counterparts in England, making comparison difficult.[53] For instance, in a recent study comparing English and Dutch almshouses, it is not absolutely clear that the English almshouse and the Dutch *hofje* (literally, 'small courtyard') under discussion were the same kind of institution, both being distinct from the parish poor house in England and the *oudeman-nenhuis* ('old men's house') and *oudevrouwenhuis* ('old women's house') of the Dutch Republic.[54] While there were these parallel developments in Europe, nevertheless the particular circumstances of the English Reformation and the evolution of a tax-based poor relief system, and the impact these had on the survival and characteristics of almshouses as a form of welfare provision in England, provide the focus here.

Chronologically, the parameters for this book are set loosely from 1550 to 1725. The period begins after the dissolution of the religious houses, guilds and chantries, and after the legislation of 1547 which established the principle of parishes providing cottages to house disabled people. It continues into the early eighteenth century, up to the legislation of 1723 which introduced workhouses as the preferred solution to the problem of the poor, legis-lation that gave overseers the right to deny relief to poor people refusing to enter a workhouse. The study is thus located between the sixteenth-century perspective of McIntosh, and the later work of Tomkins and Boulton with their focus largely on the eighteenth century. The contention is that early modern almshouses were not just a continuation of their medieval prede-cessors, despite the emphasis by historians such as McIntosh on continuity between the medieval and Tudor periods, but took on a distinct identity. As part of a mixed economy of welfare, moreover, they went on being shaped by developments in other sections of the welfare system.

---

53   Slack, *Poverty and Policy*, pp. 8–14.
54   N. Goose and H. Looijesteijn, 'Almshouses in England and the Dutch Republic *circa* 1350–1800: A Comparative Perspective', *Journal of Social History* 45/4 (2012), 1049–73.

Tomkins comments on how difficult it is to assess whether there was change over time in the character of almshouse life because the evidence is dispersed geographically and chronologically.[55] This book has both a geographical and chronological dimension, using research from three contrasting English counties – Durham, Warwickshire and Kent – chosen to represent the north, midlands and south of England respectively (see Figure 0.1). The attempt to build a comprehensive picture of provision in these particular areas by locating and identifying all known institutions in the three counties, and using them to illustrate a more general narrative of almshouse provision, follows in the tradition of earlier studies, such as that of Orme and Webster. Counties themselves may be an artificial construct for the purposes of this topic, having no direct administrative responsibility for charities, but the influence of local networks of gentry and burgesses, many of whom would have been involved in founding or running almshouses in their localities, should not be discounted. Furthermore, in their monograph on medieval hospitals Orme and Webster justify their inclusion of a regional study of Devon and Cornwall on the basis that national studies are 'selective and anecdotal', whereas in-depth study of a smaller area enables a more thorough search of possible sources to be undertaken and provides a more detailed interpretation of relevant data.[56] Certainly, some of the richest material has been uncovered in studies of single institutions or small local areas, as shown by some of the examples cited earlier.

The three counties were chosen not only to represent different geographical areas but for their markedly different characteristics. County Durham by the end of the seventeenth century was by no means the 'isolated northern backwater' it had been deemed in the sixteenth century, as the expansion of the coal trade had transformed the county's industrial and agricultural economies. It was, however, not especially prosperous, and it was a long way from the centre of government. There were comparatively few great families; the gentry were sparsely spread; and the bishopric dominated both land and office holding.[57] Warwickshire, located at the centre of England, was, in the early modern period, distant enough from London to be beyond the orbit of the court, but not so far as to be entirely remote from the metropolis. It had few great landowning magnates, and many of the seventeenth-century gentry were relative newcomers to the county.[58] The influence of the church

55 Tomkins, 'Retirement', p. 278.
56 Orme and Webster, *English Hospital*, p. 169.
57 A. Green, E. Parkinson and M. Spufford, eds, *Durham Hearth Tax Assessment Lady Day 1666* (London, 2006), pp. xxxiii, xxxvi, xlix, xc.
58 G. Tyack, *The Making of the Warwickshire Country House 1500–1650*, Warwickshire Local History Society Occasional Paper 4 (Warwick, 1982), pp. 4, 33; A. Hughes, *Politics, Society and Civil War in Warwickshire, 1620–1660* (Cambridge, 1987), p. 37.

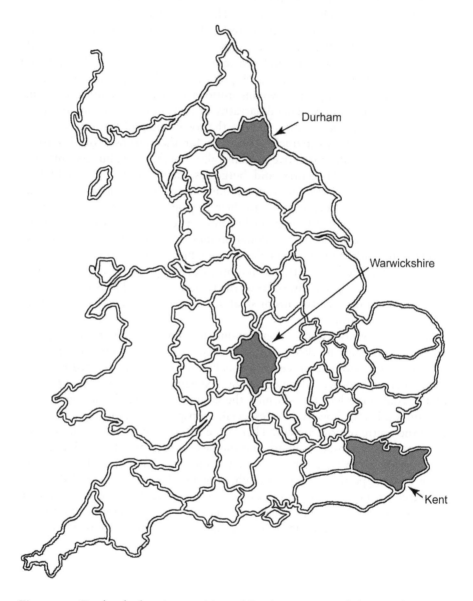

Figure o.1. England, showing position of Durham, Warwickshire and Kent

Table o.1. Almshouse numbers in three counties, 1550–1725

	Durham	Warwickshire	Kent	Total
Surviving pre-Reformation Almshouses	5	7	17	29
Almshouses founded 1550–1725	14	25	58	97
Total almshouses in 1725	19	32	75	126

Source: Online Appendix A

was weak, with the county divided between the dioceses of Lichfield and Worcester. Kent, on the other hand, was a large and populous county, seat of the archbishopric, closely linked to the centre of government and the City of London, and with close ties to the continent. In the approach to poor relief, Kent was in advance of much of the country. Many Kentish towns were 'early adopters' of organised systems of relief, often taking the lead in formulating policy and providing the government with templates for national legislation.

Unsurprisingly, there was a great difference in the number of early modern almshouses identified in the three counties, as shown in Table o.1. A total of 126 almshouses was identified for the three counties, comprising twenty-nine surviving pre-Reformation almshouses, and ninety-seven others founded between 1550 and 1725. Detailed information about the identified almshouses can be found in Online Appendix A, including, for example, the name of the founder and date of foundation, the intended occupants of the almshouse, the nature of the accommodation provided, and the level of benefits received. This data forms the empirical basis for many of the tables and the analysis in the text. While representing very different parts of the country, all three counties appear to have been well provided with almshouses compared with neighbouring areas, and together encompass a wide range of institutions. In order to counterbalance the temptation to focus only on the better-known institutions, and avoid either impressionist generalisations or a fixation on particular contexts, an attempt has been made to compile as near comprehensive a picture as possible by including all known foundations in these three locations. The broad definition of an almshouse adopted for this book has enabled the discovery of a number of quite humble foundations of a type likely to have been common across England, but usually overlooked in the literature. Their inclusion in this study has made it possible to examine what sort of institution was regarded as an almshouse by contemporaries in the period under consideration, and whether this changed over time, untrammelled by more modern and possibly anachronistic ideas of what constituted an almshouse. The use of three separate and contrasting geographical areas as the basis for the evidence discussed provides a broad-brush statistical overview, which is supplemented by data from other county surveys, and detailed, qualitative information from individual almshouses in these areas and elsewhere to augment the national perspective.

The first of the substantive chapters gives an overview of the policy background to housing the poor, tracing the development of the legislation relating to poor relief and charitable endowments, and subjecting this to a detailed analysis. It recognises the importance of housing as a component in the drive to tackle the problems associated with poverty, despite an apparent lack of policy coherence, and attempts to shed light on the intentions behind the shifts in legislation. This is followed by a chapter on the chronology and distribution of early modern foundations, which locates the detailed study of the three counties within a national context. It traces the sequence and patterns of almshouse foundation across the period and shows that, despite regional variations in pace and extent, founding an almshouse in the early modern period was widely popular as a distinct form of charity. The discussions of policy and chronology in these two chapters provide the context for the next chapter, on benefactors and their motivation in pursuing this particular form of charitable endeavour. This chapter considers the diversity of founders, and the range of different impulses which led members of different groups to become involved in founding and running almshouses. It evaluates whether these went beyond the desire for personal memorialisation, or the simple meeting of social need, to include issues of particular group identity and responsibility. The fourth chapter looks at the occupants of early modern almshouses, who they were and how they were expected to live their lives. In particular, it tests the assumption that almspeople were always the respectable, elderly, better-off poor. It examines whether there were particular expectations of the behaviour of people in almshouses, how realistic these were, and whether they differed markedly from the normal expectations of behaviour applied to other poor people in the community. The fifth chapter describes the great variety in the benefits of an almshouse place, the standard of living this might have enabled almspeople to enjoy, and how this compared to that of other poor people, particularly those on parish relief. In order to assess how well off almspeople were in relation to other poor people a statistical approach is adopted, constructing a minimum subsistence budget adjusted for inflation and comparing this to a range of almshouse stipends across the period. The sixth and final chapter is a return to the illustration with which the book opened, presenting a case study of the almshouse in Leamington Hastings, Warwickshire. Through this single example, the place of the almshouse in the range of resources available in the locality is examined, including how it operated in conjunction with other elements of the local welfare economy, and whether the people who benefited from it were markedly different from other poor parishioners.

Overall, the book sets out to assess the importance accorded to almshouses in early modern England. In the post-Reformation era, what function did they serve for donors, and were there distinct motivations specific to this period? In the context of the developing statutory system of poor relief, did they have a role to play in meeting the needs of the poor, and did this change over time? Ultimately, the study aims to judge the contribution made by early modern almshouses within the mixed economy of welfare, and whether the evidence suggests their influence and popularity in early modern England had a practical significance beyond the purely symbolic.

Housing Policy

Christ should lie no more abroad in the streets.[1]

Tudor and Stuart policy towards the poor was dominated by two perceived problems: vagrancy and idleness. The requirement to relieve the genuinely impotent poor was of long standing, and its continuation was never in doubt. Through the Tudor poor laws this requirement was discharged through an increasingly bureaucratic response which systematised and regulated local communities' traditional responsibilities. This imposed a nationwide framework of parish rates assessed and dispensed by parish officials, overseen by justices of the peace. The problems of vagrancy and idleness, on the other hand, were seen as different from the traditional requirement to relieve the impotent; while not new issues in themselves, their scale and nature in the sixteenth and early seventeenth centuries seemed to be new and threatening. Occasionally there were glimmers of an understanding that these were by-products of major socio-economic changes which were transforming England: an increase in landlessness among the rural population; the decay of traditional industries such as the cloth trade; the loss of time-honoured relief mechanisms in the monasteries, the confraternities and the guilds; the prohibition on retained armies resulting in large numbers of discharged soldiers after each military engagement; and extensive migration to the towns, particularly London, in search of work and opportunities. Mostly, however, the problems were couched in the moral rhetoric of condemnation, of masterless men, sturdy beggars, idle rogues. The solutions were seen to be settlement and work, ensuring that people were the legal responsibility of one place to which they could be returned and given employment, with punishment for the recalcitrant. This is the context within which the provision of housing for the poor must be viewed.

Housing was a key element in the welfare 'system' of early modern England. Yet there was no such thing as a coherent policy encompassing approaches to housing the poor. Prior to the late eighteenth century, there

---

1 Bishop Ridley to Cecil, 1552, in R. H. Tawney and E. Power, eds, *Tudor Economic Documents*, vol. 2 (London, 1924), p. 312.

was little interest in how the poor were housed, unless it was an issue of community safety or order. Only in London was anxiety expressed about the living conditions of the poor, where overcrowding, poor people 'heaped up together', was thought to encourage plague, disorder and food shortages.[2] There was neither an appreciation of the role of labourers' households in developing consumerism, nor a sense of the cottage and hearth as the site of honest domesticity and wholesome independence, both of which concepts were features of eighteenth-century commentary and reform.[3] As a result, seventeenth-century commentaries and guidance on the principles and operation of poor relief do not usually include anything on the provision of housing.[4] Yet housing was included in the legislation. It features in three ways: the direct provision of housing or rent for poor people through the parish poor relief system; the regulation through prohibition or licensing of cottages for the impotent poor, and of subtenants or inmates; and the encouragement of charitable endowment of institutions such as almshouses. The form of the provision which resulted, however, was often different from that intended by the legislators, as the subsequent discussion will demonstrate. The extent and nature of the housing provision which developed was influenced by a number of factors, including the availability of charitable resources; changing views on the importance of work and how best to ensure that the poor worked for their livelihood; and also the far-reaching implications of the legislation on settlement, which underlay many responses to housing need in the parishes.

Specific mention of housing for the poor makes its first appearance in early Edwardian legislation. The 1547 Act for the Punishment of Vagabonds and for the Relief of the Poor and Impotent Persons attempted to address the issue of the many maimed, aged and impotent people resorting to London and other towns and cities in order to beg. Under the terms of this act's more optimistic clauses, vagrants were to be dispersed to the place of their birth or where

2 Royal Proclamation Prohibiting New Building or Subdividing Houses, 7 July 1580: P. L. Hughes and J. F. Larkin, eds, *Tudor Royal Proclamations*, vol. 2: *The Later Tudors (1553–1587)* (New Haven and London, 1969), p. 466; W. C. Baer, 'Housing the Poor and Mechanick Class in Seventeenth-Century London', *The London Journal* 25/2 (2000), 13–39; T. G. Barnes, 'The Prerogative and Environmental Control of London Building in the Early Seventeenth Century: The Lost Opportunity', *California Law Review* 58 (1970), 1332–63.
3 J. White, 'The Laboring-Class Domestic Sphere in Eighteenth-Century British Social Thought', *Gender, Taste, and Material Culture in Britain and North America 1700–1830*, ed. J. Styles and A. Vickery (New Haven and London, 2006), pp. 247–63; S. Lloyd, 'Cottage Conversations: Poverty and Manly Independence in Eighteenth-Century England', *Past and Present* 184 (2004), 69–108.
4 For instance: Anon., *An Ease for Overseers of the Poore, Abstracted from the Statutes, Allowed by Practice, and Now Reduced Into Forme, as a Necessarie Directorie for Imploying, Releeving, and Ordering of the Poore* (1601); M. Dalton, *The Countrey Justice* (1630); M. Hale, *A Discourse Touching Provision for the Poor* (1683); Anon., *The Compleat Parish Officer*, 7th edn (1734).

they had lived for three years, and were there to be provided with 'cotages or other convenient howses to be lodged in, at the costes and charges of the said Cities ... there to be relieved and cured by the devoc[i]on of the good people of the said Cities'.[5] Those not too old or lame were to be provided with work. Whether these provisions were ever effectively implemented is not known. Many towns and villages would, theoretically, have had access to accommodation at the time in the form of guild or church housing. Although the subsequent abolition of the guilds and chantries swept much of this away, there is considerable evidence of continuity, for instance in the survival of guild almshouses in towns like Maidstone, Warwick and Stratford. The problem of vagrancy remained, however, and attempts to round up beggars and return them to their home areas were largely ineffectual, so it is unlikely that this accommodation was used in any systematic way. Although the harsh penalties of this legislation were revoked two years later, the clauses relating to the disabled were retained.[6]

The 1547 act, developing the provisions of the lapsed legislation of 1536, also ordered weekly collections of alms to be made in church, after the priest had reminded everyone of their Christian duty to relieve the poor. This was strengthened in 1552, and again in 1563, by the appointment of collectors in every parish; the recording of the names of the poor and of those contributing, with the respective amounts; and by the threat of referral to the bishop, the justices, and ultimately imprisonment, for those refusing to contribute. This was to form the basis of the parish system of poor relief which would be codified in 1598 and 1601 as the Old Poor Law.[7] Yet a curious diversion from this progression occurs in the lengthy 1572 Act for the Punishment of Vagabonds and for Relief of the Poor and Impotent, which assumes a continued role for the parishes but gives a specific responsibility to justices of the peace. They were to make a search within their divisions for 'all aged poore ympotent and decayed persons ... which lyve or of necessitye be compelled to lyve by Almes', register them in a book and then make provision within every division of 'meete and convenient places ... to settle the same poor People for their Habitacions and Abydynges', if the parish within which they were found could not or would not provide for them.[8] Any poor or

---

5   An Act for the Punishment of Vagabonds and for the Relief of the Poor and Impotent Persons, I Edw. VI c. 3 (IX). Other, more notorious, clauses included branding and enslaving of those refusing to comply.
6   A. L. Beier, *The Problem of the Poor in Tudor and Early Stuart England* (London, 1983), p. 40.
7   An Act for the Provision and Relief of the Poor, 5 & 6 Edw. VI c. 2; An Act for the Relief of the Poor, 5 Eliz. c. 3; An Act for the Relief of the Poor, 39 Eliz. c. 3; An Act for the Relief of the Poor, 43 Eliz. c. 2.
8   An Act for the Punishment of Vagabonds and for Relief of the Poor and Impotent, 14 Eliz. c. 5 (XVI).

impotent person found in a place where they were not born or had lived for three years, was to be returned to their home area, 'there to be put in the Abydynge Place or one of the Abydynge Places in that Countrey appointed ... for the Habitacion of the poore People of that Countrey'. Further clauses refer to collectors and overseers for these 'Abydynge Places', who were to be accountable to two justices of the peace living nearby. This would seem to imply that MPs envisaged not merely that the poor would be returned to their parish of settlement but that they would be accommodated in specific buildings once they got there, if they had nowhere else to live.

This suggests that the legislators had in mind the provision of supra-parochial district residences where the impotent poor could be compelled to live, and, if able enough, to work. Anyone refusing to live there would be treated as a vagrant; anyone capable but refusing to work would be whipped and stocked. The legislation is not clear exactly how these 'abiding places' were to be established; its clauses assumed that town corporations and country justices would agree among themselves where they should be and what form they should take. This vagueness resulted in a lack of clarity and uniformity in the purpose and form taken by early institutions, and is presumably the reason why 'some better Explanac[i]on' and 'nedefull Addic[i]on' to the legislation was required four years later. But it is interesting that the characteristic institution of the post-1834 new poor law unions had been anticipated as early as the sixteenth century; even more curious to imagine that, but for the deficiency of the 1572 legislation, the words 'Abiding Place' might one day have acquired the same dread redolence as 'Workhouse'.

It is hard to be clear exactly what were the intentions behind these clauses. It is not always possible to trace the origins of bills which came before the Elizabethan parliaments, so the direction and priorities of official policy can be difficult to ascertain. In each session what seems like a random selection of bills was put forward, reflecting the concerns of individual members of parliament and/or the Council. Sometimes the same bills were put forward time and again, to be rejected, amended or occasionally taken up. The legislation of 1572 had become necessary because the 1563 act expired at the end of Elizabeth's third parliament (2 April–29 May 1571). The bill which the Commons had put forward to replace it in 1571 was a private bill, initially against vagabondage, but with poor relief clauses added in committee. It was rejected by the Lords, but was revived in the new parliament of the following year, seemingly with official backing, in response to the Privy Council's increasing anxiety about the number of beggars and vagrants in London.[9]

---

9 G. R. Elton, *The Parliament of England 1559–1581* (Cambridge, 1986), pp. 269–70; P. Roberts, 'Elizabethan Players and Minstrels and the Legislation of 1572 Against Retainers and Vagabonds', *Religion, Culture and Society in Early Modern Britain*, ed. A. Fletcher and P. Roberts (Cambridge, 1994), pp. 29–55 (p. 32).

Despite the official support for this lengthy statute, the provenance and importance of its component clauses are not always clear. The main preoccupation of this parliament was the security of the realm, and the problem of how to deal with Mary Queen of Scots and the Duke of Norfolk, while the 1569 rebellion of the northern earls had increased uneasiness about aristocratic retainers and wandering bands of rebels.[10] Much of the debate seems to have been narrowly focused on who would be identified as a vagrant, particularly the inclusion or otherwise of lords' minstrels and itinerant players.[11] Frustratingly, contemporary accounts by parliamentarians throw little light on other issues which may have been included in discussion. Thomas Cromwell, MP for Bodmin, for instance, merely noted in his journal for 30 May 1572: 'This day I was absent, the most parte whereof bestowed about the bill of vagabondes.'[12]

Paul Slack assumes that the 'Abiding Places' mentioned in the 1572 act were houses of correction, as does Marjorie McIntosh.[13] Sir Francis Knollys had advocated a bridewell in every town as the solution to vagrancy during the debate the previous year, to be funded by every alehouse-keeper in the land contributing 1s per year.[14] London's Bridewell Hospital, established in 1555, was already proving influential as a model for other towns and cities. Similar institutions were founded in Oxford (1562); Salisbury (1564); Norwich (by 1565); Gloucester (by 1569); and Ipswich (1569).[15] Not all of these were necessarily bridewells; some were more likely to have been hospitals or workhouses, rather than houses of correction. That of Salisbury, for instance, was originally a place to hold idle people and set them to work, 'so that none should go begging'; while Blackfriars in Ipswich was established as Christ's Hospital 'for the poore people of this Towne'.[16] The Orders for the Poor drawn up at Norwich in 1571, however, make it clear that the workhouse at the house called the Normans was a bridewell to which the mayor or his

---

10   Paul Slack emphasises the impact of the 1569 rebellion, prompting official searches for vagabonds and calls for legislation against them: Slack, *Poverty and Policy*, p. 124.

11   This was of crucial importance as the act made vagrancy a felony for the first time.

12   T. E. Hartley, ed., *Proceedings in the Parliaments of Elizabeth I*, vol. 1: *1558–1581* (Leicester, 1981), p. 384.

13   P. Slack, *Poverty and Policy in Tudor and Stuart England* (London, 1988), p. 125; M. K. McIntosh, *Poor Relief in England 1350–1600* (Cambridge, 2012), p. 168.

14   McIntosh, *Poor Relief in England*, p. 219.

15   P. Slack, 'Hospitals, Workhouses and the Relief of the Poor in Early Modern London', *Health Care and Poor Relief in Protestant Europe 1500–1700*, ed. O. P. Grell and A. Cunningham (London, 1997), pp. 234–51 (p. 237); J. Innes, 'Prisons for the Poor: English Bridewells, 1555–1800', *Labour, Law and Crime: An Historical Perspective*, ed. F. Snyder and D. Hay (London, 1987), pp. 42–122 (p. 61); A. van der Slice, 'Elizabethan Houses of Correction', *Journal of Criminal Law and Criminology* 27/1 (1936), 45–67.

16   van der Slice, 'Houses of Correction', p. 53.

deputies could commit people as prisoners for a minimum of twenty-one days if they refused to work and preferred to beg, or were vagabonds or loiterers.[17]

The language of the 1572 act, however, and the characteristics of some of these early institutions, suggests that 'Abiding Places' were originally envisaged as something different from houses of correction, with priority given to providing accommodation for poor, aged and impotent people so that they would not need to 'begge or wander about'.[18] E. M. Leonard interprets the relevant clauses of the 1572 act to mean that the poor were to have 'habitations' found for them, without specifying the form these were to take.[19] But it seems clear that the act intended 'Abiding Places' to be some form of institution. Moreover, hints of coercion were already present in the legislation, with the threat of whipping or stocking for any aged or impotent person capable of working, but refusing to do so. The 'Abiding Place' was modified into a different sort of institution as the House of Correction four years later, in an act of 1576 ordering in every county 'One Two or more Abyding Howses or Places' to be provided 'and called the Howse or Howses of Correction'. These were not intended as places for the poor impotent people to live, but were principally places of punishment to send the idle or beggars without settlement for a period of time, to be reformed through work.[20] For instance, Reading's 'Hospitall' was converted in 1590 into a house of correction, 'as well for the settinge of the poore people to worke ... as also for the punishinge and correctinge of idle and vagrant persons'.[21] The 1576 act also included a provision to make it easier for 'well disposed persons' to found and endow 'Howses of Correction or Abydinge Howses', and to establish stocks of materials for setting the poor on work.[22]

It may be that what was originally intended was something along the lines of the continental *hôpital général*, but was transformed instead, in 1576, into a punitive work-focused institution reflecting the priorities of the legislators. This may be a result of the disproportionate influence of London on the formulation of policy. No one at court or parliament could be oblivious to the

---

17   E. M. Leonard, *The Early History of English Poor Relief* (Cambridge, 1900), pp. 311–12.

18   Interestingly, the 1610 foundation deed of John Southland's Hospital in New Romney, Kent, includes the terminology 'abiding place', referring to 'two couple of poor folke that shal be placed in the said Hospitall or Abiding place': N. G. Jackson, *Southlands 1610–1960* (Nottingham, 1960), p. 23.

19   Leonard, *Poor Relief*, p. 71.

20   An Act for the Setting of the Poor on Work, and for the Avoiding of Idleness, 18 Eliz. c. 3 (V). One of the MPs serving on the committee which formulated this act was John Aldrich, former mayor of Norwich, who already had experience of the bridewell at Norwich: Innes, 'Prisons', p. 67.

21   van der Slice, 'Houses of Correction', p. 57.

22   18 Eliz. c. 3 (IX). For the next twenty years the requirement to obtain a licence of mortmain to make such endowments was lifted.

problems of poverty and vagrancy they saw pressing around them in London, regardless of how untypical these might be compared with the situation in their home area. As a consequence, solutions appropriate to London dominated government thinking (as was pointed out by Ralph Seckerston, MP for Liverpool).[23] London's Bridewell Hospital was one of the five royal hospitals established in the capital in the reign of Edward VI, each catering for a different category of poor person, and managed jointly by a committee of London aldermen.[24] Bridewell dealt with vagrants, and the range of needs met by the other hospitals meant that it could focus on discipline; the joint strategy and management of the hospitals, meanwhile, enabled poor people to be assessed and routed to the most appropriate placement. Other cities which attempted a coordinated approach, albeit on a much smaller scale, included Coventry, where a bridewell was constructed in 1580 alongside an existing boys' hospital and Bond's Hospital for the impotent poor.[25]

The importance of discipline may have been reinforced for the policy-makers in London by the problems presented by the continued, limping existence of the Savoy Hospital, an embarrassing relic from a previous age of indiscriminate charity to homeless beggars. The Savoy had been founded as an act of piety by Henry VII in 1505, and richly endowed in his will of 1509. It was modelled on the reformed hospitals of fifteenth-century Italy, and was intended to provide nightly a bed and a meal for one hundred poor men. Although suppressed by Edward VI, and its lands and occupants transferred to Bridewell, it was refounded by Mary on a reduced income, and continued an independent existence alongside the five royal hospitals. The City authorities complained that the beggars who resorted there for relief were a cause of disorder, and undermined the good government of the city.[26] The Savoy was poorly managed, and its income misappropriated; by the time it was finally dissolved in 1702 it had last relieved a handful of poor people a quarter of a century before, and had been used as a military hospital in the intervening years.[27]

In contrast, the powers given to the City to sweep the streets of London for beggars and commit able-bodied rogues to Bridewell were initially considered a great success.[28] Further encouragement to private individuals to establish houses of correction came in 1598, with insufficient effect, and additional

23   Elton, *Parliament*, pp. 269–70.
24   St Thomas's for the aged and impotent poor; St Bartholomew's for the sick poor; Christ's for children; Bethlehem (Bedlam) for lunatics; and Bridewell for vagrants and the idle, immoral and recalcitrant poor: Slack, 'Hospitals', p. 236.
25   W. B. Stephens, ed., *A History of the County of Warwick*, vol. 8: *The City of Coventry and Borough of Warwick* (London, 1969), pp. 137–9.
26   Leonard, *Poor Relief*, p. 63.
27   R. Somerville, *The Savoy, Manor: Hospital: Chapel* (London, 1960), p. 88.
28   Innes, 'Prisons', p. 55.

measures to make houses of correction compulsory came in 1610.[29] Every county was ordered to have at least one house of correction, properly stocked and provided, by Michaelmas 1611. In any county which failed to comply, every justice of the peace would suffer a fine of £5. By now there was no uncertainty about the nature of these institutions. Gone are any references to 'abiding places'; houses of correction were clearly places of punishment, with the master authorised to use fetters and whipping to maintain discipline. Parents deserting their children, and mothers bearing bastards, were added to the list of people who could be committed for a period of punishment through labour.

After the acts of 1572 and 1576, however, there was a return to parish-based solutions as the legal foundation for the general system of poor relief. The great codifying acts of the end of Elizabeth's reign enshrined the parish as the unit of responsibility for assessing and collecting poor rates and paying poor relief, with justices of the peace given responsibility for oversight and arbitration. The 1598 Act for the Relief of the Poor gave the overseers and churchwardens powers to erect cottages at the charge of the parish on commons or waste for impotent poor people, with the agreement of the lord of the manor; and to place inmates or more than one family in a cottage or house.[30] The 1601 act repeated this clause, but with the addition that such accommodation could not be used afterwards for anyone other than impotent poor of the parish placed there by the parish officials.[31] In practice, as becomes clear from the many habitation orders and licences for cottage building given at quarter sessions, accommodation (like poor relief generally) was inevitably provided for the underemployed able-bodied poor as much as for the impotent. In this respect, the justices of the peace, like parish officials, used their powers pragmatically to extend the scope of the poor laws beyond those for whom they were legally obliged to give support. Some people for whom cottages were provided did not claim regular relief, suggesting that the provision of subsidised housing for the working poor became an essential element in the poor relief system. Many parishes built or converted cottages for poor people, and, once they had done so, the 1601 amendment ensured that such properties remained in use for the poor. In this way, during the seventeenth century, many parishes built up a considerable stock of ordinary housing in which to place poor people.[32]

---

29   An Acte for erecting of Hospitalles or abiding and working Howses for the Poore, 39 Eliz. c. 5; An Acte for the due execucion of divers Lawes and Statutes heretofore made against Rogues Vagabondes and Sturdye Beggars and other lewde and idle persons, 7 Jac. I c. 4.
30   39 Eliz. c. 3 (V).
31   43 Eliz. c. 2 (V).
32   J. Broad, 'Housing the Rural Poor in Southern England, 1650–1850', *The Agricultural History Review* 48/2 (2000), 151–70.

Yet this may well have been an unintended consequence of making the parish the unit of responsibility, as institutional solutions to housing the poor seem to have been the Elizabethan legislators' preferred response.[33] After the hiatus of the Reformation years, there was a revival in the founding of almshouses for the impotent poor in Elizabeth's reign. Robert Dudley, Earl of Leicester and member of the Council, was one of the people who gave a lead, by obtaining an act of Parliament in the 1571 session to found his hospital for old soldiers at Warwick.[34] The 1572 act exempted almshouses from the penalties for harbouring vagabonds if by the terms of their foundations they provided accommodation or alms to aged or impotent persons. Although almshouses had not been specified in the 1576 legislation which loosened the rules to encourage private benefactors to found houses of correction, it is possible that their inclusion was implied. The re-enactment in 1598 of this 1576 legislation on its expiry added hospitals and *maisons dieu* to the original abiding places and houses of correction, as long as their endowment did not exceed £200 per year.[35]

A further act in 1598 suggested that a vagrant who could not be returned to their home area, because it was not known where they were born or had lived for three years, was to be whipped and placed in the house of correction or county gaol until they could be placed in service. Those 'not being able of body' were to remain in 'some Almeshowse'.[36] This assumes that almshouses were available to which vagrants unfit for work could be sent, and that the justices would have been able to access them. We are used to thinking of almshouses as places of privilege, for the respectable deserving poor, not as holding places for disabled tramps and beggars. Yet this is the implication of this clause. Certainly, in London at least, the great hospitals under the control of the corporation could have fulfilled this role, if necessary, and this was possibly the case in some other cities too. The 1563 act had given responsibility for collecting and distributing all poor relief in London to Christ's Hospital.[37] The same arrangement was ordered for Coventry through the 'Hospitall', and extended to St Bartholomew's Hospital, Gloucester, in 1572.[38]

A further clause in the 1572 Act for the Punishment of Vagabonds and for

---

33 By 'institutional' is meant a structured, organised form of provision with a social function and expected roles and behaviours for those living there, which distinguishes it from the merely domestic.

34 13 Eliz. c. 17.

35 39 Eliz. c. 5 (I).

36 An Acte for the punishment of Rogues, Vagabond[es] and Sturdy Beggars. 39 Eliz. c. 4 (III).

37 5 Eliz. c. 3 (XIV and XV).

38 The Coventry 'Hospitall' is likely to have been Bond's Hospital, founded in 1506, sited next to the fourteenth-century College of Bablake, and run by the Corporation after the Reformation. After the dissolution of the college in 1548, a boys' hospital (later Bablake School) was established in 1560 in one part of the building, and a decision was made in 1571 to use

Relief of the Poor and Impotent instructed bishops to conduct annual visitations of any hospital in their diocese that did not have a visitor appointed
by the founder, suggesting that almshouses and hospitals were seen as
integral to the welfare system and as part of the solution to the problems
of poverty and vagrancy.[39] This is given added weight by clauses in the 1598
Act for the Relief of the Poor, providing for justices to use the county rate
to support poor prisoners and county hospitals and almshouses, and to
apply any surplus county stock to the relief of poor hospitals and people
suffering loss by fire, at sea or other casualties.[40] There is plenty of evidence
from quarter sessions records of justices of the peace ensuring that county
funds were used for poor prisoners and people losing all in house fires, but
it is less clear that almshouses were ever supported in this way. What seems
possible is that the legislators hoped for, and anticipated, the emergence of
a network of almshouses throughout the land with a specific role to play
within the attempt to impose order on the problems of poverty and vagrancy.
But the sort of institution typically founded by private benefactors did not
offer a solution in this way (with the possible exception of a few hospitals
for travellers, discussed in chapter 4). Eligibility for endowed almshouses
was often prescriptive, and access to places was controlled by patrons and
trustees. For instance, Dudley's hospital in Warwick for twelve poor men was
for former soldiers or retainers from a number of places with specific connections with his family, of which Warwick was but one; and it was its patron,
Dudley himself, rather than the local justices or town officials, who controlled
admissions.

Neither is there evidence, despite the encouragement of the legislation,
of any enthusiasm from private benefactors for founding punitive institutions such as bridewells, where the connection with the lawlessness and
immorality of their unsavoury occupants would have constituted a far less
attractive site of memorialisation than an orderly almshouse of respectable
pensioners. Despite its early success, the London Bridewell was a continual
cause of concern, with allegations of mismanagement and corruption, and it
was soon branded a 'rogues' hospital'.[41] Jordan acknowledged the failure of
bridewells, workhouses and work schemes, unlike schools and almshouses,
to attract charitable funds, calculating that over the whole of his period they
accounted for less than 1% of all charitable wealth.[42] Some of the charitable

---

another part for a house of correction or bridewell, which was constructed in 1580: Stephens,
Warwick, pp. 137–9.
39   14 Eliz. c. 5 (XXXII).
40   39 Eliz. c. 3 (XIII and XIV).
41   Innes, 'Prisons', pp. 55–6.
42   W. K. Jordan, *Philanthropy in England 1480–1660: A Study of the Changing Pattern of
English Social Aspirations* (London, 1959), p. 271.

funds applied to these purposes in the seventeenth century were actually redirected by executors and trustees, rather than bequeathed by benefactors. For instance, the Nantwich workhouse, established with a charitable bequest, was converted into a bridewell in the 1660s at the request of the townspeople; and Devon magistrates redirected a sum of money which had been left for setting the poor on work into constructing a penal 'County Workhouse'.[43] As a result, most work or correctional schemes, of which there were many examples in the seventeenth century, were founded at the public charge. With the exception of bridewells, most of these were short-lived.[44] Jordan puts this failure down to badly run schemes failing to cover their costs, or better-run schemes undercutting local businesses. He describes their efforts as an 'appealing but wholly impractical form of social rehabilitation'.[45]

Private benefactors who intended to endow a house of correction were assisted by the 1576 legislation which removed the requirement to obtain a licence of mortmain from the Crown. Despite this encouragement, the government expressed disappointment that the 1576 act 'hath not taken such effecte as was intended'.[46] A new act in 1598 simplified the legal process for endowing and incorporating almshouses, workhouses and houses of correction, an interesting amalgam that seems to differentiate little between institutions we would otherwise have expected to feature different regimes and objectives. The 1598 Act for Erecting of Hospitals has been credited with producing a remarkable surge in almshouse foundations in the early decades of the seventeenth century. Indeed, after the act, many members of the government led by example in founding or supporting institutions, such as, for instance, George Abbot, Archbishop of Canterbury (Abbot's Hospital in Guildford, commenced in 1618), and Thomas Trevor, Baron of the Exchequer (Leamington Hastings, 1633).[47] It is clear, however, that a great many more foundations such as Dudley's Lord Leycester Hospital pre-date the change, as discussed in the following chapter. Rather than being the *result* of the legislation, many early modern foundations were part of the same movement which *produced* the legislation: both were a response to the debate about the growing problem of poverty and how to deal with it, a debate which also gave rise to the poor law legislation. This is supported by the suggestion in the next chapter that the 1570s was a key decade in some places for almshouse foundation, a decade that also produced the 1572 and 1576 legislation discussed above.

For those benefactors considering founding a permanent institution, as exhorted by Elizabeth and her ministers, the capital costs could be

---

43   Innes, 'Prisons', p. 78.
44   Slack, *Poverty and Policy*, pp. 152–3.
45   Jordan, *Philanthropy*, pp. 270–2.
46   Preamble to the extending legislation of 1598, 39 Eliz. c. 5.
47   E. Prescott, *The English Medieval Hospital 1050–1640* (Melksham, 1992), p. 73.

considerable. The house of correction at Winchester, for instance, cost £1,000 to build in 1578.[48] Jordan calculated that a modest almshouse could be founded at a cost of between £100 and £500, while a larger one would require £500 – £1,000.[49] It cost William Lambarde, however, a total of £2,739 to build and endow his almshouse for twenty people at East Greenwich in 1576.[50] Private charity was unsurprisingly considered an essential contributor to projects of this sort. Jordan, whose insights were often sound even if his statistics were not, argued that charitable giving was initially expected at this time to be the principal means by which the poor were to be relieved, with parish rates only intended to fill the gaps.[51] Many founders of almshouses were childless and endowed foundations out of their estates after death; otherwise the cost to them and their families might have been prohibitive. A benefactor like Robert Dudley, who founded his almshouse during his lifetime, was fortunate to acquire the building from Warwick corporation at no cost to himself. Initially he had to support the foundation out of his income; upon his death the grant of lands he made to the hospital in his will was challenged, unsuccessfully, by his widow.[52] Nor did the parsimonious Elizabeth give a lead in charitable giving, unlike her father and brother before her. Yet in 1598 and 1601, the enactment of the Statutes of Charitable Uses, which created a legal framework for the protection of the assets and intentions of benefactors, confirms how crucially important the government saw the contribution of private charity to be.[53] The legislation provided for commissioners to investigate breaches of charitable trusts and make decrees to remedy any mismanagement. It was immediately successful, with many thorough investigations into the administration of charitable trusts in the early decades of the seventeenth century.[54]

The final element in the legislation regarding poor people's housing was the regulation of where and with whom the poor should live. During the parliamentary debate on the 1572 act, Nicholas St John, a Wiltshire landowner and MP for the town of Marlborough, had interjected that one of the reasons for the increase in rogues was their practice of building squatters'

48   van der Slice, 'Houses of Correction', p. 62.
49   Jordan, *Philanthropy*, pp. 340–1.
50   R. M. Warnicke, *William Lambarde, Elizabethan Antiquary* (London and Chichester, 1973), p. 44.
51   Jordan, *Philanthropy*, pp. 107–8.
52   E. G. Tibbits, 'The Hospital of Robert, Earl of Leicester, in Warwick', *Birmingham Archaeological Society: Transactions and Proceedings* 60 (1936), 112–44 (pp. 118–20, 129–32).
53   An Acte to reforme Deceiptes and Breaches of Trust, towching Landes given to Charitable Uses, 39 Eliz. c. 6; An Acte to redresse the Misemployment of Landes, Goodes and Stockes of Money heretofore given to Charitable Uses, 43 Eliz. c. 4.
54   G. Jones, *History of the Law of Charity 1532–1827* (Cambridge, 1969), pp. 23–5; McIntosh, *Poor Relief in England*, pp. 288–93.

cottages on commons with no land attached (and therefore little opportunity for gaining an honest livelihood). He proposed that no cottage should be built without three or four acres of ground attached, and a bill to this effect was put forward two days later, but got no further than a second reading.[55] The idea, however, was not forgotten, and legislation was enacted in 1589.[56] This set out penalties of £10 for building or converting a cottage in the countryside without at least four acres of land, 40s per month for allowing such an illegal building to remain, and 10s per month for owners or occupiers of cottages who allowed inmates or more than one family to share a cottage. This was another example of Tudor legislators mistaking cause for effect, and attempting to put the clock back to a less populous rural past where no one was idle and every able-bodied person was capable of being self-supporting.

Excluded from the act were houses in towns, or adjacent to mines, quarries, coasts and rivers, and also any cottage inhabited by 'a poore lame sicke aged or ympotent p[er]son', which in effect meant that the restrictions could not be applied to parish housing or almshouses. This legislation, which was not repealed until 1775, had the potential, in rural areas in particular, seriously to undermine poor people's attempts to house themselves, and provided ample scope for conflict and contradiction in neighbourhoods. Many landowners were happy to allow squatters to construct cottages on their land as it increased their rental income, while others were active in pulling down cottages to prevent them being occupied by poor tenants.[57] Parishioners were concerned about the arrival of poor people likely to become a burden on the poor rates, but occasional trawls by constables could result in people being presented before the magistrates who had lived undisturbed for years, including sometimes parish pensioners.[58]

Parishioners' responsibility for relieving their own poor made policing the boundaries of that responsibility imperative, and the rules of settlement, codified in law in 1662 but evolving in practice long before that, provided the framework by which people could be excluded or permitted to remain.[59] Inmates, people (including kin) lodging in others' houses, were seen as particularly evil, not having a defined relationship in society as householders, apprentices or servants, but perceived as masterless, rootless vagrants. They

---

55   J. E. Neale, *The Elizabethan House of Commons* (London, 1949) p. 156; Hartley, *Proceedings*, pp. 367, 372; Elton, *Parliament*, p. 270.
56   An Acte againste erectinge and mayntayninge of Cottages. 31 Eliz. c. 7.
57   Broad, 'Housing', p. 151; D. Tankard, 'The Regulation of Cottage Building in Seventeenth-Century Sussex', *Agricultural History Review* 59 (2011), 18–35 (pp. 24, 31).
58   S. Hindle, *On the Parish? The Micro-Politics of Poor Relief in Rural England c.1550–1750* (Oxford, 2004), pp. 303, 314–19.
59   An Act for the Better Relief of the Poor of this Kingdom, 14 Car. II c. 12; P. Styles, 'The Evolution of the Law of Settlement', *Studies in Seventeenth-Century West Midlands History* (Kineton, 1978), pp. 175–204.

were accused of sneaking and lurking to obtain an undeserved foothold in the community, consuming rather than contributing to the resources of the genuine, indigenous poor. This attitude even extended to families attempting to help one another out by taking in relatives, who were ordered to evict adult children or siblings if they were suspected of having a claim on settlement elsewhere. But parishes frequently housed people as inmates when it suited them; some parishes' standard approach to poor relief was to board out poor people on their better-off neighbours.[60] Parish housing provided for the poor was often multi-occupied, and rarely had land attached. The potential existed for endless conflict, with overseers of the poor trying to find pragmatic solutions to homelessness, and constables presenting inmates and illegal cottagers; poor people trying to find employment and somewhere to live, and parishes trying to keep them out. Quarter sessions records demonstrate the extent to which the arbitration of settlement disputes became a significant component of magistrates' workload. Once settlement had been determined and the person returned to their parish of settlement, they might then need to be housed by the parish, increasing the pressure on parish resources. In practice, the poor were at the mercy both of their neighbours and of the justices. The prohibition and licensing of cottages, and the operation of the settlement laws, brought ordinary people into the reach of the developing welfare bureaucracy, even if they were not recipients of poor relief. In this respect, commentators such as Dalton were right that poor laws undermined independence – poor people's attempts to find their own solutions were continually sabotaged by their better-off neighbours.

In this climate, almshouses were not immune from similar concerns. Most almshouses only catered for the poor of their immediate locality, and entry criteria often specified a minimum length of time an applicant had to have been resident in that locality to qualify.[61] Where some of the wealthier almshouses such as the Lord Leycester Hospital took some of their residents from outside the immediate locality, stipends were sufficiently generous to place the almspeople outside the concern of the poor law authorities. At other places, such as New Cobham College, which admitted recipients of poor relief from a number of surrounding parishes, the parish of origin had to provide the almshouse with a bond of £20 'to save the parish of Cobham harmless', guaranteeing not only that the poor person met the criteria for

---

60 Hindle, *On the Parish?*, pp. 63–6; D. Marshall, *The English Poor in the Eighteenth Century: A Study in Social and Administrative History* (London, 1926), p. 111.
61 For instance, applicants to New Cobham College, Kent, had to have resided in their parish for a minimum of three years; for Hutchinson's almshouse at Romaldkirk it was seven years: MALSC VF COB 726.709 Rules and Ordinances made for the New College of Cobham in the Countie of Kent [undated]; DRO EP/Rom 12/2 Romaldkirk Regulations for the management of the Bowes and Romaldkirk charities 1891.

admission but that the parish of origin retained responsibility for them.[62] Almshouse rules often specifically prohibited the lodging of inmates, for fear the attraction of free accommodation could lead to them becoming a haven for the ineligible yet needy poor from outside the area. In Elizabethan Warwick, for example, where Lee Beier used the 1587 census to calculate that 45% of the poor were either inmates themselves or lived in households with inmates, these included the beggar Margery Watts and her two children lodging illegally in the Westgate almshouses. They were ordered to be evicted and returned to their home parish of Bishops Itchington.[63]

Although it ostensibly protected the interests of parish ratepayers, the settlement merry-go-round to which many poor people were subjected probably contributed in the longer term to the well-documented steady increase in sums paid out in poor relief throughout the seventeenth and eighteenth centuries.[64] The problem was still conceived as one of idleness; the solutions, yet again, were seen to be work and discipline. Attitudes to the poor hardened, with the introduction of compulsory badges to be worn by those on poor relief in 1697, and the denial of relief to anyone refusing.[65] Despite earlier failures, there was a revived interest in work schemes towards the end of the seventeenth century. London's experiment with a Corporation of the Poor in the Commonwealth years was adopted, first by Bristol in 1696, then by another thirteen provincial towns by 1712.[66] These schemes enabled work and relief to be organised in larger units across parish boundaries.

In 1723, Knatchbull's Act, or the Workhouse Test Act, encouraged parishes to set up workhouses, or to join with other parishes in doing so, but, more importantly, gave overseers the right to withdraw relief from anyone refusing to enter the workhouse.[67] Workhouses were not a new phenomenon; many towns and villages had experimented with them in the sixteenth and seventeenth centuries. However, the degree of compulsion or incarceration involved in many early work schemes is hard to establish, and certainly not all were intended to be residential. For instance, the Frampton parish workhouse

---

62   MALSC P336/5/1 Shorne Churchwardens' accounts 1630–1681, rules relating to Cobham College.
63   A. L. Beier, 'The Social Problems of an Elizabethan Country Town: Warwick, 1580–90', *Country Towns in Pre-Industrial England*, ed. P. Clark (Leicester, 1981), pp. 46–79 (p. 61); T. Kemp, ed., *The Book of John Fisher, Town Clerk and Deputy Recorder of Warwick (1580–1588)* (Warwick, 1900), pp. 170–1.
64   Slack, *Poverty and Policy*, p. 179; Hindle, *On the Parish?*, pp. 275–6.
65   An Act for supplying some Defects in the Laws for the Relief of the Poor of this Kingdom, 8 & 9 Will. III c. 30.
66   P. Slack, *From Reformation to Improvement: Public Welfare in Early Modern England* (Oxford, 1999), p. 103.
67   An Act for Amending the Laws relating to the Settlement, Employment and Relief of the Poor, 9 Geo. I c. 7.

in Lincolnshire may perhaps be better described as a workshop in its first incarnation in the 1630s and 1640s, and there is no evidence that it housed paupers before the eighteenth century.[68] The short-lived workhouse established in 1633 in the former church house in Fillongley, Warwickshire, was intended to house any of the poor who had nowhere else to live, but there is no suggestion that people would be compelled to live there.[69] The 1723 act, however, enshrined the principle that housing the poor was now to be in a punitive environment: the aim was deliberately to put people off applying for relief, rather than to meet the accommodation needs of those with nowhere else to go.

Yet, as Broad has shown, even after 1723, parish paupers continued to be placed in ordinary housing in the community. He argues that this was because ordinary people retained a belief that even the poor were entitled to a home of their own. This may be an overly romantic notion: many parish paupers were forced to share accommodation, and the Webbs believed that parish housing always tended to revert to the 'general mixed workhouse' type, where were housed together an unsavoury mix of the derelict, the aged, the immoral and the innocent.[70] But the actions of many justices of the peace – themselves a landowning class – in licensing cottages, making habitation orders and intervening in parish affairs when the actions of the overseers were deemed negligent or unjust, also shaped the nature and scale of parish provision. This suggests that contested ideologies were at play, with the theoretical desire for order and discipline counterbalanced by philanthropy, liberalism and pragmatic economics.

The overarching theme of welfare policy on housing seems to be that the preferred option of the political elite, as reflected in the legislation, tended towards institutional solutions, but that implementation produced very different results.[71] Policymakers, in England as much as in continental Europe, wanted provision for the poor that was ordered and institutional, although not necessarily (at least at first) penal or punitive. Yet in only a few places, such as London, did they succeed. Slack discusses a number of reasons why the system of English poor relief did not develop along the lines of continental institutions.[72] Only in London were there large-scale welfare institutions equivalent to those found in continental cities, although early attempts to replicate the London system of coordinated relief were conducted in, for instance, Coventry. The emphasis on the parish as the unit of responsibility

---

68 Hindle, *On the Parish?*, p. 184.
69 WQS, vol. 1, p. 223.
70 S. Webb and B. Webb, *English Local Government*, vol. 7: *English Poor Law History, Part I: The Old Poor Law* (London, 1927), pp. 213, 218.
71 For 'institutional', see n. 33 above.
72 Slack, *Poverty and Policy*, pp. 8–14.

in England, confirmed in the codified poor laws of 1598 and 1601, ensured that provision, including accommodation for the poor, necessarily remained small scale and local, and hindered the development of the large welfare institutions that were typical of many continental cities. Even in London, where the responsibility for the collection of poor rates through Christ's Hospital was enshrined in law, tensions existed with the parishes, and by 1598 this attempt at central control was abandoned.[73] Meanwhile, private charitable provision was similarly fragmented and on a small scale. Despite government encouragement, very few individual benefactors had sufficient wealth or inclination to found large-scale institutions. The abolition of the guilds and fraternities meant that, apart from the London livery companies, there was no real framework for collective charitable provision until the development of subscription charities in the eighteenth century.

Had the justices and burgesses retained the powers and responsibilities implied in the 1572 act and developed the means of collecting and spending resources for provision on a larger scale, such as the 'abiding places' mentioned in the act, the outcome might have been different. But the confirmation of the parish as the unit of responsibility in 1598 meant that, for most of the period, there was no coordinated provision of either public or private institutions across the towns and counties of England in the way the legislators may have hoped: most housing provided for the poor in the early modern period was neither institutional nor punitive, but consisted of small-scale almshouses and ordinary cottages, until harsher attitudes made workhouses commonplace from the eighteenth century.

73   Slack, 'Hospitals', p. 238.

2

Chronology and Distribution of
Almshouse Foundations

Surely this is an annal of a magnificent and a noble achievement.[1]

The remarkable surge in the founding of almshouses in the early modern period has been widely noted, and is usually viewed as a direct response to increasing problems of poverty and homelessness at the time. Elizabeth Prescott, for instance, asserts that 'in the mid sixteenth century there was a desperate need for accommodation of this kind', exacerbated by the loss of monasteries and hospitals through the Dissolution.[2] More recently, Marjorie McIntosh has calculated that 291 hospitals and almshouses, out of a total of 601 pre-Reformation institutions, were closed in the period between 1530 and 1559.[3] The many ancient foundations which had been monastic in origin were swept away; such was the fate, for instance, of St Giles' Hospital for the poor at Kepier, Durham, founded in 1112 and dissolved in 1545.[4] Out of that county's eighteen medieval hospitals, only five survived the Reformation, and these could hardly have been sufficient for the population of the county.[5]

The impact of these losses is, nonetheless, hard to quantify, and may have been exaggerated by contemporary commentators. Both Clay and Prescott use a single quotation about the impotent poor from the 1546 polemic, *A Supplication of the Poor Commons*: 'The[n] had they hospitals, and almshouses to be lodged in, but nowe they lye and storve in the stretes. Then was their number great, but nowe much greater'.[6] This may well be a nostalgic reference to an imagined golden age when the poor were properly looked after, rather

1 W. K. Jordan, *Philanthropy in England 1480–1660: A Study of the Changing Pattern of English Social Aspirations* (London, 1959), p. 260.
2 E. Prescott, *The English Medieval Hospital 1050–1640* (Melksham, 1992), p. 72.
3 M. K. McIntosh, *Poor Relief in England 1350–1600* (Cambridge, 2012), CUP Online Appendix 2, Number of institutions founded, closed, and in existence per decade.
4 M. Harvey, *Lay Religious Life in Late Medieval Durham* (Woodbridge, 2006), p. 178.
5 H. L. Robson, 'The Medieval Hospitals of Durham: Paper Read to the Sunderland Antiquarian Society 17 November 1953', *Antiquities of Sunderland and its Vicinity*, ed. H. Simpson, Sunderland Antiquarian Society 22 (Sunderland, 1960), pp. 33–56 (p. 47).
6 Anon., *A Supplication of the Poor Commons* (1546), p. 291.

than an accurate portrayal of the past; and, given the forty-three pages of vivid anticlerical complaints within which it is embedded, this single quotation has possibly been ascribed too much significance. More recent scholarship, however, has revised upwards the proportion of monastic income estimated to have been spent on the poor, although this was unlikely to have been evenly distributed throughout the country.[7] At a time of rapidly rising population, moreover, any loss of provision for the poor was likely to have been felt more keenly.

There is no doubt, however, that many medieval hospitals had decayed to the point of uselessness well before their dissolution.[8] In a town such as Warwick, which was not well endowed with functioning medieval hospitals, the Dissolution itself probably had little impact. The leper hospital of St Michael's had been absorbed by St Sepulchre's Priory in the fifteenth century, and there was no master at the time of the Dissolution, but a few pensioners continued to be supported by St Mary's parish and the new owners of the priory in the later sixteenth and seventeenth centuries.[9] The other Warwick hospital, St John the Baptist's, catered principally for travellers, and appears to have had no residents by the time of the Dissolution.[10] In contrast, the city of Coventry lost twenty beds for the poor upon the dissolution of their St John's Hospital in 1545.[11] It is not clear, however, whether all lost hospital places were still fulfilling a useful function by the time of the Dissolution. For instance, Clay gives many examples of institutions like St John's, Warwick, which had decayed to the point where there were no longer any inmates, or where the poor had been replaced by permanent corrodians (better-off people who had paid for their place).[12]

Orme and Webster assert that after the Dissolution 'a very large body' of working hospitals and almshouses survived intact into the post-Reformation era, but Marjorie McIntosh is the first historian to attempt to assess the actual number.[13] By her calculations, over half of the 601 institutions existing

7   N. S. Rushton, 'Monastic Charitable Provision in Tudor England: Quantifying and Qualifying Poor Relief in the Early Sixteenth Century', *Continuity and Change* 16/1 (2001), 9–44.
8   The many abuses in late medieval hospitals are detailed by Clay and McIntosh: R. M. Clay, *The Medieval Hospitals of England* (London, 1909), pp. 212–25; McIntosh, *Poor Relief in England*, pp. 124–6; M. McIntosh, 'Negligence, Greed and the Operation of English Charities, 1350–1603', *Continuity and Change* 27 (2012), 53–81.
9   The owners of the priory continued to make these payments at least until 1737: WRO CR 556/164 Correspondence between Matthew Wise and Warwick Corporation 1747–1755, 1781.
10   W. Page, ed., *A History of the County of Warwick* (Victoria County History), vol. 2 (London, 1909), pp. 115–17. The Henrician survey of chantries found that neither of the two hospitals in Warwick was 'used nor the possessions thereof employed according to the intent of their foundations': Alan Kreider, *English Chantries: The Road to Dissolution* (Cambridge, MA and London, 1979), p. 65.
11   Prescott, *English Medieval Hospital*, p. 168.
12   Clay, *Medieval Hospitals*, p. 225.
13   N. Orme and M. Webster, *The English Hospital 1070–1570* (New Haven and London, 1995), p. 161.

on the eve of the Reformation survived the dissolution of the monasteries, guilds and chantries in the mid sixteenth century.[14] The king's commissioners and the Court of Augmentations made a theoretical distinction between revenues used for superstitious and charitable uses, confiscating the former but in many cases reassigning revenues to the latter.[15] Although there were 291 almshouses assumed closed between 1530 and 1559, McIntosh also notes a surprising number, seventy-five, were founded in the same period, many of which are likely to have been refoundings. Thus it seems that more than two-thirds of pre-Reformation hospitals and almshouses either survived the Reformation or were refounded in subsequent years.[16] As Jordan asserts in typically robust fashion, 'Among the many myths still clustering around the English Reformation, not the least is the one persuading us that the medieval hospitals were destroyed.'[17]

Survival was often as a result of the intervention of powerful advocates, or petitions from town and city corporations who valued their local institutions and were allowed to acquire the dissolved foundations and their lands from the Crown. Archbishop Parker, for instance, intervened to save St Thomas's Hospital in Canterbury, founded to accommodate pilgrims coming to the shrine of St Thomas a Becket. He refounded it as Eastbridge Hospital for wounded and travelling soldiers, and supported it out of his own resources. After his death in 1575, attempts were again made to seize its revenues. This time Archbishop Whitgift rescued it, and refounded it as an almshouse for the poor of Canterbury, with ten in-brothers and sisters, and ten out-brothers and sisters.[18] Two other Canterbury hospitals also survived: St John's Hospital in the city, and St Nicholas Harbledown, just outside the city and originally for lepers, managed jointly with St John's. Yet in the whole of County Durham only five medieval hospitals survived, and two of these struggled against attempts at expropriation throughout Elizabeth's reign. Christ's Hospital at Sherburn, just outside Durham, and the Hospital of God at Greatham seem to have enjoyed the protection of the Bishops of Durham, yet the bishop's own hospital at Northallerton did not survive and the wealthiest institution in the diocese, Kepier Hospital, was surrendered.[19] The tiny hospitals of St Edmund King and Martyr in Gateshead and St John's, Barnard Castle, suffered many attempts at confiscation of their lands and revenues. Barnard Castle was the

14   McIntosh, *Poor Relief in England*, CUP Online Appendix 2.
15   Kreider, *English Chantries*, pp. 175–6.
16   McIntosh, *Poor Relief in England*, CUP Online Appendix 2. According to McIntosh's figures, the total number of institutions in existence fell from 601 in the 1530s to 429 in the 1550s (71% of the 1530s total).
17   Jordan, *Philanthropy*, p. 259.
18   CCA CC/S/24/1 Alderman Bunce's Register of Loans and Charitable Donations to the City of Canterbury (1798), pp. 371, 400–14.
19   Clay, *Medieval Hospitals*, p. 233.

site of a pitched battle in Elizabeth's reign between rival claimants for the hospital, who showed no interest in or concern for the three poor almswomen; while St Edmund's position was finally settled by a new charter from James I and its refounding as King James' Hospital.[20]

The picture was not uniform throughout the country. Westmorland had lost all four of its medieval hospitals by 1550.[21] The county of Warwickshire, which had few monastic foundations among its medieval hospitals, retained none after the Reformation, possibly because of the relative lack of church influence in the county, divided as it was between the bishoprics of Worcester and Lichfield. In other places the lack of survival may be principally a reflection of the poor response to need shown by the medieval church locally, or of the corruption of many foundations and the resulting lack of local interest in saving institutions of dubious usefulness. Where institutions were valued for the service they provided to the local poor, strenuous efforts were often made by local people to save them from the king's commissioners. This was the case, for instance, at Norwich where St Giles', known as the Great Hospital, was transferred to the city corporation in 1547 and was providing fifty-seven beds by 1645.[22] Similarly, St Bartholomew's Hospital in Gloucester was granted to the city corporation in 1564, whereupon it was extensively rebuilt for forty almspeople.[23]

Other potential casualties of the Dissolution were the many almshouses attached to guilds and chantries, when these too were abolished in Edward VI's reign. These chantry almshouses, which often provided genuine support for poor people in return for their prayers, had a good chance of surviving, albeit with the loss of their priests and their function, as did almshouses provided by guilds. In many towns, guild almshouses were able to survive when town corporations were allowed to buy back the guild's property, as at Stratford-upon-Avon, when the almshouses of the Guild of the Holy Cross came under the control of the new town corporation in 1553, or in Coventry, where the city commonalty bought Ford's Hospital and its lands after their forfeiture to the Crown in 1547.[24]

While the survival of pre-Reformation almshouses and hospitals may have been greater than previously thought, and certainly greater than many contemporary commentators seemed to suggest, McIntosh believes those that survived were often the smaller institutions, resulting in a proportionally greater loss of places. She argues that with the increased population and rise in

20 DRO D/HH 10/17/170 St John's Hospital, Barnard Castle 1592–1593; NRO SANT/ BEQ/5/1/3 Thomas Bell's Collections re King James' Hospital.
21 McIntosh, 'Negligence, Greed', p. 66n.
22 Prescott, *English Medieval Hospital*, p. 143.
23 McIntosh, *Poor Relief in England*, p. 190.
24 HCPP, no. 15 (1826), p. 544, and no. 28 (1834), p. 166.

poverty in the second half of the sixteenth century, almshouses and hospitals were making far less of a contribution to total need than they had in the past, with 'two to three times more people per place at the end of the century than in the 1520s'.[25] Nor was survival according to any systematic plan.[26] The institutions which remained intact were not necessarily in the places where the need was most pressing. For example, neither of the surviving Sherburn and Greatham Hospitals in County Durham were located in centres of population (the former having originally been intended for lepers). Their rural locations would probably have limited their usefulness in meeting the needs of the local population.

As well as these survivors, and the numerous institutions that were refounded in the years after the Reformation, there were also very many completely new foundations in the second half of the sixteenth century. Despite the development of statutory relief for the poor, provided out of local taxation, it was still the government's expectation that private charity would provide for most necessities, and the public were continually exhorted to contribute. McIntosh argues that regulating and securing charitable donations and endowments was a key element in the Elizabethan state's approach to tackling the problem of poverty, with almshouses an important component in the relief system.[27] Many notable late-sixteenth-century founders were members of the court or Privy Council, such as Robert Dudley, who founded his hospital in Warwick in 1571 and William Cecil, Lord Burghley, who founded his almshouse in Stamford in 1597. Other examples include Sir William Cordell, Solicitor General and Master of the Rolls (Long Melford, Suffolk, 1580); William Brooke, Lord Cobham and Warden of the Cinque Ports (New Cobham College, 1596); Matthew Hutton, Archbishop of York (Warton, Lancashire, 1596); and John Whitgift, Archbishop of Canterbury (Croydon, 1596). These men all founded almshouses during their lifetime, as did other prominent government officials such as Sir Roger Manwood, judge and Chief Baron of the Exchequer (Hackington, Kent, 1570); William Lambarde, Master in Chancery, Deputy Keeper of the Rolls and royal archivist (Queen Elizabeth Hospital, Greenwich, 1576); and Sir John Hawkins, Admiral and Treasurer of the Fleet (Chatham, 1592). This group of men, concerned as they were with the government of the kingdom and the maintenance of social order, were thoroughly versed in the debates surrounding the Tudor legislation and how best to address social need, and may have felt a responsibility on an individual basis to take a lead in implementing the government's policy agenda.

---

25   McIntosh, *Poor Relief in England*, p. 198.
26   Orme and Webster, *English Hospital*, pp. 157–60, provides a useful description of the confused position of the hospitals during the period of the Reformation, and the lack of a coherent government policy towards them.
27   McIntosh, *Poor Relief in England*, p. 3.

Other late-sixteenth-century founders were of more humble origin, such as the Warwick merchant Thomas Oken and his friend, the glazier Nicholas Eyffler (Warwick, 1571 and 1591); Devon merchant John Waldron (Tiverton, 1574); and Northamptonshire schoolmaster Owen Ragdale (Rothwell, 1591). Jordan identified the new mercantile wealth, particularly in London, evident in the period 1480–1660 on which he concentrated his studies, as the driver behind much of the philanthropy of the time. It was certainly a factor in the foundation by London grocer Lawrence Sheriff of a school and almshouse in his birthplace of Rugby in 1567, for example, and in the foundation of almshouses at Sutton Valence in Kent in 1574 by London cloth-worker and merchant William Lambe. Jordan calculated that over 40% of Kent's charitable endowments in his period (1480–1660) came from London mercantile wealth, with the capital's 'merchant aristocracy' vying to emulate and exceed the generosity of their predecessors.[28] Marjorie McIntosh refers to 'the great burst of support for almshouses and hospitals in the Elizabethan period'.[29] Although seeing this as chiefly a continuation of late medieval practice, she acknowledges that these institutions were evolving from their late medieval predecessors, with a new 'social role as providers of care within the community'.[30] She suggests that the donors founding these new institutions at an increasing rate in the latter part of the sixteenth century were not only manifesting an interest in the personal memorialisation which came to replace prayers for the soul, but were responding to growing need and to Protestant teachings about charity.

The chronology of new foundations supports the idea that many benefactors were influenced by contemporary concerns about social need. Elizabeth Prescott suggests it was the 1598 act for erecting hospitals which 'encouraged an outburst of building', with the foundation of almshouses reaching 'a new climax' about 1600.[31] McIntosh believes that the legislation of the same year securing the status of charitable trusts was crucial in placing almshouses on a solid legal and economic footing, encouraging the subsequent growth.[32] Yet McIntosh's tables show the 1580s as a key decade in her period, pre-dating the legislation she and Prescott deem so significant.[33] In the counties of Warwickshire and Kent the noteworthy decade is the 1570s, once again pre-dating the legislation (see Figure 2.1). In Kent this was the single decade with the highest number of foundations across the whole early

---

28   W. K. Jordan, *The Social Institutions of Lancashire: A Study of the Changing Patterns of Aspirations in Lancashire, 1480–1660*, Chetham Society (3rd series) 11 (Manchester, 1962), p. 223.
29   McKintosh, *Poor Relief in England*, p. 188.
30   McKintosh, *Poor Relief in England*, p. 186.
31   39 Eliz. c. 5; Prescott, *English Medieval Hospital*, p. 73.
32   39 Eliz. c. 6; McIntosh, *Poor Relief in England*, p. 187.
33   McIntosh, *Poor Relief in England*, Appendix B, p. 302.

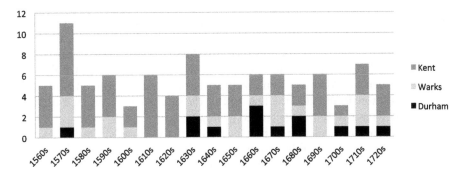

Figure 2.1. Almshouse foundations by decade
Source: Online Appendix A

modern period. This decade also saw the only post-Reformation foundation in County Durham until the 1630s: the Kepier Free Grammar School and Almshouse.[34] In this table also, of the six foundations from the 1590s in Warwickshire and Kent, four came into being before the 1598 legislation, implying this was not the major motivating factor. Rather, these Elizabethan foundations suggest a link with poor relief policy formation and legislation, particularly the debates surrounding the important 1570s statutes. In other words, they were a direct response to the contemporary welfare agenda.

Jordan identified the early decades of the seventeenth century as the peak years in his study period of 1480–1660 for charitable endowments of all kinds, including almshouses. The chart he presents of 'gifts for almshouse foundations' shows a sharp increase from 1600 to a peak in 1620, followed by an equally steep decline to 1650.[35] He ascribed this growth in giving to the aspirations of the 'urban aristocracy' of merchants and burgers, and the newly influential county gentry. These men, in his view, were taking responsibility for public welfare by establishing lasting social and cultural institutions through charitable trusts to address the pressing social problems of the time.[36] Jordan's figures are based on capital bequests, not numbers of foundations, and take no account of inflation. Thomson suggested, in his critique of Jordan, that it was the existence of greater surplus wealth in this period which was the determining factor driving philanthropy, rather than the aspirations that Jordan

---

34 Kepier Free Grammar School and Almshouse was founded by John Heath and Bernard Gilpin in Houghton-le-Spring in 1574, but no accommodation for the almshouse was built.

35 Jordan, *Philanthropy*, p. 260. Jordan's chart is based on the ten 'counties' he surveyed (Bristol, Buckinghamshire, Hampshire, Kent, Lancashire, London, Norfolk, Somerset, Worcestershire and Yorkshire), which represented by his estimation one-third of England's population.

36 Jordan, *Philanthropy*, p. 18.

identified.[37] Nevertheless, Jordan was correct in observing in many places an increase in almshouse foundations after 1600, often led by merchants and local gentry. This can be seen, for instance, in Dorset, where eleven almshouses were founded between 1611 and 1630, two of them by Matthew Chubb, the leading citizen of Dorchester, and in Bristol and Somerset where twenty-two almshouses were founded in the first half of the seventeenth century, mostly by Bristol merchants or Somerset landed gentry.[38]

Nigel Goose has calculated that by 1660, at the close of Jordan's study period, there were probably around 1,019 almshouses in England, accommodating between 1.8% and 2.24% of the elderly population.[39] This is a considerable increase on Marjorie McIntosh's figure of 494 almshouses in 1600, housing between 1% and 1.8% of the over-sixty population.[40] It is also greatly in excess of the 617 almshouses identified by McIntosh in her 'peak' year of 1520. McIntosh acknowledges her numbers may be an underestimate as it is impossible to guarantee that all almshouses in England for her period have been identified. Goose's calculations meanwhile use the probably unrealistic average of eight to ten residents per almshouse to estimate total places, which may inflate the later figures. McIntosh considers the median of six places per institution to be 'probably more accurate', because the average can be distorted by a few exceptionally large establishments.[41] While it is possible that the apparent scale of this achievement over the country as a whole may be exaggerated, there is a clear increase in the number of almshouses and available places between 1550 and 1670 in the three counties of Durham, Warwickshire and Kent, as shown in Table 2.1. The increase in places over the period was lower in Durham than in either Warwickshire or Kent, and started later; and there were undoubtedly similar differences elsewhere in the pace and extent of the increase in almshouse numbers. Despite these caveats, the overall increase in almshouse foundations and places is undeniable.

Prescott's survey concludes in 1640, and that of Jordan in 1660 so, while they both draw attention to an apparent peak in almshouse foundations in

37 J. A. F. Thomson, 'Piety and Charity in Late Medieval London', *Journal of Ecclesiastical History* 16 (1965), 178–95 (p. 184).
38 E. O. Cockburn, *The Almshouses of Dorset* (Dorchester, 1970), pp. 23–4, 41; W. K. Jordan, 'The Forming of the Charitable Institutions of the West of England: A Study of the Changing Pattern of Social Aspirations in Bristol and Somerset, 1480–1660', *Transactions of the American Philosophical Society* (new series) 50/8 (1960), 29–58.
39 N. Goose and M. Yates, 'Charity and Commemoration: A Berkshire Family and their Almshouse, 1675–1763', *Population, Welfare and Economic Change in Britain 1290–1834*, ed. C. Briggs, P. M. Kitson and S. J. Thompson (Woodbridge, 2014), pp. 227–48 (p. 230).
40 McIntosh, *Poor Relief in England*, pp. 188, 198.
41 McIntosh, *Poor Relief in England*, p. 197. The table in Appendix 2 shows the size of early modern almshouses in eight English counties, confirming a median size of six places. Average sizes ranged from 6.4 in Lincolnshire to 8.6 in Shropshire, not the 8–10 assumed by Goose.

Table 2.1. Almshouses and places, 1550–1670

	Almshouses in 1550		Almshouses in 1600		Almshouses in 1670		Percentage increase in places 1550–1670
	Number	Places	Number	Places	Number	Places	
Durham	5	40	5	40	12	73	83%
Warwickshire	7	64	14	109	21	148	131%
Kent	17	198	36	331	60	480	142%
Total	29	302	55	480	93	701	132%

Source: Online Appendix A

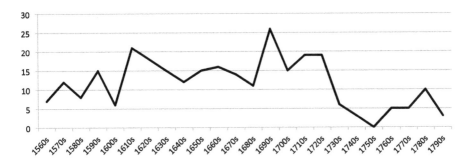

Figure 2.2. Almshouse foundations by decade for eight counties
Source: See n. 41

the early decades of the seventeenth century, they fail to reflect the fact that almshouses continued to be founded in large numbers after these dates. Figure 2.1 shows almshouse foundations carrying on into the 1720s in Durham, Warwickshire and Kent. In other counties, further peaks are also evident in the late seventeenth and early eighteenth centuries: in the period between 1690 and 1730, for example, eighteen almshouses were founded in Lincolnshire and twenty-two in West Yorkshire.[42] Figure 2.2 charts the chronology of almshouse foundation in eight sample English counties (including Durham, Warwickshire and Kent) between 1560 and 1800.[43] It shows not only the

42   L. Crust, *Lincolnshire Almshouses: Nine Centuries of Charitable Housing* (Sleaford, 2002), pp. 27–44; H. Caffrey, *Almshouses in the West Riding of Yorkshire 1600–1900* (King's Lynn, 2006).

43   The eight counties are Durham, Warwickshire and Kent (using data from Online Appendix A); Dorset (information extracted from Cockburn, *Almshouses*); Lincolnshire (from Crust,

early-seventeenth-century peak observed by Prescott and Jordan, but an even greater increase in the later seventeenth and early eighteenth centuries. This is important because it indicates that almshouses continued to be a popular form of charity, despite the almost universal implementation of statutory poor relief during the course of the seventeenth century.

Variations in the pace and scale of foundation are, however, evident in different parts of the country. As can be seen from the three counties in Table 2.1, the early growth in the number of almshouse foundations was not uniform. In Durham, a northern county, the increase began later than in Kent or Warwickshire, and this seems to have been the case elsewhere in the country. The early peak in Warwickshire and Kent seen in Figure 2.1, for instance, differs from the later seventeenth-century peaks from the mainly midlands and northern examples of the eight counties as seen in Figure 2.2. Thus the early surge in post-Reformation foundations apparent in McIntosh's statistics and remarked upon by Prescott seems to have been principally a southern phenomenon, as McIntosh acknowledges. While much of the deficit in almshouse places nationally had been made up by 1600, with 210 new foundations between 1540 and 1599, their geographical spread was very uneven.[44]

An imbalance had already been in evidence before the Reformation, with late medieval institutions concentrated in East Anglia and the south-east, with a 'secondary cluster' in the north and north-west, but the position was worsened by the Dissolution.[45] By the end of the sixteenth century there were no almshouses in Westmorland, and only one, a medieval survivor, in Cumberland. While there were seven medieval survivors in the city of Newcastle upon Tyne, there were no new foundations there in the second half of the sixteenth century, and no provision at all in rural Northumberland (see Appendix 1).[46] As mentioned previously, the county of Durham saw no foundations between 1500 and 1632, apart from the Kepier Free Grammar School and Almshouse. In Lancashire, which had only two surviving pre-Reformation establishments, there was one new foundation in 1595, and just two more in the early seventeenth century, providing a total of only fourteen places across that large county.[47]

In all, eight counties in England saw no new almshouse foundations in the

---

Lincolnshire Almshouses); Nottinghamshire (from E. A. Earl, *Nottinghamshire Almshouses, from Early Times to 1919* (self-published, 2011)); Shropshire (S. Watts, *Shropshire Almshouses* (Woonton Almeley, 2010)); and West Yorkshire (Caffrey, *Almshouses*). The contribution made by each of the eight counties to the total is shown in Online Appendix B.

44 McIntosh, *Poor Relief in England*, p. 301.

45 McIntosh, *Poor Relief in England*, p. 94.

46 Figures from Marjorie McIntosh's database. I am extremely grateful to Professor McIntosh for giving me access to her data.

47 Jordan, *Social Institutions*, pp. 21–5.

second half of the sixteenth century[48] (see Appendix 1, column a). This is in marked contrast to Kent, with fifteen new foundations in the same period; Essex with twelve; and Suffolk and Devon with ten each.[49] By 1600, the only southern counties with little or no almshouse provision, whether new foundations or medieval survivors, were the small or sparsely populated counties of Huntingdonshire (none), Bedfordshire (one) and Cornwall (three). Essex meanwhile had twenty-seven almshouses by 1600; Kent and Devon had twenty-six; Suffolk had twenty-three; Norfolk had twenty-one; and Somerset had twenty. Some of the greatest concentrations, inevitably, were in the cities, with forty-four foundations in London and Middlesex, fifteen in Bristol, and eleven in Exeter and Norwich. In Yorkshire, which was better provided than the rest of northern England, there were concentrations in Hull with twelve foundations by 1600 and York with nine.

Not all of the observed variation in almshouse provision can be explained by differences in population alone. According to Jordan, in Buckinghamshire, which was a largely rural but reasonably prosperous southern county with half the population of Lancashire and only four pre-Reformation almshouses surviving, twenty-two almshouses were founded between 1557 and 1644, against Lancashire's three in the same period.[50] A similar contrast can be shown between Kent and Durham. Calculating the number of almshouses places in 1670 as a proportion of the population aged over sixty, it seems the disparity in almshouse places only partly reflects the differing population of each county (Table 2.2). Kent not only had many more almshouses numerically, but also significantly more places for its late-seventeenth-century population than either Durham or Warwickshire. The difference between Kent and Durham is most marked, with Kent having more than twice the almshouse places available for its elderly population than Durham.

One explanation is the differing levels of prosperity between the counties and regions of early modern England. This difference can be seen, for instance, in the late-seventeenth-century hearth tax returns for the three counties, where the percentage of households exempt from paying the tax can be used as a rough indicator of poverty.[51] Here Durham had a much higher percentage of households exempt from paying the tax than Kent, with Warwickshire placed between the two. Similarly Durham had twice as many single-hearth households than Kent, and hardly any homes with ten or more

---

48 These were the counties of Cumberland, Westmorland, Northumberland, Durham (apart from the Kepier Free Grammar School and Almshouse), Cheshire and Cornwall, together with the small East Midlands counties of Huntingdonshire and Bedfordshire.

49 Figures from Marjorie McIntosh's database.

50 W. K. Jordan, *The Charities of Rural England 1480–1660* (London, 1961), pp. 24, 42.

51 Although Tom Arkell suggests a more nuanced interpretation: T. Arkell, 'The Incidence of Poverty in England in the Later Seventeenth Century', *Social History* 12 (1987), 23–47.

Table 2.2. Almshouse places in relation to the elderly population in 1670

	Durham	Warwickshire	Kent
Number of almshouses	12	21	60
Total almshouse places	73	148[1]	480[2]
Late seventeenth-century population[3]	52,946	82,328	c.150,000
Places per head of over 60 population[4]	1:72	1:55	1:31
Places as percentage of over 60 population	1.39%	1.82%	3.23%

1   This number excludes 5 of the 12 places at the Lord Leycester Hospital, Warwick, as these were for men from outside Warwickshire.
2   This total uses the latest figure where almshouse numbers changed over the period. It excludes all the places at the Royal Naval Hospital, Greenwich, as it was a national resource, and also those places at Trinity Hospital Greenwich (8) and Quested's almshouse, Harrietsham (6) which were specifically for people from outside Kent.
3   Population figures obtained for Durham and Warwickshire by multiplying total hearth tax households by 4.3: T. Arkell, 'Multiplying Factors for Estimating Population Totals from the Hearth Tax', *Local Population Studies* 28 (1982), 52–7 (p. 57); A. Green, E. Parkinson and M. Spufford, eds, *Durham Hearth Tax Assessment Lady Day 1666* (London, 2006), pp. cxxiii; T. Arkell and N. Alcock, eds, *Warwickshire Hearth Tax Returns: Michaelmas 1670* (Stratford-upon-Avon and London, 2010), pp. 60–1. For Kent an approximate figure has been given from Chalkin, as Hearth Tax assessments are missing for large sections of the county: C. W. Chalkin, *Seventeenth-Century Kent* (London, 1965), p. 27.
4   Older people are assumed to constitute 9.89% of the population in 1671: E. A. Wrigley and R. S. Schofield, *The Population History of England 1541–1871: A Reconstruction* (Cambridge, 1989), p. 528.
Source: Online Appendix A

Table 2.3. Hearth Tax Returns c.1670 for three counties

	Durham	Warwickshire	Kent
Percentage of exempt households	44%	38%	32%
Percentage of 1 hearth homes	73%	59%	36%
Percentage with 10 or more hearths	0.78%	1.01%	2.48%

Source: Green, Parkinson and Spufford, *Durham Hearth Tax*, p. cxxxix; Arkell and Alcock, *Warwickshire Hearth Tax*, p. 60; D. Harrington, S. Pearson and S. Rose, eds, *Kent Hearth Tax Assessment Lady Day 1664* (London and Maidstone, 2000), p. lix.

hearths (Table 2.3). This disparity in wealth would have affected the availability of resources for endowing almshouses, and there can be no obvious or simple correlation between social need and charitable provision. For example, the late-eighteenth-century parliamentary returns of the amounts raised by parish poor rates and charitable donations (the Gilbert Returns) show clear regional disparities when calculated per head of population.[52] Unlike the government-instigated hearth tax, parish poor rates were collected in response to need identified in the parishes, but it does not follow that need was necessarily highest where the amounts raised were greatest. Figure 2.3 shows the average amounts raised in poor relief per person between 1783 and 1785 in four quartiles. The top and second quartiles are only found south and east of a line from the Severn to the Wash, with the county of Warwickshire in the second quartile straddling that line. Conversely, all the counties in the third and lowest quartiles are located in the north and west of the country.[53]

Steven King identified a similar regional variation in the aggregate amounts actually paid out to paupers in the eighteenth century, which he attributed to a cultural difference between the north and west of the country and the south and east in terms of attitudes to the poor and the relative generosity of parish poor relief. He suggested that there was a more ingrained culture of independence and 'making do' among the poor in the north and west (and possibly greater opportunities for economic self-sufficiency in developing industries), together with harsher attitudes exhibited by overseers and magistrates towards the poor. Conversely, in the south and east he identified a greater acceptance of dependence on the part of the poor, and a readiness by the poor law authorities to provide relief earlier and more generously to those in need.[54] These differing cultural attitudes are as likely to have affected patterns of private philanthropy, with the Gilbert returns for charity income demonstrating, for instance, that Berkshire had ten times the charitable wealth per head of population than Cumberland.[55]

Comparisons *within* counties also show that the distribution of almshouses does not simply correlate with patterns of social need. In Warwickshire, for example, using the proportion of households exempt from paying the seventeenth-century hearth tax as an indication of the areas with the greatest

---

52   HCPP, *Report from the Committee on Certain Returns, Relative to the State of the Poor, and to Charitable Donations; &c. Reported by Thomas Gilbert, Esq.* (23 May 1787), p. 546.

53   The average annual amounts collected ranged from just over 2s per person in Cumberland to 11s per person in Sussex.

54   S. King, *Poverty and Welfare in England 1700–1850: A Regional Perspective* (Manchester, 2000).

55   Unfortunately the Gilbert Returns for charity income do not distinguish support for almshouses from other charitable causes. The returns reveal wide variations between counties in per capita charitable income, but their accuracy cannot be relied on: D. Owen, *English Philanthropy 1660–1960* (Oxford, 1965), p. 86.

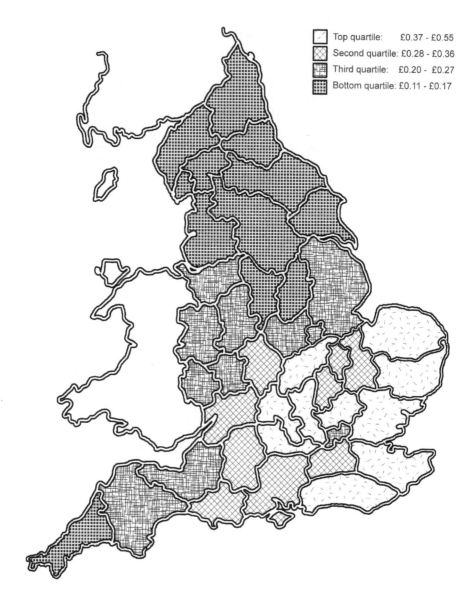

Figure 2.3. Annual amounts raised by poor rates per head of population
Source: The Gilbert Returns

poverty, only one parish in the group with the highest proportion of exempt households had an almshouse, namely, Nicholas Chamberlaine's almshouse at Bedworth (no. 8 on Figure 2.4).[56] Most of Warwickshire's almshouses were located in the next highest band, so that in almost three-quarters of parishes where almshouses were located, the proportion of exempt households was above the Warwickshire average.[57] These were mostly town parishes, such as Stratford-upon-Avon, Tamworth and Rugby, but they also included the rural parishes of Leamington Hastings and Dunchurch. Conversely, four of the five almshouse locations where the percentage of exempt households was below the Warwickshire average were rural areas, namely, Coughton, Stoneleigh, Shustoke and Temple Balsall. Here the gentry and aristocratic founders were landowners, motivated principally by a desire to enhance their local status while providing for their tenants and dependants. Unlike many of the gentry and aristocracy, the clergymen Humphrey Davis and Nicholas Chamberlaine founded their almshouses, in Leamington Hastings (1607) and Bedworth (1715) respectively, in parishes with apparently significant levels of social need.[58] Yet elsewhere in the very poorest areas, it is possible that there were insufficient people of substance able to indulge in generous acts of philanthropy, thus confirming the availability of wealth as the necessary prerequisite for founding an almshouse, rather than the existence of social need itself.

Even in urban areas where social need was greatest, the founding of new almshouses was dependent on the availability of resources. For example, in the city of Coventry, once the corporation had successfully battled to save the early-sixteenth-century Bond's and Ford's Hospitals, giving them access to possibly twenty residential almshouse places, only one additional almshouse appears to have been founded in the early modern period, namely the small almshouse for four founded at West Orchard by Alderman John Clark in 1638.[59] This is in marked contrast to the much smaller town of Warwick, also under pressure in the sixteenth century but growing more prosperous throughout the seventeenth century, which benefited from a surprising number of almshouse foundations in this period. In Warwick, almshouse places increased from twelve (or possibly sixteen) before the Reformation to

56 Eight Warwickshire parishes had over 55% of households exempt from paying the hearth tax; Bedworth's percentage was 79%: T. Arkell and N. Alcock, eds, *Warwickshire Hearth Tax Returns: Michaelmas 1670* (Stratford-upon-Avon and London, 2010), pp. 55, 155.

57 The average percentage of exempt households across Warwickshire was 38%. Fourteen of the nineteen parishes with almshouses were above this value; nine parishes were 45% or above: Arkell and Alcock, *Warwickshire Hearth Tax*, pp. 55–61.

58 Leamington Hastings was a rural parish of ninety-four households where 48% were exempt: Arkell and Alcock, *Warwickshire Hearth Tax*, p. 58. For Bedworth, see n. 54 above.

59 There were places for ten men and a housekeeper at Bond's Hospital, and five couples and a nurse at Ford's: J. Cleary and M. Orton, *So Long as the World Shall Endure: The Five Hundred Year History of Ford's and Bond's Hospitals* (Coventry, 1991), pp. 12, 14.

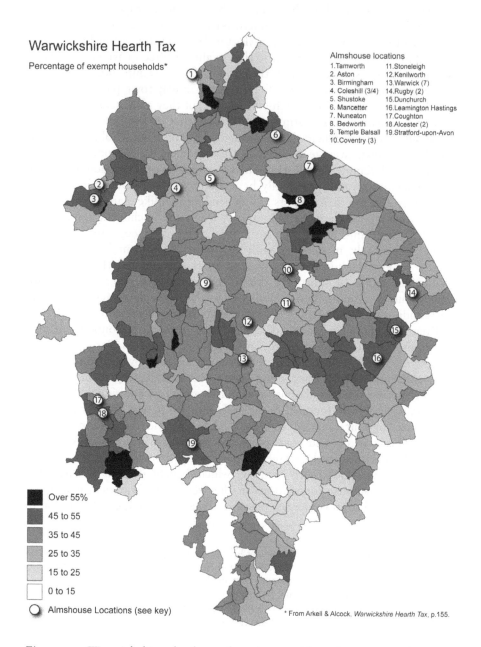

Figure 2.4. Warwickshire almshouse locations and hearth tax exemption

around forty by 1600, and thereafter to a total of approximately eighty places by 1712.[60] The addition of thirty-four places after the Great Fire of 1694 was a significant part of this increase, yet even so the contrast with the much larger city of Coventry is striking.[61]

Yet despite these local and regional disparities in wealth, and apparent variation in responses to need, the idea of the almshouse seems to have held an almost universal appeal. Different areas of the country may each have had their own trajectory of almshouse foundation, influenced by the extent of medieval survival, the availability of wealth, existing charitable networks and differing local priorities; but the overall picture is surprisingly uniform. By the second half of the nineteenth century there were almshouses in every English county, although the numbers were still low in Cumberland, Lancashire, Cheshire and Cornwall (see Appendix 1, column c). Goose estimates that by around 1870 almshouses constituted more than a quarter of the expenditure from all endowed charity.[62]

The scale of almshouse foundation in early modern England was undoubtedly impressive, particularly in comparison with other periods. While Goose's figures show an overall decline in the percentage of the elderly population accommodated in almshouses from 1520 through to the twenty-first century, during the seventeenth century this trend was reversed.[63] For the early modern period, the accumulation of new almshouse foundations in a period of stabilising population growth in the mid-to-late seventeenth century, enabled almshouse provision in many places to maintain its relative position. In Durham and Warwickshire, for instance, the percentage of the elderly population who could be accommodated in almshouses in 1800 was similar to the position in 1670 (see Appendix 3).

After about 1730, however, there was a steep decline in almshouse foundation in many parts of the country, as can be seen in Figure 2.2.[64] In the county of Warwickshire, for instance, no almshouses were founded from 1725 until after 1800, while in Dorset there were no new foundations at all in the eighteenth

---

60   That is, if all twelve places at the Lord Leycester Hospital are counted, and the Rosemary Lane almshouse is included.

61   After the fire, twenty-eight places were created by the corporation in two converted barns for the Rosemary Lane almshouse, and a further six places with the rebuilding of Oken's almshouse: WRO, 'To Divers Good Uses': A Directory of the Warwick Charities Past and Present (Warwick, 1993), p. 16; P. Bolitho, Warwick's Most Famous Son: The Story of Thomas Oken and his Charity (Warwick, 2003), p. 29.

62   Goose and Yates, 'Charity and Commemoration', p. 236.

63   There was a reduction from between 2.32% and 2.9% in 1520 to 0.28% in 2012, but with an increase between 1600 and 1660: Goose and Yates, 'Charity and Commemoration', p. 230.

64   Although this was followed by a partial revival later in the Victorian era, the increase in places was insufficient to keep pace with nineteenth- and twentieth-century population increases, hence the overall decline identified by Goose and Yates.

century.[65] Even in the populous county of Kent, only six almshouses were founded between 1726 and 1800, adding a mere twenty-five additional places to the previous total of 593. In County Durham there were three almshouses founded in the early years of the eighteenth century, but then only one more before the start of the nineteenth century.[66] After 1728, Lincolnshire had no new foundations until 1770, and then a further seven almshouses established in the last decades of the century. Even in West Yorkshire, where almshouses continued to be founded throughout the eighteenth century, the fact that only thirteen almshouses were founded in the seventy years between 1730 and 1800 compares unfavourably with fifteen being founded between 1700 and 1730.[67]

This eighteenth-century decline resulted not only in fewer new foundations, but in the neglect and abuse of some existing institutions, to which the many reports of the Brougham Commission attest.[68] A newly hostile charitable environment produced the Mortmain Act of 1736, which placed restrictions on testamentary bequests to charity which deprived the testator's natural heirs.[69] Almshouses had to compete with alternative models of charity which were developing to meet social needs, such as the voluntary subscription charities and the increasingly popular medical charities, hospitals and dispensaries.[70] As a practical response to the problem of the poor, moreover, almshouses were overtaken by the need to deal with greater numbers more economically. Parish workhouses became the preferred option for dealing with the problem of the poor after the 1723 Workhouse Test Act, many of them built at the cost of a single benefactor.[71] By the 1740s it has been estimated there were 600 parish workhouses nationally, 3,765 by 1802, and 4,000 by 1815. Almshouses, meanwhile, were still only 1,336 in number by 1870.[72]

---

65 Cockburn, *Almshouses*; A. Langley, 'Warwickshire Almshouses: To What Extent Were They "affording comfortable asylums to the aged and respectable poor"?', *The British Almshouse: New Perspectives on Philanthropy ca. 1400–1914*, ed. N. Goose, H. Caffrey and A. Langley (Milton Keynes, 2016), pp. 121–37 (p. 124).

66 This was the almshouse for six women at Greatham, founded in 1762 by Dormer Parkhurst, Master of Greatham Hospital.

67 Crust, *Lincolnshire Almshouses*; Caffrey, *Almshouses*.

68 There were, however, many new donors who left legacies to support existing foundations, enabling them to survive: N. Goose and L. Moden, *A History of Doughty's Hospital, Norwich, 1687–2009* (Hatfield, 2010), p. 35.

69 G. Jones, *History of the Law of Charity 1532–1827* (Cambridge, 1969), p. 110.

70 P. Slack, 'Hospitals, Workhouses and the Relief of the Poor in Early Modern London', *Health Care and Poor Relief in Protestant Europe 1500–1700*, ed. O. P. Grell and A. Cunningham (London, 1997), pp. 234–51 (pp. 245–6).

71 An example is the workhouse constructed in Poole in 1739 with £500 from Thomas Missing: Cockburn, *Almshouses*, p. 39.

72 P. Slack, *From Reformation to Improvement: Public Welfare in Early Modern England* (Oxford, 1999), p. 133; King, *Poverty and Welfare*, p. 3; Goose and Yates, 'Charity and Commemoration', p. 230.

A complete chronology of post-Reformation almshouse foundation has yet to be written, but it seems that, in the years up to 1725, founding an almshouse was a widely popular form of charity, regional differences in pace and extent of foundation notwithstanding. Almshouse founders were frequently responding to generalised rather than specific concerns about poverty, influenced by public debate, polemic and sermons. The location of their foundations was influenced as much by where there were resources available as by where need was greatest, and the decision to found an almshouse could itself be influenced by a number of other considerations. Social need was not the only, or overriding, factor; other motivations will be explored more fully in the following chapter.

3

Almshouse Founders and Their Motivations

> To classify men's charitable acts into neat categories according to the
> impulses assumed to have prompted them would be dangerous and absurd.
> Human behaviour rarely exhibits such helpful singleness of motive.[1]

The motivation behind any philanthropic gesture is open to a number of
interpretations, and altruism and self-interest may, as Clive Burgess observes,
be 'hopelessly entangled'.[2] As a particular form of philanthropy with a long
history, almshouses lent themselves to a wide range of motivations which
went beyond the obvious meeting of social need. Founders, too, were a diverse
group, ranging from town tradesmen, country gentry and local clergymen
to city merchants, great magnates and church prelates. Many were involved
in local or state government and administration, and their philanthropy was
as much a public as a private gesture, influenced by a range of complex and
overlapping agenda. While the Christian imperative to provide for the poor
was accepted by Catholics and Protestants alike, and for many founders this
was probably sufficient motivation, for others there is some suggestion that
the founding and administration of almshouses might have played a part in
forging particular religious and cultural identities. In the continuing debate
on the correct response to the problem of the poor, moreover, members of the
government and court publicly led by example in founding almshouses and in
other charitable works. For the landowning classes, accepting responsibility
for providing for aged tenants and other poor people in the neighbourhood
was an obvious expression of their status, virtue and moral leadership, while
their charitable foundations could themselves become sites of memorialisation. Among the urban oligarchies, involvement in the provision of
almshouses was likewise an opportunity to demonstrate or acquire prestige
and respect through the exercise of civic responsibility. Consequently, the
beneficiaries of almshouses might be not only the poor inhabitants themselves,
but also the donors, the administrators, and society more generally.

---

1   D. Owen, *English Philanthropy 1660–1960* (Oxford, 1965), p. 36.
2   C. Burgess, '"A fond thing vainly invented": An Essay on Purgatory and Pious Motive in
Later Medieval England', *Parish, Church and People: Local Studies in Lay Religion 1350–1750*,
ed. S. Wright (London, 1988), pp. 56–84 (p. 67).

In these circumstances, identifying the specific impulses which motivated individual donors is a necessarily speculative exercise. The conservatism of many donors, whereby benefactors were influenced by the philanthropic acts of their contemporaries or local predecessors, also makes it difficult to judge how far individuals were subject to a precise set of motivations. Yet the enduring popularity throughout the early modern period of almshouses as a specific form of charitable provision requires at least some attempt at explanation. There were two crucial mid-sixteenth-century changes which might have been expected to obviate the need for, or reduce the attraction of, almshouse foundation for potential donors. The first was the abolition of intercessory institutions, which was the function of many medieval hospitals; and the second was the development of statutory poor relief, which included parish responsibility for housing their poor. Neither of these changes, however, appears to have had any such impact. On the contrary, from the second half of the sixteenth century, almshouses continued to be founded in great numbers.

This chapter will explore some of the possible motivations influencing the founders and benefactors of almshouses in the early modern period, and the societal and cultural pressures to which they were responding. Their objectives, specifically what they hoped to achieve through this particular form of philanthropy, will be examined in succeeding chapters discussing the identity of the beneficiaries and the nature of the provision for them.

Who were the donors?

Founding an endowed almshouse required a major investment, and this act must have held considerable significance for benefactors. Even an unendowed almshouse, perhaps the donor's own house or a couple of cottages, represented an important gift of property. It assumes the donor to have been in possession of disposable wealth; wealth, moreover, surplus to that which was required for supporting a family or heirs. In her study of Warwickshire landed society in the fifteenth century, Christine Carpenter claims that merchants, new gentry and rising yeomen farmers were able to spend more on roads, bridges, education and the poor, not from ideological motives but because they held more of their wealth in surplus goods rather than land. It was the priority of established landowners, on the other hand, to preserve the integrity of their estates for future generations, so their charitable bequests were often of 'peripheral or specially acquired properties' which were not fundamental to the estate they were trying to preserve.[3] Surplus disposable wealth was

3 C. Carpenter, *Locality and Polity: A Study of Warwickshire Landed Society, 1401–1499* (Cambridge, 1992), pp. 224–5, 238, 241.

consequently a prerequisite for founding an almshouse. For childless founders there were fewer competing claims for their available wealth, and founding an almshouse could be one way of benefiting posterity in the absence of heirs. Thomas Oken, Warwick mercer, died childless in 1573 and left the bulk of his fortune for the benefit of the town, including an almshouse of three cottages for six poor people. Similarly, Rev. Nicholas Chamberlaine, another Warwickshire almshouse founder, declared in his will of 1715, 'I having no child do dispose of my temporall Estate to the charitable uses following'.[4] Anne Langley has calculated that, of the twenty-one individual founders of almshouses in Warwickshire before 1900 that she identifies, just over half were childless.[5]

Unsurprisingly, most founders were men, though this probably under-represents women's influence. In Warwickshire, for instance, of the thirty-one almshouses definitely known to have been founded between 1500 and 1725, only one is known to have been founded solely by a woman; the figures for Durham are one out of fourteen, and for Kent one out of fifty-nine.[6] Women were sometimes involved, either as founders themselves or acting jointly with their husbands, or as executors of their husband's estates. Dame Alice Leigh, for instance, who built the Stoneleigh almshouses in Warwickshire in 1576 after the death of her husband Sir Thomas, said that she was acting on her husband's wishes, and the almshouses were credited to the couple in the founding letters patent.[7] John and Ann Smith, wealthy Londoners, founded their almshouse at Longport in Canterbury together in 1644, apparently in thanks for the birth of a son after twenty years of marriage.[8] Acting as his executrix, Nicholas Eyffler's wife arranged with Robert West for the conversion into an almshouse for eight women of the barn in Warwick that her husband had bought from West.[9] The administration of trusts, and of almshouses under the control of parishes and town corporations, was almost universally at this period undertaken by men alone, and there were no boards of female governors or regents to match those in seventeenth-century Holland, for instance.[10]

4   TNA PROB/11/548/170 Will of Nicholas Chamberlaine, Clerk of Bedworth Warwickshire, 24 June 1715.
5   A. Langley, 'Warwickshire Almshouses, 1400 to 1900: "Affording comfortable asylums to the aged and respectable poor"', *Warwickshire History* 14/4 (2009/10), 139–55 (p. 141).
6   See Online Appendix A.
7   HCPP, no. 18 (1828), p. 521.
8   D. I. Hill, *The Ancient Hospitals and Almshouses of Canterbury* (Canterbury, 2004), p. 45.
9   WRO CR 1618/WA12/34 Will of Nicholas Eyffler 1591, and CR 1618/WA12/36/13 Building accounts for the almshouse on Castle Hill 1597.
10   See, for instance, the many seventeenth-century group portraits of regentesses of Haarlem hospitals in the Frans Hals Museum, Haarlem, http://www.franshalsmuseum.nl/en/collection/search-collection/?q=regentesses&medium=&category=&artist= (accessed 5 December 2013).

In his works on English philanthropy between 1480 and 1660, W. K. Jordan claimed that, whereas medieval charity had been largely provided by the church and the nobility, in the period he studied these were largely replaced by the gentry and the people he described as the mercantile aristocracy.[11] He used fourteen different groups to categorise donors of testamentary bequests in ten English counties, and tabulated the amount and percentage of their contribution to various causes to demonstrate the dominance of the gentry and, particularly, the merchant classes. He showed, for instance, that tradesmen donated more in total to charity than the nobility (an entirely spurious comparison when one considers the great disparity of the numbers within each group).[12] Despite Jordan's assertions, almshouse foundations by churchmen and nobility were still in evidence in the early modern period. While the absence of foundations by the monarch for almost two hundred years is perhaps remarkable, the Crown's financial difficulties for most of the sixteenth and seventeenth centuries is the likely explanation.[13] Noble founders were certainly few in number with notable examples being: Robert Dudley, Earl of Leicester (Warwick, 1571), the Countesses of Cumberland and Pembroke (Beamsley Hospital in North Yorkshire, 1593 and 1650), and Henry Howard, Earl of Northampton (Clun, 1607; Castle Rising, 1609; and Trinity Hospital, Greenwich, 1613). Almshouses continued to be founded throughout the early modern period by great churchmen, such as Archbishops of Canterbury Whitgift (Croydon, 1596) and Abbot (Guildford, 1617), Archbishops of York Robert Holgate (Helmsley, 1555) and Matthew Hutton (Warton, 1596), and Bishop of Durham John Cosin (Bishop Auckland, 1662 and Durham, 1666). In addition, and particularly after the Restoration, almshouse founders are present among the lesser clergy: for instance, Abraham Colfe (Lewisham, 1658); George Davenport (Houghton-le-Spring, Durham, 1666); Nicholas Chamberlaine (Bedworth, Warwickshire, 1715); John Bowes (Bishopwearmouth, Durham, 1712); and Oliver North (West Farleigh, Kent, 1725).[14]

Obviously, the assets required to found an endowed almshouse means that one would expect benefactors to come from the wealthier groups: merchants rather than tradesmen, gentry rather than husbandmen.[15] Yet despite the

---

11   W. K. Jordan, *Philanthropy in England 1480–1660: A Study of the Changing Pattern of English Social Aspirations* (London, 1959), pp. 18–19.

12   These groups included the Crown, nobility, upper and lower gentry, upper and lower clergy, yeomen, husbandmen and agricultural labourers, merchants, tradesmen, burghers, artisans and lastly the professions and public officials. Jordan, *Philanthropy*, Tables X and XI, Structure of Class Aspirations, pp. 384–7.

13   There were no foundations by the reigning monarch between the Savoy Hospital, founded by Henry VII in 1505, and the Royal Hospital at Chelsea founded by Charles II in 1682.

14   See Online Appendix A.

15   Jordan's interest was endowed charity, demonstrated through testamentary bequests. As such, he ignored many smaller gifts, including houses and cottages, with which a wider section

assurance with which Jordan uses his categories, the exact occupation and status of many almshouse founders is unknown, and for others the categories are blurred. For instance, nothing is known of George Ingram, who founded the Bleachfield almshouses in Alcester, Warwickshire, in 1680, beyond the fact that his family were local mercers and that he was probably brother-in-law to John Bridges, founder of the Priory almshouses in the same town in 1659.[16] The Bridges family owned land in Alcester and served as stewards to Lord Brooke. John Bridges was a 'minor lawyer' who served as a colonel in the Parliamentary forces and, as governor of Warwick castle, earned the enmity of the Warwickshire gentry.[17] It is not clear in which of Jordan's categories he would have placed either man. Just as elusive are two other Warwickshire almshouse founders: Thomas Newcombe, founder of almshouses at Dunchurch in 1690, about whom the only known fact appears to be that he was printer to King Charles II; and Humphrey Davis, founder of the almshouse at Leamington Hastings in 1607. Davis was an ordained clergyman and schoolmaster, but does not appear to have been occupied in either capacity in Warwickshire, and how he came by his wealth is a mystery.[18] He left his own house to be lived in by eight poor, and charged his brother's family with their support from the lands he left them.

This was a typical gesture of many less wealthy donors, particularly if they were childless. Quite ordinary people had for generations left houses and cottages for the use of the poor, either to be rented out and the income used for the good of the church or the poor, or to be used as a base for communal activities such as church ales. Often, however, they were also used to provide accommodation for poor people of the parish at little or no rent.[19] The property might be left to the parish church to be managed by the churchwardens, rather than to relatives as in Davis's case, or to town corporations or guilds. For example, Peregrine Horden notes from the 1517/18 churchwardens' accounts of St Mary's Lambeth that the parish was running an almshouse.[20] Miri Rubin cites the similar example of St Mary's parish in Cambridge, where Thomas Jakenett and Thomas Ebbon

---

of the population had traditionally benefited their local communities. See the critique of Jordan by Steve Hindle in *On the Parish? The Micro-Politics of Poor Relief in Rural England c.1550–1750* (Oxford, 2004), pp. 98–9.

16   G. E. Saville, *Bleachfield and Swan Streets and Stratford Road*, Alcester and District Local History Society Occasional Paper 35 (Alcester, 1985), p. 4; John Bridges' son Brooke Bridges refers to Ingram as 'my uncle' in his will: WRO CR 2219/13 Codicil to Brooke Bridges' will 1702.

17   A. Hughes, *Politics, Society and Civil War in Warwickshire, 1620–1660* (Cambridge, 1987), p. 235.

18   See Leamington Hastings case study, chapter 6.

19   P. Cowley, *The Church Houses* (London, 1970), pp. 63, 82; M. K. McIntosh, *Poor Relief in England 1350–1600* (Cambridge, 2012), p. 64.

20   P. Horden, 'Small Beer? The Parish and the Poor and Sick in Later Medieval England', *The Parish in Late Medieval England*, ed. C. Burgess and E. Duffy (Donington, 2006), pp. 339–64 (p. 346).

established almshouses near the church in 1479. These were maintained by the churchwardens and appear in the sixteenth- and seventeenth-century church-warden accounts, where the almsfolk are occasionally mentioned as cleaning the church.[21] Pat Cullum describes the ubiquitous but often ephemeral *maisons dieu* of late-medieval Yorkshire where provision could be as basic as a room reserved for the poor in the donor's house.[22] The extensive property of the Guild of Corpus Christi in Maidstone, Kent, taken over by the town corporation in 1549, included very many small cottages used as almshouses, which had probably been gifted by members in the past.[23]

This tradition of housing the poor was probably more widespread than surviving documentation suggests, as indicated by the occasional references to vestiges of early provision about which very little else is known. For instance, there was a medieval hospital in Henley-in-Arden, Warwickshire, for the poor and wayfarers which was rebuilt in 1449, but apart from that nothing is known of it.[24] Yet the reference in the hearth tax returns of 1670 to 'Foure almes houses' in Henley-in-Arden could suggest some form of provision survived from this medieval hospital.[25] Similarly, the reference in the 1587 will of William Willoughby to the almshouses in Nuneaton churchyard suggests they were an earlier foundation, possibly supported by the church or a guild.[26] Historians such as Horden and Marjorie McIntosh have demonstrated that the development of statutory poor relief in Tudor England came on the back of an already well-embedded tradition of formal and informal giving within parishes, which included the provision of housing. As with much of the Tudor poor relief legislation, the provision of cottages for the impotent poor seems to have acknowledged this tradition, rather than initiated it.[27]

The role of religion

Prior to the Reformation, the motivation behind all philanthropy is thought to have been principally religious. Rosenthal, for instance, declared that 'almost

---

21   M. Rubin, *Charity and Community in Medieval Cambridge* (Cambridge, 1987), p. 128.
22   P. Cullum, '"For Pore People Harberles": What Was the Function of the Maisondieu?', *Trade, Devotion and Governance: Papers in Late Medieval History*, ed. D. J. Clayton, R. G. Davies and P. McNiven (Stroud, 1994), pp. 36–54 (p. 38).
23   P. Clark and L. Murfin, *The History of Maidstone: The Making of a Modern County Town* (Stroud, 1995), p. 56.
24   W. Page, ed., *A History of the County of Warwick* (Victoria County History), vol. 2 (London, 1909), p. 112.
25   T. Arkell and N. Alcock, eds, *Warwickshire Hearth Tax Returns: Michaelmas 1670* (Stratford-upon-Avon and London, 2010), p. 235.
26   HCPP, no. 29 (1835), p. 993.
27   McIntosh, *Poor Relief in England*, p. 111.

all medieval philanthropy had the purchase of prayers as their ultimate goal'.[28] The Reformation altered the nature and motivation of philanthropy, if not its effects. In the fifteenth century, in particular, it is assumed that the preoccupation of many benefactors was with the afterlife, and specifically with the progress of their souls and those of their loved ones in Purgatory. Many pre-Reformation almshouses, for example, were essentially chantries, of which one of the best-known examples is God's House at Ewelme in Oxfordshire, founded by William and Alice de la Pole, Earl and Countess of Suffolk, in 1437.[29] The poor men in these almshouses, often a symbolic twelve or thirteen in number, were charged with an onerous programme of daily prayer, including for the souls of the founders, in return for which they received accommodation, a stipend, and sometimes food and clothing. Other almshouses in towns and villages were run by religious guilds, which also sought to ensure prayers after death for the souls of their members. For example, the fifteenth-century Hosyer's Almshouse in Ludlow was run by the Palmers' Guild, which existed to relieve poor members and provide prayers for the souls of members and their families.[30] The Guild of Corpus Christi in Maidstone, which had its chantry chapel in All Saints' Church, also maintained several small almshouses in the town.[31] As McIntosh suggests, once almshouses were no longer able to offer prayers for the dead, the reasons for founding and maintaining such establishments 'had to be reassessed'.[32]

The linking of philanthropy with reciprocal obligations such as prayers for the soul has led some historians to utilise anthropological constructs, notably the theory of gift exchange developed by Marcel Mauss and his successors, to understand late-medieval philanthropy.[33] Mauss's observation, put very simply, was that gifts were never free, but bound the recipient in a social relationship with the giver which required them to reciprocate. As a consequence, an unreciprocated gift left the recipient as the inferior in an unequal relationship, dishonoured and under a permanent obligation to the giver.[34] In this hypothesis, the abolition of the doctrine of Purgatory at the Reformation, by removing the direct purpose behind the exchange in chantry almshouses, required other sources of 'return' to be identified for post-Reformation

---

28   J. T. Rosenthal, *The Purchase of Paradise: Gift Giving and the Aristocracy, 1307–1485* (London, 1972), pp. 10, 126.
29   J. Goodall, *God's House at Ewelme: Life, Devotion and Architecture in a Fifteenth-Century Almshouse* (Aldershot, 2001).
30   S. Watts, *Shropshire Almshouses* (Woonton Almeley, 2010), p. 67.
31   C. Cooper, *Maidstone, A History* (Chichester, 2008), p. 13.
32   McIntosh, *Poor Relief in England*, p. 186.
33   Rosenthal, *Purchase*; S. Sweetinburgh, *The Role of the Hospital in Medieval England: Gift-Giving and the Spiritual Economy* (Dublin, 2004).
34   M. Mauss, *The Gift: Forms and Functions of Exchange in Archaic Societies*, trans. Ian Cunnison (originally *Essai sur le don*, 1925; London, 1966).

benefactors of almshouses. Also, once prayers for the dead had been abolished, there was no longer the same clear, reciprocal relationship between the donor and the poor recipient. The 'rewards' for benefactors were thus perceived and received in other ways, for instance through memorialisation, honour and status enhancement, where the poor were not themselves the reciprocators but part of a more complex set of relationships. Meanwhile, the development of poor relief funded by compulsory taxation both undermined the charitable principle of the gift freely given, and placed the poor recipient under an obligation with less opportunity for reciprocation.

It is possible, however, that there has been an overemphasis on the importance of Purgatory and prayers for the dead in the pre-Reformation period. Margaret Aston and Colin Richmond give examples of fifteenth-century benefactors who did not request prayers for their souls, such as Sir Thomas Latimer and his wife Anne; Sir Thomas Broke of Holditch in Devon and his son Thomas; and John Tasburgh, who in 1473 'left a house and land for poor people to live in, with no provision for prayers for his soul'.[35] Colin Richmond also remarks on the 'careless' attitude of the Paston family towards Purgatory, neglecting to create the perpetual chantry intended by their forebear Judge William Paston.[36] Even when prayers for the dead were specified, in some cases this seems to have been mere convention rather than the result of heartfelt conviction. The fifteenth-century mercer Richard Whittington, for instance, who was mayor of London three times during the reigns of Richard II and Henry IV, gave an enormous fortune to various charitable causes in London. These included a library, a refuge for unmarried mothers, and a 120-seat public lavatory on the banks of the Thames. In his will of 1421 he made more than thirty separate bequests, for only half of which he asked that the recipients should pray for his soul and that of his wife. His largest single bequest was for the relief of poor prisoners in London gaols. He asked his executors to dispose of the residue of his estate in works of charity for the good of his soul, from which they established the almshouse attributed to him.[37] This seems a somewhat casual instruction if concern for the afterlife was his overriding motivation. Also, a concern for public toilets and poor prisoners, while of public benefit, does not seem to be the most obvious priority for someone wanting to guarantee that prayers for their soul were diligently delivered after their death.

---

35 M. Aston, '"Caim's Castles": Poverty, Politics and Disendowment', *The Church, Politics and Patronage in the Fifteenth Century*, ed. B. Dobson (Gloucester, 1984), pp. 45–81 (pp. 65, 80 n. 111).

36 C. Richmond, 'Religion and the Fifteenth-Century English Gentleman', *Church, Politics and Patronage*, ed. Dobson, pp. 193–208 (p. 195).

37 J. Imray, *The Charity of Richard Whittington: A History of the Trust Administered by the Mercers' Company, 1424–1966* (London, 1968), pp. 2–8.

Whittington was mayor of London at the time Lollardy was at its height. The Lollards disparaged chantries because they advantaged the souls of wealthy benefactors over those of poorer people, diverted resources from the poor, and enriched a corrupt church.[38] Although Wycliffe's writings were condemned as heretical in 1382 and his Lollard followers irredeemably tainted with treason after Oldcastle's rising in 1414, Lollard beliefs arguably continued to influence popular attitudes to piety and charity throughout the fifteenth and early sixteenth centuries.[39] So it is that, for at least some pre-Reformation founders of almshouses, easing their soul's passage through Purgatory was not the overriding motivation, even perhaps for those whose establishments came in the guise of chantries. Donors tended to follow tradition, using the structures and forms of giving familiar to them, and as historians such as Miri Rubin and Elizabeth Prescott have shown, almshouses in the medieval period proved themselves to be remarkably adaptable institutions, often borrowing traditional forms even when their function had changed, to reflect changing attitudes and meet new needs.[40] Many almshouses founded in the fifteenth century, moreover, were very modest, providing accommodation only as a 'bare act of relief', with no attempt at creating a quasi-religious institution, and this was also true for many sixteenth-century foundations.[41]

The emergence of civic humanism in the early sixteenth century has also been credited with influencing attitudes to the poor and the intentions of donors.[42] Much medieval philanthropy could be viewed as principally for the good of the donor, with the benefit to poor recipients being merely incidental rather than the major purpose of the donation, as poverty was assumed to be an ineradicable part of the human condition.[43] Humanists such as Juan Luis Vives, however, argued for a rational, organised approach to poor relief in European cities, which would lead not only to the eradication of social ills such as crime and begging, but would have a rehabilitative purpose, enabling

38   Number seven of the Lollards' Twelve Conclusions: H. S. Cronin, 'The Twelve Conclusions of the Lollards', *The English Historical Review*, 22/86 (1907), 292–304 (p. 299); Aston, 'Caim's Castles', p. 56.

39   R. Lutton, *Lollardy and Orthodox Religion in Pre-Reformation England: Reconstituting Piety* (Woodbridge, 2006), pp. 100–1.

40   E. Prescott, *The English Medieval Hospital 1050–1640* (Melksham, 1992); M. Rubin, 'Development and Change in English Hospitals, 1100–1500', *The Hospital in History*, ed. L. Granshaw and R. Porter (London and New York, 1989), pp. 41–59; M. Rubin, 'Imagining Medieval Hospitals: Considerations on the Cultural Meaning of Institutional Change', *Medicine and Charity Before the Welfare State*, ed. J. Barry and C. Jones (London, 1991), pp. 14–25.

41   Rubin, 'Development and Change', p. 56.

42   McIntosh, *Poor Relief in England*, p. 21.

43   Kreider, *English Chantries: The Road to Dissolution* (Cambridge, MA and London, 1979), p. 66.

the poor to lead ordered lives of Christian piety.[44] While this arguably had more of an influence in Continental cities, there is evidence, particularly in the Kentish towns, of well-organised systems of poor relief pre-dating the Tudor legislation. Historians of the late medieval and early modern periods are increasingly acknowledging continuities across the fifteenth and sixteenth centuries, and emphasising the gradual rather than the cataclysmic nature of the social and religious changes occurring. The recent historiography of the Reformation in England, for instance, suggests a gradual, albeit fundamental, shift in beliefs and practice over time, rather than the previously competing ideologies which depict either abrupt, imposed disjunction or the survival, unchanged, of popular religion. Similarly, aspects such as the secularisation of charity and the development of parish-based structures of poor relief have been shown convincingly by historians such as Peregrine Horden and Marjorie McIntosh to have been not uniquely Tudor achievements but a continuation of developments occurring in the fifteenth century or earlier.[45]

Almshouses, a form of welfare provision with a long history, appear to be an example of this continuity, with many early modern benefactors motivated by similar philanthropic considerations as their late medieval predecessors, and adopting the same traditional forms for their establishments. Jordan's claim that the rise in charitable giving he observed (itself a contested claim) was part of a cultural revolution, 'a momentous shift from men's primarily religious preoccupations to ... secular concerns' is difficult, if not impossible, to substantiate.[46] His problematic distinction between religious and secular concerns is misleading, and a gross oversimplification, as historians such as Thomson have been quick to point out.[47] The use of the term 'secular' by Jordan was in fact intended to denote a lay institution, one that was not *ecclesiastical*, rather than not *religious*. He included bequests to almshouses in the secular category of 'the poor', despite the religious character of many of them. As he himself acknowledged, many donors were deeply pious, even those making bequests for purposes he categorised as secular, and religion and personal piety remained powerful drivers in much of the philanthropy of the age.

Subsequent historians have shown that there was little distinction between

44   J. L. Vives, 'De subventione pauperum' (1526), *Some Early Tracts on Poor Relief*, ed. F. R. Salter (London, 1926), pp. 4–31.
45   M. McIntosh, 'Local Responses to the Poor in Late Medieval and Tudor England', *Continuity and Change* 3/2 (1988), 209–45; Horden, 'Small Beer?'; McIntosh, *Poor Relief in England*.
46   Jordan, *Philanthropy*, p. 16.
47   J. A. F. Thomson, 'Piety and Charity in Late Medieval London', *Journal of Ecclesiastical History* 16 (1965), 178–95.

Protestants and Catholics in charitable giving.[48] Although Protestants no longer officially believed in good works as a route to salvation, they were eager to promote charitable giving and concern for the poor as a reflection of their faith and piety, which suggested that God had chosen them to be saved. The nuances of the theology of justification by faith probably passed the majority of the population by, and for many the link between Christian salvation and charity remained unbroken.[49] The Christian tradition of charity based on the seven works of bodily mercy survived the Reformation and underpinned a wide range of social provision gifted to their communities by individual benefactors. This connection is made explicit in the inscription from Matthew 25 on the wall of the almshouses (now demolished) founded at Bromham in Wiltshire by Sir Henry Baynton in 1612:

> I WAS HUNGRIE AND YEE
> GAVE MEE MEATE. I WAS
> THIRSTIE AND YEE GAVE MEE
> DRINKE. I WAS NAKED AND
> YEE CLOTHED MEE. I
> WAS HARBARLES AND YEE
> GAVE MEE LODGINGE. CUM
> YEE BLESSED OF MY FATHER
> INHERIT THE KINGDUM
> PREPARED FOR YOU.[50]

The injunction to treat the poor as if they were Christ himself was unaffected by the Reformation and would have been instantly recognised by Christians of all allegiances. Yet the inclusion of the last sentence 'Come ye blessed of my Father, inherit the kingdom prepared for you', seems to suggest a direct link between good works and salvation which ought to have been at odds with the family's Protestantism.[51] More unusually, Sir Henry's name does not appear on the inscription, neglecting the opportunity to be commemorated in perpetuity. For many other benefactors, this was an obvious 'return' to be achieved through their charitable acts.

---

48 For instance, P. Slack, *Poverty and Policy in Tudor and Stuart England* (London, 1988), pp. 8–10.
49 McIntosh, *Poor Relief in England*, pp. 20–1.
50 S. Heath, *Old English Houses of Alms: A Pictorial Record with Architectural and Historical Notes* (London, 1910), p. 29. The inscription is now in the Church of St Nicholas, Bromham.
51 A. Wall, 'Baynton family (*per.* 1508–1716)', *ODNB* (Oxford, 2004; online edn, May 2010), http://www.oxforddnb.com/view/article/71877 (accessed 18 January 2013).

Memorialisation

Medieval chantries, with their rounds of obits and prayers for the souls of the departed, had functioned as perpetual remembrance of the lives and works of the founders. Peter Marshall has shown how the abolition of prayers for the dead resulted in their replacement by a post-Reformation emphasis on individual memorialisation, through tombs, monuments, sermons, even dinners; and the development of a culture of commemorative charity which was distinctly Protestant.[52] Almshouses, with their combination of explicit charitable purpose and their distinguishing features of permanence and physicality, presented particular opportunities for memorialisation. For example, the Devon merchant John Waldron inscribed his almshouse in 1579: *Remember the Poor*, but, with the insignia of a merchant ship and his initials also on the plaque, the subtext is clearly: 'Remember John Waldron' (Figure 3.1). In one of the most spectacular examples of self-aggrandisement masquerading as philanthropy, the slightly later Hospital of the Blessed Trinity in Guildford, founded in 1622 by George Abbot, Archbishop of Canterbury, has a magnificent gatehouse towering over the High Street in the town of his birth (Figure 3.2).

Memorialisation was not only achieved through architecture but also variously through the liveries and insignia worn by the almspeople, through communal events such as the trustees' annual dinner, and through the naming of the foundation. For instance, Robert Dudley instructed that the almshouse he founded in Warwick for old soldiers should be known as 'The Hospital of Robert, Earl of Leycester'. His almsmen wore uniform cloaks of black or blue, and silver badges with his insignia of the bear and ragged staff, suggesting household livery, and they processed to church on Sundays to sit in allocated seats in the centre of the nave where they were most visible to the rest of the congregation. Yet there were obviously less expensive ways of ensuring that benefactors were remembered. A weekly distribution of bread in church on Sunday would ensure the gratitude of the greatest number, most often; while a grand memorial in church would only entail a one-off payment, and be seen by all. Some almshouse benefactors managed a memorial as well (for instance, Dudley and Abbot).

The wording of the Bromham inscription interestingly suggests that the type of social need considered worthy of charity was already circumscribed by the early years of the seventeenth century. The line 'I was harbourless and ye gave me lodging' has been substituted here for its equivalent from the King James Bible, 'I was a stranger and ye took me in', with its dangerous suggestion of indiscriminate charity to strangers – outsiders, the unknown – who could

52   P. Marshall, *Beliefs and the Dead in Reformation England* (Oxford, 2002), pp. 265–308.

Figure 3.1. Plaque on John Waldron's almshouse, Tiverton, Devon

Figure 3.2. Gateway to Abbot's Hospital, Guildford High Street

not be vouched for as deserving.[53] As well as the ubiquitous leper hospitals, very many medieval hospitals had been founded to provide accommodation for poor travellers, including pilgrims. With the abolition of pilgrimages and the major concern about vagrancy in the sixteenth century, this was no longer considered an appropriate function. Despite this, a few almshouse founders did still try to cater for poor travellers in the sixteenth century (see chapter 4). Most almshouses, however, did little to address what were seen by contemporaries as among the most pressing social evils of the time: that is, idleness and vagrancy. Traditional foundations for poor travellers were mostly allowed to decay, and despite government encouragement, few benefactors chose to endow workhouses and houses of correction. There were exceptions, such as Sir Roger Manwood, whose portfolio of philanthropic endowments in the late sixteenth century appears to be a direct response to the government's policy agenda discussed in chapter 1. His endowments included not only the provision of wool, flax and hemp to set the poor on work in six Kent parishes, a free grammar school in Sandwich 'for help of youth', and an almshouse at Hackington 'for help and reliefe of age', but also a house of correction to restrain 'middle age & lusty bodyes' who were 'to be sett at work with straite and hard dyett and lodging and due punishment till they do so amend'.[54] The wording of Manwood's will suggests that he was deliberately aiming to establish a coordinated, rational scheme of assistance to meet the social needs of eastern Kent. Very many almshouse founders also established schools, often as a joint foundation or charity with the almshouses (such as at Rugby, Sevenoaks, Abingdon and Charterhouse), but few founded workhouses or houses of correction, despite government encouragement to do so.

    While a house of correction was considered a desirable institution for any community aiming to get to grips with the problems of idleness and vagrancy, and was required by law after 1576 (an injunction repeated, with more effect, in 1610), it was hardly to be expected that the inmates of such an institution would feel gratitude towards the individual who had provided the funds to set it up, however much the local community felt it had benefited from such a gift. This suggests that the anticipated gratitude of the recipients of charity was important for all but the most public-spirited benefactors, and determined

---

53   According to the Victoria County History for Wiltshire, 'the text does not appear to be drawn from any one contemporary version of the Gospel and it is probable that the mason drew on a faulty memory when incising this familiar almshouse text': R. B. Pugh, *The Victoria History of Wiltshire*, vol. 7 (London, 1953), p. 186. It seems hardly likely, however, that the inscription on such an important building was left to the discretion of the mason; and though inaccurate or misremembered, was most probably a deliberate rendition of what was seen as a more acceptable version of the text.

54   Sir Roger Manwood's will 12 December 1592: CCA CC Supp Ms/6 Alderman Gray's Notebook 1737–1780, pp. 240–4.

the type of institution by which they chose to be remembered.[55] The more usual, popular type of provision, therefore, was for the obviously deserving aged and impotent poor. The effects of ageing could be catastrophic for the working poor if they were unable to save enough to support themselves in later life. Once they became too old to earn a living, whether labouring, following a trade, or as a servant or farm tenant, they were at risk of destitution and of losing their homes. The precariousness of many poor people's existence was thus compounded by old age and disability. As a result those who could no longer support themselves, through no fault of their own, were universally acknowledged as appropriate recipients of compassion and charity from the better-off members of society. When the Warwickshire justices, for example, agreed Joyce Edwards, 'aged and poor', must surrender her tenancy, they ordered the owner to pay her 10s per year for the rest of her life.[56] Unsurprisingly then, the great majority of almshouse foundations were for elderly and disabled people, or became used in this way.

Status, reputation and responsibility

Sir Henry Baynton was typical of the newly influential county gentry, the magistrates who, along with town burgesses and the 'urban aristocracy' of merchants identified by Jordan, took responsibility at a local level for implementing legislation and keeping the peace. According to Jordan, these were the people whose charitable efforts were directed at creating lasting social and cultural institutions such as schools and almshouses, to address the pressing social problems of the time.[57] Yet almshouses only ever made a minor contribution to the total relief of the poor, and many donors were of lesser wealth and status than the groups Jordan regarded as typical. Similar to the earlier tradition in the fifteenth century, many new almshouses were very small, sometimes little more than cottages left to the parish for the use of the poor, and often hard to distinguish from parish housing. McIntosh has shown that, in her period, most almshouses catered for only a few people, with a median size of only six places in the second half of the sixteenth century, and this remained the case throughout the early modern period.[58] The average size of

55 Slack, *Poverty and Policy*, p. 165. Gratitude from the community could also be anticipated and expected. Thomas Guy, having served as Tamworth's MP since 1695 and been a town benefactor, barred Tamworth residents from his almshouse there after failing to be re-elected as their MP in 1708: N. Hervey, 'Guy, Thomas (1644/5?–1724)', *ODNB* (Oxford, 2004; online edn, Jan. 2008), http://www.oxforddnb.com/view/article/11800 (accessed 25 March 2016).
56 WQS, vol. 1, p. 262.
57 Jordan, *Philanthropy*, p. 18.
58 McIntosh, *Poor Relief in England*, pp. 197–8.

almshouses in eight English counties was 7.6, with a median of six places; some only had two or three places (see Appendix 2). Many small almshouses were the donor's own house, left to the parish for use as an almshouse, but without any endowment. Robert Serlys of Wye in Kent, for instance, left his house called Puntowes as an almshouse for three people in 1567, while Edward Colthurst of Westerham, also in Kent, left his house called Wimbles to the parish in 1572 to be lived in by six of the parish poor.[59] This practice was given added impetus in the seventeenth century as parishes increasingly provided housing for poor parishioners as part of their poor law responsibilities such as, for example, Anthony Rawlins' three cottages left to the parish officers of Beckenham in 1694.[60] These bequests, like donations to the parish stock, were a popular and cost-effective way for less wealthy donors to benefit their local community.

Permanent, endowed almshouses on the other hand were an expensive way to provide for the poor, and would have required a more considered motivation. Creating a large new foundation presupposes commitment and vision as well as disposable wealth, especially since care had to be taken to organise the establishment and protect the investment. As an illustration, William Lambarde, the Elizabethan antiquary and lawyer, spent a total of £2,739, a vast sum for the time, on building and endowing his Queen Elizabeth Hospital at East Greenwich in 1576. To give some idea of the scale of investment involved, he had to grant lands to the hospital worth more than £2,000 in order to generate an annual income of £83 6s 8d, which would be sufficient to pay the pensions of the twenty almspeople and to allow for repairs to the building.[61] He also spent £16 on five acres of woodland to provide the almshouse with fuel. Even small almshouses, if they were to be properly endowed, required considerable sums. James Gramer's almshouses in Mancetter, Warwickshire, a simple row of six one-room cottages, cost £2,000 to build and endow in 1728.[62] These are great sums to benefit relatively small numbers of people, but the permanent nature of these endowments means that the total number of people helped over the years is considerable.[63] The large initial expense, nevertheless, contrasts with equally permanent but less ostentatious forms of supporting the poor. Unsurprisingly, Jordan found that charitable endowments for 'outright relief' of the poor outweighed any other category of giving for the poor.[64] Providing bread for the poor, or even

59   HCPP, no. 30 (1837), pp. 440, 610.
60   HCPP, no. 30 (1837), p. 441.
61   R. M. Warnicke, *William Lambarde, Elizabethan Antiquary* (London and Chichester, 1973), p. 44.
62   B. Bailey, *Almshouses* (London, 1988), p. 148.
63   This is Slack's point about Jordan's calculations: Slack, *Poverty and Policy*, p. 163.
64   Jordan, *Philanthropy*, Appendix, p. 369.

paying the schoolmaster's wages, however, while valuable in themselves, did not provide the same opportunities to publicise and memorialise the donor's generosity.

Many almshouses were located in places of significance to the founder and their family. Thus, Robert Dudley obtained his licence from the queen to found an almshouse in either Kenilworth, the site of his castle, or Warwick, where his brother Ambrose, Earl of Warwick, had his ancient seat. Henry Howard, Earl of Northampton founded three almshouses: at Clun in Shropshire (1607), the family's ancestral lands and the favourite hunting ground of his brother; at Castle Rising in Norfolk (1609), in memory of his grandfather, the Duke of Norfolk; and at Greenwich (1613), the place where his father's death warrant had been signed.[65] Robert Dudley's granddaughter, Lady Katherine Leveson, wife of a wealthy Staffordshire landowner, made many bequests to the poor in various counties, but chose to place her almshouse for poor women in the rural hamlet of Temple Balsall, Warwickshire. She also chose St Mary's Church, Warwick, 'where my ancestors are interred' for her memorial.[66] Thus Lady Katherine chose to place her most visible, enduring monuments in Warwickshire, to emphasise her noble family connections there.

For the nobility and gentry, emphasising their territorial connections was a way of displaying local status, which in turn conferred respect and influence. In the febrile and precarious early modern world of social mobility and political uncertainty, the status of many members of the gentry and nobility was very insecure, and founding an almshouse could be one means of establishing or shoring up a reputation. It is noteworthy that both Robert Dudley and Henry Howard were the sons and younger brothers of men who had been executed for treason, and both owed their current positions of wealth and influence entirely to the favour of the current monarch: to Elizabeth for Dudley and to James I for Howard. Similarly, the wealthy Lady Leveson had her early years blighted by scandal and insecurity. She was the youngest daughter of Dudley's illegitimate son Robert, and her father abandoned his family after failing to prove his legitimacy. Even that conscientious public servant Lord Cobham was anxious enough about his position and reputation to demand that the Falstaff character in Shakespeare's *Henry IV* originally called Sir John Oldcastle (the rebel executed for treason in the fifteenth century, and a previous holder of the Cobham title), should be renamed in case any opprobrium should attach to himself.[67] For Howard, the change in his fortunes could not have been more

---

65   Prescott, *English Medieval Hospital*, p. 84.

66   WRO CR 1540/6 Transcript of the Will of Lady Katherine Leveson (1671). Robert Dudley and his brother Ambrose both have their memorials in St Mary's, Warwick.

67   J. Lock, 'Brooke, William, tenth Baron Cobham (1527–1597)', *ODNB* (Oxford, 2004; online edn, Jan. 2008), http://www.oxforddnb.com/view/printable/61735 (accessed 24 April 2012).

dramatic, as he embarked on a political career at last at the age of sixty-three: he was made a privy counsellor by James, created Earl of Northampton, and had his family's lands restored. As his biographer states, 'After a lifetime of poverty and danger, he could now lay claim to his inheritance of power and influence'.[68] The great mansion he built on the Strand was considered 'one of the finest residences in Europe' and he amassed one of the largest art collections of the period.[69] Building three sets of almshouses was another extravagant demonstration of his restored status.

For the gentry founders of almshouses, taking the lead in providing for the poor in their localities was part of the accepted network of obligation to tenants, servants, neighbours and to the community more generally. These obligations came with land ownership, often with specific responsibilities attached to the land itself, such as that expected of the new owners of former monastic lands to maintain 'hospitality' to the poor (obligations which were not always scrupulously carried out).[70] There were also obligations of status, the honour code by which people of gentle or noble birth, or those who aspired to these ranks, demonstrated through virtuous conduct their fitness for gentility. Many almshouses are thus the physical representations of the status and influence in the locality of the benefactor.

Even modest foundations without spectacular buildings provided perpetual, visible testament to the donor's generosity, a reflection of their position in society rather than a tribute to their philanthropy necessarily. Sir Thomas Holte, founder of almshouses at Aston, was one of the new baronets created by James I. His family had held land in the area for a century, and he was Sheriff of Warwickshire in 1599. He had been rewarded with a knighthood for being part of the delegation that went to meet James I on his progression south to take the throne in 1603, and subsequently paid the fee to become one of the first cohort of baronets in 1612. Despite leaving £300 in his will to found the almshouses, Sir Thomas was not noted as being particularly philanthropic. In fact, he was described by his biographer as 'proud, obstinate and revengeful'; he was accused of murdering his cook in 1605; and he remained implacably unreconciled to his son throughout the latter's life despite an attempt at mediation by the king. On completion of his magnificent Aston Hall in 1635, which surpassed in grandeur and sophistication any other house in Warwickshire at the time, he drew up an indenture for a set

---

68   L. L. Peck, *Northampton: Patronage and Policy at the Court of James I* (London, 1982), pp. 21–3.
69   Peck, *Northampton*, p. 73.
70   According to Richardson, most of the lands passing through the Court of Augmentations were legally encumbered in some way, with debts, corrodies, pensions, rentals or assignments: W. C. Richardson, *History of the Court of Augmentations, 1536–1554* (Baton Rouge, 1961), pp. 75, 428.

of almshouses to be located outside its gates, to the east of the parish church (see Figure 3.3 for a surviving example of almshouses located at the gates of the founder's hall).[71] The almshouses for ten poor of the parish of Aston were evidently intended to complement the hall, and provide the finishing touch to the grand project which stamped Sir Thomas's position as a great landlord upon the local countryside. The almshouses do not appear to have been a priority, however, as they were not built until after his death in 1654, being completed by his grandson and heir Sir Robert Holte.

It is arguable that the physical representation of one's virtue in this way might have been of the greatest importance for those with most to prove, those whose position in society was less secure or only newly established. For the nobility and gentry, and those who aspired to be considered as such, gentility was based on birth and behaviour. Many of the county gentry in the late sixteenth and seventeenth centuries were 'new' men whose families had acquired wealth through public office or trade, and who had used the immense opportunities provided by the sale of monastic lands to acquire property and country estates. For those unable to provide evidence of an impeccable pedigree, or whose ancestors' honour was suspect in some way, it was doubly important that their gentility or nobility could be demonstrated through their own virtuous conduct. This included not only moral and civic responsibility and leadership, but also hospitality to one's neighbours and dependants, and charitable acts for the community.[72]

Sir John Puckering was a successful lawyer, speaker of the House of Commons in Elizabeth's reign, serjeant-at-law, lord keeper of the great seal and a member of the Privy Council.[73] He purchased St Sepulchre's Priory, Warwick, in 1582. His son Thomas was a companion to Henry, Prince of Wales, but after Henry's death missed out on royal preferment through choosing to remain abroad on tour, and subsequently settled into the life of a country gentleman on the estates his father had purchased in Warwick. Relations with the town corporation were not always easy, however, and Sir Thomas had the misfortune to be compared unfavourably by the townspeople with a neighbouring gentry family, the Lucys of Charlecote Park. Arriving with William the Conqueror, the Lucys had owned Charlecote since the thirteenth century. In 1626 Warwick Corporation chose Francis Lucy rather than Thomas Puckering as their member of parliament, alleging

71 A. Davidson, *A History of the Holtes of Aston, Baronets; with a Description of the Family Mansion, Aston Hall, Warwickshire* (Birmingham, 1854), pp. 18–26. The almshouses were demolished in 1931 and rebuilt in Erdington.

72 F. Heal and C. Holmes, *The Gentry in England and Wales, 1500–1700* (Basingstoke, 1994), pp. 9–10, 283, 372.

73 N. G. Jones, 'Puckering, Sir John (1543/4–1596)', *ODNB* (Oxford, 2004; online edn, May 2007), http://www.oxforddnb.com/view/article/22860 (accessed 19 November 2012).

Figure 3.3. Hare Almshouses (1603) at the gates of Stow Hall, Stow Bardolph, Norfolk

that Puckering was 'but a stranger in the country' and not 'a man of such noble hospitality as that worthy family the Lucyes'. Yet it was Puckering who maintained the poor of the now dissolved St Michael's hospital, which became his responsibility through ownership of the priory; established an almshouse in the Saltisford for St Michael's pensioners; maintained the women in the Westgate almshouses from his ownership of former guild lands; and who, in 1633, provided six houses for tradesmen in Warwick on condition that they each took three poor apprentices.[74] The Lucy family presumably felt that their status and honour were sufficiently well established to require no enhancement through spectacular acts of public charity.

Puckering was not alone in being considered a 'stranger' in the shire. According to Ann Hughes, many of the seventeenth-century Warwickshire gentry 'were comparative newcomers to the shire, and the minor gentry were often of very insecure status'.[75] Sir Thomas Leigh, a wealthy mercer of London who was lord mayor in the year of Elizabeth's accession, and knighted by her, bought the estate of Stoneleigh Abbey in Warwickshire. At his death he left large sums to charitable causes, including to 'poor householders' in his home parishes in London and Warwickshire; to poor scholars at the universities and the poor prisoners of Newgate, King's Bench and Marshalsea; and the London hospitals of Christ's, St Bartholomew's and St Thomas's.[76] After his death, according to his wishes, his widow Dame Alice founded almshouses for ten poor people in the village of Stoneleigh, creating a permanent symbol of his munificence in his adopted county, where his ennobled descendants subsequently turned the abbey into a spectacular country mansion. Both Puckering and Leigh can be considered as examples of the new owners of monastic lands putting wealth to 'proper' use. In this, as in the form of foundation chosen, they were responding to cultural norms about status and appropriate behaviour.

Some of the same sort of considerations could influence an urban benefactor such as Sir John Duck, a Durham butcher, alderman and mayor, who founded an almshouse at Great Lumley, Chester-le-Street in 1686. Duck's biography suggests that despite the wealth he amassed, his grand town house and his baronetcy (acquired in 1687 for helping to fund the defence of Ulster), he was never accepted by his peers. The story that he liked to promote about the origins of his prosperity that when he was down on his luck a raven dropped a gold coin at his feet, thus providing him with the wherewithal to build his commercial wealth, functions as a creation myth similar to the story of 'Dick

---

74   M. Merry and C. Richardson, eds, *The Household Account Book of Sir Thomas Puckering of Warwick 1620*, Dugdale Society 45 (Warwick, 2012), pp. 11, 16, 19.
75   Hughes, *Politics*, p. 37.
76   SBT DR18/13/9/1 Will of Sir Thomas Leigh.

Whittington' and the Bow bells.[77] In reality, he probably owed his success to trading in stolen cattle. The Butchers' Company initially refused to accept his apprenticeship, and later in life he was suspected of shady dealings by Bishop Cosin.[78] The almshouse was perhaps intended to cement his reputation, imitating what someone of his standing would be expected to do; and the timing of the foundation may have been intended to influence the decision over the award of his baronetcy. His foundation, however, was not located in his home town of Durham, but in a place where he had recently bought land and where there was no local allegiance to him. He gave the oversight of the almshouse to trustees and the mayor of Durham, but no such oversight appears to have been exercised after his death. This arrangement seems to show a fundamental misreading on Duck's part of how civic and social responsibility worked. There was no reason why the mayor of Durham should want to be involved in an institution for the benefit of people outside his jurisdiction, and the responsibility offered him no reward in terms of status or patronage. This was in contrast to Sir Roger Manwood's almshouse at Hackington, just outside Canterbury, where the oversight of the mayor of Canterbury was rewarded with an annual dinner and the sum of 10s. As a result, successive mayors of Canterbury exercised their duties, including intervening in a legal dispute when the almspeople were not being paid their allowances, and taking responsibility for raising funds by distress on the holders of the hospital lands.[79]

While benefactors made individual decisions regarding their charitable disbursements they were very much influenced by their peers or forebears. So, for instance, Nicholas Eyffler, a Westphalian glazier living in Warwick, founded an almshouse for four (later eight) women in 1591 similar to that established by his friend Thomas Oken twenty years earlier. He even specified that his charity was to use the same collectors as those of Oken.[80] In Coventry, two almshouses founded in the early years of the sixteenth century, Bond's and Ford's Hospitals, were endowed and supported by a small tight-knit group of local merchants, related by marriage and acting as one another's executors.[81]

77   Duck had the scene depicted in a painting in his house in Silver Street (now in the Durham Museum and History Centre, St Mary-le-Bow).
78   Letter from Bishop Cosin to his secretary 20 August 1670, and editor's note: G. Ornsby, ed., *The Correspondence of John Cosin D.D. Lord Bishop of Durham: Together with Other Papers Illustrative of his Life and Times, Part II*, Surtees Society 55 (Durham, 1872), p. 249.
79   CCA CC/S/7/1 St Stephen's Hospital Memorandum and Disbursements Book 1593–1828, ff. 27–35 (1625–1630).
80   WRO CR 1618/WA12/34 Will of Nicholas Eyffler 1591.
81   Thomas Bond, draper and mayor of Coventry in 1497/8, founded his almshouse for the poorer members of the Holy Trinity and Corpus Christi guilds in his will of 1506. His executors included his son John, mayor in 1519/20, who built the almshouse, and William Ford, wool merchant and member of the Staple of Calais, who had been mayor in 1496/7. On his own death in 1509, Ford left money for a similar almshouse, which was built and further endowed by his executors, William Pisford, grocer and mayor in 1500/1, and William Wigston, wool merchant

There was a similar grouping around William Lambarde at the end of the sixteenth century. Lambarde, Lord Cobham and Archbishop Whitgift each founded his own almshouse and also worked together as the first governors of Sir John Hawkins' Hospital in 1592. Cobham's daughter Elizabeth married Robert Cecil, whose father Lord Burghley was another almshouse founder. Donors tended to follow tradition, making the same sort of bequests that were common in their social circle and using the forms of charity their predecessors had favoured. It is possible that the very small number of early modern almshouse foundations in Lancashire remarked upon by Jordan, for instance, may be a result of the few surviving examples of this form of provision in the county by the end of the fifteenth century, leaving only two existing institutions as examples to inspire future generations of benefactors.[82]

Philanthropy, in any case, was not necessarily an individual activity; but, particularly in the towns, could be a communal expression of social responsibility, shared values and reciprocal benefits. Some foundations were a communal endeavour from the start, such as the Trinity House almshouses in Deptford, maintained by a tax on seamen after the mariners' guild was incorporated in 1514.[83] The Keelmen's Hospital was similarly established two centuries later in Newcastle upon Tyne with the contributions provided by the keelmen from each load of coal they carried out to the colliers' ships.[84] The London livery companies had established many almshouses for aged members in the fifteenth and early sixteenth centuries, and the tradition of merchant philanthropy among Londoners was particularly extolled by Jordan.[85] Town merchants, like their London counterparts, often gave money and property for a range of social benefits, as typified by Thomas Oken's will in 1573. Among the 'godlie uses and purposes' he bequeathed to the town of Warwick were the almshouses; maintenance of the town's bridges, wells and roads; twelve leather fire buckets; wages for a preacher, a schoolmaster, the town's herdsman and beadle; and money for bonfires, festivities and an annual dinner, thereby locating his almshouses within a portfolio of essential and imaginative public services.[86]

Oken set up an independent charity with its own collectors and trustees; but many donors left their endowment to an existing organisation, to

---

of Leicester. Wigston was married to Pisford's daughter Agnes, who was formerly the wife of William Ford: J. Cleary and M. Orton, *So Long as the World Shall Endure: The Five Hundred Year History of Ford's and Bond's Hospitals* (Coventry, 1991), pp. 11–14.

82   Jordan, *Philanthropy*, pp. 261–2.

83   A. A. Ruddock, 'The Trinity House at Deptford in the Sixteenth Century', *English Historical Review* 65/257 (1950), 458–76 (p. 462).

84   NRO SANT/DEE/3/20/9 Keelmen's Hospital Indenture 1700.

85   I. Archer, *The Pursuit of Stability: Social Relations in Elizabethan London* (Cambridge, 1991), p. 120; W. K. Jordan, *The Charities of London 1480–1660* (London, 1960).

86   WRO CR 1618/WA3/84 Nineteenth-century copy of Thomas Oken's will 1570.

manage the assets, collect the rents, and maintain the charity's work. Often this was the town corporation, which took over many of the activities of the dissolved fraternities and guilds in running local services, or in London one of the livery companies. In some places the administration of almshouses was amalgamated with responsibility for important public works such as bridges. Lord Cobham, Warden of the Cinque Ports, gave the administration of New Cobham College to the Rochester Bridge Wardens, a prestigious incorporated body with responsibility for maintaining the vital crossing over the Medway, while conversely it was Christ's Hospital, Abingdon which was given responsibility in its charter of 1553 for maintaining several important bridges over the Thames and keeping the Dorchester road in repair.[87]

In a well-endowed town such as Faversham in Kent in the seventeenth century, the corporation's assets and responsibilities were so extensive that specific officials were appointed to oversee them. A mayor of Faversham, Robert Allen, had given a house in Partridge Lane to the town in 1601, which had been made into two almshouses; John Foad left the corporation his house behind Middle Row in 1633 to be used as an almshouse; and Thomas Knowler, mayor in 1688, gave the town two unendowed almshouses in Tanner Street. Even the house of correction was left to the town by the master of the grammar school, Robert Stone, in 1604.[88] The town officers for Faversham, appointed annually, included two governors for the almshouses, together with governors for the school, the house of correction, and the sluice and channels, as well as receivers of the corn for the poor.[89] The wardmote minute books, which record the decisions and orders of the common council, reveal the detailed business of running the town including arrangements for poor relief (1560); for setting the poor on work (1638); letting a contract to provide coals for the poor from a charitable bequest (1635); and commissioning repairs and arranging admissions to the various almshouses. The expanded opportunities for office-holding and patronage offered by these extensive responsibilities in towns like Faversham created 'networks of interest' and enabled many otherwise 'obscure individuals' to become involved in the public sphere of town government and welfare provision.[90] In this way charitable works, for those involved in them, were as much the architects as the products of status and reputation.

---

87 A. A. Arnold, *Cobham College* (London, 1905), p. 18; J. Carter and J. Smith, *Give and Take: Scenes from the History of Christ's Hospital, Abingdon, 1553–1900* (Abingdon, 1981), p. 2.
88 E. Jacob, *History of Faversham* (1774; new edn, Sheerness, 1974), pp. 135, 137, 141; D. Harrington and P. Hyde, eds, *The Early Town Books of Faversham, c.1251 to 1581* (Folkestone, 2008), pp. 527–8.
89 CKS Fa/Ac4/1 Faversham Wardmote Minutes 1633–1740 part 1.
90 S. Cavallo, 'The Motivation of Benefactors: An Overview of Approaches to the Study of Charity', *Medicine and Charity*, ed. Barry and Jones, pp. 46–62 (p. 52).

Religious identity

Although there appears to have been little evidence to justify their anxieties, many early Protestants were sensitive to suggestions that they gave less to charity than their Catholic forebears. In a sermon from 1578, Laurence Chaderton complained, 'the papistes alwayes cast in our teeth the great and famous hospitalitie of their nobility and cleargy ... which in deede are such as do stoppe our mouthes and put us Protestants to silence'.[91] Many almshouse benefactors in the immediate post-Reformation period, nevertheless, were unequivocally Protestant. Dame Alice Leigh, widow of Sir Thomas, who built the Stoneleigh almshouses in 1576, was the niece and heir of Sir Rowland Hill, the first Protestant mayor of London. Another Warwickshire benefactor, Lawrence Sheriff, founder of almshouses in Rugby and Rugby School in 1567, received a mention in *Foxe's Book of Martyrs*. Most notable of all, Robert Dudley was the leader of the puritan faction at court. He used his almshouse's independence from the church authorities to provide a secure base for the controversial puritan theologian Thomas Cartwright, whom he appointed master of the Lord Leycester Hospital on his return from exile in 1586.[92] Dudley had already been instrumental in appointing another puritan preacher and Marian exile, Thomas Lever, to the mastership of Sherburn Hospital in County Durham in 1562. Lever remained at Sherburn until his death in 1577, and was succeeded by his brother Ralph, an equally radical cleric described as 'a troublesome Nonconformist, and very disobedient to his Patron', the Bishop of Durham.[93] Almshouse positions like this could provide a secure base for radical preachers, and a captive community for the exercise of their religious zeal. According to Strype's *Life of Archbishop Parker*, Thomas Lever was so concerned at the disorder and lack of obedience at Sherburn that he reported matters to his bishop, and this proving unsuccessful, complained thereafter to Archbishop Parker. Lever protested that the almsmen 'he supposes were favourers of the old Superstition, and too negligent of the worship of God'.[94]

Not all benefactors were as unambiguous as these Protestant paragons. The testamentary bequests of the second half of the sixteenth century were often made by people who had lived through the religious changes, and seen

---

91 Laurence Chaderton, sermon (1578), quoted in I. W. Archer, 'The Charity of Early Modern Londoners', *Transactions of the Royal Historical Society* 12 (2002), 223–44 (p. 226).

92 E. G. Tibbits, 'The Hospital of Robert, Earl of Leicester, in Warwick', *Birmingham Archaeological Society: Transactions and Proceedings* 60 (1936), 112–44 (p. 123).

93 G. Allan, *Collectanea Dunelmensis: Collections Relating Sherburn Hospital in the County Palatine of Durham* (1771), pp. 91–2.

94 Allan, *Collectanea Dunelmensis*, p. 176. The allegation was probably true, for at least one of the almsmen in Lever's time, Cuthbert Bell, had been one of the four priests attached to the hospital in Mary's reign (pp. 166, 187).

the despoliation of the church. This must have had a powerful influence; for some, there may have been regrets, possibly a sense of obligation. Thomas Oken, Warwick mercer and almshouse founder, was the last master of the town's Guild of Holy Trinity and St George in 1545, and he arguably retained traditional beliefs until his death in 1573. Oken's memorial brass in St Mary's Church probably originally read 'Of your charitye pray for the Soules of Thomas Oken and Jone his wyff'. It has clearly been altered at a later date: a replacement piece of brass has been carefully inserted with the words 'give thanks' instead of 'pray'.

The motivations of a contemporary of Thomas Oken's, the goldsmith Martin Bowes, were more ambivalent (or opportunistic). He was mayor of London in 1545/6, and represented London in five parliaments. As alderman he profited from the sale of nine alabaster tombs and 'seven-score gravestones of Marble' at the dissolution of London's Greyfriars.[95] During Mary's reign in 1557 he proposed to establish a chantry in his home town of York, but dropped this plan on Elizabeth's accession. Instead he gave generously to poor relief, played a key role in establishing London's five hospitals, and endowed his own almshouse at Woolwich in 1560.[96] William Lambe was another whose earlier, more traditional, religious affiliation was replaced by a more expedient Protestant identity in later life. A London clothworker and courtier to Henry VIII, he founded his almshouse at Sutton Valence in Kent in 1574, and was vaunted on his death in 1580 as 'an exemplar of protestant piety' despite (or because of) his friendship with the conforming Catholic Sir William Cordell, and 'privie whisperings' that he was a papist sympathiser.[97]

Like their predecessors, many of the Protestant almshouses were still places of prayer, their statutes (looking very similar to those of earlier institutions) specifying daily rituals of prayer and regular church attendance. William Lambarde is of particular interest in this respect because he not only founded his own almshouse in 1576, but was involved in the founding and management of two other late-sixteenth-century almshouses: Sir John Hawkins' Hospital in Chatham (founded in 1592), where he was a governor; and New Cobham College in Kent (founded in 1597), for which he acted as executor and as one of the first governors. Lambarde was a committed Protestant, and a friend of Archbishop Parker. The rules which he devised for his own almshouse included the provision that applicants must be honest and godly persons who could recite, in English, the Lord's Prayer, the Articles of the Christian Faith, and the Ten Commandments. Morning and evening

95 J. Stow, *A Survey of London*, quoted in Marshall, *Beliefs and the Dead*, pp. 88–9.
96 C. E. Challis, 'Bowes, Sir Martin (1496/7–1566)', *ODNB* (Oxford, 2004; online edn, Jan. 2008), http://www.oxforddnb.com/view/article/3055 (accessed 25 April 2012).
97 I. W. Archer, 'Lambe, William (d.1580)', *ODNB* (Oxford, 2004; online edn, Jan. 2008), http://www.oxforddnb.com/view/article/15929 (accessed 25 April 2012).

the almspeople were to gather for prayer; if they were absent they were fined 4d. This sounds very like a Protestant reworking of the rule for God's House at Ewelme, or at the Gainsborough almshouse founded by Lord Burgh in 1496, where even illiterate almsmen had to be able to recite the paternoster, ave and creed.[98] Lambarde's almshouse was in many ways a model. In his role as governor, he drafted similar statutes for New Cobham College and Hawkins' Hospital. These rules were also copied by Sir John Jolles, Master of the Drapers' Company to which Lambarde had bequeathed the management of his Queen Elizabeth Hospital, when Jolles founded his own almshouse at Bow in 1617.

Lambarde was particularly concerned that acts of charity should be performed in life, rather than by will after one's death. He himself was aged only forty when he founded his almshouse, and he lived for a further twenty-five years. In 1578 he presented to the Drapers' Company, of which his father had been warden, a silver cup inscribed: 'A Proctour for the poore am I, remember theim before thou dye.'[99] As executor to Lord Cobham he took the unusual step of persuading Cobham to transfer his property to his executors before his death so that work on the college could begin immediately. Many other sixteenth-century benefactors such as Robert Dudley, Dame Alice Leigh, Sir John Hawkins, and Sir Roger Manwood founded their almshouses in their lifetime, rather than by testamentary bequest. For Protestants such as themselves, it was important to demonstrate that their charitable endeavours were uncorrupted by superstitious redemptive practices.

Yet, despite their Protestantism, many late-sixteenth-century founders chose explicitly to emphasise tradition. In Houghton-le-Spring, County Durham, the noted preacher Bernard Gilpin, who had left England for the safety of the continent in Mary's reign, dedicated the Kepier Grammar School and Almshouse he helped to found in 1574 to the Holy Trinity. The name was taken from the lands of the former Kepier Priory used for the endowment; and Holy Trinity had been the name of the guild which maintained an altar in the parish church at Houghton. Many of the founders of almshouses in the immediate post-Reformation decades made similarly self-conscious efforts to retain links with older institutions. Robert Dudley's hospital was based in Warwick's medieval guildhall buildings, which he acquired from the town corporation.[100] William Cecil, Lord Burghley, founded his

---

98   C. Richmond, 'Victorian Values in Fifteenth-Century England: The Ewelme Almshouse Statutes', *Pragmatic Utopias: Ideals and Communities, 1200–1630*, ed. R. Horrox and S. Rees Jones (Cambridge, 2001), pp. 224–41 (p. 228); C. Richmond, 'Religion', *Fifteenth-Century Attitudes: Perceptions of Society in Late Medieval England*, ed. R. Horrox (Cambridge, 1994), pp. 183–201 (p. 199).
99   Warnicke, *William Lambarde*, p. 49.
100   T. Kemp, ed., *The Black Book of Warwick* (Warwick, 1898), pp. 33–42.

almshouse at Stamford in 1597 on the site of the twelfth-century hospital of St John the Baptist and St Thomas the Martyr, and incorporated part of the remains in his new building.[101] Similarly, Lord Cobham founded New Cobham College using the site and the buildings of the dissolved medieval college.[102] Meanwhile, the intervention of the Protestant Archbishops Parker and Whitgift ensured the survival of two of the quasi-monastic medieval foundations in Canterbury, Eastbridge Hospital and St John's, which might otherwise have been confiscated.[103]

Alexandra Walsham has argued that Protestantism required the preservation of 'objects of iconoclastic annihilation' such as monastic ruins, in order to demonstrate that the corrupt doctrines which they represented had been extinguished.[104] But many medieval almshouses and hospitals were retained as flourishing institutions rather than as ruins, or their remains were sometimes even incorporated into new establishments. Even completely new foundations adopted traditional forms, in a deliberate attempt by their founders to emphasise continuity with true religion and reclaim an honourable institution believed to have been corrupted by popery. Almshouses were an ideal vehicle through which to make these claims. They held a special place in the public consciousness, going back at least two centuries. A petition presented to Henry IV by the Commons in 1410 had declared that the lands of the church, occupied and wasted by the bishops, abbots and priors could, if taken by the king, provide one hundred almshouses throughout the land, as well as a host of earls, knights and squires to serve the king.[105] The response, however, had merely been a statute in 1414 reforming decayed hospitals.[106]

The ideal of one hundred almshouses had appeared before, in the Twelve Conclusions of the Lollards (1395), alongside criticism of the practice of using almshouses as chantries.[107] The 'hundred almshouses' proposal reappears in the first scene of Shakespeare's *Henry V* (1599), when the Archbishop of Canterbury and the Bishop of Ely are discussing the bill in parliament by which the Commons urge the stripping of the church's temporal lands and putting the revenue to better use.[108] In an echo of Lollardy, and arguably

---

101   L. Crust, *Lincolnshire Almshouses: Nine Centuries of Charitable Housing* (Sleaford, 2002), p. 41.
102   W. H. Godfrey, *The English Almshouse, with Some Account of its Predecessor, the Medieval Hospital* (London, 1955), pp. 51–2.
103   Hill, *Almshouses of Canterbury*, pp. 14, 28.
104   A. Walsham, *The Reformation of the Landscape: Religion, Identity, and Memory in Early Modern Britain and Ireland* (Oxford, 2011), p. 148.
105   A. H. Thomas and I. D. Thornley, eds, *The Great Chronicle of London* (London, 1983), pp. 88–90.
106   2 Hen. V. c. 1, Power given to ordinaries to enquire of the government of hospitals.
107   Cronin, 'Lollards', p. 299.
108   Shakespeare, *Henry V*, act I, scene i.

validating the claims of Jordan, sixteenth-century almshouse founders were demonstrating the proper use to which wealth should be put, supporting the poor rather than the church. Protestants could answer the Catholic accusers in Chaderton's sermon by transforming these archaic institutions into showcases of reformed religion where the godly life could be seen in action, both in the charity of the donor, and in the idealised community of deserving poor, living out pious, quiet lives of work, prayer, and neighbourliness.

Meanwhile, few Catholic gentry or nobility were in a position to counter Protestant propaganda through their own acts of charity. The Earl of Northampton, with his three great almshouses, was an exception, as was Sir William Cordell, a discreet but openly acknowledged conforming Catholic, who founded the almshouse at Long Melford.[109] The insecure and impoverished position of many Catholic gentry, however, meant that few were in a position to finance large works of charity, and in any case their priorities lay elsewhere. As Pauline Croft has emphasised, after the Gunpowder Plot in James I's reign the overriding need for many Catholics was to demonstrate their loyalty to the Crown, hence the large numbers coming forward to purchase the new baronetcies in 1611.[110]

> For all these men, the purchase of the new honour reinforced their county status, shaking off or at least mitigating their extensive Catholic connections. The financial outlay enabled them to outflank their Protestant neighbours' suspicion and hostility, while at the same time ingratiating them with central authority.[111]

They were required to have assets worth at least £1,000 per annum, and to pay £1,090 for the privilege of the baronetcy, and it is clear that some at least of the new Catholic baronets could barely afford the outlay.[112] Recusancy fines and lack of access to public office meant that Catholic families were increasingly disadvantaged financially, and most were not in a position to be notable benefactors. Recusant gentry may have continued to support their poorer tenants and retainers as far as possible: the Throckmortons, for example, continued to support the almshouses in Coughton, Warwickshire founded by Sir Robert Throckmorton in 1518 and administered by them as a wholly private family charity, but new acts of public charity were beyond their

109 M. C. Questier, *Catholicism and Community in Early Modern England: Politics, Aristocratic Patronage and Religion, c.1550–1640* (Cambridge, 2006), pp. 154–5.

110 Croft calculates that twenty-six of the eighty-eight baronets created in 1611 to fund the colonisation of Ulster had recusant connections: P. Croft, 'The Catholic Gentry: The Earl of Salisbury and the Baronets of 1611', *Conformity and Orthodoxy in the English Church, c.1560–1660*, ed. P. Lake and M. Questier (Woodbridge, 2000), pp. 262–81 (p. 262).

111 Croft, 'Catholic Gentry', p. 272.

112 Croft, 'Catholic Gentry', pp. 273, 276.

resources.[113] As a result, the great majority of almshouses, whether medieval survivors or new foundations, were conspicuously Protestant in character.

Order and good governance – the Commonwealth and the Anglican Restoration

Writers such as Prescott consider that the peak of post-Reformation almshouse foundations was over by 1630, and the 1640s inevitably saw few new foundations. Yet there were new almshouses established during the Commonwealth, such as the unendowed almshouses in Alcester founded in 1659 by the will of John Bridges, lawyer, steward to Lord Brooke and colonel in the Parliamentary army.[114] This period was also characterised by examples of efforts to maintain good local administration. Thus Thomas Delaval, landowner of Hetton-le-Hole, County Durham, was in 1657 appointed one of the governors of the Kepier Free Grammar School and Almshouse in Houghton-le-Spring, founded in 1574. Delaval kept admirable records of income and expenditure for the charity, and was evidently concerned to carry out his duties correctly. In the accounts he noted that after he had been elected governor, perusing the statutes he found that five poor scholars and 'three poore Almsfolkes' were supposed to be paid 7d per week from the school's income, but this had been neglected for many years. He redressed this problem by choosing and appointing the scholars and almsfolk, and duly paying them their allowances.[115] He then went on to devise a procedure and oath on admission for subsequent appointments.

The puritan George Lilburne, uncle of the radical John Lilburne, was a neighbour of Delaval's, and together they signed the churchwardens' accounts for Houghton-le-Spring for the year 1656.[116] Lilburne was a coal merchant in Sunderland, and mayor in the 1630s and early 1640s. During the Civil War he was the only magistrate acting in the borough of Sunderland, and was a member of Cromwell's Parliament in 1654. His son Thomas was an officer in Monck's army, and a member of parliament for Durham in 1656 and Newcastle in 1659. On John Cosin's appointment as Bishop of Durham at the Restoration, Cosin demanded that 'neither George Lilburne nor his son Thomas may have any public employment in Durham', and Lilburne's house was searched for arms in 1662. Yet Lilburne gave £50 to the poor plague victims of Sunderland in 1665, and acted with Cosin's

---

113 HCPP, no. 15 (1826), p. 523.
114 Hughes, *Politics*, p. 235.
115 DRO EP/Ho 613 Thomas Delaval's Notebook 1657–1663.
116 Anon., *Churchwardens' Accounts of Pittington and Other Parishes in the Diocese of Durham from AD 1580 to 1700*, Surtees Society 84 (Durham, 1888), p. 309.

chaplain George Davenport to enhance the Kepier Free Grammar School and Almshouse Charity by building six almshouses in Houghton-le-Spring in 1666.[117] Davenport had been in exile in Paris with Cosin, and was appointed Rector of Houghton-le-Spring in 1664, the wealthiest living in the diocese. As well as building one-half of the almshouses, he rebuilt the Rectory, added the chapel, and in his will left £40 to the poor of Houghton, £20 to the poor of his birthplace (Wigston in Leicestershire), and £10 to be distributed to the poor of Houghton at his funeral.[118] He is alleged to have said that 'he feared to die with any of the Church's goods in his hands' (a danger which, Surtees notes, he probably avoided). In a letter to Sancroft he wrote, 'we priests that have no wives, ought to look upon the Church and poor as our next heires'.[119] Lilburne, for his part, had the inscription 'All things come of thee O Lord And of thine own have wee given thee' placed on his part of the almshouse building.[120] It is tempting to speculate that with the almshouse the two men, Lilburne and Davenport, were engaged in a bout of competitive philanthropy, where each, while representing a very different view of how society should be ordered, would not be outdone by the other in caring for the poor. The completely separate endowment and administration of the two parts of the almshouse (known as Davenport's wing and Lilburne's wing) would certainly suggest that there was only the barest minimum of cooperation between the two founders.

Bishop Cosin himself founded two almshouses in his diocese, at Bishop Auckland in 1662 and in Durham in 1666. These do not appear to have been acts of self-aggrandisement, like Archbishop Abbot's, but part of Cosin's programme of restoring authority and good order to the Anglican Church in his diocese after the Restoration. The almshouses, for four and eight poor people respectively, were relatively simple foundations without grand buildings, which Cosin wished to be called 'the Bishop of Durham's Hospitalls', in other words commemorating his office rather than himself personally (see the drawing and plan of the Palace Green almshouses in Figure 5.2).[121] Cosin also restored the ruinous bishop's palace at Bishop Auckland and rebuilt its chapel as well as the two schools on Palace Green at Durham, and founded and endowed his magnificent public library on the opposite side of the Green in 1668. The library cost him £500 to build, and the collection of books with which he furnished it was apparently valued at £2,000.[122] The

117 H. L. Robson, 'George Lilburne, Mayor of Sunderland', *Antiquities of Sunderland and its Vicinity*, ed. H. Simpson, Sunderland Antiquarian Society 22 (Sunderland, 1960), pp. 92–102.
118 R. Surtees, *The History and Antiquities of the County Palatine of Durham*, vol. I (London, 1816), p. 171.
119 G. Ornsby, ed., *Miscellanea*, Surtees Society 37 (Durham, 1861), p. xvii n.
120 DULSC MSP 25 Mickleton and Spearman Manuscripts 1635–1691, f. 81v.
121 Ornsby, *Correspondence of John Cosin, Part II*, p. 295.
122 Ornsby, *Correspondence of John Cosin, Part II*, pp. xxii, xxv.

achievement is even more notable considering that Cosin was so impoverished in exile that in 1659 he had been on the point of selling his books to maintain himself.[123]

The religious turbulence of the Civil War and Commonwealth period followed by the restoration of the monarchy and the Anglican Church led to numerous disputes for the masters of almshouses who were ordained clergymen. John Machin, Master of Sherburn Hospital in Durham, was deprived of the mastership by the Scottish army in the early years of the Civil War, and subsequently engaged in a lengthy legal battle to obtain his rights.[124] Similarly Raphael Pearce, Master of Lawrence Sheriff Hospital in Rugby, had his income withheld for years, leading, according to his widow, to his complete destitution and premature death.[125] It may have been conscience which prompted John Cogan, Commonwealth administrator of seques-tered church lands in Kent, to leave in his will of 1657 his own house in Canterbury as an almshouse to accommodate six poor clergy widows and a servant. Ironically, the land with which he endowed the almshouse had formerly belonged to the Archbishop, and was recovered at the Restoration, leaving the almshouse seriously impoverished.[126] The Restoration also led to the expulsion of ten of the residents of St John's Hospital in Canterbury in 1660, but there is no explanation given for this action in the register book. It is possible that admissions during the Commonwealth had not been carried out correctly; but one of those expelled, Jane Dun, is probably Jane Dunkin, a minister's widow admitted in 1652, suggesting that religious affiliation may have been a reason.[127] Certainly, whereas in the immediate post-Reformation period the emphasis had been on ensuring that almspeople were Protestant rather than Catholic, in the late seventeenth and early eighteenth century it was dissenters who were likely to be excluded. Rev. Nicholas Chamberlaine, for instance, in 1715 insisted that applicants for his almshouse in Bedworth should be members of the Church of England, in a town where a sizeable part of the population was nonconformist.[128]

123   G. Ornsby, ed., *The Correspondence of John Cosin D.D. Lord Bishop of Durham: Together with Other Papers Illustrative of his Life and Times, Part I*, Surtees Society 52 (Durham, 1869), pp. xxxviii–xxxix.
124   W. Hutchinson, *The History and Antiquities of the County Palatine of Durham*, vol. 2 (Newcastle, 1785), pp. 596–7.
125   W. H. D. Rouse, *A History of Rugby School* (London, 1898), p. 67.
126   Hill, *Almshouses of Canterbury*, p. 48.
127   CCA U13/2 St John's Hospital Admissions Book 1538–1557 and 1625–1653, and U13/3 The Register Book of St John's Hospital 1659–1843.
128   According to the Compton census of 1676, the parish had 291 conformists, and 100 nonconformists: A. H. Lawrence, *The Rev. Nicholas Chamberlaine Rector of Bedworth: His Times and his Charity 1715–1965* (Nuneaton, n.d.), p. 10.

Conclusion

It is evident, therefore, that while founding an almshouse was an essentially philanthropic gesture, undertaken in response to social need, it was not necessarily a rational response to particular problems of poverty and homelessness in old age. As the foregoing discussion has shown, almshouses might fulfil a number of other functions for donors. An increase in disposable wealth among certain sections of the population may not in itself have led to greater charitable giving, but it did enable a wider group of people than previously to become involved as benefactors of organised, endowed charitable institutions such as almshouses. The visibility of almshouse buildings and the presence of almshouse residents in their local communities were attractive to founders who wished to be remembered and honoured by posterity, while those responsible for the administration of their establishments could benefit by association from the founder's status and reputation. Although post-Reformation almshouses were necessarily secular institutions, their founders were often deeply pious and adopted many overtly religious features from earlier establishments. For some, the religious imperative was distinctly partisan, inspiring them to use the almshouses they founded or ran to promote a particular religious identity. While the existence of an almshouse could help landowners fulfil their obligations to aged tenants and servants and other local poor, managing an almshouse provided opportunities for local elites to exercise patronage, involve themselves in implementing and shaping local resources for the poor, and establish a culture of good governance and social stability in their communities.

4

Almshouse Residents and the Experience of Almshouse Life

Respectable, gowned, Trollopian worthies?[1]

There is a general assumption that most, if not all, almshouse occupants were respectable, elderly, poor men and women, living quietly ordered lives in sheltered retirement. With the variety of founders and institutions outlined in the preceding chapter, however, it might be expected that the recipients of an almshouse place would be similarly diverse. Medieval almshouses and hospitals had catered for a range of different needs, including the sick, lepers and travellers, but with the development of more permanent accommodation from the fifteenth century onwards, the clientele became more commonly elderly and disabled people, but not exclusively so.[2] In the brief analysis from which the epigraph to this chapter is taken, Paul Slack suggests that by the end of the sixteenth century there was an 'increasing fastidiousness' about who should benefit from an almshouse place, with lepers, lunatics and victims of infectious diseases increasingly excluded.[3] The process by which this marginalisation took place may be seen not only in the categorisation used by founders in determining eligibility for an almshouse place, but also in the type of person that trustees actually admitted. As the following discussion will demonstrate, these suggest a varied and pragmatic approach to the selection process by founders and those administering almshouses throughout the early modern period, but with a discernible shift by the early eighteenth century towards a more limited range of beneficiaries. Yet, as with

---

1   P. Slack, *From Reformation to Improvement: Public Welfare in Early Modern England* (Oxford, 1999), p. 25.
2   M. K. McIntosh, *Poor Relief in England 1350–1600* (Cambridge, 2012), p. 71.
3   As, for instance, in the rules of admission for Lord Burghley's almshouse at Stamford, quoted by Slack, and those of his son Sir Thomas Cecil's Lyddington Bede House: C. Woodfield and P. Woodfield, *Lyddington Bede House Rutland* (English Heritage: London, 1988), p. 18. But these restrictions occur much earlier too, for instance in the regulations for the fifteenth-century almshouses at Ewelme and Heytesbury: C. Richmond, 'Victorian Values in Fifteenth-Century England: The Ewelme Almshouse Statutes', *Pragmatic Utopias: Ideals and Communities, 1200–1630*, ed. R. Horrox and S. Rees Jones (Cambridge, 2001), pp. 224–41 (pp. 227, 232).

the parallel introduction of statutory poor relief in England, while the overall trajectory of this transformation in almshouse function may be unarguable, the pace and timing of these changes varied considerably.

Many almshouses were governed by rules set down by the founder, or by later patrons or trustees, covering such matters as who was eligible for a place, how they were to be chosen and with what resources they were to be provided. Some also included directions regarding the way the almshouse was to be run, and how the almspeople were expected to behave. Sometimes these were simply expressed in the founder's will, or not at all, in which case those administering the almshouse interpreted their duties in accordance with their own wishes and assumptions, reflecting contemporary cultural expectations about what an almshouse was and who it was for. While some almshouses had clear structures of supervision to ensure compliance with the rules, most did not, and the degree of autonomy and independence experienced by almspeople must have varied considerably. This chapter will examine who were the occupants of early modern almshouses, and how they were expected to live their lives. In particular it will attempt to address the questions: were they old, were they poor, and were they orderly?

Rules of eligibility

The terms almshouse and hospital were not only used interchangeably throughout the early modern period, but both could be used to denote very different types of institution, meeting the needs of very different people. This is shown most clearly in the great sixteenth-century London hospitals, which met the needs, respectively, of travellers (the Savoy); the sick (St Bartholomew's); the old and incurable (St Thomas's); the mentally ill (Bethlehem); orphaned children (Christ's); and the idle vagrant (Bridewell). In no other city or town in England was there such a comprehensive range of provision, but in many places such as at Coventry and Ipswich there were several establishments grouped together trying to provide a similar level of coverage, or institutions attempting to cater for more than one type of need.[4] Sometimes the name 'almshouse' might be used very loosely, merely as a place where alms were received. For instance, the Kepier Free Grammar School and Almshouse in County Durham was founded in 1574 as a school with three poor pensioners, but no accommodation was provided for these pensioners in the initial foundation.[5] At other places, for instance the medieval St Bartholomew's, Chatham, and St Mary Magdalene Hospital in

4 Slack, *Reformation*, p. 21.
5 DRO EP/Ho 559 Foundation Document of Kepier School and Almshouse 1570–1571.

Newcastle upon Tyne, while the foundation survived the accommodation had long since disappeared.[6] But generally the single unifying characteristic of an almshouse or hospital was the provision of accommodation for a number of poor people.

Yet even where accommodation was provided, it was not always envisaged that this would be for permanent residents. Travellers were still catered for in a few almshouses in the post-medieval period; for example, the almshouse 'in the moat' at Durham Castle established by Ralph Squire in 1474, which provided thirteen beds for poor travellers. It was probably intended for pilgrims coming to the shrine of St Cuthbert and survived through the sixteenth century, run by the churchwardens of St Margaret's parish, providing lodging of one day and one night for visitors to the city. In 1610 its foundation deed was altered 'as poor people were no longer allowed to wander'; it was now to cater only for the poor of St Margaret's parish.[7] Other almshouses for travellers probably met the same fate, or disappeared altogether. Some pre-Reformation almshouses were refounded after the Reformation, still with the function of serving travellers, such as Eastbridge Hospital in Canterbury, restored by Archbishop Parker; or Henry VII's Savoy Hospital in London, suppressed by Edward but refounded by Philip and Mary, and remaining an embarrassing anachronism until it was finally dissolved in 1702. But there were also new foundations for travellers. In Coleshill, Warwickshire, George Butler was one of the trustees of Richard Chapman's almshouse, founded in 1507. The original purpose of this almshouse is not known, but Butler appears to have re-established it in 1591 as an almshouse for poor travellers. Although only a small town, Coleshill was an important staging post on the main route from London to Chester and Holyhead, and by the time the Travellers' Rest was rebuilt in the early nineteenth century, it was accommodating 1,300 travellers per year.[8] A more famous Poor Travellers' Rest was established in Rochester, Kent, by Richard Watts in 1579, in an existing almshouse adjacent to the market cross, on the main London to Dover highway. By the terms of Watts' will the almshouse was extended to provide six comfortable lodging rooms for travellers to stay one night. This was in addition to the accommodation for the permanent poor almspeople who were expected to look after the almshouse and the travellers' rooms.[9]

6   E. Hasted, *The History and Topographical Survey of the County of Kent*, vol. 4 (1798), p. 191; NRO SANT/GUI/NCL/6/6/2 St Mary Magdalene Hospital Act (1867).

7   G. Allan, *Collectanea Dunelmensis: Collections Relating Sherburn Hospital in the County Palatine of Durham* (1771), p. 225; M. Harvey, *Lay Religious Life in Late Medieval Durham* (Woodbridge, 2006), pp. 176–7.

8   HCPP, no. 29 (1835), p. 1030.

9   E. J. F. Hinkley, *A History of the Richard Watts Charity* (Rochester, 1979), pp. 11, 39, 131. According to Hinkley, travellers continued to be accommodated at the Travellers' Rest until 1947 (p. 24).

Travellers presented a significant challenge to the authorities in early modern England, and local officials needed to distinguish between people travelling on legitimate business and disorderly vagrants. Churchwardens' accounts of the period are full of payments to people 'with a pass' to help them on their way. This can be seen, for instance, in the numerous entries in the churchwardens' accounts for St Mary's, Chatham, often for sailors with passes en route to their home, from France to Cornwall, for example, or even Scotland.[10] The Parsonage Barn at Aylesford, Kent (on the London to Maidstone road) was so frequently used as a refuge by travelling people in the early eighteenth century that it was alternatively known as the Travellers' House or Beggars' House.[11] Even when relief of travellers was not part of the official remit, it is interesting that this ancient duty of hospitality was taken on by some almshouses. Christ's Hospital in Ipswich, founded by the town in 1569 at the heart of a complex of welfare provision including Tooleys' Hospital, was frequently used by the authorities to provide lodging for people passing through. These included William Lowe, 'a pore sycke man', who stayed five days in 1574, and Mary Weste, a blind wayfaring woman with three children, who remained for a fortnight over Christmas that year.[12] The seventeenth-century stewards' accounts for the Lord Leycester Hospital in Warwick show numerous small payments made at the gate to poor people including travellers, such as 1d given in 1672 to a poor sailor 'that came from Tangiers'.[13] Sherburn Hospital outside Durham was still observing this custom as late as 1735. The new rules for the Hospital that same year indicate the unease that this practice provoked. In future, idle vagrants were to be discouraged and punished, and only 'necessitous travellers on their honest occasions supplied'; care was to be taken that those with no legal settlement should not become burdensome to the hospital 'by an indiscreet relief'.[14]

While medieval and monastic infirmaries have received considerable attention from historians, it is often overlooked that some early modern almshouses continued to provide temporary care for the sick just as those earlier institutions had done. The great London hospital of St Bartholomew's was refounded in 1546 to care for London's sick, and there is evidence from the records of Kent parishes such as Hoo that people were sent from outside

10 MALSC P85/5/2 Chatham St Mary's Churchwardens Accounts 1673–1686. In the eighteenth century, Hasted reported that 800–900 travellers journeyed annually by water from Milton (Gravesend) to London at the parish's expense: Hasted, *History and Topographical Survey*, vol. 3 (1797), Milton charities, pp. 335–46.

11 CKS P12/12/3 Aylesford Overseers' accounts 1713–1746.

12 J. Webb, *Poor Relief in Elizabethan Ipswich*, Suffolk Records Society 9 (Ipswich, 1966), pp. 80–1.

13 WRO CR 1600/42/10 Hospital accounts for 1672.

14 HCPP, no. 23 (1830), p. 125.

London to be treated there.[15] The city of Bath, which drew many sick people to use the thermal baths, had a small almshouse for poor visitors built by John Feckenham in 1576. It had seven beds and was known as the Lepers' Hospital. In 1608 a further almshouse for poor 'diseased' people coming to Bath was built and endowed by Thomas Bellott, steward to William Cecil, Lord Burghley. It was open for three months of the year during the bathing season, and could accommodate twelve people, who had to bring a certificate of support from their home parish. They were provided with their accommo- dation, gowns, the attendance of a surgeon, the sum of 4d per day, and could stay for up to twenty-eight days in one year. People with infectious diseases were excluded, but they could be accommodated at the Lepers' Hospital, which had direct access into its own small bath.[16] Other almshouses with permanent occupants, such as the former guild almshouses in Maidstone, provided care to sick townspeople in times of need, such as during plague visitations.[17] This was also the responsibility of poor widows (though not necessarily almshouse occupants) in Faversham, who were paid 10s by the corporation for keeping people visited by the plague in 1579/80.[18]

In the towns in particular, almshouse charities might be used to meet a number of social needs. Richard Watts' charity was also designed to assist the working poor of Rochester by the provision of flax, hemp and yarn for them to spin and work into cloth, for which they would be paid. From the accounts it seems that the charity's stock of flax and hemp was physically kept at the almshouse. In 1615 the almshouse itself (apart from the travellers' rooms) was turned into a work training centre for young children of the city. Sixteen of the 'most indigent' children (ten boys and six girls) were to be chosen and placed in the custody of the almshouse until they were aged eighteen (boys) or sixteen (girls), unless they were apprenticed before then. The charity accounts for the year 1619–20 show that ten children were in residence, supervised by a weaver.[19] This was still the arrangement in 1650, when the town decided that the mayor and aldermen should be the overseers of the children. It seems that other children were also attending the almshouse on a daily basis at this time,

15   For example, the Overseers of Hoo paid John Cartar 7s in 1671 for his journey to London to get Mary Hicks, a parish pauper, into the hospital. MALSC P/188/12 Hoo Overseers' Accounts 1601–1760.
16   J. Manco, The Spirit of Care: The Eight Hundred Year Story of St John's Hospital, Bath (Bath, 1998), pp. 61, 74–7.
17   In 1563 the occupants of the Maidstone town almshouses were ordered to look after plague victims or be turned out of their accommodation: C. Cooper, Maidstone, A History (Chichester, 2008), p. 23.
18   D. Harrington and P. Hyde, eds, The Early Town Books of Faversham, c.1251 to 1581 (Folkestone, 2008), p. 476.
19   Hinkley, Watts Charity, Appendix 3 Provider's Accounts, pp. 138, 142, and Appendix 4 The Agreement of 1615 Affecting Poor Children, pp. 144–5.

as the overseers were to 'take accompt what children doe Daily come thither to worke' and to 'send for the defaulters'.[20] In 1663 the Rochester corporation resolved to research the governance of the almshouse at Canterbury and the instruction there of poor children in spinning and carding, indicating that there was a similar arrangement in Canterbury.[21] It was very common for an almshouse to be linked to a school, as at Kepier, and, for example, at Rugby, Sevenoaks and Jesus Hospital, Canterbury. Often the school and almshouse were built together, as in the example from Great Linford illustrated in Figure 4.1, and the schoolmaster also acted as the warden of the almshouse, as at Southlands Hospital, New Romney, and at Sir Thomas Dunk's almshouse in Hawkhurst, Kent. The arrangements cited above suggest that the Rochester establishment was not a school but was primarily an introduction to paid work for poor children, and from the Rochester corporation minutes it is clear that the children's families were compelled to send them to the 'almshouse' for instruction.

Other towns also had children in their almshouses. The city of Coventry had references to men, women, and children as almsfolk in 1640.[22] Bablake Boys' Hospital in Coventry was founded by Thomas Wheatley in 1566 for orphans and other poor children, and was located alongside Bond's Hospital for poor men and the house of correction in a group of welfare institutions. It is not always evident, as seen at Faversham, whether the children referred to in these almshouses were placed with their families or on their own (as in the boys' hospital at Coventry). In a few almshouses, however, it was clearly anticipated that occupants would be families and have their children with them. The Reverend Oliver North left a tenement in West Farleigh, Kent, as an almshouse for two poor families in 1725. The vicar and churchwardens were to select the occupants, who were to be 'industrious men' and their families, either 'past labour' or with a 'charge of children to maintain'.[23] Similarly, John Styleman, a director of the East India Company, in his will of 1734, endowed almshouses in Bexley, to be run by the minister and churchwardens for 'twelve poor and distressed familys'.[24] According to the rules of the much earlier New Cobham College (1598), the poor, their wives *and children* were to work either within the College itself or in the local area. Another of the college's rules refers to the pensioners *and their children and servants* having to wear

20   MALSC RCA/A1/1 Rochester City Corporation Meeting Book 1621–1653, 25 January 1650.
21   MALSC RCA/A1/2 Rochester City Corporation Meeting Day Book 1653–1698, 21 December 1663.
22   CHC BA/H/3/17/1 Coventry Council Minute Book 1557–1640, f. 371v.
23   The first two beneficiaries were Thomas Manser and William Stretfield and their families: HCPP, no. 30 (1837), p. 350.
24   K. M. Roome, *Styleman's Almshouses* (Bexley, 1985), p. 6.

Figure 4.1. Great Linford almshouses and school house (1696), Milton Keynes

the college badge.[25] Elsewhere, the presence of children caused consternation. Thomas Maunton was only allowed to enter the Stratford almshouses in 1608 on condition that his wife and children did not come to the almshouse 'to trouble the almsfolk or dwell with him'.[26] The widow Franciscus Pynder was admitted to the same almshouse in 1597 on condition that she placed the child she was caring for in service as soon as the child was old enough.[27] Presumably this was a pragmatic decision by the corporation, who might otherwise have had to take responsibility for boarding out the child elsewhere. In 1591, Archbishop Whitgift raised the worrying possibility of the children of brethren and sisters of St John's Canterbury and St Nicholas Harbledown being left orphans and a charge on the hospitals in the event of their parents' death. He made an order similar to one he had laid down for his own hospital at Croydon, expressly forbidding the admission of children, and ruled that if parents were admitted their children must not be a charge on the hospital but provided for 'otherwise'.[28] This clearly remained a problem at St John's and St Nicholas, however, because an order was made in 1663 against brethren or sisters marrying strangers 'such as sometimes as bring a traine of children along with them'; hereafter, anyone marrying after admission would forfeit their place. Again in 1686, the rule was reiterated that residents were forbidden to have children or grandchildren with them except to nurse them, and only by permission of the master.[29]

A perhaps surprising feature of many almshouses was the requirement that the almspeople should work. As will be seen in the next chapter, this was an economic necessity for many almspeople, especially in less well-endowed establishments. But some almshouses in the earlier part of the period made work compulsory by a specific requirement in the rules, for instance the foundations with which William Lambarde was involved. At Hawkins' Hospital, Chatham (founded in 1592), the poor were required to 'occupie and exercise themselves dayly in such honest labors as the habilities of their bodyes will suffer'. If employment were available either within the hospital or within one mile of it, nobody who was capable of work was permitted to 'live ydlie'. They would forfeit a week's allowance for a first offence, and expulsion for a third.[30] At New Cobham College (1598), Lambarde's rules stated that 'every of those poore & their wives & children being able to labor shall dayly on

25   MALSC P336/5/1 Shorne Churchwardens' accounts 1630–1681, Copy of Rules relating to Cobham College.
26   J. Jones, *Family Life in Shakespeare's England: Stratford-upon-Avon 1570–1630* (Stroud, 1996), p. 121.
27   L. Fox, ed., *Minutes and Accounts of the Corporation of Stratford-Upon-Avon and Other Records*, vol. 5: *1593–1598*, Dugdale Society 35 (Stratford-upon-Avon, 1990), p. 100.
28   CCA U13/16 Memorandum Book, entry for 20 May 1591.
29   CCA U13/16 Memorandum Book, entry for 19 February 1663; 1686.
30   MALSC CH108/21 Minute Book 1617–1691.

the working days doo some Honest labour either within the Coll. or abroad'.
They were also required to work for any honest person within the hundred
of Shamwell who offered to employ them on tasks they could do, and were
to be fined if they refused. At his own foundation, Queen Elizabeth Hospital,
Greenwich (1576), Lambarde had provided a plot behind the almshouse for
hemp to be grown for the almspeople to work into cloth. They were forbidden
from selling their share of the hemp crop, but could pay one of the other
inmates to work it for them. They were also to be available to work anywhere
within the Blackheath hundred if required, and fined for refusing.[31] The rules
for Sir Thomas Cecil's Bede House at Lyddington, Rutland (1600), required
the twelve almsmen 'not to be idle but to take on some handicraft while they
were able'. Among the first almsmen at Lyddington were a tailor, a weaver and
a shoemaker, and these were convenient occupations they would presumably
have been able to continue in their rooms, although it is not known to what
extent, if any, these rules were implemented.[32]

Henry Pinnock's almshouses in Gravesend, known as St Thomas's
almshouses from their position on the site of an earlier chapel, operated on
a slightly different basis in that work was the primary emphasis. They were
founded in 1624 for 'poor decayed persons' of Milton and Gravesend, with a
house for a master weaver to employ them.[33] In 1633 Sir Thomas Puckering
established six almshouses in Warwick, to be let at nominal rents to poor
tradesmen who agreed to take on apprentices.[34] The early seventeenth century
was a time of innovation, when many towns in England were experimenting
with various schemes for assisting the poor and providing work, and both
these sets of almshouses can be viewed in this context.[35] Although the
requirement to work occurs most often in the early part of the period, the
expectation that almspeople would continue in employment is evidenced
later in the period as well. For instance the Ironmongers' Company, who were
given responsibility for establishing Robert Geffrye's almshouses in London
by his will of 1704, considered a site near the City would give the almspeople
opportunities for employment.[36]

Other more conventional almshouses were intended specifically for retired

31   MALSC P336/5/1 Shorne Churchwardens' accounts 1630–1681, Abstract of rules relating
to Cobham College; R. M. Warnicke, *William Lambarde, Elizabethan Antiquary* (London and
Chichester, 1973), p. 47.
32   Woodfield and Woodfield, *Lyddington Bede House*, p. 18.
33   Hasted, *History and Topographical Survey*, vol. 3, p. 335; R. H. Hiscock, *A History of
Gravesend* (Chichester, 1976), p. 7.
34   WRO CR 1618/WA3/89 Review of Puckering's Charity [undated, post-1809]; WRO, 'To
Divers Good Uses': A Directory of the Warwick Charities Past and Present* (Warwick, 1993), p. 18.
35   See, for instance, S. Hindle, *On the Parish? The Micro-Politics of Poor Relief in Rural
England c.1550–1750* (Oxford, 2004), pp. 174–91.
36   N. Burton, *The Geffrye Almshouses* (London, 1979), p. 52.

members of particular occupational groups such as decayed tradesmen, for example Thomas Fulnetby's almshouse in Sandwich (1625); and Napleton's almshouse in Faversham (1721). Fulnetby left four dwellings for poor tradesmen of the parish of St Mary the Virgin, Sandwich, 'in consideration of the great and dayly increase of poore people' in the parish. The tradesmen had to have been born or 'long dwelt' in the parish, and only in default of these could other poor of the parish be considered, which suggests that Fulnetby was concerned to provide for a group of tradesmen who were under pressure from the influx of poor, rather than those poor themselves.[37] On a much grander scale, for business people of higher rank, was Morden College, Blackheath, founded in 1695 for merchants who had been engaged in overseas trade, and who were 'fallen to decay by accidents of the sea or otherwise'.[38] There were similar merchant establishments in Bristol, such as the Merchant Venturers' almshouses and Colston's almshouses, founded in 1696 and 1691 respectively. There was a long tradition of almshouses for particular occupational groups, many founded by craft guilds and the London livery companies.[39] Even before Hawkins' Hospital was founded at Chatham there had been almshouses for sailors in ports around the country, for instance the Trinity House almshouses in Deptford (1514), which were based on those of an earlier fraternity, the Company of Mariners; and the Seamen's Hospital in Dover, run by the town corporation, in existence before 1552.[40] Other almshouses founded for seafarers were the Royal Hospital for Seamen at Greenwich (known as the Royal Naval Hospital, 1694), the Fishermen's Hospital, Great Yarmouth (1702), and the Keelmen's Hospital in Newcastle upon Tyne (also 1702).[41] A number of early modern benefactors gave the management of the almshouse they founded to a London livery company, which was then able to nominate their members to a certain number of places. For instance, Mark Quested's almshouse at Harrietsham, Kent, founded in 1646, was managed by the Fishmongers' Company until 2010. Six of the twelve places were for residents of Harrietsham, but the other six were reserved for members of the Fishmongers' Company itself.[42]

---

37 CCA U3/173/25/6 Fulnetby's Charity, Sandwich.
38 P. Joyce, *Patronage and Poverty in Merchant Society: The History of Morden College, Blackheath 1695 to the Present* (Henley-on-Thames, 1982), p. 50.
39 F. Rexroth, *Deviance and Power in Late Medieval London*, trans. P. E. Selwyn (Cambridge, 2007), pp. 236–8.
40 A. A. Ruddock, 'The Trinity House at Deptford in the Sixteenth Century', *English Historical Review* 65/257 (1950), 458–76 (p. 462); J. Bavington Jones, *The Records of Dover* (Dover, 1920), p. 203.
41 B. Howson, *Houses of Noble Poverty: A History of the English Almshouse* (Sunbury-on-Thames, 1993), pp. 32, 110; W. H. Godfrey, *The English Almshouse, with Some Account of its Predecessor, the Medieval Hospital* (London, 1955), pp. 71–2.
42 HCPP, no. 12 (1825), p. 121.

Some occupational groups were singled out because of the particular circumstances to which they might be vulnerable, such as Fulnetby's Sandwich tradesmen. John Cogan, for instance, gave his house in Canterbury in 1658 for six widows of clergymen and a servant to assist them. Cogan was a lawyer and administrator of sequestered church lands under the Commonwealth, and would have been acutely aware of the difficulties experienced by many clergy widows, particularly those whose husbands had been ejected from their livings in the religious turmoil of the Civil War and Commonwealth. A few years later and prompted by the same need, John Warner, Bishop of Rochester, founded an extremely grand and well-appointed almshouse for the widows of loyal clergy at Bromley College. The husbands of many of these women would have suffered financially during the Interregnum. The restriction to widows of 'loyal' clergy would, however, have specifically excluded the widows of clergy unable to subscribe to the Act of Uniformity in 1662, that is, those whose husbands had also lost their livings, and were consequently as likely to have been in need.

This emphasis on orthodox belief, rather than merely a godly life, was increasingly a feature of the criteria for admission in many almshouses, and of the regime by which the almspeople were expected to live. Whereas sixteenth-century foundations had emphasised religious orthodoxy in opposition to Catholicism, in the later seventeenth and early eighteenth centuries this tended to be replaced by hostility to dissenters. Thus, for instance, Rev. Nicholas Chamberlaine made membership of the Church of England one of the criteria for admission to his Bedworth almshouse in 1715, in a deliberate exclusion of the 25% of his parishioners who were nonconformist.[43] According to its new rules of 1725, St Thomas's Hospital, Sandwich, became reserved exclusively for members of the Church of England. The reaction among nonconformists to these exclusions was to provide institutions of their own for worship, education and welfare. For instance, Mary Duke, around 1727, gave three houses in Maidstone to be lived in by Presbyterian women.[44] The merchant Michael Yoakley founded the Drapers' Homes in Margate in 1709, with a meeting house and burial ground attached. All the early trustees would appear to have been Quakers, and Yoakley was also a supporter of the Quaker workhouse in Clerkenwell.[45]

Sometimes a particular relationship with the founder was specified, for instance, family members or servants.[46] Robert Dudley's hospital at

43   A. H. Lawrence, *The Rev. Nicholas Chamberlaine Rector of Bedworth: His Times and his Charity 1715–1965* (Nuneaton, n.d.), p. 10.
44   P. Clark and L. Murfin, *The History of Maidstone: The Making of a Modern County Town* (Stroud, 1995), p. 92.
45   HCPP, no. 30 (1837), p. 551.
46   I. W. Archer, 'The Charity of Early Modern Londoners', *Transactions of the Royal Historical Society* 12 (2002), 223–44 (pp. 235, 243).

Warwick was not only for old soldiers but for those who had served him: 'the Servauntes and Tenauntes of Us and our heires shalbe preferred before all others'.[47] One of his hospital's almsmen, for example, was admitted from the parish of St Martin-in-the-Fields in London, because he had previously been a servant in the patron's family, and was now 'poor, aged and blind'.[48] In his will of 1693, William Hutchinson did 'indifferently respect' whether the people admitted to his almshouse for ancient and impotent poor people at Romaldkirk were men, women, single, married or widowed, but he specified that any of his kindred in need should be 'first admitted before any other'.[49] Elizabeth Tewart of Chester-le-Street left two houses in 1718 to trustees to be used to accommodate 'two poor widows of my kindred or relations' or, if there were none, to other poor widows nominated by the minister of the parish church.[50] Similarly, Jane Gibson, founder of an almshouse for twelve in Sunderland in 1725, gave her heirs the right of nomination, and stated that her relatives were to be preferred.[51]

The most frequent and most important criteria, however, were geographical: almost invariably, people admitted had to come from the immediate neighbourhood or parish. Some founders were very specific about this, particularly in scattered rural populations. For instance, eighteen of the twenty places at New Cobham College were distributed between the surrounding parishes in specified proportions.[52] William Hutchinson's six almspeople were to come from the various villages or townships constituting the vast upland parish of Romaldkirk.[53] In these cases, community ties and belonging appear to be the overriding test of deservingness. Even when the founder had not specified who the poor were to be, or where they were to come from, the locality was

47 WRO CR 1600/2 Founder's Statutes: Ordinances of the Hospital of Robert Earl of Leicester 26 November 1585, no. 7.
48 WRO CR 1600/19/33 Patron of admission for John Duglas, 13 December 1658.
49 Will of William Hutchinson, DRO EP/Rom 12/2 Romaldkirk Regulations for the management of the Bowes and Romaldkirk Charities 1891, p. 5.
50 Will of Elizabeth Tewart, DRO EP/CS 4/104 Chester-le-Street Memorandum Book of Charities 1626–1919, p. 28.
51 HCPP, no. 23 (1830), p. 68.
52 There were three each from Cobham and Hoo; two each from Shorne and Strood; and one each from Cooling, Cliffe, Chalke, Gravesend, Higham, St Mary's, Cuxtone, and Hallinge. They were to be elected by the parson, churchwardens, sidesmen, overseers, constables and borsholders of each parish. The remaining two places were one each in the nomination of Lord Cobham and the president of the Rochester Bridge Wardens): MALSC P336/5/1 Shorne Churchwardens' accounts 1630–1681, Abstract of rules relating to Cobham College and the method of their election.
53 One almsperson to come from the village of Cragg; the second from Lartington and Naby; the third from Cotherston; the fourth from Hunderthwaite, Briscoe, Hury or Baldersdale; the fifth from Mickleton, Holwick, or Lune; and the sixth from the town of Romaldkirk itself: Will of William Hutchinson, in DRO EP/Rom 12/2 Romaldkirk Regulations for the management of the Bowes and Romaldkirk Charities 1891, p. 5.

usually assumed as the basis for selection as in, for example, Humphrey Davis's almshouse in Leamington Hastings (see chapter 6). Where places beyond the immediate locality were permitted or specified, often these held special significance for the founder. Henry Howard, the Earl of Northampton, for instance, gave twelve of the places at his Trinity Hospital, Greenwich (1613), for poor men from Greenwich, and eight for men from Shotesham, his birthplace in Norfolk.[54] Lady Katherine Leveson's Hospital at Temple Balsall in Warwickshire was intended for women from the parish of Balsall. If there were insufficient of these, then women were to be chosen from areas where she owned land: Long Itchington, Warwickshire; Trentham, Staffordshire; and Lilleshall, Shropshire.[55] Lady Leveson's grandfather, Robert Dudley, had specified that the twelve places at his hospital in Warwick should be allocated in turn between five towns or villages with which his family had connections.[56] This can be seen partly as the accepted responsibility of landowners, the aristocracy and gentry, for their aged tenants, servants and poor relatives. In other words, the geographical criteria for admission were heavily overlaid with personal connections, allowing individual founders and their successors to exercise patronage in the award of an almshouse place. For instance, in 1638 Alderman John Clark endowed two small houses in West Orchard, Coventry, for the benefit of the poor people of Cross Cheaping ward in the city, the selection of beneficiaries to be made by his successors as aldermen of that ward.[57]

Sometimes this exercise of patronage could trump local connections and other criteria laid down by the founder. For instance, as will be seen later, personal servants of people associated with the almshouse appear to have been admitted to Lady Leveson's Hospital at Temple Balsall. Similarly, at the Lord Leycester Hospital, John Stowe, admitted in 1650 on the recommendation of Earl Spencer to whom he had been a personal servant, was dismissed in 1656 when he was found to be ineligible.[58] A visitation of the hospital in 1705 examined allegations that the patron had appointed people from outside the five named towns who were not otherwise qualified.[59] Again, in the eighteenth

54   P. K. Kipps, 'Trinity Hospital, Greenwich', *Transactions of the Greenwich and Lewisham Antiquarian Society* 3/6 (1935), 294–301 (p. 294).

55   WRO CR 1540/6 Transcript of the Will of Lady Katherine Leveson (1671).

56   The five were Warwick, Kenilworth, and Stratford-upon-Avon in Warwickshire; and Wotton-under-Edge and Erlingham in Gloucestershire. In default of sufficient of these, brethren could be admitted from any town in Warwickshire: WRO CR 1600/2 Founder's Statutes: Ordinances of the Hospital of Robert Earl of Leicester 26 November 1585, no. 10.

57   HCPP, no. 28 (1834), p. 290.

58   Extracts from Lord Leycester Hospital Old Book 1660–1926, in WRO CR 1741/57 Philip Styles' notebook, p. 46. Stowe was deprived of his place because he was found to have 'an estate of his own for life and has absented himself for 3 years past'.

59   E. G. Tibbits, 'The Hospital of Robert, Earl of Leicester, in Warwick', *Birmingham Archaeological Society: Transactions and Proceedings* 60 (1936), 112–44 (p. 138).

century there was conflict between local interests and the patron, John Shelley Sidney, when he resisted attempts by the Earl of Warwick to place his nominees in the hospital.[60] The earl had no right of patronage, but appeared to assume that his greater position of local power and influence in the town gave him the authority to countermand the regulations, and usurp the position of the patron. Incidents such as these suggest that not all almshouse places were occupied by the founder's intended beneficiaries, but sometimes by those who owed their place to their personal connection to people of influence.

Age

The assumption is that almshouse residents were usually elderly, but in the early modern period it was often not actually specified in eligibility criteria that residents should be old, and it was even rarer for a minimum age to be stated. In the three counties of Durham, Warwickshire and Kent only about a quarter of almshouses specified that occupants must be old (see Table 4.1).

Some almshouse founders required applicants to be 'old', but without specifying a particular age. These are shown in the tables as '"Old" only'. Examples include Eyffler's almshouse in Warwick (1591) for poor old maids or other poor old women, and John and Ann Tilden's small almshouse at Wye in Kent (1642), which was for 'ancient and well reputed widows of the town'.[61] Some included old age as one of a number of conditions conferring eligibility ('"Old" or other' in the tables). For instance, New Cobham College gave first priority to a poor person who had previously been a labourer, and who had now 'become aged and ... past worke and labour'. The establishment also admitted, in descending order of priority: those lamed and maimed in the service of the monarch; people born or become blind; those overtaken by 'sudden casualty' such as robbery, fire or shipwreck; the sick (but not if they were infectious); and poor people 'overcharged with a burden of children'.[62]

Medieval almshouses often had no age specification. Almshouses which were originally for lepers or pilgrims would have catered for all ages, and chantry almshouses with their onerous prayer regimes would have been unable to perform their function effectively if all their almsmen had been too old and frail to undertake their duties.[63] Yet even post-Reformation almshouses

60   Tibbits, 'Hospital', p. 138. The Sidney family of Penshurst in Sussex were patrons of the hospital by descent from Philip Sidney, nephew of Robert Dudley.
61   HCPP, no. 30 (1837), p. 439.
62   MALSC VF COB 726.709 Rules and Ordinances made for the New College of Cobham in the Countie of Kent [undated], pp. 4–5.
63   Colin Richmond, for instance, likened the almsmen suffering the regime at Ewelme to 'toilers in a Dickensian workhouse': Richmond, 'Victorian Values', p. 226.

Table 4.1. Age criteria for admission to almshouses, 1550–1725

Admission criteria	Durham	Warwickshire	Kent	Total
Specific age	3	5	8	16
'Old' only	0	1	7	8
'Old' or other	1	2	5	8
Subtotal OLD	*4 (21%)*	*8 (25%)*	*20 (27%)*	*32 (25%)*
Unspecified	13	21	51	85
Not known	2	3	4	9
TOTAL	19	32	75	126

Source: Online Appendix A

commonly had no age criteria, for instance the Lord Leycester Hospital almsmen were merely to be 'poore and ympotent persons', with no age specified.[64] Table 4.2 shows post-Reformation almshouses only, for the three counties, together with the inclusion of Eastbridge Hospital in Canterbury, which was refounded after the Reformation. Eastbridge was issued with new ordinances by Archbishop Whitgift, which included a minimum age of fifty on admission. Even with the exclusion of the other surviving medieval almshouses, which rarely specified old age, Table 4.2 shows that less than a third of almshouses founded in the early modern period in the three counties were specifically for old people.

Yet old age and the problems it brought were a well-known feature of the early modern period. Average life expectancy at birth remained around thirty-five throughout the period because of the large numbers of children dying in infancy and high mortality rates in general in the expanding towns. Nonetheless, a person who survived into adulthood had a reasonable chance of living on to their forties or fifties, or even older. People over sixty constituted approximately 7–8% of the total population in the later sixteenth century, rising to about 10% in the early eighteenth century, so older people made up a considerable proportion of the adult population and would have been a visible presence in most communities.[65] Dependent as they were on their own labour, the effects of ageing could be catastrophic for the working poor when their physical capabilities deteriorated, particularly if they had been unable to accumulate sufficient assets to buffer them in their old age.

64 WRO CR 1600/2 Founder's Statutes: Ordinances of the Hospital of Robert Earl of Leicester 26 November 1585, no. 7.
65 E. A. Wrigley and R. S. Schofield, *The Population History of England 1541–1871: A Reconstruction* (Cambridge, 1989), pp. 528–9.

Table 4.2. Age criteria for post-Reformation almshouses only

Admission criteria	Durham	Warwickshire	Kent	Total
Specific age	3	3	8	14
'Old' only	0	1	7	8
'Old' or other	1	2	4	7
Subtotal OLD	*4 (29%)*	*6 (24%)*	*19 (32%)*	*29 (30%)*
Unspecified	9	17	39	65
Not known	1	2	1	4
TOTAL	14	25	59	98

Source: Online Appendix A

Margaret Pelling's analysis of the 1570 Norwich census of the poor shows that 42% of those over sixty in the city were assessed as poor, compared with 22% of adults under sixty, a stark demonstration of older people's economic vulnerability.[66] The life-cycle character of poverty notwithstanding, the lack of specific age requirements for almshouse admission is unsurprising, not least because old age in the early modern period was generally defined functionally rather than chronologically, by the physical signs of ageing or the inability to perform certain tasks rather than by the attainment of a specific age. Lynn Botelho suggests that women were considered 'old' at a younger age than men, as the menopause brought obvious physical changes.[67] Similarly, poor people were seen as 'old' at an earlier age than those who were better off, as a poor diet, hard labour and lack of physical comfort took their toll.

Illness and disability could affect people's capacity to support themselves while relatively young. The great majority of early modern almshouses, in consequence, did not have an age definition in their criteria for admission, and there was no consistency among those that did. For instance, Bowes almshouse at Woolwich (1560) was for poor people aged over fifty, and occupants of Cooper's almshouse in Sedgefield (1702) similarly had to be over fifty, while Hutchinson's almshouse at Romaldkirk (1674) was for men or women, married or unmarried, but all had to be over sixty on admission unless they were disabled. Sir John Duck's almspeople in Chester-le-Street (1686) also had to be over sixty, as did those of James Gramer's almshouses in Mancetter (1728). Bond's Hospital in Coventry (1506) was for men over

66   M. Pelling, *The Common Lot: Sickness, Medical Occupations and the Urban Poor in Early Modern England* (Harlow, 1998), pp. 75–6.
67   L. Botelho, 'The Seventeenth Century', *The Long History of Old Age*, ed. P. Thane (London, 2005), pp. 113–74 (p. 115).

forty, while Ford's Hospital in the same city, founded a few years later, was for couples aged about sixty. Boone's almshouse in Lee, Kent (1683) was for those above a very precise fifty-seven years of age.[68] Compulsory registration of baptism was not introduced until 1538, and so there would not have been any method of verifying an older person's exact age until the late sixteenth century at the earliest. As a result, the use of approximations for age ('about sixty') and the rounding of ages was commonplace in official records, and continued well into the eighteenth century.[69]

As it became more usual over the course of the early modern period for people to know, and be able to verify, their exact age, a precise age criteria for almshouse admissions became more common. Applicants for Lady Hewley's almshouse, for instance, founded in York in 1704, had to 'prove their age to be above fifty-five, by good testimonials if required'.[70] Two ancient foundations, Sherburn Hospital, Durham, and St Thomas's Hospital, Sandwich, were given new rules in the eighteenth century which introduced an age limit for the first time. The rules for St Thomas's drawn up by the trustees in 1725 established a minimum age of fifty on admission, while the 1735 rules for Sherburn Hospital introduced a minimum age of fifty-six.[71] Even so, only half of the new foundations in the three counties from the first quarter of the eighteenth century specified that they were for older people, as shown by Table 4.3.

Even when no age criteria were specified, however, many people involved with almshouse admission assumed older people to be the intended beneficiaries. For instance, Thomas Delaval, governor of Kepier Free Grammar School and Almshouse in 1658, who discovered that the appointment of almspeople by the charity had been hitherto neglected, put this right by choosing three men over seventy years of age, despite the founder Bernard Gilpin not having specified that the pensioners were to be elderly.[72] It is, however, only possible in a very few cases to establish exactly how old in practice were the people admitted to early modern almshouses. Like most

---

68 HCPP, no. 8 (1823), p. 327; HCPP, no. 23 (1830), p. 102; DRO EP/Rom 12/2 Romaldkirk Regulations for the management of the Bowes and Romaldkirk charities 1891, p. 4; HCPP, no. 23 (1830), p. 29; HCPP, no. 29 (1835), p. 953; HCPP, no. 28 (1834), p. 135; J. Cleary and M. Orton, *So Long as the World Shall Endure: The Five Hundred Year History of Ford's and Bond's Hospitals* (Coventry, 1991), p. 45; M. Adams and C. MacKeith, *Boone's Chapel: History in the Making* (London, 2010), p. 1.

69 S. Ottaway, *The Decline of Life: Old Age in Eighteenth Century England* (Cambridge, 2004), pp. 45–6.

70 Anon., *The Foundation Deeds and Other Documents Relating to Dame Sarah Hewley's Charity* (London, 1849), p. 31.

71 CKS U187/7/1 St Thomas's Hospital, Sandwich, 1725 hospital rules; Allan, *Collectanea Dunelmensis*, p. 302.

72 The three almsmen were Edward Moory, aged seventy-four; John Birkfield, seventy-five; and Henry Baker, seventy-four. DRO EP/Ho 613 Thomas Delaval's Notebook 1657–1663.

Table 4.3. Age criteria for almshouses founded between 1700 and 1725

Admission criteria	Durham	Warwickshire	Kent	Total
Specific age	1	2	1	4
'Old' only	0	0	1	1
'Old' or other	0	1	2	3
Subtotal OLD	1	3	4	8 (50%)
Unspecified	3	2	3	8
TOTAL	4	5	7	16

Source: Online Appendix A

of the poor generally, almshouse occupants tend to be anonymous, leaving very little mark in the historical records. Surviving admissions registers are rare, and even those that do exist, such as that for Lady Leveson's Hospital at Temple Balsall, rarely provide much in the way of biographical information about residents.[73] Occasionally information on current occupants is provided by survey or other investigation. For instance the Warwick census of the poor in 1587 records the six women in Oken's almshouses as one aged 60, three aged 80, and the last two at 100 and nearly 100 years of age.[74] This information is highly unlikely to have been accurate; here, the census clerk was merely recording his subjective impression that most of Oken's almswomen were very old indeed and amply demonstrates just how problematic stated ages in early modern records can be, particularly in the earlier part of the period.

Similarly, the master of Greatham Hospital in County Durham, responding to an official inquiry in 1594, was fairly imprecise about the ages of the nine brethren there, recording them as 'about the age of 50 years', or 'about the age of 70 years'. Only one of the nine, John Worme, had an actual age recorded, but this was similarly qualified as 'about 74'. The range of ages was from forty to seventy-four, with an average of fifty-eight years of age.[75] The master of Sherburn Hospital replied to the same 1594 investigation, and gave more precise ages for Sherburn's fifteen in-brothers and fifteen out-brothers. Their ages ranged from thirty to ninety, with seven brothers in their thirties (two aged 30, two aged 32, two aged 34 and one aged 38), and an average

---

73   The register of the women at Temple Balsall begins in 1678, but their ages are not recorded on a regular basis until 1799: WRO DRB36/5 Temple Balsall Register of Admissions 1678–1890.
74   T. Kemp, ed., *The Book of John Fisher, Town Clerk and Deputy Recorder of Warwick (1580–1588)* (Warwick, 1900), p. 169.
75   DULSC DCD/T/YB York Book 1567–1599, f. 120.

also of fifty-eight years of age.[76] These were all given as current ages, rather than that on admission, which suggests it was usual for the men at Sherburn to be admitted at ages well below that which would normally be accepted as 'old'. Perhaps to justify this situation, at the end of his list the master of Sherburn Hospital stated that the men were all 'lame blinde impotent or other waies decaied persones'. It is possible that the men in their thirties and forties admitted to Sherburn and Greatham Hospitals in the late sixteenth century were invalided soldiers, although this is not stated in the records.

The Bishop of Durham's 1593/4 investigation into almshouse provision in the diocese was part of a national survey prompted by Burghley to see whether places could be commandeered by the government for wounded soldiers.[77] Disbanded and disabled soldiers and sailors were held partly responsible for the increase in vagrancy, and the need for provision of this kind had been addressed by a number of founders in the second half of the sixteenth century. Henry Tooley's almshouse in Ipswich, for example, the plans for which were set out in his will of 1550, was to be for ten people 'lame by occasyon of the kynges warres', or who otherwise could not get their living.[78] Robert Dudley's hospital in Warwick (1571) was intended for old and disabled soldiers; Dudley's protégé, Thomas Coningsby, founded a similar institution for old soldiers or mariners in Hereford in 1612, to be known as Coningsby's Company of Old Servitors.[79] The Elizabethan sea captain and adventurer Sir John Hawkins had similarly founded his hospital for sailors in Chatham in 1592. He had previously been one of the instigators, with Sir Francis Drake and Lord Howard of Effingham, behind the creation of the Chatham Chest, the official welfare fund for disabled seamen. The ages of Dudley's and Hawkins' original almsmen are, unfortunately, not known. In the Hawkins' Hospital minute book covering the seventeenth century, men's ages on admission were recorded occasionally, and these men were usually elderly. William Ashby, for instance, admitted in 1643, was eighty-one; Thomas Battle, admitted in 1645, was seventy-three; Edmund Spillman, admitted in 1647, was sixty; Nicholas Neale, admitted the following year, was seventy-seven; and Richard Smith, admitted in 1651, was seventy-six. Nicholas Neale had apparently served in the navy for over fifty years.[80]

Although ages are not given for the seventeenth-century Lord Leycester almsmen, the length of stay for some of them can be calculated from recorded admissions and deaths. Between 1625 and 1689, the length of stay for

76   DULSC DCD/T/YB York Book 1567–1599, f. 117v.
77   Slack, *Reformation*, p. 56.
78   J. Webb, *Great Tooley of Ipswich: Portrait of an Early Tudor Merchant* (Ipswich, 1962), p. 150.
79   E. Prescott, *The English Medieval Hospital 1050–1640* (Melksham, 1992), p. 128.
80   MALSC CH108/21 Minute Book 1617–1691.

forty-five of the brethren ranged from five months to thirty-six years, with an average of eleven to twelve years. This is not dissimilar to the length of time some recipients of poor relief spent on parish pensions in the seventeenth century.[81] A very few men were near the end of their lives on admission to the Lord Leycester Hospital, including Thomas Carte who was granted the place of Thomas Palmer in January 1667/8, but died before he could be admitted. Six men appear to have lived at the hospital for more than twenty years, and it is unlikely that they were particularly old when admitted.[82] Using length of residence again, some of the brethren and sisters of St Nicholas Harbledown and St John's in Canterbury must have been very young on admission. The register taken by the master of both institutions in 1629 records each person's name and the date of their admission. The in-brothers and sisters at St John's had an average length of stay by then of between seven and eight years, with a range from a few months to twenty-four years. At St Nicholas the average was ten years, with a range from two to twenty-two years. Startlingly, a few of the out-brothers and sisters had been receiving their pensions for many decades. Thomas Purt had been an out-brother of St John's since 1567, and he did not die until 1631, suggesting he was a very young man when first appointed. Richard Frisbye had been admitted an out-brother at St Nicholas in 1587, and Margaret Walker an out-sister in 1597. They were both still alive in 1631.[83]

It is possible that these out-brothers and sisters were all disabled in some way. The Stratford-upon-Avon corporation determined in 1586 that none should be admitted to the Church Street almshouses under the age of sixty, but made exceptions for those who were blind or crippled. For example, Mary Symson, 'the blind wench', was admitted in 1596 when she was only twenty-six.[84] George Lilburne's daughter objected to the placement by the parish overseers of a blind boy in her father's almshouse in Houghton-le-Spring in 1697, not because of his youth but because her father had specified that his almspeople must be widows or widowers.[85] However, it is also likely that at least some people who would not normally be considered eligible were admitted to the benefits of an almshouse place through patronage

---

81   Lynn Botelho identified some single women supported by the parish 'for startlingly long periods' in Suffolk, for instance ten, twenty-four and thirty-five years: L. A. Botelho, *Old Age and the English Poor Law, 1500–1700* (Woodbridge, 2004), p. 113. Steve Hindle estimated that the typical recipient of a parish pension was on relief for between five and twelve years, with occasional individuals receiving a pension for twenty-one, thirty-six or even forty-eight years: Hindle, *On the Parish?*, pp. 278–9.
82   WRO CR 1600/19/2 Thomas Carte's patent of admission 1667; WRO CR 1741/57 Philip Styles' notebook, collation of admissions, pp. 44–7.
83   CCA U13/16 Memorandum Book, October 1629.
84   Jones, *Family Life*, p. 93.
85   DRO EP/Ho 300 Letter from Jane Tooley, daughter of George Lilburne of Sunderland, 11 June 1697.

and connections, as described earlier. In the long-running dispute between two rival factions trying to gain control over Lawrence Sheriff's school and almshouse in Rugby in the century after its foundation, for example, one of the accusations made against Sir William Boughton in 1642 was that he 'placed and displaced almsmen at his pleasure'. On one occasion he had apparently placed an able-bodied youth of twenty, one of his own tenants, in the almshouse.[86] In a similar example of an attempt by persons of influence to subvert an establishment's rules of eligibility, Samuel Jemmat, Master of the Lord Leycester Hospital, had to deal with an application in 1689 by Thomas Bredon, London pipe-maker and former inhabitant of Warwick, who brought a mandate for admission from William III. Jemmat brought this embarrassing breach of the admissions procedure to the attention of the patron, saying that 'his Majesty hath been misinformed. For ye man is young & able: of a base, thievish family: and, if I mistake not, forced from this town, for some such practises.'[87]

It is clear from this evidence that not all residents of almshouses were old. Moreover, given the involvement of particular almspeople in tasks relating to the running of their establishment, it seems that in some almshouses there were residents who, regardless of age, were neither particularly frail nor disabled. The 1625 patent of admission to the Lord Leycester Hospital for Francis Whetstone, yeoman of Kenilworth, stated that he was 'now growne aged and altogether unable to labour and travaile for any meanes of his livelyhood'. Yet he was fit and active enough to travel to London on hospital business in February 1631/2, and he appears to have lived on at the hospital for twenty-eight years.[88] Similarly, some of the almspeople of New Cobham College undertook an arduous journey by horse and boat in 1693 to view the college lands at Thurrock, Essex, which had been inundated by the Thames and permanently lost.[89] At the very generously endowed Virgin Mary Hospital in Newcastle, Richard Godson, one of the almsmen, was given the uncomfortable task of going round the hospital's tenants and attempting to collect rent arrears.[90] The range of labouring tasks undertaken by some of the almsmen at Jesus Hospital, Canterbury, suggests that the residents

86   W. H. D. Rouse, *A History of Rugby School* (London, 1898), p. 62.
87   WRO Z725/5 Correspondence relating to the Lord Leycester Hospital, 1689–1775.
88   WRO CR 1600/42/1 Hospital accounts for 1631; WRO CR 1741/57 Philip Styles' notebook, collation of admissions, pp. 44–7.
89   Accounts for 1693/4: 'Paid for horse hier and Boat hier when I went into Essex with sum of the Poore of Cobham to certifie them that their land was under water, 7s': A. A. Arnold, *Cobham College* (London, 1905), p. 30.
90   Although he did not meet with physical violence, he was abused and called a 'shabby fellow' by Charles Horsley, who owed rent of 8s and considerable arrears for his house: NRO 309/A/2 Virgin Mary Hospital, Newcastle, Account Book no. 2, 1686–1699, entry for 1 August 1687.

included people who were by no means incapable of physical work. Four of the brothers had to go to the hospital's wood to survey and lay out the timber in 1613; and several almsmen are named in the seventeenth-century accounts as employed in various building trades and undertaking repairs around the almshouse.[91]

Despite occasional abuses, nonetheless, it seems that there was a general expectation that most almspeople would be elderly. The new ordinances issued by the Bishop of Durham for Sherburn Hospital in 1735, specifying that the men were to be aged '56 and upwards' on admission, resulted from a visitation by the Bishop that year.[92] Prompted by this, the ages of the brethren had again been recorded. This time the youngest in-brother was fifty-two, and the youngest out-brother forty-eight, with the eldest being eighty-six and eighty-four respectively. It is, unfortunately, not known how old they were at the time of their admission. Many had clearly been admitted at an earlier age than the new minimum for admission, but as a group they were considerably older than the late-sixteenth-century brethren. It is possible to see here at Sherburn a deliberate attempt to move the focus of the provision towards an older age range. The ability to know and verify given ages was by now well established through reference to parish records, and this would have enabled age criteria for almshouse admission to be more effectively implemented.[93] But the change would also seem to be a reflection of a developing culture of welfare which increasingly saw almshouse provision limited to older people. This was not a consistent or smooth progression, and exceptions and abuses doubtless still occurred, but the idea that almshouses should be mainly for older people seems to have become fixed as the norm by the end of the period.

Gender

The majority of almshouses in the three counties did not specify the gender of the inmates, or were intended for both men and women, with almshouses solely for men in an overall minority (see Table 4.4). Even medieval foundations were not exclusively for men, somewhat belying traditional assumptions and the picture painted by Trollope.[94] There is a bias towards poor men in the foundations surviving from the pre-Reformation era in County Durham (three foundations for men but only one for women – see Table 4.5), but this was not

91   CCA U204/F/1 Jesus Hospital Ledger 1610–1637.
92   Allan, *Collectanea Dunelmensis*, p. 302.
93   In the parish register for Leamington Hastings, for instance, Jane Man's birth has a mark beside it in the register, presumably from where the vicar William Binckes had been checking the register to establish when and where she had been born (see chapter 6).
94   R. M. Clay, *The Medieval Hospitals of England* (London, 1909), pp. 25–6, 147.

Table 4.4. Gender of almshouse occupants, 1550–1725

	Durham	Warwickshire	Kent	Total
Men	3	5	6	14
Women	6	8	8	22
Either/both	8	14	51	73
Not known	2	5	10	17
Total	19	32	75	126

Source: Online Appendix A

Table 4.5. Gender of occupants of surviving pre-Reformation almshouses

	Durham	Warwickshire	Kent	Total
Men	3	1	2	6
Women	1	1	0	2
Either/both	0	2	11	13
Not known	1	3	4	8
Total	5	7	17	29

Source: Online Appendix A

Table 4.6. Gender of occupants of almshouses founded 1700–1725

	Durham	Warwickshire	Kent	Total
Men	0	1	1	2
Women	2	2	0	4
Either/both	2	1	6	9
Not known	0	1	0	1
Total	4	5	7	16

Source: Online Appendix A

replicated elsewhere or in later centuries. In the period after the Reformation, foundations for women outnumbered those for men, but both were significantly less common than those foundations which were for either or both genders. Yet in practice, women often came to outnumber men in institutions which took both men and women, unless the numbers of each gender were specified (for instance at St Nicholas Harbledown, where there were fifteen in-brothers and fifteen in-sisters, and also fifteen out-brothers and fifteen out-sisters). This is shown, for instance, by a comparison of the occupants of the Leamington Hastings almshouse in 1633 and in 1698, when the first group comprised seven men and one woman, but the later group consisted of one man, two couples and five widows (see the case study in chapter 6). Martin Bowes founded his almshouse at Woolwich (1560) for poor people, gender unspecified, but it became used exclusively for widows.[95] Similarly, Thomas Oken's almshouses in Warwick, founded in 1571 for married couples or single people of either sex, were rebuilt exclusively for women after the Great Fire of Warwick in 1694.

It might seem that, in the same way that parish poor relief became dominated by the needs of poor widows in the seventeenth century, so mixed almshouses were increasingly colonised by poor women.[96] Even so, in the early years of the eighteenth century, new foundations in Durham and Warwickshire were only slightly more likely to be exclusively for women than for men (see Table 4.6).

Many widows receiving regular parish pensions were not elderly, but were the heads of households with children.[97] These were not generally the circumstances of women admitted to almshouses. Lynn Botelho argues that women's experience of poverty in old age differed from that of men, with the availability of low-paid employment in some places enabling women to retain a degree of self-sufficiency in old age, but often only at a level which required some parish assistance.[98] Low-paid widows working hard to avoid penury may have become the very epitome of the deserving poor, and thus more likely be considered suitable for an almshouse place. In the Netherlands the gender bias in almshouses was even more extreme, with women overwhelmingly the clientele by 1800 (154 foundations reserved entirely for women, compared with only twenty-one for men, and thirty-seven for both men and women).[99] As an explanation, Goose and Looijesteijn suggest that women in almshouses were

---

95   HCPP, no. 8 (1823), p. 330.
96   T. Wales, 'Poverty, Poor Relief and the Life-Cycle: Some Evidence from Seventeenth-Century Norfolk', *Land, Kinship and Life-Cycle*, ed. R. M. Smith (Cambridge, 1984), pp. 351–404.
97   Hindle, *On the Parish?*, p. 273–4.
98   Botelho, *Old Age*, pp. 112–13.
99   N. Goose and H. Looijesteijn, 'Almshouses in England and the Dutch Republic *circa* 1350–1800: A Comparative Perspective', *Journal of Social History* 45/4 (2012), 1049–73 (p. 1059).

expected to be able to look after themselves in old age, whereas men were less likely to be able to do so. The parallel development of the *oudemannenhuis* ('old men's home') in many Dutch cities from the start of the seventeenth century, for elderly men who were unable to look after themselves, may have enabled Dutch almshouses (*hofje*) to cater exclusively for women.[100] There was no equivalent to the *oudemannenhuis* in England until workhouses became common.[101] Instead, old men's strategies for survival might include remarriage to a younger spouse or being taken in by sons or daughters, both of which were more likely for older men than older women.[102] Admitting men to an almshouse was thus likely to require the provision of some form of additional support, either from relatives, from female fellow-residents, or from paid staff. The existence of servants in better-off almshouses for unmarried or widowed men, such as Sherburn Hospital and Trinity Hospital, Greenwich, may thus have been not only a mark of status but necessary to provide this essential support.

Although women residents may have been in the majority overall, it does appear, however, that in some almshouses women were viewed as problematic. The ordinances drawn up in 1601 for the Lyddington Bede House by Sir Thomas Cecil, specified that men need only be aged over thirty on admission, but women had to be over forty-five.[103] Similarly, while Sir John Hawkins made no age requirement for the sailors and shipwrights admitted to his hospital in Chatham (1592), if their wives were also to be admitted they must be over fifty, and the men were not allowed to marry or remarry after admission.[104] The concern here was evidently that only women past childbearing age should be admitted. Eyffler's almshouses for 'oulde Maydens of Warwicke' or other old women, made this a specific order. In 1608 the trustees required a bond on the admission of Margery Griffin, 'a poore maimed Maid, lacking one hand', stating that, as it was 'doubtfull whether yet the said Margery may bringe forth a Child or noe', the sureties had to guarantee that in the event of her becoming pregnant she would leave the hospital upon ten days' notice.[105] On

100   Goose and Looijesteijn, 'Almshouses', p. 1064.

101   Early findings from the FACHRS Almshouse Project suggested that in nineteenth-century Hertfordshire, at least, older men were more likely to be resident in workhouses than women, while women predominated in almshouses: N. Goose and S. Basten, 'Almshouse Residency in Nineteenth-Century England: An Interim Report', *Family and Community History* 12/1 (2009), 65–76 (pp. 67–8).

102   In the Norwich census of 1570, Margaret Pelling identified many examples of older men married to much younger spouses, while Alexandra Shepard calculated that as many as 50% of men over sixty-five co-resided with a child: Pelling, *Common Lot*, pp. 147–51; M. Pelling, 'Who Most Needs to Marry?', *Women and Ageing in British Society Since 1500*, ed. L. Botelho and P. Thane (Harlow, 2001), pp. 31–42 (p. 34); A. Shepard, *Meanings of Manhood in Early Modern England* (Oxford, 2003), p. 241.

103   Woodfield and Woodfield, *Lyddington Bede House*, p. 18.

104   MALSC CH108/21 Minute Book 1617–1691.

105   WRO CR 1618/WA12/33/7 Bond 1608.

admitting Matthew Blithe in 1618, Hawkins' Hospital refused admission to his wife because she was not yet forty and had five children.[106]

In many almshouses, such as Henry Howard's Trinity Hospital at Greenwich, only unmarried or widowed men were admitted. This caused problems for Howard's secretary, John Griffith, who had the eight poor men that Howard had specified from Shotesham transported by cart from Norfolk to Greenwich in time for the grand opening on 24 February 1617, only to have to send two of them back when it was found they were married.[107] At Hawkins' Hospital, the men were permitted to have their wives with them; the statutes specified that widows were allowed to stay on in the hospital if their husbands predeceased them, and to receive the full stipend.[108] The governors noted in 1607 that the foundation was intended for twelve residents, yet there were only ten houses. As two of these were occupied by widows, the governors considered making them share a room and a stipend, as had been the case for widows in Ford's Hospital, Coventry before 1609.[109] This was possibly what happened at Jesus Hospital, Canterbury, when Margaret Knight and Jane Forebrace shared a sister's salary from 1630 to 1634.[110] The new rule was not implemented at Hawkins' Hospital, however, and in 1609 the numbers were officially reduced to ten. However, again in 1649 the governors determined to investigate whether they were obliged to maintain the widows, as they could find no evidence that they were indeed liable.[111] In 1651 the governors decided they would only admit 76-year-old Richard Smith into the almshouse if he disposed of his wife elsewhere, as she was 'a scandalous liver'. She seems to have managed to gain admission, however, because in 1656, by which time she was widowed, the governors ordered that she was to have her pension suspended whenever she was 'distempered w[i]th drinke'. She was finally expelled in 1658 for disorderly behaviour, having been frequently drunk; the governors belatedly realised she had 'noe cleare admittance at the first'.[112]

Even in almshouses that allowed wives, it seems that sometimes they were there only on sufferance. The occupants of Sir Roger Manwood's Hospital

---

106   MALSC CH108/21 Minute Book 1617–1691.

107   J. Imray, 'The Early Days of Trinity Hospital', *Transactions of the Greenwich and Lewisham Antiquarian Society* 9/3 (1981), 117–36 (pp. 118, 121).

108   'Anyone then lawfully married, if his wife is at least 50 years old, to be admitted also in to the hospital to cohabit with him, both to be relieved as one single person. If she outlives him, to have the whole pension for life so long as she remain in the hospital and unmarried': MALSC CH108/21 Copy of the Charter and Statutes at the front of the Minute Book 1617–1691. Reduced pensions were eventually introduced for women in the later eighteenth century.

109   Cleary and Orton, *So Long as the World*, p. 45.

110   CCA U204/F1/1 Jesus Hospital Ledger 1610–1637.

111   MALSC CH108/21 Minute Book 1617–1691, p. 172.

112   The Deputy Governor paid 1s for a warrant from the justices to order the Chatham overseers of the poor to provide for her: MALSC CH108/21 Minute Book 1617–1691, pp. 179, 192, 203, 205.

at Hackington, Kent, for example, were six married couples at the time of Manwood's death in 1592. Manwood's son listed them by name in the hospital records, and beside the name of each wife he added 'of curtesye duringe pleasure', indicating that the wives were there by permission rather than by right.[113] At the Lord Leycester Hospital, the marital status of the men was never specified, but there do occasionally appear to have been wives living with their husbands. Sometimes wives took on the role of nurse to the other men, as did 'Nurse' Falconer, widow of almsman Edward Falconer, appearing in the accounts in 1667, and it may have been through performing tasks such as this that their presence was tolerated.[114] Although St Edmund's, Gateshead was apparently intended only for men, 56-year-old Alice Pickering was one of the three occupants named in the 1593/4 inquiry. It is not known whether she was the widow of a former almsman, or was unofficially the nurse. The two other almspeople were men aged seventy and seventy-six, and it is possible that Alice was there to look after the two elderly men.[115] This is also suggested by the changes to the foundation of Ford's Hospital in Coventry in the early sixteenth century. Ford originally specified in 1509 that the foundation was for five men and one woman, but in 1517 one of his executors, William Pisford, changed this to six poor men and their wives aged over sixty. Pisford's co-executor, William Wigston, however, amended this again in 1528 to five couples aged over sixty, and a nurse, who was to be aged between forty and fifty.[116] Wigston's rationale for the nurse was that many people of that age (over sixty) were impotent and 'not able well to keep themselves clean of their bodies'. The nurse was to wash them, cook their food and clean their houses, 'ministering all things necessary to them when and as often as need should require'.[117]

Younger women, as long as they were not *too* young, were thus regarded as useful in helping to care for other almspeople as they became old and frail. At Temple Balsall Hospital, for instance, the younger women were expected to look after the older ones, with two of them paid extra as nurses from 1708.[118] At Lyddington Bede House the two women over forty-five were presumably there

---

113   For instance, 'In ye seconde howse next the streete Percevall Foster (and Elizabeth his wyffe of curtesye duringe pleasure); in the thirde Edwarde Watts (& Joane his wyffe of curtesye duringe pleasure)' etc., CCA CC/S/7/1 St Stephen's Hospital Memorandum and Disbursements Book 1593–1828, p. 11.

114   WRO CR 1600/31 'The House Book', stewards' accounts. According to the former master, Lt Col. Gerald Lesinski, the current rules for the Hospital officially still require widows to leave the Hospital once their husband dies, so their appointment as nurse may have been one way for them to remain in residence.

115   DULSC DCD/T/YB York Book, f. 116v.

116   Cleary and Orton, *So Long as the World*, pp. 13–15.

117   HCPP, no. 28 (1834), p. 166.

118   E. Gooder, *Temple Balsall: From Hospitallers to a Caring Community, 1322 to Modern Times* (Chichester, 1999), pp. 60–1.

to look after the twelve men. This mirrored the situation at Browne's Hospital, Stamford (1475), which was founded for two chaplains, ten men and two sisters, and which would have been well known to Sir Thomas Cecil, Lyddington's founder.[119] Women in almshouses frequently seem to have been obliged to take on caring tasks, not only looking after other frail residents, but even people in the neighbourhood who were sick. The women of the ancient foundation of St John's in the centre of Sandwich were awarded 20s yearly in 1614 for looking after poor people that the town sent to them.[120] While women may have been expected to be carers, men were often expected to take on senior positions, locking gates and reading prayers. The first twelve inhabitants of Sir John Duck's almshouse in 1686, chosen by him personally, were eleven women and one man. It is possible that the man, John Pots, was appointed specifically to take charge of the women.[121] Unusually, Samuel Lock's wife was paid 5s in 1658/9 for reading the prayers to the other almspeople at Hawkins' Hospital, although the normal payment for this task was 10s when performed by a man.[122]

While it would probably not be accurate, from the evidence available, to describe almshouses as gendered spaces, the position of women residents did differ from that of men. Women in almshouses, as in early modern society generally, were likely to have been subordinated to men, whether that was to other occupants for whom they had to provide caring services, or to male masters, wardens or stewards appointed over them. They were also more likely to be subject to suspicious and discriminatory admission criteria. Conversely, however, it was rare for stipends to be discriminatory in almshouses which accepted both men and women, with only a handful of almshouses paying lower stipends to women than to men (as will be seen in chapter 5). For many older women, this would have contrasted favourably with their experience of employment, while the relative comfort, status and autonomy of an almshouse place for an elderly woman was likely to have been a significant improvement on her previous circumstances.

Poverty

All almshouses were intended for poor people, but poverty is a relative concept, and there is no absolute measure to determine the economic status

---

119 Cecil had his seat at Burghley just outside Stamford, and his father William's almshouse was in the same town.
120 Sandwich Local History Society, *Sandwich Almshouses 1190–1975*, Occasional Paper 2 (Sandwich, n.d.), p. 6.
121 DULSC MSP 25 Mickleton and Spearman Manuscripts 1635–1691, f. 135r, Foundation Charter of Sir John Duck's Hospital, Great Lumley.
122 MALSC CH108/172 Deputy Governor's Accounts 1658–1659.

of people admitted to early modern almshouses. The likelihood is that this varied considerably, with sought-after places in the better-off almshouses, where stipends and benefits were generous, becoming the preserve of those with greater access to patronage and influence. Such people were unlikely to be among the poorest.

William Lambarde's regulations for his own Queen Elizabeth Hospital at Greenwich (1576), and for Lord Cobham's New Cobham College (1598), specified that applicants must have been supported by their parish for three years prior to admission. In other words they were expected to be very poor, and unable to support themselves without help.[123] Yet other late-sixteenth-century almshouses clearly had rather different expectations. The ordinances for the Lord Leycester Hospital, Warwick, drawn up in 1585, specified that applicants were not to be admitted if they had any other living of more than £5 per year, and at Sir John Boys' Jesus Hospital in Canterbury (1599) the upper limit was £10.[124] These limits would have allowed for the admission of people well above destitution levels. The process of admission for Jesus Hospital entailed the patron putting forward two candidates for one place, with one to be selected by the mayor. Boys' rules specified that the poorer of the two should be chosen, but it is not possible to judge whether this ever happened in practice as there is no surviving documentation giving the reason why the successful candidate was preferred. A comparison of the surnames of Jesus Hospital almspeople from the 1664–87 payments ledger with entries in the 1663 or 1664 hearth tax assessments provides many examples of people who shared the same surname as almshouse occupants being charged on two, three, four and even six-hearth houses, and just two names of non-chargeable residents, both in two-hearth houses.[125] Of course it is not possible to say for certain whether these people sharing surnames were related, but it is likely that some were; also exemption or otherwise from the hearth tax is no absolute guarantee of people's relative poverty.[126] The overall impression, however, is that the Jesus Hospital almspeople were members of Canterbury's better-off families, perhaps predominantly craftsmen and small tradespeople. Occupations only began to be recorded in the register book that commences in 1727. Between 1728 and 1742, apart from two relatives of the founder and

123   Warnicke, *William Lambarde*, p. 46; MALSC VF COB 726.709 Rules and Ordinances made for the New College of Cobham in the Countie of Kent [undated], p. 4.
124   WRO CR 1600/2 Founder's Statutes: Ordinances of the Hospital of Robert Earl of Leicester 26 November 1585, no. 24; CCA CC Supp Ms/6 Alderman Gray's Notebook 1737–1780, p. 155.
125   CCA U204/F1/3 Jesus Hospital Ledger no. 3, 1664–1687; D. Harrington, S. Pearson and S. Rose, eds, *Kent Hearth Tax Assessment Lady Day 1664* (London and Maidstone, 2000), pp. 375–6, 380–2, 436–49.
126   T. Arkell, 'The Incidence of Poverty in England in the Later Seventeenth Century', *Social History* 12 (1987), 23–47.

two women appointed as nurses, the admissions were of a paper maker, a gardener, a husbandman and six silk-weavers.[127]

There is evidence from other Kent almshouses that the occupants were not very poor in an absolute sense. Fifteen probate inventories of residents of St Bartholomew's, Sandwich, from 1568 to 1593, show them each occupying a suite of rooms in this medieval establishment, and leaving goods valued at between £5 and £82. The brewer Oliver Stromble and his wife, for instance, admitted to St Bartholomew's in the 1540s, were owners of valuable property in the town.[128] In 1677 Mary Wheeler, one of the sisters of St Bartholomew's, was sufficiently well-educated and experienced in business matters to compile a list of the rentals of the property of the hospital. She then represented the almspeople in a complaint to the Sandwich mayor and jurats that former hospital lands had been misappropriated, resulting in two jurats being accused of illegal possession of hospital property.[129] According to a memorandum written by the master inside the seventeenth-century accounts book of St Thomas's Hospital, Sandwich, it was the custom at both St Thomas's and St Bartholomew's for a new almsperson to pay 32s on admission, to be distributed among their fellows.[130] This was a sizeable sum, unlikely to have been payable by the genuinely poor, and the origin of this unusual requirement is unknown.

Admission fees in some form, however, were not unknown. In some other Kent almshouses, and elsewhere, the sum of 6s 8d was paid on admission by new almspeople. At Stratford-upon-Avon, for example, this had been the sum traditionally paid by members of the Guild of the Holy Cross on admission to the guild almshouses, and these payments continued once the almshouses were taken over by the town corporation. John Ashwell, for instance, paid the fee in 1598, but died so soon after entering the Stratford almshouses that the chamberlains charitably returned 3s 4d to his widow Elizabeth.[131] This payment of 6s 8d was not the equivalent of a medieval corrody, by which better-off people purchased a place for life in a monastery or hospital; it is probably more accurate to view it as a kind of entry fine, payable on taking up a tenancy. At the Maynard and Cotton almshouses in Canterbury, the 6s 8d fee first appears in 1607 upon the admission of Robert Bynge, when it was actually referred to as a 'fyne of his entrance'.[132] At St John's

127 CCA U204/R2 Jesus Hospital Register Book 1727–1844.
128 H. Clarke, S. Pearson, M. Mate and K. Parfitt, Sandwich, 'the completest medieval town in England': A Study of the Town and Port from its Origins to 1600 (Oxford, 2010), p. 212–13.
129 Sandwich Local History Society, Sandwich Almshouses, p. 12.
130 Sandwich Local History Society, Sandwich Almshouses, p. 14.
131 J. Jones, ed., Stratford-upon-Avon Inventories, vol. 1: 1538–1625, Dugdale Society 39 (Stratford-upon-Avon, 2002), p. 55.
132 CCA CC/S/8/1 Maynard and Cotton Almshouses, Accounts 1599–1653 and Admissions 1630–179.

Hospital in the same city, the register book records William Phipps as being admitted on 26 October 1625, 'and at his admission paid 6s 8d according to Custome'.[133] Here a 'corrodie' is also mentioned, but as the warrant or patent of admission from the Archbishop. Subsequent admissions of both in- and out-brothers and sisters are recorded with the same formula: 'by a corrodie from my Lords Grace and payd 6s 8d'. For the admission of Elizabeth Wallett in 1629, and all subsequent admissions until 1699, the 6s 8d fee was referred to as 'the Reparation noble', suggesting that it was seen as a contribution towards repairs of the almshouse. In another example, the 1587 rules for the Drapers' Company almshouses in Shrewsbury included the stipulation that, on admission, almspeople should bring with them a shroud with 4d tied in a corner, presumably as their contribution towards their (eventual) burial.[134]

The residents of the Maynard and Cotton almshouses, chosen by the mayor, and those of St John's, nominated by the Archbishop of Canterbury, were likely to have been drawn from better-off inhabitants of the city, for whom paying a noble on admission would not have presented any difficulty. One of the brethren admitted to the Maynard and Cotton almshouses by the mayor George Miller in 1661/2, was referred to as 'James Masters Gent, some time Alderman of the city'.[135] From a comparison with hearth tax listings of the few admissions to this almshouse in the 1660s and 1670s, the impression is that the economic status of almspeople was similar to Jesus Hospital, where occupants were also chosen by the mayor. Two surnames of almspeople appear in the hearth tax assessments, both chargeable on two-hearth houses; and Daniell Wakeley, chosen as 'prior' (warden) in 1668 had previously been chargeable on a three-hearth house in Newingate Ward in the city.[136]

It is not clear that occupants of other almshouses would have been as well off as these almspeople, even in places where 6s 8d was chargeable on admission. For instance at Stratford-upon-Avon, where the 6s 8d entry fee continued to be paid throughout the sixteenth century, the surviving probate material from two sixteenth-century almshouse residents does not suggest great wealth. Thomas Patrick, a tailor, and his wife Joan entered the almshouses in 1582. They had owned their own house, and when Joan died in 1597 her inventory was worth £4 12s. But John Ashwell, who entered the almshouses the following year and died shortly after, was a wheelwright, and at his death his possessions were valued at only 18s 10d. He left his working tools to his son Thomas, and 12d to each of his other three children. His widow had not entered the almshouse with him, perhaps because they

---

133   CCA U13/2 St John's Hospital Admissions Book 1538–1557 and 1625–1653.

134   S. Watts, *Shropshire Almshouses* (Woonton Almeley, 2010), p. 101.

135   CCA S/8/1 Maynard and Cotton Almshouses, Accounts 1599–1653 and Admissions 1630–1795.

136   Harrington, Pearson and Rose, *Kent Hearth Tax*, p. 442.

could not afford to pay two entry fees.[137] It is not often that almspeople left wills; the few identified show considerable variation, but relatively modest possessions. Richard Hargrave, a husbandman who died in the Stoneleigh almshouses in Warwickshire in 1640, had assets worth £47 15s 8d, but debts owed to him made up £43 of this total amount. His actual possessions were fairly typical of a poor householder, including a 'joyned chest', an 'olde bedsted' and 'woolbedde' with a pillow, two blankets and two pairs of sheets; two 'Little kettle', four 'little stooles', an 'Old lanthorne' and a 'Forke'.[138] Dorothy Clarke, an almswoman at Temple Balsall Hospital in Warwickshire, subscribed her will with her mark in 1729. Her inventory has not survived, but she left 1s to her brother and the rest of her possessions to her kinsman and executor Thomas Harris, who was a labourer. In contrast Bridget Phipps, spinster and one of the first almswomen admitted to Temple Balsall Hospital, left possessions valued at £34 1s 2d in 1713. Her bequests included one guinea to her cousin, a Dr William Phipps.[139]

It might have been the intention of an almshouse founder to benefit the very poor, but after their death the actual disposition of places was in the hands of trustees with possibly differing priorities. Lady Katherine Leveson, for example, in designing her almshouse at Temple Balsall, had specified that her almspeople were to be chosen 'out of the poor inhabitants' of Balsall, and 'in the choyce of the said poore persons the poorest persons and such as be lame and in greatest distress shall be ever preferred'. Only if there were insufficient applicants from Balsall were women to be admitted from elsewhere.[140] Yet in a complicated lawsuit in Chancery in 1685, one of the complaints made was that poor widows were being brought out of other parishes, given a settlement for a short time in Balsall, and then admitted to the almshouse, 'while severall poore widows ancient inhabitants of the said parish of Balsall … are kept out'.[141] At least two of the almswomen leaving wills in the early eighteenth century appear to have been personal servants, one to the master of the hospital and the other to Lady Leveson's steward, who acted as principal trustee. It may be that the trustees were using their powers to provide for their own dependants rather than Lady Katherine's intended beneficiaries, prompting the parishioners' complaint.[142]

137 Jones, *Inventories*, pp. 55, 171.
138 N. W. Alcock, *People at Home: Living in a Warwickshire Village, 1500–1800* (Chichester, 1993), p. 143.
139 WRO CR 112/Ba45 Will of Bridget Phipps 16 November 1713, and CR 112/Ba65/47 Inventory of Bridget Phipps 9 March 1713/4.
140 WRO CR 1540/6 Transcript of the Will of Lady Katherine Leveson (1671).
141 WRO DR18/15/3 Temple Balsall lawsuit by the overseers of the poor regarding the administration of the hospital, 1685–1700, Petition to Lord Guildford 20 July 1685, p. 62.
142 WRO CR 112/Ba47/1 Will of Lucie Leek 3 November 1718, and CR 112/Ba52/1 Will of Joan Miles 14 August 1726.

While some of these examples show that many almspeople could be considered among the better-off sections of society, other evidence exists to show that some almspeople were undoubtedly poor. The six inhabitants of Oken's almshouses at the time of the Great Fire of Warwick in 1694 were simply described as 'poore' in the official estimates of the fire losses. Elizabeth Dyer, Sarah Cooper and Anne Dunne each lost goods worth just over £1, representing their meagre household goods, bedding, bedclothes and wearing clothes. William Pestell, lodging in the almshouse with his mother Mary, lost linen and woollen cloth worth £3 3s; Widow Mary Bolton claimed a slightly more substantial loss of £6 10s worth in 'bedsteds, beding, linen, woollen, brass, household goods and fewel'. Comparison with fire losses sustained by other citizens of Warwick indicate the level of poverty experienced by Oken's almspeople, with only live-in servants such as Elizabeth Pain and Mary Carter having possessions of as little value as the three almswomen, Elizabeth, Sarah and Anne.[143] The trustees of Hawkins' Hospital began to provide a burial grant of 17s 6d in 1719, presumably because many of the almsmen, existing only on their stipends with no additional resources, were unable to meet these costs themselves. Prior to this, the Minute Books show that 5s had been expended on John Wardell's burial in 1639, he 'having noe meanes left to bury himself'; and in 1684 George Oliver had been described as 'an Almes man so poor yt he left nothing to bury him'.[144] The admission criteria for the Kent almshouses with which William Lambarde was involved specified that applicants should have been relieved by the parish for three years prior to admission. Applicants had to be nominated by the parish officers, and it seems safe to assume that parishes would have complied with this restriction, as it was in their interests to place in these almshouses parishioners who were proving a burden on the rates. At New Cobham College, for example, although parishes were supposed to give the almshouse a bond of £20 to ensure that no one 'unmeet' was admitted, by the early eighteenth century there were complaints that parishes were getting rid of their most disreputable residents in this way.[145]

There is also evidence from a number of other almshouses that applicants were dependent, or partially dependent, on parish poor relief before admission, and, in the poorest almshouses, retained that dependence even after admission. Anne Davison, for instance, one of Sir John Duck's original almswomen from Chester-le-Street, County Durham, appears in the overseers' accounts as receiving poor relief in 1666, 1675, 1684 and 1685, prior to her

---

143   M. Farr, ed., *The Great Fire of Warwick 1694*, Dugdale Society 36 (Stratford-upon-Avon, 1992), pp. 175, 203–4, 238.
144   MALSC CH108/21 Minute Book 1617–1691, p. 124, and CH108/115/41 Loose accounts 30 May 1684.
145   Arnold, *Cobham College*, p. 21.

admission to the almshouse in 1686.[146] She was described as blind, and, like the other almswomen, is recorded as a widow in the 1686 list of inmates.[147] She also appears in the hearth tax records as exempt in 1673, as does another of Duck's first occupants, widow Barbara Robinson.[148] Six others of the original twelve almspeople share surnames with people listed as exempt, and one person shares a surname with someone paying on a one-hearth house.[149] This suggests that most if not all of Duck's original almspeople were from genuinely poor families. It is occasionally possible to trace other almshouse occupants being helped through parish poor relief before admission to an almshouse, such as widow Margaret Sharpe who entered Sir Roger Manwood's hospital in Hackington, in 1595. She appears as Mother Sharpe in the accounts of the churchwardens of St Stephens, Hackington, receiving 5s and a load and a half of wood in 1593, and another load of wood in 1594.[150] Marjorie McIntosh also gives a number of examples of residents in the almshouses at Hadleigh, Suffolk, in 1594 who had received parish relief before they were admitted to one of the town almshouses.[151]

Examples of parish paupers being admitted as almspeople continue throughout the period, for instance in seventeenth-century Leamington Hastings, Warwickshire (see the case study in chapter 6). In 1719 the overseers of East Farleigh in Kent, who had been providing Widow Baldock with regular relief of 1s or 2s, paid 3s 'for carrying Widd Bauldock and her housall goods to the Almes house'.[152] Widow Ann Austin, one of the first inhabitants of Sir Thomas Dunk's almshouse in Hawkhurst, Kent, had previously been on regular poor relief. From 1720 until her admission to the almshouse she had her rent of 15s per year paid by the parish, and regular relief of 4s per month. Another widow, Elizabeth Stunt, admitted in 1730, was having her rent paid from the commencement of the overseers account book in 1711; she also received half a cord of wood and half a cord of faggots, and occasional relief of 2s per month.[153] Apart from Ann Austin, three more of the original six inhabitants of Dunk's almshouses, had previously received payouts

146   DRO EP/CS 4/92 and 4/93 Churchwardens and Overseers Account Books 1606–1666 (three volumes) and 1670–1702.

147   DULSC MSP 25 Mickleton and Spearman Manuscripts 1635–1691, f. 135r, Foundation indenture of the Hospital of Sir John Duck, Baronet, at Lumley.

148   A. Green, E. Parkinson and M. Spufford, eds, *Durham Hearth Tax Assessment Lady Day 1666* (London, 2006), pp. 251, 265.

149   Green, Parkinson and Spufford, *Durham Hearth Tax*, pp. 77–8, 168, 251–2, 263–51.

150   CCA CC/S/7/1 St Stephen's Hospital Memorandum and Disbursements Book 1593–1828, and U3/39/28/13 Hackington Churchwardens' Accounts 1588–1601 (typed transcripts).

151   For example, Agnes Berdwell and Katherine Debenham: M. K. McIntosh, *Poor Relief and Community in Hadleigh, Suffolk 1547–1600* (Hatfield, 2013), pp. 175–6.

152   CKS P142/12/1 East Farleigh Overseers' Accounts 1715–1751.

153   CKS Ch147/A2 Thomas Dunk's Charity Register, and P178/11/1 Hawkhurst Overseers' Poor Book 1711–1726.

from Thomas Iddenden's Charity, administered by the Hawkhurst church-wardens.[154] John Evans, who was admitted to the almshouse in 1727, dying the following year, was never in receipt of poor relief, but was probably on the margins of poverty. He was assessed to pay poor rates, but by 1723 this was at the insignificant amount of 13½d for the half year. He was a shoemaker, regularly paid by the overseers to repair poor people's shoes, and in 1720 he had a poor man, John Reynolds, boarded out with him for a year.[155]

These examples demonstrate the diversity in the economic circumstances of almshouse residents before admission. It may well be that in this diversity they were not so very different from other recipients of relief and charity in early modern communities. The parish of St Mary's, Gateshead, for instance, paid 5s 6d in 1684 towards the burial of Mr Whitehead, a schoolmaster.[156] It seems that people from very different economic backgrounds could end up in old age needing the support of the parish. This can be seen, for example, in the inventories of goods assigned to the parish by parish paupers. The overseers of Leigh in Kent supported John Hayselden with lodging and food at the end of his life in 1661/2, and paid for his funeral. In return they received a meagre 14s 6d for his 'apparell'. After the death of Widow Child in 1680, the overseers of Ipsley in Warwickshire received just £1 6s 2d for her goods.[157] Yet Dorothy Harding's goods, sold in 1687 to the overseers of West Malling in Kent, were worth £6 and included chairs, beds, dishes, chests of drawers, curtains, rugs, feather beds and bolsters, and she was able to sign her own name.[158] Joseph Gillham of Chatham owned two houses, but still needed parish support in 1724. The vestry minutes of Chatham St Mary's record that the parish officers were ordered to take into custody his two houses and put the rent towards the maintenance of Gillham and his wife.[159] The town of Maidstone received £22 1s 8d, a considerable sum, from the goods of a Widow Ward who had died leaving three children to the care of the town of Maidstone in 1673, in recompense for the money spent on nursing and burying her, and the care of the children.[160] In a poignant example of how families' fortunes could change and parish support be required, widower John Bodkins was apparently an independent smallholder, contributing to the poor rate in New Romney, when he died in 1669 leaving two young children to the care of the parish. The overseers took his goods, valued at £14 9s 10d, rented out his house, and sold his two horses and his apple crop. In return they

---

154   CKS Ch153/F1 Thomas Iddenden's Charity Accounts.
155   CKS P178/11/1 Hawkhurst Overseers' Poor Book 1711–1726.
156   DRO EP/Ga.SM 5/1 Gateshead St Mary's Resolutions of Vestry Meetings 1681–1807.
157   WRO CR 1741/28 Ipsley Overseers' Accounts 1661–1730.
158   CKS P223/5/1 Leigh Churchwardens' and Overseers' Accounts 1631–1683, and P243/18/164 West Malling Overseers' records, Sale of household goods of Dorothy Harding to the Overseers 1687.
159   MALSC P85/8/2 Chatham St Mary's Vestry Minutes 1715–1739.
160   CKS P241/11/1 Maidstone Poor Book 1668–1677.

maintained the children. Mary was apprenticed in 1674; her little brother John died in 1678, by now a 'poore boy', orphaned and disinherited.[161]

This sort of personal catastrophe was all too common in early modern England. Contemporaries were acutely aware of the precariousness of life; how people could work to secure economic independence for themselves and their families, and yet be so rapidly overtaken by misfortune. As a result, many almshouse founders emphasised that the beneficiaries of their endowments should be people who had previously worked to support themselves, and been reduced to want through no fault of their own. This has sometimes been interpreted as a desire to benefit only the 'deserving' poor, and exclude the profligate and idle. While this was no doubt an important factor, the emphasis might actually have been more inclusive than this would suggest, recognising and sympathising with the predicaments of a wide range of people who might require help.

However, there is a definite suggestion of more discrimination in the allocation of almshouse places as the period progressed. By Dunk's will, his almshouses at Hawkhurst had been intended as 'plain and useful habitations' for 'decayed housekeepers' of the parish, and the first almspeople would appear to fit that description.[162] They seem to have been a relatively diverse group, as were the occupants of the Leamington Hastings almshouse (see chapter 6). There is some suggestion, however, that, as with admissions to the Leamington Hastings almshouse in the early eighteenth century, access to Dunk's almshouse soon became more restricted. William Turley, church-warden in 1722 and one of the guardians of the new workhouse built in 1726, was admitted to the almshouse in 1734.[163] Meanwhile, in contrast, the poor man John Reynolds (mentioned above), had to petition the justices for relief in 1723, and in 1726 he was forced to enter the newly built workhouse.[164] There was no possibility of a place in the almshouse for him. By the early eighteenth century, almshouse founders also appear to have become more discriminatory, sometimes explicitly excluding those on poor relief. Thomas Harris, for example, who founded his almshouse in Canterbury by will in 1719, specified that each applicant had to produce a certificate from the parish officers vouching that they had settlement in the parish, were aged over fifty, and were not receiving parish poor relief.[165] The numbers of people who were genuinely poor in early modern England were much greater than the minority who received parish poor relief, so this stipulation does not imply that Harris's almspeople would necessarily have come from among the better

---

161   CKS P309/11/1 New Romney Overseers' Accounts 1653–1710.
162   CKS Ch147/A10 Copy of will of Sir Thomas Dunk.
163   CKS P178/5/9 Hawkhurst Churchwardens' Accounts 1717–1759.
164   CKS P178/13/315 Hawkhurst warrant 1723, and P178/13/316 Hawkhurst order 1726.
165   HCPP, no. 30 (1837), p. 267.

off. It does hint, however, at the introduction of a new element of discrimination, whereby the occupants of an almshouse came to be seen as a different
category of poor from the recipients of parish poor relief, despite the many
similarities there might once have been between them.

Rules of behaviour

Some almshouses had rules of behaviour for their almspeople, but the
majority did not. The interest in this aspect of almshouse life, while fitting
the social control paradigm once in favour among historians, is probably
disproportionate. Angela Blaydon, for instance, has found that only a fifth
of the almshouses she investigated in Surrey appeared to have had any rules
and regulations.[166] In County Durham, only three early modern almshouses
have extant rules.[167] In Warwickshire the number is similarly small, only six,
although there may have been more which have not survived.[168] While some
of the archaic rules governing occupants' behaviour may dismay modern
readers, such rules are often formulaic, seemingly copied from earlier
examples of almshouse statutes.[169] In many respects, moreover, they were
no different from contemporary expectations of the conduct of the poor in
general, particularly those in positions of economic dependence. For instance,
a disabled soldier in 1660 had the pension of 40s per year awarded him by the
Durham quarter sessions, made conditional on his good behaviour: he was
to receive it 'soe long as [he] doth well demeane himselfe'.[170] The majority of
almshouses did not have explicit rules laid down; those that did were mostly
the better-endowed institutions. Examples include the lengthy ordinances for
the Lord Leycester Hospital, drawn up by Robert Dudley in 1585; the series
of regulations devised by William Lambarde for the almshouses with which

---

166   A. Blaydon, 'Almshouse Rules and Regulations for Trustees and Almspeople with Particular
Reference to Surrey', *The British Almshouse: New Perspectives on Philanthropy ca. 1400–1914*,
ed. N. Goose, H. Caffrey and A. Langley (Milton Keynes, 2016), pp. 211–31 (p. 211).
167   The three were Sherburn Hospital, which had several sets of rules made at different times
by Bishops of Durham; the rules laid down by John Cosin, Bishop of Durham for his Palace
Green almshouses; and those set out by William Hutchinson for his almshouse at Romaldkirk.
168   Three of those with extant rules are the foundations of Robert Dudley, Earl of Leicester;
Lady Katherine Leveson; and Sir Thomas Holte of Aston Hall. The others are Ford's Hospital
and West Orchard almshouses, administered by Coventry corporation, and James Gramer's
almshouses at Mancetter. Eyffler's almshouse may once have had rules, as there is a reference
to orders 'in the book of the said house', but this has not survived: WRO CR 1618/WA12/33/7
Bond 5 Aug 6 James.
169   See, for instance, the discussion of the Ewelme statutes and comparison with other
fifteenth-century examples in Richmond, 'Victorian values'.
170   DRO Q/S/OB5 Quarter Sessions Order Book 1660–1668, p. 72.

he was involved in Kent; and the simple instructions for the Palace Green almshouses in Durham set out by John Cosin, Bishop of Durham, in 1668.[171] As Goodall helpfully emphasises in discussing the complex set of fifteenth-century rules for God's House at Ewelme, these rules should not be read as a description of daily life. Rather, they were the contract between the patron and the almshouse community, between the donor and the recipients of his charity, setting out what was expected from the almsmen in return for their place.[172] In the case of the almsmen of Ewelme, for instance, their main duty was to pray for the souls of the living and the dead, for the founders and their ancestors, the king and all Christian people.

Most early modern almshouses with formal rules also specified prayers and attendance at church. Robert Dudley, for instance, ordered that his almsmen were to attend prayers daily in the former guild chapel over the West Gate in Warwick which had been appropriated to the almshouse. On Sundays and holy days they were to process in their gowns to the parish church of St Mary's, where their allocated seats towards the front of the central nave were a mark of their high status.[173] William Hutchinson, in his will of 1693, appointed the parish clerk as custos of his almshouse in Romaldkirk, and required him to read prayers on Wednesdays and Fridays, and see that the almspeople attended the parish church on Sundays.[174] Bishop Cosin's almspeople had to attend Durham Cathedral twice daily, for the morning and evening services. They were also expected to pray privately on their knees in their chambers on rising and going to bed, Cosin specifying the Lord's Prayer and the second and third collects from the services of Morning and Evening Prayer for their private devotions. These prayers were to be displayed on the wall in their rooms for their daily use. The rest of their time they were expected to spend in their rooms, not to indulge in carding or dicing, and to allow no tippling or gaming in their chambers.[175] This exceedingly dull life must have been the nearest equivalent to monasticism in seventeenth-century Protestant England; yet a resolutely Anglican bishop considered it the ideal model for his poor almspeople.[176] We have no means of knowing

171   Tibbits, 'Hospital'; Warnicke, *William Lambarde*, pp. 45–7; DULSC MS/91 Mickleton and Spearman Manuscripts late 16th to early 18th centuries, f. 170.

172   J. Goodall, *God's House at Ewelme: Life, Devotion and Architecture in a Fifteenth-Century Almshouse* (Aldershot, 2001), p. 213.

173   WRO CR 1600/31 'The House Book', 10 April 1664, records the agreement with the churchwardens of St Mary's: the Lord Leycester Brethren 'were settled in two seates in ye middle Isle being the 4th and 5th formes'.

174   Copy of William Hutchinson's will, in DRO EP/Rom 12/2 Regulations for the management of the Bowes and Romaldkirk charities 1891.

175   DULSC MS/91 Mickleton and Spearman Manuscripts late 16th to early 18th centuries, f. 170.

176   While in exile on the Continent during the Commonwealth, Cosin had resisted attempts to convert him to Catholicism, despite his son John and many other English exiles becoming

how far Bishop Cosin's rule was obeyed, but if the conduct of other cathedral appointees at Durham was typical, it probably remained an unattained ideal. For instance, the cathedral organist Richard Hutchinson was admonished in 1628 for breaking the head of one of the singing men with a candlestick in an alehouse, 'wounding him verie dangerously'.[177] The cathedral bedesmen, who were poor men appointed by the Crown charged with keeping the cathedral clean and assisting at services, seem to have been very lax in undertaking their duties. Many of them appear to have been absent from Durham, possibly having sold their pensions to others, and with one even continuing to claim his allowance from prison in Rochester.[178]

The evidence from other almshouses suggests that not all almspeople embraced a life of prayer enthusiastically. Sir John Boys' Jesus Hospital in Canterbury had its own chapel where the almspeople were supposed to assemble daily for prayers, but attendance appears to have been somewhat reluctant. Boys issued revised ordinances in 1599, expressing his chagrin that, despite their living 'at the chapel door', the Brothers and Sisters often did not arrive until the prayers were almost over. Henceforth, he ordered that if they were late, they were to be fined as if they had been absent.[179] The requirements at Hawkins' Hospital were less onerous: there was no chapel, and the almspeople only had to attend church on Sundays and holy days. But the almsmen were expected to learn by heart a set of prayers, and be tested on them by the minister of the parish once a quarter.[180] Anyone who could not manage to say them after three months was to be expelled, unless they did not have the use of their tongue, or extreme old age (eighty or more) made anyone 'of soe bad memory that he may not carry the same prayers in mynd', which suggests that Hawkins (or Lambarde) was realistic about the likely capabilities of aged and illiterate seamen.[181] At Hawkins' Hospital a Bible in English 'of the allowed translation' and a Book of Common Prayer were also to be in a 'convenient place' for the use of the almsfolk. The governors went

---

Catholics: A. Milton, 'Cosin, John (1595–1672)', *ODNB* (Oxford, 2004), http://www.oxforddnb.com/view/article/6372 (accessed 2 December 2013).

177   DCL Add MS 375/1 Transcription (1898) of Chapter Act Book vol. 1, 1578–1726.

178   DULSC DCD/L/BB/51 Treasurer's Book no. 51, 1710/11–1728/9, f. 163v. The 1595 rules at Sherburn Hospital specifically forbade the selling of pensions, suggesting it was a known practice (although, interestingly, this prohibition was not included in the new rules of 1735): Allan, *Collectanea Dunelmensis*, p. 230.

179   Copy of revised ordinances in the back of CCA U204/R2 Jesus Hospital Register Book 1727–1844.

180   Possibly the same prayers written by William Lambarde for his own Queen Elizabeth College, and approved by the Bishop of Rochester: Warnicke, *William Lambarde*, p. 46.

181   MALSC CH108/21 Minute Book 1617–1691. This requirement is similar to that of the fifteenth-century St John's Hospital in Heytesbury, Wiltshire, where those who could not read had to learn the prayers by heart and be tested on them quarterly: Richmond, 'Victorian values', p. 231.

further at their meeting on 6 April 1648: 'Taking into consideracon the great want of the Almesffolkes as to instrucon in the ways of God', they asked the minister of Chatham to visit weekly.[182] In 1674 they suspended Widow Mann from her place for refusing to go to divine service. She, however, petitioned the governors, arguing that the rules only imposed fines rather than suspension for this offence, which fines were supposed to be distributed among the other almsfolk. She asked for the suspension to be withdrawn, and in her petition 'humble desires to submit to such forfeiture as often as she breaks ye sd Institution'.[183] In other words, she had no intention of conforming, but seems to have been prepared to pay the fines as a tax on her nonconformity.

The purpose of all this prayer was not ostensibly, as in pre-Reformation Ewelme, to benefit the founder's soul, although some early modern founders of almshouses seem to have hoped to benefit from the prayers of their beneficiaries. Thomas Oken, who died in 1573 and whose memorial in St Mary's Warwick appears to have originally asked for prayers for his soul, requested his almspeople to pray daily for the queen, the good estate of the town of Warwick, and to praise God for his soul and that of his wife Joan.[184] Lady Katherine Leveson ensured that she was remembered daily as 'our renowned Benefactress' by writing the prayer for her almswomen herself before her death in 1674.[185] The emphasis on prayer was a means of promoting godliness, as well as gratitude, in the hearts of the almspeople, which in itself would mark them out as fit recipients of charity. Promoting godliness in old age, moreover, for those approaching death and the last judgement, may have been seen as especially important, as vital as instilling godliness in young people in preparation for their adult lives. Thomas Delaval, the Commonwealth magistrate, on rediscovering Bernard Gilpin's intention that there should be three poor men attached to the Kepier Free Grammar School and Almshouse in County Durham, not only appointed the poor men in 1658 but devised a form of agreement for their appointment. Each 'poor almsbody' was to attend divine service twice on Sundays, and 'spend the short remaining part of his dayes religiously, peaceably, and unblameably'.[186] This is a similar aspiration to that expressed in the Ewelme statutes that the rules were devised 'to the increase of virtue in the inhabitants'.[187] This suggests an ideal model for a pious old age.

Many founders specified in their rules that almspeople were to live peaceably and cleanly, and to refrain from swearing, drinking, and fornication.

182 MALSC, CH108/21 Minute Book 1617–1691, p. 169.
183 MALSC, CH108/21 Minute Book 1617–1691, p. 228, and CH108/36 Petition by Susanna Mann [undated, late seventeenth century].
184 WRO CR 2758/1 Oken's Charity Accounts 1574–1596.
185 WRO DRB36/5 Temple Balsall Register of Admissions 1678–1890, vol. 1.
186 DRO EP/Ho 613 Thomas Delaval's Notebook 1657–1663.
187 Statute LXXXI, Goodall, *God's House*, p. 251.

For instance, the ordinances drawn up for the Lord Leycester Hospital in 1585 forbade physical violence, specified expulsion for the offences of adultery and fornication, and required each brother to 'keep his Chamber sweete without wilfull anoyenge any of his Bretheren in any fylthie or unseemelye maner'. They also included such rules as not keeping 'Dogge or Hawke', using no 'unlawfull Game', and not 'unlawfullie breakinge anye hedge' nor 'cuttinge or carryenge awaye any Wood'.[188] In contrast, Dudley's granddaughter, Lady Katherine Leveson, left fairly simple instructions for the behaviour of her almswomen at Temple Balsall. They were to be widows or unmarried, 'of good lives and conversations'; they were at all times to wear the provided gowns of grey cloth with the letters 'KL' in blue; and to have the benefit of their place and annual stipend for their respective lives, unless they were removed by the trustees 'for their miscarriage (and demeanour)'.[189] Gratitude and deference to their benefactors were expected of almspeople, for instance by accepting the distinctive livery. Sometimes this was made even more explicit; for instance the poor almsmen at Hawkins' Hospital had to present themselves at the gate of the almshouse, humbly and with 'some words of prayer for their health and prosperitie' if any of the four most important trustees should pass by.[190] At New Cobham College, all the able poor were expected to present themselves at Cobham Hall on the second Sunday of every quarter, if Lord and Lady Cobham were at home, 'in thankfull manner for theire mainetance'.[191]

Penalties for misdemeanours were usually fines, or the stopping of the almsperson's allowance, with expulsion for repeat offenders. It is not easy to find evidence of fines being levied for breach of the rules, however, and expulsions were rare. John Black of Jesus Hospital, Canterbury, was fined 'according to the statute' in 1620 and 1621 'for his perditions', but what these were is not specified. The fines appear to have had the desired effect, however, as he received his full allowance in 1622.[192] In another rare example, John Vaughn of Christ's Hospital, Abingdon, 'was restored to his full wages' in 1608 after being fined three weeks' pay for 'misbehaving himself' towards the governors and fellow residents. Earlier in the year he had been admonished, but not fined, for being 'a man very turbulent, a brawler and a fighter'.[193] Only three men appear to have been expelled from the Lord Leycester Hospital during the whole of the seventeenth century, and three were in the

---

188   WRO CR 1600/2 Founder's Statutes: Ordinances of the Hospital of Robert Earl of Leicester 26 November 1585, nos 13, 20, 21, 23, 27, 29.
189   WRO CR 1540/6 Transcript of the Will of Lady Katherine Leveson (1671).
190   MALSC CH108/21 Minute Book 1617–1691.
191   Abstract of rules relating to Cobham College, in MALSC P336/5/1 Shorne Churchwardens' accounts 1630–1681.
192   CCA U204/F1/1 Jesus Hospital Ledger 1610–1637.
193   J. Carter and J. Smith, *Give and Take: Scenes from the History of Christ's Hospital, Abingdon, 1553–1900* (Abingdon, 1981), p. 53.

1650s, possibly indicating a tightening of the rules at that time. Two were for prolonged absences of several years from the hospital, suggesting these might have been almsmen who had been inappropriately admitted, or who had other resources. The third was 'deprived for drunkenness, misdemeanours and marrying without the consent of the Master'.[194] How hard it was to deprive an almsperson of their place is shown by two examples from Bond's Hospital, Coventry. Henry Leech was expelled in 1611 after many complaints of 'his misdemeanour against his fellows', and the corporation ordered that 'an other of better manners' should be admitted in his place.[195] But he was mentioned again in 1615, when his allowance was stopped and he was 'putt forth' from the place for 'many misdemeanours' which had been documented over a period of time, and 'conclude him a man unfitt for that place'.[196] John Eden was expelled in 1666 for his 'debauchedness, fighting, quarrelling', but was allowed to stay until a place at the neighbouring Ford's Hospital became vacant. He was still at Bond's the following year, when he was again expelled for 'disquietness and ill carriage'. Yet the Corporation minutes record his death in the almshouse in 1678.[197]

It is possible that these expulsions were only temporary, and Henry Leech and John Eden had been readmitted after short absences. John Griffin was suspended from his place in Hawkins' Hospital, Chatham, in April 1622 for behaving obstinately and disobediently towards the deputy governor, 'unquietlie' among his fellows, and even being 'very peremptorily behaved' towards the governors. A week later the Deputy Governor reported that he 'dothe humblie intreate forgivenes for all his former abuses both in the howse and towards those unto whome he oweth both obeidnce reverence & duty'. He promised to give no future cause for complaint 'but will bee a true convert', and the governors agreed to allow him back in.[198] They were particularly concerned for the 'miserable condicon' of his poor wife, to whom several additional payments had been made for surgery and salve for her leg.[199] However, in August that year he was expelled again, with another almsman Robert Wilson, for having 'clamorously' petitioned the Archbishop of Canterbury, on behalf of all the almsfolk, about the government of the hospital. Despite the governors regarding Wilson as the ringleader and their description of him as being 'of a factious and contentious disposition', he was readmitted 'on his humble petition' five days later.[200] Although the Griffins

194   WRO CR 1741/57 Philip Styles' notebook, p. 46.
195   CHC BA/H/3/17/1 Coventry Council Minute Book 1557–1640, p. 188.
196   CHC BA/H/3/17/1 Coventry Council Minute Book 1557–1640, p. 205v.
197   Cleary and Orton, *So Long as the World*, pp. 49–50.
198   MALSC CH108/21 Minute Book 1617–1691.
199   MALSC CH108/135 Deputy Governor's Accounts 1621–1622.
200   MALSC CH108/21 Minute Book 1617–1691.

were not reinstated, the governors appear to have retained some sympathy for them, or for Griffin's poor wife at least, and in May 1623 paid 10s to John Lasey's wife for the care she had given them, including 'in the tyme of their sickness after their expulsion'.[201]

It seems that despite the strictures in the rules, these were not necessarily applied rigorously, and in practice it appears that it was extremely difficult to deprive an almsperson of their place once it had been awarded. This might have been because there was nowhere else practically for the person to go; but there also seems to have been a widely accepted view that the award of an almshouse place was for life, similar to an annuity. The existence of official rules, constituting a contract as in Goodall's suggestion, was thus a necessary counterbalance to the almsperson's rights, giving trustees and governors the power to act if they needed to do so. Rules were consequently more in evidence in the wealthier establishments where the award of an almshouse place constituted a particularly valuable resource. This had the paradoxical effect of making the inhabitants of higher-status almshouses more likely to be subjected to rules governing their behaviour, and to be more rigorously controlled in their day-to-day activities.

This is shown most clearly perhaps at Morden College, Blackheath, founded by Sir John Morden in 1695 for 'decayed Turkey merchants', that is, those who had been engaged in overseas trade with the east. According to Morden's wishes his college was run by trustees from the Levant (or Turkey) Company (and after its demise by the East India Company). The building, a grand quadrangle, is believed to have been designed by Wren; the forty-four almsmen, who were to be widowed or unmarried, were provided with a sitting room and bedroom each, a generous allowance, and resident servants to look after their needs. Morden built the college in his lifetime, and his charity was designed to enable the almsmen to live as gentlemen, despite their reduced circumstances: 'The provision made for College members was a badge of their status as once men of worth and now gentlemen of a sort again.'[202] Yet the rules could not have been more irksome to men who had previously run their own businesses and occupied a respected position in society. They had to attend service in the chapel twice a day in their gowns, receive holy communion four times a year, and attend evening lectures or 'expositions'. A resident chaplain and treasurer were responsible for their day-to-day super-vision, under the direction of the trustees. The almsmen were to 'employ themselves in acts of piety and devotion', 'demean themselves civilly', and not 'intermeddle with the business of the college'.[203] Swearing, drunkenness and quarrelling could lead to immediate expulsion, although drunkenness seems

201   MALSC CH108/137 Deputy Governor's Accounts 1623–1624.
202   Joyce, *Patronage and Poverty*, p. 49.
203   Joyce, *Patronage and Poverty*, pp. 46, 50.

to have been quite common. The gates were locked at nine in the summer and eight in the winter, and the men could not be absent from the college for more than twenty-four hours. Hardly surprisingly, there seems to have been a 'powerful current of disorder, disobedience and resistance' running through the college's history.[204]

Other high-status almshouses provide similar evidence of disorderly behaviour, for instance the many examples from the London Charterhouse, which suggests that the attempt to impose discipline upon residents had only limited success.[205] Joseph Stanley, for example, an occupant of the Geffrye almshouses in Shoreditch run by the Ironmongers' Company (founded in 1714), had to appear before the Company Court in 1721 charged with being drunk and helping another almsman, also drunk, over the almshouse wall at an unreasonable time of night, and then leaving his companion on the ground all night so that he died soon after.[206] One suspects that climbing over the almshouse wall after the gates had been locked at night was probably a regular occurrence, and Stanley was only apprehended in this instance because of the fatal accident. At the Geffrye almshouses there was a resident chaplain responsible for the good behaviour of the almsmen, but in 1729 even he was dismissed for rudeness and misbehaviour, including throwing a cushion over a desk and refusing to read prayers.[207] Stephen Porter ascribes this sort of disorder at early modern almshouses to the common standards of behaviour of the times, which were in contrast with the unrealistic expectations of founders and governors attempting to establish model communities. He also blames the poor selection of residents and staff, as a result of patronage and corruption.[208] But it could just as easily have been a response to the provocations of the restricted communal existence the men were forced to lead.

Interesting as these anecdotes are, however, they should not be given undue emphasis. The great majority of almshouse residents left no mark in official records of any kind, and may well have displayed exemplary behaviour while being duly grateful for their good fortune. It is possible that a lifetime of deference and subjection to authority through economic dependence better prepared the genuinely poor than those of higher status for the intrusive supervision of masters, chaplains, trustees and members of the corporation, which residence in an almshouse could entail. Moreover, most almshouses did not have the mechanisms for on-site supervision and surveillance employed by wealthier establishments. Many of the surviving pre-Reformation almshouses

204 Joyce, *Patronage and Poverty*, p. 54.
205 S. Porter, 'Order and Disorder in the Early Modern Almshouse: The Charterhouse Example', *The London Journal* 23/1 (1998), 1–14.
206 Burton, *Geffrye Almshouses*, p. 37.
207 Burton, *Geffrye Almshouses*, p. 55.
208 Porter, 'Order and Disorder', p. 13.

and hospitals had a master, such as the Durham hospitals of Greatham and Sherburn, who was usually an ordained minister, responsible for the governing of the almshouse and supervision of the almspeople. This traditional form was adopted by a small number of wealthier establishments in the late sixteenth and early seventeenth centuries, such as Robert Dudley's Lord Leycester Hospital at Warwick (1571), and the Earl of Northampton's Trinity Hospital, Greenwich (1613). The master was not necessarily resident, however, and many posts were treated by their incumbents as valuable sinecures, often combined with other valuable livings. The Bishops of Durham, for instance, appear to have regarded the masterships of Greatham and Sherburn as useful posts with which to reward their protégés.[209]

In poorer establishments which could not afford to fund the salary of a master, such as the King James' Hospital at Gateshead, the master was also the rector of the parish. Elsewhere local officials took on this role. At Dover the town mayor acted as the master of the Seamen's Hospital, and Sir Roger Manwood appointed the parish clerk of Hackington to act as warden of his almshouses. In those almshouses which were joint foundations with a school, as at Lawrence Sheriff's foundation at Rugby and Lady Leveson's Hospital at Temple Balsall, it was usual for the master of the school to combine the supervision of the two establishments. At Hawkins' Hospital one of the trustees, usually a naval captain living nearby, was appointed deputy governor to manage the hospital's day-to-day affairs. Elsewhere there might be a prefectorial system in place, by which one or two of the almspeople would be appointed or elected to supervise the rest. For instance, at Lambarde's Queen Elizabeth Hospital and at Trinity Hospital, Aylesford, one of the almspeople was appointed to act as warden. At the Lord Leycester Hospital, while the master had responsibility for such things as letting leases of the hospital's lands, two of the senior almsmen were appointed as stewards, and they conducted the day-to-day business of the hospital, paying bills and keeping accounts.[210] These 'senior' almspeople might also have had the task of reporting on the conduct of their fellows to the governors at their official meetings, as did paid employees such as the chaplains at Morden and Bromley Colleges. At New Cobham College, an 'honest man' was to have 5s per year in return for informing the paymaster of any disorders among the poor in

209 Anthony Bellasis, for example, was master of both Sherburn Hospital and St Edmund's Hospital in Gateshead in the sixteenth century: Allan, *Collectanea Dunelmensis*, p. 88. Bishop John Cosin himself had been master of Greatham Hospital for a short time in 1624 while chaplain to Bishop Neile, succeeding the bishop's brother in the post: G. Ornsby, ed., *The Correspondence of John Cosin D.D. Lord Bishop of Durham: Together with Other Papers Illustrative of his Life and Times, Part I*, Surtees Society 52 (Durham, 1869), p. 21.
210 See, for instance, WRO CR 1600/31 'The House Book', containing the elections and accounts of the stewards.

the College.[211] This responsibility for peer surveillance, unpleasant though it sounds, was no different from that undertaken by, for instance, church-wardens in the parishes, and should be seen in that context. While one might have expected that the rewards for snooping and reporting to officialdom would have led to bad feeling among the occupants of an almshouse, the scant evidence of fines and expulsions suggests that, as in the parishes, turning a blind eye in the interests of solidarity and good neighbourliness commonly led to the response 'all well' to the enquiries of officialdom.[212]

For the majority of almshouses with no on-site or official supervision, this responsibility would have fallen on the minister and parish officials in the normal exercise of their authority and moral oversight. This can be seen, for instance, in the example of Rev. William Binckes' intervention in Jane Man's expulsion from the Leamington Hastings almshouse (see chapter 6). This does not imply some quasi-Foucauldian role for almshouses in disciplining the poor; they were not institutions of incarceration and punishment.[213] Officialdom intruding in the lives of the poor, regulating how they lived their lives, was commonplace in early modern England. Even as the influence of the relatively toothless church courts waned, the increase in legislation on moral behaviour and the ubiquitous houses of correction gave the secular courts plenty of work. Jane Man was sent from the almshouse to the Warwick house of correction for bastardy, but the courts were also ready to intervene without any offence being committed. The Warwick quarter sessions, for instance, ordered Elizabeth Jervyes to be removed from her house and to go into service in 1654, she 'being a young woman and living in a late built house by the highway at Allesley remote from any other house ... and in danger to be made a place for receipt of ill-disposed people'. James Wilson's house near Rugby was ordered to be pulled down in 1664, because it 'stands in a place very inconvenient being far from neighbours and fit to entertain rogues and vagabonds'.[214] Apart from the few surviving medieval leper houses such as St Nicholas Harbledown, Kent and Sherburn Hospital, Durham, the great majority of early modern almshouses were located in the centre of their towns and villages, on the high street or next to the church. Here the surveillance of neighbours and parish officials would have been routine and expected, but probably no more intrusive than that to which other poor people in the community were subjected.

211   Abstract of rules relating to Cobham College, in MALSC P336/5/1 Shorne Churchwardens' accounts 1630–1681. Similarly, at Ewelme one of the poor men was appointed to report on the behaviour of the others: Richmond, 'Victorian Values', p. 226.
212   K. Wrightson, *English Society 1580–1680*, 2nd edn (London, 2003), p. 174.
213   Unlike houses of correction, or the sixteenth- and seventeenth-century beggars' hospitals on the Continent: R. Jütte, *Poverty and Deviance in Early Modern Europe* (Cambridge, 1994), pp. 169–77.
214   WQS, vol. 3, Epiphany 1654, p. 207; WQS, vol. 4, Epiphany 1664, p. 262.

It could be argued, moreover, that the circumstances of many almspeople, those in the great majority of almshouses without on-site supervision, gave them a degree of autonomy greater than that afforded to most other poor people. Tomkins suggests that the level of independence created by the permanent appointment to an almshouse place was always regarded as inherently problematic, hence the attempts at regulation.[215] This can be shown in the bitter struggle between the keelmen and the hostmen (merchants) in Newcastle upon Tyne for control of the Keelmen's Hospital and its charitable funds, the hospital having been founded in 1702 by the contributions of the keelmen themselves. The dispute was in large part driven by the hostmen's fears that the keelmen having control of their own welfare fund would give them sufficient independence to determine their own terms of employment, and resist the demands of their employers.[216] The grant of a permanent place in an almshouse could be regarded in the same way, as freeing the occupants from the control of an employer or master in a dangerous fashion.

Conclusion

Perhaps unsurprisingly, then, the picture that emerges of early modern almshouses is often that of a disorderly and motley array of residents. They were not always old, although this seems to have become more usual by the end of the period. Women residents were often viewed as problematic, as were children, although their presence might be tolerated in practice, particularly if they performed domestic or caring tasks for other residents. The economic circumstances of occupants could differ markedly, with some suggestion of greater discrimination in who was admitted in the later part of the period. The majority of almspeople seem not to have been subject to any greater degree of surveillance than ordinary poor people in the community. It was in the wealthier establishments where formal rules were more likely to be in evidence, but even here there appear to have been only occasional and largely ineffectual attempts by trustees and governors to impose some discipline. Nevertheless the rules, although formulaic and frequently ineffective, do reveal the anxieties of those in charge of almshouses about the dangerous freedoms potentially enjoyed by their occupants. For instance, rules about residence suggest that with an independent income many almshouse residents would have chosen to be absent if they could. Rules requiring almspeople

215   A. Tomkins, 'Retirement from the Noise and Hurry of the World? The Experience of Almshouse Life', *Accommodating Poverty: The Housing and Living Arrangements of the English Poor, c.1600–1850*, ed. J. McEwan and P. Sharpe (Basingstoke, 2011), pp. 263–83 (p. 272).
216   J. M. Fewster, *The Keelmen of Tyneside: Labour Organisation and Conflict in the North-East Coal Industry, 1600–1830* (Woodbridge, 2011), p. 25.

to keep their rooms and communal areas clean suggest that, freed from the structure of a normal household, these were tasks that would not have been performed. There were breaches of the rules by almspeople and patrons alike, with masters abusing their position to benefit from almshouse property, and trustees abusing their patronage to admit people with no right to a place. But although the reality may frequently have fallen short, the rules of eligibility and behaviour represented an ideal, one which found ready acceptance in early modern contemporary opinion.

5

The Material Benefits of an Almshouse Place

> For every ancient pensioner maintained comfortably there was at least one
> almsperson whose entitlements and receipts were thin indeed.[1]

The previous two chapters concluded that there was considerable range and
variety among the people founding and living in early modern almshouses, and
that the motivations of founders and the experience of occupants were equally
diverse. Similarly, the benefits the occupants received in these almshouses were
surprisingly variable, and it would be hard to say that there was such a thing
as a typical almshouse. Some provided residents with comfortable accommodation, a regular monetary allowance or stipend, clothing, fuel and practical
support. Other foundations, with modest or non-existent endowments,
provided little more than rent-free accommodation. The result was a range of
institutions providing greatly varying material benefits. Whether benefactors
built their almshouses in their lifetime or specified to executors the accommodation and stipends that they intended their almspeople to receive, or
whether the provision was developed and adapted by subsequent trustees and
interested parties, early modern almshouses reflected contemporary views of
what was appropriate for the recipients of charity. This chapter will examine
what was provided for the occupants of almshouses in early modern England,
and what these benefits might have represented in terms of the social and
economic status of almspeople within the wider community. The first two
sections describe a broad array of material benefits: first, the accommodation provided, and then secondly, stipends, food, fuel and clothing. In the
third section, a more statistical approach is adopted, in order to evaluate the
standard of living these benefits enabled almspeople to achieve, and how this
compared with the living standards of other poor people at the time. Overall
the discussion demonstrates that, in many respects, there were similarities
between almshouses dwellers and those on parish poor relief, but it also
outlines some crucial differences.

---

1   A. Tomkins, 'Retirement from the Noise and Hurry of the World? The Experience of
Almshouse Life', *Accommodating Poverty: The Housing and Living Arrangements of the
English Poor, c.1600–1850*, ed. J. McEwan and P. Sharpe (Basingstoke, 2011), pp. 263–83 (p. 264).

Accommodation

The single distinguishing feature of most almshouses is a building providing accommodation for people in need. Much of what has been written in the past about early modern almshouses concentrated on the architectural design of these buildings.[2] For instance, Godfrey's *The English Almshouse* focuses on a series of 'remarkable' buildings, and charts their 'changing architectural character'; while Prescott uses architecture to trace the changes and developments in the function of almshouses from 1050 to 1640.[3] Many examples in the literature are drawn from a small group of notable foundations, usually those with buildings of particular architectural merit or interest. This leads Heath, for instance, to assert that 'almost without exception', sixteenth- and seventeenth-century foundations consisted of 'an audit room, a suite of rooms for the master or warden; an infirmary for the sick, a common hall; a suite of living rooms for the inmates; and a chapel'.[4] In fact, it is hard to find any early modern foundation precisely conforming to this description.[5] More typical were almshouses, often a simple row of cottages, with no chapel or communal facilities, where each almsperson had a room to themselves, or possibly two, with their own fireplace and front door. Most were small, with four-fifths having less than twelve residents (Appendix 2). Godfrey acknowledges that most almshouses of the early modern period were just a single row of dwellings, yet he pays most attention to the design of more complex buildings, particularly the way these developed from the medieval infirmary hall to the collegiate quadrangle.[6]

The traditional model of the medieval hospital had been the infirmary hall, where a long dormitory lined with beds opened onto a chapel at one end, so that those who were too infirm could see the mass being celebrated from their beds.[7] From the fifteenth century, along with the increase in secular foundations, there was a retreat from communal living in the design and operation of almshouses and hospitals, reflecting the changes in domestic architecture

---

2 For example S. Heath, *Old English Houses of Alms: A Pictorial Record with Architectural and Historical Notes* (London, 1910); W. H. Godfrey, *The English Almshouse, with Some Account of its Predecessor, the Medieval Hospital* (London, 1955); B. Howson, *Houses of Noble Poverty: A History of the English Almshouse* (Sunbury-on-Thames, 1993).

3 Godfrey, *English Almshouse*, p. 7; E. Prescott, *The English Medieval Hospital 1050–1640* (Melksham, 1992).

4 Heath, *Old English Houses*, p. 24.

5 The closest examples would probably be the wealthy early-seventeenth-century foundations of the London Charterhouse; Trinity Hospital, Greenwich; Abbot's Hospital, Guildford; and Sackville College, East Grinstead. Even so, none of these has all the features described by Heath.

6 Godfrey, *English Almshouse*, pp. 76, 45 (*passim*).

7 For example, the illustration in Godfrey of the infirmary hall at Beaune with beds down either side and the altar screen beyond: Godfrey, *English Almshouse*, plate 10.

of the time.[8] It became more common for almspeople to be accommodated in individual rooms or chambers, each with its own hearth. Prescott relates this development to improvements which were taking place within domestic housing of the period, when living standards for many ordinary people began to be transformed.[9] For instance, the traditional medieval hall house, open to the rafters, with its central fire and smoke filtering out through the roof, began to be partitioned into separate rooms. The open fire was replaced with fireplaces and chimneys, which allowed for the boarding over of upper floors, and the heating of individual rooms. Glazed windows became widely available, with John Evelyn remarking in 1671 that even poor people on alms now had window glass.[10]

W. G. Hoskins argued that this 'rebuilding of rural England', occurring first in the homes of the wealthy and then filtering down to the housing of ordinary people, was driven by a desire for greater privacy and material comfort.[11] From the fifteenth century similar changes can be seen in almshouse foundations, such as God's House at Ewelme in Oxfordshire (1437), where thirteen individual rooms are arranged around a courtyard; or the spectacular Hospital of St Cross at Winchester, known as the House of Noble Poverty, refounded in 1445 by Cardinal Beaufort. As the name suggests, this was a high-status almshouse for decayed gentlemen, where each almsman had not only his own room but an individual *garderobe*. Even where the traditional hall type was retained, as in Browne's Hospital in Stamford, founded around 1485, or the late-Tudor Lord Leycester Hospital in Warwick, which used the town's medieval guildhall, the almsmen had individual wooden cubicles built within the hall to give them some privacy. The disadvantage of the hall type, along with the lack of privacy, was warmth. At Stamford there was a single fireplace to heat the hall. A century later at Warwick, the Lord Leycester almsmen appear to have constructed a number of fireplaces in 'outrageous' positions in their living quarters in the unheated guildhall, with ramshackle flues 'carried out most recklessly through the walls encalcining many timbers'.[12] At St Mary's Chichester, a thirteenth-century almshouse

---

8   Prescott, *English Medieval Hospital*, pp. 4, 102–3.

9   McIntosh describes the change as also mirroring that taking place in monasteries and convents: M. K. McIntosh, *Poor Relief in England 1350–1600* (Cambridge, 2012), p. 65.

10   C. Platt, *The Great Rebuildings of Tudor and Stuart England: Revolutions in Architectural Taste* (London, 1994), p. 149. See also M. Johnson, *Housing Culture: Traditional Architecture in an English Landscape* (London, 1993).

11   W. G. Hoskins, 'The Rebuilding of Rural England, 1570–1640', *Past and Present* 4 (1953), 44–59.

12   Two fireplaces were actually based with their chimneys upon first-floor timbers: S. A. Pears, 'The Lord Leycester Hospital, Warwick', *Transactions of the Ancient Monuments Society* (new series) 13 (1965/6), 35–41 (p. 41). The flues were 'no more than drainpipes ran up the roofs, and the house had frequently been on fire, but providentially, from the age and hardness of the oak

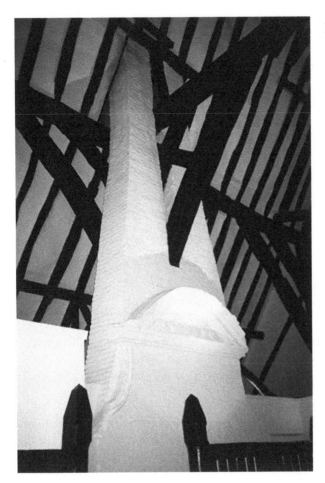

Figure 5.1. Chimney inserted inside hall at St Mary's Chichester

for women, improvements did not take place until the seventeenth century. Here there was no fireplace, but the scoring of a groove on one of the roof beams indicates there was a hanging brazier to heat the hall. In 1680 eight small brick houses, each with its own individual chimney, were built inside the medieval hall for the eight women, a startling transformation which graphically demonstrates the changing expectations of privacy and material comfort (Figure 5.1).

At both St Mary's and the Lord Leycester the individual rooms were accessed internally from within the building, and there was a similar

timbers the fire had only smouldered': extract from the old Minute Book, 1851, quoted in E. G. Tibbits, 'The Hospital of Robert, Earl of Leicester, in Warwick', *Birmingham Archaeological Society: Transactions and Proceedings* 60 (1936), 112–44 (p. 144).

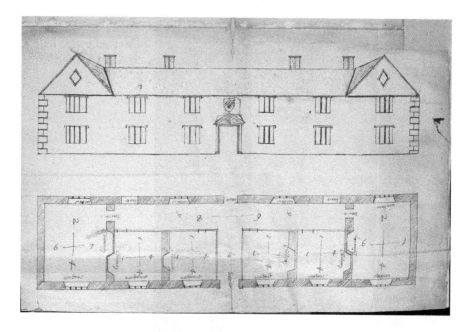

Figure 5.2. John Langstafe's plan of the Palace Green almshouses, Durham, showing internal doors and no staircases

Source: DULSC MS/91, f.2 (reproduced by permission of Durham University Library)

arrangement at the high-status College of Matrons in Salisbury (1682), and also at Bishop Cosin's Palace Green almshouses in Durham (see Figure 5.2). By the early modern period, however, it was more usual for almspeople's rooms to have their own front door providing direct external access: for example, the upstairs rooms at Eyffler's almshouse in Warwick had external staircases giving independent access to each apartment.[13] How highly this was valued is demonstrated by the way additional external doorways were often created in those existing domestic buildings that were converted to almshouses. For instance, Lawrence Sheriff left his own house in Rugby for the accommodation of four poor men in 1567, a foundation which eventually became Rugby School. Each almsman had two rooms, and the accounts show that new doorways were made in the walls so that each almsman could have his own entrance.[14] Similarly, in 1607 Humphrey Davis left his house in Leamington Hastings as an almshouse for eight poor people. The building was probably converted into three or four apartments, and once again additional external

13   WRO CR 1618/WA12/36/13 Building accounts for the almshouse on Castle Hill 1597.
14   W. H. D. Rouse, *A History of Rugby School* (London, 1898), p. 34.

doorways were cut through the walls to give each almshouse its own front door.[15] At the end of the seventeenth century, when new accommodation had to be built to replace Oken's three little almshouses destroyed in the Great Fire of Warwick, six new rooms were built onto Eyffler's almshouse, three above and three below. From the plans for the rebuilding work it can be seen that each of the six rooms had a window, a fireplace and its own door giving independent access to the outside.[16] This required two external staircases to be constructed to serve the upper rooms, as at Eyffler's almshouse next door. This was a relatively expensive arrangement, in marked contrast to the much simpler design at the Palace Green almshouses in Durham, where the upper rooms appear to have been accessed via the lower rooms (Figure 5.2).[17] Perhaps it was due to the pressure on accommodation with so much property destroyed by the fire, that each of Oken's replacement almsrooms was now to be shared by two women, providing an extra six places. It would seem from this example that, while privacy might not have been considered essential for almspeople, autonomy and independence were very highly valued.

Jordan suggested that the purpose of an almshouse was to withdraw the poor from society, but this does not seem to be substantiated by the evidence of the majority of almshouse buildings. Unlike the medieval hospitals for lepers or travellers, most early modern almshouses were situated in the centre of their communities, often close to the parish church, and the separate entrances would have enabled the almspeople to come and go freely. This was true to an extent even in grander establishments where the almspeople's rooms were grouped around a courtyard or quadrangle, occasionally with a gatehouse, in imitation of many Tudor gentry houses, as at New Cobham College or Abbot's Hospital. In these establishments the almspeople were not confined inside but still able to access the outside world, while the gatehouse provided an additional level of privacy, which itself enhanced the status of the residents within and controlled intrusion by the public.[18] Paradoxically, however, if the gates were locked at night, then the residents of these higher status almshouses were deprived of some of their independence in a way that occupants of lower-status almshouses were not.

Even modest almshouses, such as the simple cottage row without architectural pretension or grandeur, were often notable buildings, designed to be seen and to be instantly recognisable. They might be marked out in some way, as

---

15   L. F. Salzman, ed., *The Victoria History of the County of Warwick*, vol. 6: *Knightlow Hundred* (Oxford, 1951), p. 150.

16   WRO M287 'The Estemat of Sam Dunckley for the Almseshowes upon the backhills' (microfiche of original documents in the Folger Shakespeare Library, Washington DC).

17   'Draught for the schoole and Almseshouses at Durham by John Langstafe', in DULSC MS/91 Mickleton and Spearman Manuscripts late 16th to early 18th centuries, f. 2.

18   F. Heal and C. Holmes, *The Gentry in England and Wales, 1500–1700* (Basingstoke, 1994), p. 284.

were Thomas Oken's three little houses in Pebble Lane, Warwick, where the building accounts for 1574 show 2s paid to Roger Pigeon for painting the three almshouse doors 'and writing Texte letters therapon'.[19] Caffrey describes the sometimes 'inessential' architectural details that graced several of the West Yorkshire almshouses she studied, which would have had a similar distin-guishing effect as the attractive Dutch gable ends on the Longport almshouses in Canterbury (Figure 5.3).[20]

Lady Katherine Leveson's Hospital at Temple Balsall, Warwickshire, was built in 1677 to her own very detailed specification. Everything was to be 'well wrought' from quality materials, with suitable embellishment. The master's house was to tower over the almswomen's accommodation, emphasising the difference in status and reinforcing the hierarchy of the establishment, while the roof was to be capped with a 'fitting bell to call to prayers'.[21] Even in a much simpler example, the building accounts for the barn in Black Lane, Warwick, converted into Eyffler's almshouse in 1597, show that, although unadorned, the walls were of brick, with stone lintels for doors and windows, and that the roof was tiled and the windows glazed.[22] These were all relatively new features in vernacular housing of the 1590s in Warwickshire, and would have combined to create a very modern-looking, substantial building. Similarly, the row of ten cottages built as almshouses in Stoneleigh in 1576 by Dame Alice Leigh were originally timber framed, like the majority of houses in the locality at that time. Twenty years later they were faced with stone, creating a distinctive image in the centre of the village among the surrounding half-timbered buildings.[23]

Many almshouse founders used their buildings as sites of memoriali-sation and display, where the appearance of the building was designed to draw attention to the status and generosity of the founder. This could be through the character or grandeur of the building itself, as at Abbot's Hospital, Guildford (Figure 3.2); Morden College, Blackheath; and the College of Matrons, Salisbury; or through decorative features such as coats of arms and inscriptions, as at John Waldron's almshouse in Tiverton, Devon (Figure 3.1). At Robert Berkeley's Hospital in Worcester, founded in 1692, a statue of the founder appears in a niche above the door of the chapel, which itself towers over the cottages for the twelve poor men. The

19   WRO CR 2758/1 Oken's Charity Accounts 1574–1596.
20   H. Caffrey, *Almshouses in the West Riding of Yorkshire 1600–1900* (King's Lynn, 2006), pp. 29–30.
21   WRO CR 112/Ba177/1 Agreement for Building the first Hospital. The women's accommo-dation was to be single storey, eight feet high to the eaves, compared with the master's house which was nineteen feet to the eaves.
22   WRO CR 1618/WA12/36/13 Building accounts for the almshouse on Castle Hill 1597.
23   N. W. Alcock, *People at Home: Living in a Warwickshire Village, 1500–1800* (Chichester, 1993), p. 142.

Figure 5.3. John and Ann Smith's almshouses at Longport, Canterbury

doorways to each of these are also richly decorated with the Berkeley arms. Through these physical representations of their status and charity, founders were also exhibiting social and economic power. Buildings convey meaning, or as Whyte expressed it: 'buildings are more than utilitarian; they are instruments by which emotions, ideas and beliefs are articulated'.[24] Observers are left in no doubt about the virtue and status of these founders, and, by association, of the humble poor people fortunate enough to have been honoured with a place. Markus regarded it as the 'covert programme of all buildings' to 'reproduce the sponsors' position of power which gave them access to the resources to invest in the first place'.[25] Unsurprisingly, then, one of the most spectacular buildings was the Royal Naval Hospital, Greenwich, founded by William and Mary by royal charter in 1694 for aged seamen, and designed by Sir Christopher Wren. Yet here there were complaints almost immediately about the grandeur of the building being unsuitable as accommodation for poor seamen, with Dr Johnson apparently remarking after a visit in 1763 that it was 'too magnificent for a place of charity'.[26] The status of the founder did not necessarily dictate the quality of the building, however. The Holte almshouses at the gates of Aston Hall, for instance, while ornamented to mirror the architectural style of the exquisite hall itself, were very mean buildings by comparison.[27]

Spectacular architecture may have served to enhance the status of the institution and honour the memory of the founder, but was not essential to the comfort of the residents. Yet substantially built accommodation, kept in good repair, might well have provided a degree of comfort for those almspeople above that which other poor people would usually have experienced. Only a minority of early modern almshouses have survived in their original buildings, however, and even then, modern improvements mean that it is often not possible to discern the original internal arrangement of the accommodation. For instance, the wooden cubicles at the Lord Leycester Hospital were removed in extensive renovations in the 1960s which returned the medieval guildhall to its original state, and no record appears to have been made of the men's accommodation before its destruction. The wooden partitions and the windows, moreover, appeared to date from the eighteenth century, raising

---

24   W. Whyte, 'How Do Buildings Mean? Some Interpretations in the History of Architecture', *History and Theory* 45/2 (2006), 153–77 (p. 155).
25   T. A. Markus, *Buildings and Power* (London, 1993), p. 317.
26   B. Howson, *Almshouses: A Social and Architectural History* (Stroud, 2008), p. 51.
27   A note on their condition just prior to demolition in the 1930s describes them as 'very dilapidated' single-room dwellings with 'floors of blue brick paving': two typewritten pages dated 13 April 1931 and signed by C. E. Bateman (presumably a trustee of the almshouses), inserted between pp. 28 and 29 of the Warwick University Library copy of A. Davidson, *A History of the Holtes of Aston, Baronets; with a Description of the Family Mansion, Aston Hall, Warwickshire* (Birmingham, 1854).

intriguing questions about how the men were housed before that date.[28] This lack of interest in the details of the men's accommodation, in comparison with the attention paid to the medieval guild buildings, might be considered typical of the time. It has, however, been replicated more recently: a collection of essays on the Guild of the Holy Cross and its buildings at Stratford-upon-Avon devotes very few pages to the almshouses which form an integral part of the building complex, and none whatsoever to the accommodation which would have been provided.[29] In contrast, an informative doctoral thesis on Henry VII's royal almshouse at Westminster has used contemporary drawings to carefully reconstruct a floor-plan of the almsmen's living accommodation, showing that each man had two rooms and a *garderobe*, though the building itself was demolished in 1779.[30] At Hawkins' Hospital in Chatham, the current small almshouse buildings date from the eighteenth century, and the only record of the original accommodation is to be found in seventeenth-century inventories from which we can deduce that each almsman had his own set of rooms, furnished with a bed, bedding, tables, stools and chairs.[31] This provision of furniture might have been essential for men who had spent most of their lives at sea, and may have usually lived in lodgings when ashore.

It seems that furniture was also provided at some other almshouses. At Eyffler's in Warwick, the building accounts of 1597 show that the women's rooms were equipped with a table board and a bed (to be shared between two), and, in a nice touch of domesticity, were even decorated with several yards of painted cloth.[32] Sherburn and Greatham Hospitals in County Durham provided the men with beds; at Sherburn, in addition, they were given bedding and bedlinen as well. At Browne's Hospital, Stamford, an inventory taken in 1731 showed that each man was provided with a bed, a shelf, a candlestick

---

28 P. B. Chatwin, 'The Hospital of Lord Leycester, Formerly the Hall and Other Buildings of the Medieval Guilds in Warwick', *Birmingham Archaeological Society: Transactions and Proceedings* 70 (1952), 37–47 (p. 46). Chatwin suggests that some of the men might have been accommodated in the rooms formerly provided for the four guild chaplains, but there were twelve almsmen, so they either had to share accommodation (unusual for men at the time) or the guildhall was partitioned at an earlier date. The seventeenth-century stewards' accounts clearly refer to individual men's rooms and windows, for example WRO CR 1600/42/9 Hospital accounts for 1671, and CR 1600/42/10 Hospital accounts for 1672.

29 J. R. Mulryne, ed., *The Guild and Guild Buildings of Shakespeare's Stratford: Society, Religion, School and Stage* (Farnham, 2012), pp. 20, 26, 154–6.

30 C. M. Fox, 'The Royal Almshouse at Westminster c.1500–c.1600' (PhD thesis, Royal Holloway, University of London, 2012), p. 152.

31 For instance, the inventory of 1618 in MALSC CH108/21 Minute Book 1617–1691, pp. 53–4.

32 WRO CR 1618/WA12/36/13 Building accounts for the almshouse on Castle Hill 1597. This was not the only attention paid to the women's comfort in this relatively poor almshouse, for they were also provided with mats for their seats in church: McIntosh, *Poor Relief in England*, p. 209.

and a snuffer; by 1766 they had acquired a second shelf and a cupboard.[33] In the surviving wills of a handful of Lady Leveson's almswomen from the beginning of the eighteenth century, none mentions a bed among their possessions, which suggests that the beds the women slept in were provided by and belonged to the almshouse. This was the case at Abbot's Hospital, Guildford, where the rooms were equipped with 'halfe headed Bedsteds'.[34] The provision of beds suggests that it was expected that many older people would be admitted from lodgings, or from a relative's home, where they may not have owned their own bed. In contrast, the inventory drawn up on the death of Richard Hargrave, husbandman, who died in the Stoneleigh almshouse in 1640, included among his possessions a 'joyned chest', and an 'olde bedsted' and 'woolbedde', with associated bedlinen, suggesting that he had been a householder and owned these himself.[35] Occasionally almspeople had to agree on entering the almshouse to leave their possessions to the establishment, to be sold or passed on to their successor, as was commonly expected of parish paupers. Indeed, the entry in the Leamington Hastings almshouse accounts for 1694, recording Nicholas Jelly's funeral expenses and the sale of his clothes to recoup some of the costs, could easily have come straight from an overseers' account book: 'Charges in burying him more than his clothes sold for 10s 1d.'[36]

An important feature of most almshouses was the provision of an individual hearth. Unlike the unheated medieval infirmary hall, individual almshouse cottages or rooms were usually heated, with the ubiquitous row of chimneys often a first indicator of the identity of the building. Individual fireplaces supplied both warmth and cooking facilities, as in the great majority of almshouses food was not provided. At Frieston Hospital, Kirkthorpe (1595), the seven men's rooms were unheated but led off a central hall where there was a fireplace and seating area. This is in contrast to Beamsley Hospital, also in West Yorkshire and founded two years earlier, where the women's rooms are similarly located around a central space, in this case a chapel, but where each room had an individual hearth. At Frieston there was provision for an eighth almsperson, a woman who lived in an adjoining cottage, and the implication is that she would have cooked for the men together, whereas the women at Beamsley would have cooked for themselves in their own rooms.[37] Where there were communal facilities, as in some of the grander almshouses,

33   Royal Commission on Historical Monuments, *An Inventory of Historical Monuments: The Town of Stamford* (London, 1977), p. ix.
34   B. Taylor, *Abbot's Hospital, Guildford* (Guildford, 1999), p. 45.
35   Alcock, *People at Home*, p. 143.
36   WRO DR43a/195 Leamington Hastings Davis/Wheler Charity records 1686–1799. For pauper burials, see S. Hindle, *On the Parish? The Micro-Politics of Poor Relief in Rural England c.1550–1750* (Oxford, 2004), p. 281.
37   Caffrey, *Almshouses*, pp. 21–4.

the expectation was that the almspeople would eat and spend time together, as for instance in the Earl of Northampton's Trinity Hospital at Greenwich, where there was a sub-hall for the men to congregate in, and fires were only lit in the men's own rooms if they were ill.[38] But most almshouses had no communal facilities and people lived in their rooms. Inventories of almspeople's personal possessions are uncommon, but, in the few which survive, cooking implements are recorded. For instance, Joan Patrick who died in the Stratford-upon-Avon almshouse in 1597 left a brass pot, four kettles, a skillet, chafing dish and platters, and also bellows, pot hooks and a fire shovel.[39] When Eyffler's almshouse in Warwick was constructed in 1597, the building accounts record expenditure on four pot hangings in the chimneys 'to hang on their potts', indicating that the women would be cooking in their rooms.[40] The basis of most poor people's diet at the time would have been pottage (a basic soup or stew), cooked in a single pot over the fire and made from vegetables, hedgerow herbs, barley or oatmeal, and occasional small pieces of meat.[41] Although wheat-flour bread cooked by commercial bakers was becoming the norm, particularly in southern England and in the towns, older people may still have baked barley bread or oatcakes on the hearth in the traditional way.[42] Without a fire, poor people would have been limited to a more expensive and restricted diet of baker's bread and cheese.[43]

The extent of the accommodation provided to each almsperson is not always known, but information exists for about two-thirds of the almshouses in Durham, Warwickshire and Kent (see Table 5.1). This accommodation ranged from the simple cubicles of the Lord Leycester and the 'huts' at Sherburn Hospital, to the luxurious three rooms provided by Sir John Banks at Maidstone and the five rooms each for clergy widows at Bromley College (which included a bedroom for a maid) at the other extreme. The most usual form of provision, however, was for each almsperson to have their own accommodation of one or two rooms. There were, however, distinct regional differences in the generosity of the accommodation provided. For instance, the accommodation in County Durham is poor compared with the other two

38 P. K. Kipps, 'Trinity Hospital, Greenwich', *Transactions of the Greenwich and Lewisham Antiquarian Society* 3/6 (1935), 294–301 (plan of the hospital between pp. 296–7; J. Imray, 'The Early Days of Trinity Hospital', *Transactions of the Greenwich and Lewisham Antiquarian Society* 9/3 (1981), 117–36 (p. 131).
39 J. Jones, ed., *Stratford-upon-Avon Inventories*, vol. 1: *1538–1625*, Dugdale Society 39 (Stratford-upon-Avon, 2002), p. 171.
40 WRO CR 1618/WA12/36/13 Building accounts for the almshouse on Castle Hill 1597.
41 J. Thirsk, *Food in Early Modern England: Phases, Fads, Fashions, 1500–1760* (London, 2007), p. 149.
42 M. Barker-Read, 'The Treatment of the Aged Poor in Five Selected West Kent Parishes from Settlement to Speenhamland (1662–1797)' (PhD thesis, Open University, 1988), p. 91.
43 Thirsk, *Food*, p. 217.

Table 5.1. Accommodation in almshouses, 1550–1725

Type of accommodation	Number of almshouses			
	Durham	Warwickshire	Kent	Total
Cubicles/huts	1	2	0	3
Shared room	4	1	0	5
Shared house or two rooms	1	9	13	23
One room each	6	4	15	25
Two rooms each	0	8	22	30
Three or more rooms each	0	0	3	3
Subtotal	12	24	53	89
Not known	7	9	22	38
Total	19	33[1]	75	127[1]

1   Chamberlaine's almshouse had two different types of accommodation, on the upper and lower floors, hence the totals come to 33 and 127 (instead of 32 and 126 as in Table 0.1).
Source: Online Appendix A

counties, being either shared or, at best, single rooms for each almsperson. The three women of St John's Hospital, Barnard Castle, for example, lived in a 'low thatched building containing one room only'.[44] The seal of King James' Hospital in Gateshead (formerly the ancient hospital of St Edmund), depicts the almshouse as a low, single-storey building with a central chimney, suggesting that there were two rooms at most for the three almsmen. This difference remained constant over the period and probably reflects lower norms and reduced expectations of domestic comfort in the northern region. The contrast is particularly noticeable with Kent, where only a small proportion of almspeople had to share accommodation and where the largest single category is two or more rooms per person. Only in Kent were there almshouses where more than two rooms each were provided, probably reflecting the greater wealth and higher standard of living in the county. This is borne out by the marked difference shown in the hearth tax returns for the three counties (Table 2.3), where Durham had twice the number of single-hearth homes as Kent, while Kent had more than three times the number of large houses with ten hearths or more.

    If the provision of accommodation merely reflected local wealth and expectations, however, it might be expected that almspeople's accommodation generally improved over time, as material standards of living rose.

44   HCPP, no. 21 (1829), p. 75.

Certainly the three most generous Kent almshouses (Bromley College (1666), Banks's almshouses in Maidstone (1679), and Philipot's almshouse at Eltham (1680)), all date from the second half of the seventeenth century and not from the early eighteenth century as might be expected. In Warwickshire there is no evidence of a general improvement over time. The provision of two rooms each occurs in two sixteenth-century Warwickshire almshouses (Ford's and Stoneleigh), while an eighteenth-century foundation (Gramer's at Mancetter) was still built with only single rooms. After the Great Fire of Warwick in 1694, Oken's almspeople, previously sharing a small house between two, now had to share two to a room in the rebuilt accommodation. Adrian Green suggests that the housing conditions of poor people did indeed improve in the latter part of the seventeenth century, but this was followed by a deterioration in the eighteenth century. It may be that the design of some almshouses followed this pattern, reflecting changing cultural expectations about what was suitable accommodation for poor people.[45]

Green cautions against assuming that all poor people lived in miserable conditions, as suggested by late-eighteenth-century commentators, and it is hard to know by what standard to judge the accommodation provided in almshouses.[46] Nonetheless, for the many almshouse occupants who did not have to share rooms, the provision of private living space in almshouses may have been generous in comparison with the accommodation of other poor people. Simple one-room cottages inhabited by poor people, often with families, would have been a common feature in both rural and urban areas.[47] A surviving example of a pair of sixteenth-century cottages from Berkswell in Warwickshire shows each to have consisted of a ground-floor room approximately 15 feet square, with a fireplace, front door and boarded loft above.[48] According to Alcock these are the same dimensions as the rooms in the Stoneleigh almshouses built in 1574 (also in Warwickshire), where the ground-floor room with fireplace and upper room were described by Prescott as 'spacious houses'.[49] These almshouse room sizes were comparable with, but slightly larger than, two other small cottages in Stoneleigh surveyed by Alcock.[50] Similarly, Oken's new almsrooms at Warwick of 1696 are shown on the plan attached to Dunkley's estimate as roughly 15 feet by 12 feet, with two of them 15 feet square.[51] Philipot's almshouses in Eltham, Kent, built around the same time, had ground-floor rooms approximately 14 feet

---

45 A. Green, 'Heartless and Unhomely? Dwellings of the Poor in East Anglia and North-East England', *Accommodating Poverty*, ed. McEwan and Sharpe, pp. 69–101 (pp. 90–1).

46 Green, 'Heartless and Unhomely?', p. 69.

47 Green, 'Heartless and Unhomely?', p. 73.

48 The building, now the Berkswell Museum, was originally of timber and wattle-and-daub construction.

49 Prescott, *English Medieval Hospital*, p. 165.

50 Alcock, *People at Home*, pp. 126–42.

51 WRO M287 'The Estemat of Sam Dunckley for the Almseshowes upon the backhills'.

square, with a small scullery behind, and a bedroom above 14 feet by 12 feet.[52] These dimensions appear to have been fairly typical of single-bay buildings at the time.[53] A seventeenth-century manorial survey from Urchfont in Wiltshire lists small cottages ranging from 16 feet square down to a tiny 10 feet by 8 feet, with most described as being 13 or 14 feet by 10 feet.[54] Joseph Bettey describes these buildings as little more than cabins or hovels, but it is possible, even with these dimensions, that they were single-bay cottages with one room, a fireplace and a boarded loft.[55]

Larger accommodation often migrated down the housing scale over time, to become subdivided and multi-occupied by people poorer than the original occupants. For many poor people, moreover, lodging in someone else's home would have been a common occurrence. From the Warwick census of 1587 Lee Beier has calculated that 45% of the poor were either inmates themselves or lived in households with inmates.[56] The list of poor people receiving a disbursement in Gateshead in 1681, with their amounts, shows several names grouped, as in, for example, 'Mary Porter & Widow Woodburne 8d'; 'Timothy Walton, Ann Thompson, Ann Taylor 2s 2d'; suggesting that these unrelated individuals were living in the same household.[57] Many poorer people could not have expected to retain a home of their own in old age, particularly once widowed; others, who had never married, or who had spent a lifetime in service, might never have had a home to call their own. Parish paupers were often expected to share accommodation, often against their will and with little say about with whom they had to share. Lynn Botelho, among others, has described the 'combined households' of many of the elderly poor in Cratfield, in Suffolk, while in Poslingford, the other Suffolk parish in her study, it was usual for the parish authorities to board out poor older people with neighbours.[58] The parish officers of Cranbrook in Kent, for example, frequently lodged older people with other poor pensioners, and seemed to

52   J. Kennett, *Thomas Philipot's Almshouse Charity of Eltham and Chislehurst* (Eltham, 1997), p. 6.
53   A bay, the area between two supporting timber uprights, was used as a unit of measurement, and could be anything from 9 feet to 16 feet, the actual size depending on the timber available. In the Stoneleigh cottages examined by Nat Alcock, a bay varied between 10 feet and 15 feet: Alcock, *People at Home*, pp. 126–38.
54   J. Bettey, ed., *Wiltshire Farming in the Seventeenth Century* (Trowbridge, 2005), pp. 322–4. As a comparison, the main room of the medieval cottage from Hangleton, reconstructed at the Weald and Downland Open Air Museum, Singleton, West Sussex, is approximately 13 feet square.
55   A manorial survey for Brailes in Warwickshire records three cottages of a single bay only: A. Tennant, 'The Property and Landholding Survey of 1607', *Brailes History: Episodes from a Forgotten Past* 4 (2005), 1–28 (p. 28).
56   A. L. Beier, 'The Social Problems of an Elizabethan Country Town: Warwick, 1580–90', *Country Towns in Pre-Industrial England*, ed. P. Clark (Leicester, 1981), pp. 46–79 (p. 61).
57   DRO EP/Ga.SM 5/1 Gateshead St Mary's Resolutions of Vestry Meetings 1681–1807.
58   L. A. Botelho, *Old Age and the English Poor Law, 1500–1700* (Woodbridge, 2004), p. 123.

have moved people around at will.[59] Similarly, when the parish of Southam in Warwickshire needed to house Thomas Basley in 1680, they moved two elderly widows in together and gave the spare cottage to Basley.[60]

While for many older people sharing accommodation would have been the norm, only a minority of residents of almshouses were expected to share, usually women, with most having at least a room to themselves. For instance, the two-room apartments of Eyffler's almshouse in Warwick were each shared by two women, and it seems this was also the arrangement initially at Lady Leveson's Hospital at Temple Balsall. At Ford's almshouse in Coventry for five couples, if a woman was widowed she was expected to share her room with another widow; if she died first, her husband was allowed to continue to occupy the room on his own. This suggests that it was considered acceptable, possibly even desirable, for women to share. Conversely it was rare for men in almshouses to be expected to share, although the north-east of the country may have been an exception to this rule. It is possible that the men of King James' Hospital in Gateshead, and some of the men of Sherburn Hospital, Durham, may have had to share. According to an anonymous commentator, in the mid eighteenth century the master of Sherburn, Dr David Gregory, demolished 'all the little wretched huts in which they were huddled together before', and erected new apartments 'that each of the Old Men might have one entirely to himself'.[61] For younger people such as household servants, accommodation would usually have been in shared rooms, and for the many almswomen who had been personal servants before admission, such as those at Lady Leveson's Hospital, this might have been all that they had known. For many almspeople, then, and for women in particular, the sole occupancy of a rent-free room would have been a considerable benefit.

Whether this would have marked them out from most other poor people is harder to say. While many recipients of poor relief would be placed in multi-occupied houses or in lodgings, this does not imply that they were necessarily in shared rooms. The overseers of Lapworth, Warwickshire, for instance, were ordered by the justices in 1672 to provide Elizabeth Fowler with 'a convenient room in some house at Lapworth', and pay her 6d per week.[62] When, in 1655, the overseers of Kenardington, Kent, paid for 'hous roome' for Goodwife Maunt, they also paid for a key for her, suggesting that she had her own, lockable room.[63] The importance of having one's own secure space is shown

59 Barker-Read, 'Aged poor', pp. 76–9.
60 WQS, vol. 7, Epiphany 1680, p. 174.
61 Anon., *A Brief History of Sherburn Hospital in the County of Durham, with Observations on the 'Scheme' Proposed by the Charity Commissioners 'for the Application and Management and the Estates and Possessions Thereof'* (London and Oxford, 1855), p. 13.
62 WQS, vol. 5, Trinity 1672, p. 187.
63 CKS P206/12/1 Kenardington Churchwardens' and Overseers' Accounts 1642–1707.

by Joyce Astley's series of complaints to the Warwickshire justices. She had
to share a house in Willoughby with Elizabeth and Anne Radway. They cut
up her clothes and shut her out of the house, for which they were sent to the
house of correction.[64] In County Durham the quarter sessions ordered the
parish of Castle Eden to provide 'a convenient house' for Magdalen Lamb
'to live in alone by her selfe' and not be made to share with her mother, as
her mother's house was 'but a very small cottage & not able to containe both
their said familyes'.[65] Access to one's own hearth also appears to have been
highly valued for the independence and privacy it afforded. Isabel Robinson
found it impossible to live peaceably in the same house as her brother's
family in Berkswell, Warwickshire, sharing the single hearth. She complained
to the quarter sessions, and in 1641 the court ordered the parish to build
another chimney in the cottage to resolve the matter.[66] Edmund Verney
despaired of the four families occupying the church house in East Claydon,
Buckinghamshire, who were allowed to 'do what they please'. This included
refusing to use the single hearth provided, 'because every one will be private',
and instead making their own 'fires without chimneys' against the walls.[67]

From these examples it seems that many poor people had a clear sense of the
standard of housing to which they were entitled, and it bore a distinct resem-
blance to the accommodation usually available in almshouses. As a minimum,
this was a room of their own, with their own hearth, for themselves and their
family.[68] Until the advent of large workhouses brought the segregation of men,
women and children into dormitories, there is also evidence that this was not just
an ideal, but was achieved in much of the housing provided for the poor. A register
of all the occupants of Faversham's poor houses taken in 1754, for instance,
shows that each individual or family had at least one room to themselves,
occasionally two. Gabriel Berry and his wife, for example, had a house with two
rooms. Widow Butler and her daughter had two rooms, one of which was noted
as being without a fireplace (suggesting the other rooms had hearths); while
Daniel Deale, his wife and six children lived in just one large room. Nobody was
sharing a room with anyone with whom they were not related, although a note
beside Mary Pillay's name suggested this might occasionally be required: 'One
Room, drinks and is not fit to be put with ano[the]r'.[69]

64   WQS, vol. 3, Epiphany, Easter and Trinity 1651, pp. 52, 56, 64.
65   Order made 14 January 1679/80, in DRO Q/S/OB6 Quarter Sessions Order Book January
1668–January 1681.
66   WQS, vol. 2, Michaelmas 1641, p. 100.
67   Letter of Edmund Verney to Sir Ralph Verney, 29 January 1677/8, quoted in J. Broad,
'Housing the Rural Poor in Southern England, 1650–1850', The Agricultural History Review
48/2 (2000), 151–70 (pp. 158–9).
68   This accords with Broad's finding that poor people retained a belief in their right to their
own home, even after workhouses had become the preferred solution: Broad, 'Housing', p. 158.
69   CKS Fa/Ac5/1 Faversham Wardmote Minutes 1741–1820 part 1.

The representation of the town poorhouse on a 1684 estate map of Chilvers Coton, Warwickshire, shows that it was occupied by six paupers, four men and two women (and possibly their families). It appears to be a two-storey property, and is drawn showing at least three chimneys, several windows and at least two external doors. In other words, it was a substantial building, subdivided, with more than one entrance and at least three hearths.[70] It seems distinctly possible that each of the occupants had their own room and most could have had their own fireplace, as they would in most almshouses of the time. Another multi-occupied building in nearby Ansley 'filled with poor people' was a three-hearth house.[71] The advantage of almshouse accommodation over parish housing may not therefore have been in the size and amount of accommodation, nor even always in the provision of discrete space for each poor person, so much as in the secure nature of that accommodation, and in the autonomy and independence allowed the occupants through features such as having one's own front door.

Ascribing a monetary value to the benefit of rent-free almshouse accommodation is not easy. Parish poor relief accounts in the seventeenth and eighteenth centuries show that many parishes paid rent for poor people, either instead of, or in addition to, regular relief. In Terling, Essex, for instance, the overseers paid rents of between £1 and £1 10s per year for poor families at the end of the seventeenth century, leading Wrightson and Levine to estimate the sum of £1 as a typical annual rent in their construction of a poor family's budget.[72] But it is hard to know how typical this actually was. At the opposite end of the scale, Sir Richard Newdigate of Arbury in Warwickshire charged rents of as little as 1s or 2s per year for many of his small tenements. These were clearly not market rates, but peppercorn rents on tied accommodation for his workforce.[73] The churchwardens of St Oswald's in Durham rented out three small houses owned by the church for 4s each per year to Widows Tomlinson, Turner and Tayler in 1595. In 1664 the rents of these cottages were still only 4s 4d per year, and only a little more in 1699, suggesting that

70 WRO CR 136/M14 Map of the three common fields of Chilvers Coton 1684. This house is possibly the same as the 'towne houses' at Griff in Chilvers Coton, recorded as having four hearths in 1670: T. Arkell and N. Alcock, eds, *Warwickshire Hearth Tax Returns: Michaelmas 1670* (Stratford-upon-Avon and London, 2010), p. 371.

71 This property was recorded in the hearth tax assessment for the following year as 'full of poore people and given by a gent to the parish for that use', but it was then certified as having just one hearth: Arkell and Alcock, *Warwickshire Hearth Tax*, p. 370.

72 K. Wrightson and D. Levine, *Poverty and Piety in an English Village: Terling, 1525–1700* (Oxford, 1979; new edn 1995), p. 40.

73 For instance, Thomas Knight and William Mortimer: S. Hindle, 'Work, Reward and Labour Discipline in Late Seventeenth-Century England', *Remaking English Society: Social Relations and Social Change in Early Modern England*, ed. S. Hindle, A. Shepard and J. Walter (Woodbridge, 2013), pp. 255–80 (pp. 272–3).

they were let out at deliberately low rents to poor parishioners.[74] More typical perhaps are the rents of 8s and 10s per year paid by the Pittington overseers for several poor people in 1695, and the 12s per year paid by the parish of St Mary-le-Bow for Dorothy Davison in 1680. Yet in Winston, three paupers were having their rents of 5s per year paid in 1683, while in the same year Gateshead was paying several rents of only 1s or 2s per year.[75] In most cases we have no means of knowing what this accommodation consisted of, but where rents of 3s or 4s per year or less were being paid for poor widows, it is likely that these referred to one-room cottages or a room in someone's house.

Many early modern almshouses were new foundations with purpose-built accommodation. Usually the trustees of the almshouse charity ensured that the buildings were kept in good condition and, while there were sometimes specific funds dedicated to repairs and renovations, the maintenance of almshouse property was often prioritised over support of the poor residents. Katherine Wrott, for instance, founded an almshouse for four people at Sutton-at-Hone, Kent, in 1596 with only sufficient endowment to maintain the property, but not the residents.[76] At Jane Gibson's almshouse in Bishopwearmouth, founded in 1725, the residents had to forego their stipend for the first six months after admission as a contribution to the repair fund.[77] Repairs were expensive and a constant issue for both almshouse trustees and parish officials; parish overseers' accounts record many examples of payments made to repair paupers' houses.[78] This does not necessarily imply that houses were poorly built but timber-framed buildings with wattle and daub, or mud walls and a thatched roof, would have needed regular attention to keep them weatherproof, while the use of brick, stone and tiles, where available, would have reduced the level of maintenance required. It is possible that the impression of early modern almshouses providing good-quality accommodation is biased by the better survival rates of the more substantial buildings using more durable materials, and these are not necessarily representative of all almshouse accommodation. It is nonetheless likely that most almshouses provided a degree of comfort and privacy, possibly greater than that available to most poor people

74   DRO EP/Du.SO 203–4 St Oswald's Durham Churchwardens' Accounts 1580–1656, 1658–1822.

75   DRO EP/Pi 22 Pittington parish records, EP/Du.MB 10 St Mary-le-Bow Durham Parish Book 1678–1760, EP/Wi 18 Winston Overseers' books 1632–1728, and EP/Ga.SM 5/1 St Mary's Resolutions of Vestry Meetings 1681–1807.

76   W. K. Jordan, *Social Institutions in Kent: A Study of the Changing Pattern of Social Aspirations*, Archaeologia Cantiana 75 (Maidstone, 1961), p. 44.

77   HCPP, no. 23 (1830), p. 69.

78   For instance, the parish of Leamington Hastings in Warwickshire paid £5 9s 5d for repairing Nicholas Jelly's house in 1672. Widow Ann Tarsey's house was repaired several times, costing £4 4s in 1661; a further 16s in 1664; and £1 3s 6d in 1669: WRO DR43a/19 Leamington Hastings Overseers' Accounts 1655–1679.

in ordinary housing. Whether this was superior to parish accommodation of the time is not entirely clear; it may be that paupers' expectations of the standard of housing to which they were entitled, coupled with the desire of parish officials to protect their long-term investments, created a congruity between parish housing and almshouses which is perhaps unexpected.

The paradox is that not all almspeople valued their accommodation as much as we might expect. The frequent rules against non-residence suggest that for many poor people the stipend, where it existed, was the more important benefit, and that recipients in many cases would have preferred to be non-resident if given the chance. Certainly, where rules were non-existent or not enforced, some almspeople seem to have taken the opportunity to be non-resident, as at St Bartholomew's Hospital, Oxford, in the eighteenth century.[79] Some surviving medieval almshouses had out-pensioners as well as (or instead of) resident almspeople, such as St John's Canterbury and St Nicholas Harbledown in Kent, and Sherburn and Greatham Hospitals in Durham. Kepier Grammar School and Almshouse was founded in 1574 without accommodation; there was no actual almshouse building until almost a century after its foundation. In establishments such as these, out-pensioners could receive the stipend and make their own living arrangements.[80] Sometimes this was necessary because of the inadequacy of the accommodation. When Sherburn Hospital was refounded by act of Parliament in 1585, the number of almsmen was increased, but without any corresponding increase in the amount of accommodation. Yet when new buildings were erected at Sherburn in the early nineteenth century, only a few of the out-brethren chose to become resident.[81] Accommodation may have been a valuable resource, but it was not necessarily desired by all.

Stipends and material benefits

In the earliest forms of almshouse, the medieval hospitals, which had often been modelled on monastic institutions, residents lived communally and had all their needs met within the institution. For instance, the charter of the twelfth-century

79 A. Tomkins, *The Experience of Urban Poverty 1723–82: Parish, Charity and Credit* (Manchester, 2006), p. 93.
80 There was a similar arrangement for the cathedral almsmen of Durham and Rochester. While they were required to live 'in or near' the cathedral, there is no evidence that they were provided with accommodation in addition to their pensions: DCL Add.MS 375/1 Transcription (1898) of Chapter Act Book vol. 1, 1578–1726, p. 196; C. S. Knighton, 'The Reformed Chapter, 1540–1660', *Faith and Fabric: A History of Rochester Cathedral, 604–1994*, ed. N. Yates and P. A. Welsey (Woodbridge, 1996), pp. 57–76 (p. 67).
81 DRO DU/6/1/6 Charity Commissioners, Further Report 30 January 1830.

St Cross Hospital, Winchester, provided thirteen poor men with 'necessary clothing ... and beds for their infirmities; and daily a good loaf of wheaten bread of the weight of five measures, three dishes at dinner, and one for supper, and drink in sufficient quantity'.[82] The later development of individual accommodation in almshouses, providing greater privacy and comfort for the occupants, had implications, however, for the way that almshouse life was lived. The move away from communal living necessitated the introduction, in many almshouses, of monetary allowances or stipends with which almspeople could purchase their own food and necessities. Rexroth has suggested that the provision of individual rooms, each with its own hearth, in fifteenth-century guild almshouses allowed aged members to retain the autonomy and status of a householder, even once they had become poor pensioners.[83] It is likely that the stipend or allowance performed the same function. Even at an institution like St Cross where the men were still expected to eat together, the design of the accommodation suggests a greater emphasis on individuality and autonomy, with much of the brethren's time spent in their own chambers rather than in the common hall.

A very few traditional foundations continued to provide food for their residents in addition to a monetary allowance. After its refounding, for instance, Sherburn Hospital in Durham continued to feed and clothe fifteen in-brethren, but it is unlikely that this was done to a lavish standard. Bishop Chandler's visitation in 1735, which resulted in new rules being drawn up, established the diet of the Sherburn brethren, probably as a result of complaints, and ordered that all who were not sick should eat together in the common hall. As at Greatham Hospital, the master and brethren at Sherburn appear to have been supported by a large establishment of servants, and the men had all their food supplied and cooked for them. The prescribed diet was nutritious if monotonous, consisting of one pound of boiled or roasted meat daily for each man, a quart of beer, and a weekly allowance of bread and cheese. On Fridays and fast days the meat was replaced by a pudding.[84] The quantities seem generous, particularly for elderly men, and certainly compare favourably with nineteenth-century workhouse diets.[85] At Trinity Hospital, Greenwich, modelled on traditional lines, there were a cook, a butler and a nurse to meet the needs of the almsmen. During Lent in 1617 the Warden reported that the men had been fed 'milk pottage, butter, herrings and dried cod for dinner and pottage, butter, dried cod and cheese for supper, with herb pottage, buttered wheat and carrot roots for variety'.[86]

82   J. McIlwain, *The Hospital of St Cross and St Cross Church* (Andover, 1993), unpaginated.
83   F. Rexroth, *Deviance and Power in Late Medieval London*, trans. P. E. Selwyn (Cambridge, 2007), p. 254.
84   HCPP, no. 23 (1830), p. 128.
85   T. May, *The Victorian Workhouse* (Princes Risborough, 1997), pp. 23–4.
86   Imray, 'Trinity Hospital', p. 123.

Prescott describes how the men of the fifteenth-century Higham Ferrers Bede House used their allowance of 7d per week to buy their own meat, which they each gave to the nurse to cook for them in the communal pot.[87] This may well have been the arrangement at the Lord Leycester Hospital in Warwick. Here the seventeenth-century stewards' accounts list payments to a nurse, and to a woman and a boy to weed the gardens and scare away the birds; also for the purchase of vegetable seeds and nets. No food items appear in the accounts other than the celebration wassail cake at Christmas, indicating that the men usually provided their own food (or otherwise existed wholly on a diet of vegetables and cake). The shared vegetable plot suggests that the nurse may have cooked up a communal vegetable stew or pottage to which she added the men's individual portions of meat, as at Higham Ferrers.[88] Many almshouses had gardens, with often an individual plot for each resident for them to grow their own food. How practical this was for many elderly almspeople is debatable, but along with the domestic architecture of many almshouse buildings, it may reflect an idealised representation of almspeople as sturdily independent poor cottagers.[89]

A few other almshouses are known to have given their residents some basic provisions. For instance, the 1617 foundation document for Coningsby Hospital in Hereford specified a regular supply of bread, ale, cheese, butter and firewood for the men, and cows to be kept to supply them with milk. Over and above their weekly allowance, they were also to have a dinner of roast beef and supper of mutton and broth served in the common hall on the main festivals.[90] Sir Roger Manwood's almspeople at Hackington in Kent were to be served dinner in the patron's house every Sunday, although it is not clear whether this was continued after Manwood's death. This stipulation appears to have been a reflection of the ancient tradition of household hospitality towards the poor, the passing of which was already being lamented in Manwood's time.[91] In times of dearth, it could be argued that the provision of food rather than money was of greater benefit to the poor, but despite this, only a small proportion of early modern almshouses provided any form of food. The great majority of almspeople would have purchased their own food and cooked it themselves.

---

87   Prescott, *English Medieval Hospital*, p. 68.
88   WRO CR 1600/42/3 Stewards' Accounts 1669/70.
89   S. Lloyd, 'Cottage Conversations: Poverty and Manly Independence in Eighteenth-Century England', *Past and Present* 184 (2004), 69–108 (pp. 78, 82–5). See also the discussion of almshouse gardens in S. Hare, 'Almshouse Gardens with Particular Reference to Somerset', *The British Almshouse: New Perspectives on Philanthropy ca. 1400–1914*, ed. N. Goose, H. Caffrey and A. Langley (Milton Keynes, 2016), pp. 298–314.
90   HCPP, no. 32, part 2 (1837–38), p. 54.
91   F. Heal, 'The Idea of Hospitality in Early Modern England', *Past and Present* 102 (1984), 66–93 (p. 68).

Not all almshouses provided stipends or financial allowances, but many did. The value of these could vary considerably, however. In late medieval almshouses, the stipend was often 1d per day, equivalent to £1 10s 4d per year. With rent-free accommodation, it has been argued that in the fifteenth century this amount would have been adequate but not over-generous, sufficient perhaps to provide a 'decent but sparse living'.[92] The 1495 statutes of St John's Hospital in Lichfield specified that each almsperson was to receive 7d per week, with which 'the poor men are to remain contented, nor must they presume to beg'.[93] The assumption here is that 7d should be a sufficient sum for an almsman to live on, with no necessity to supplement his income by begging. The twelve almsmen at God's House at Ewelme, Oxfordshire, founded in 1437 by the Earl and Countess of Suffolk, received 2d per day, but this was a particularly well-endowed and high-status establishment, where the almsmen had to undertake an onerous daily regime of prayer.[94] Indeed, the wealth and status of the founder of the almshouse often dictated the amount of the almsperson's stipend. The London grocer Lawrence Sheriff, who founded an almshouse in 1567 for poor men in his home town of Rugby, Warwickshire, specified the medieval allowance of 7d per week for his almsmen; while in 1571 Thomas Oken, mercer and local burgess, gave the occupants of his almshouse in Warwick even less, at only 4s per year. In contrast, Robert Dudley's almshouse in Warwick was a much wealthier foundation, as befitted his status as one of the leading peers of the realm and Queen Elizabeth's confidant. His almsmen received £4 each per year in stipend, together with a share in the dividends from the rents of almshouse property.[95]

A particularly nice example of a founder using the stipend to indicate the status he ascribed to his establishment, is provided by Bishop John Cosin in the second half of the seventeenth century. Cosin was appointed Bishop of Durham on the restoration of Charles II in 1660 at a time when this bishopric was one of the most powerful in the land, where the Prince Bishops exercised temporal as well as ecclesiastical jurisdiction in the County Palatine. Cosin founded two almshouses near his palaces, one for two men and two women

---

92   C. Dyer, *Standards of Living in the Later Middle Ages: Social Change in England, c.1200–1520* (Cambridge, 1989), p. 253. More recently, Dyer has judged this amount 'was enough to provide an individual with a more than adequate daily diet, including some meat and fish': C. Dyer, 'Poverty and its Relief in Late Medieval England', *Past and Present* 216 (2012), 41–78 (p. 65).
93   HCPP, no. 7 (1822), p. 388.
94   J. Goodall, *God's House at Ewelme: Life, Devotion and Architecture in a Fifteenth-Century Almshouse* (Aldershot, 2001), pp. 231–7.
95   Rouse, *Rugby School*, p. 24; P. Bolitho, *Warwick's Most Famous Son: The Story of Thomas Oken and his Charity* (Warwick, 2003), p. 19; WRO CR 1600/31 'The House Book'; Tibbits, 'Hospital', p. 128.

in Bishop Auckland in 1662, and a larger one for eight in the cathedral city of Durham in 1666. The four Bishop Auckland almspeople received stipends of £4 each per year, plus cloaks worth £3 6s 8d every three years. The eight men and women in the Durham almshouse, however, received £6 13s 4d annually, and cloaks or gowns worth £5 every three years, together with 15s of fuel. This was considerably more than the stipends at other late-seventeenth-century foundations in County Durham. For instance, George Lilburne's almshouse in Houghton-le-Spring (also founded in 1666) gave £3 6s 8d per year; William Hutchinson of Romaldkirk gave £2 per year in 1674; and Sir John Duck's almshouse established in 1686 at Great Lumley gave each of the twelve almspeople £3 8s 8d per year.[96]

Bishop Cosin's Durham stipend of £6 13s 4d is not only a very generous but also a very *precise* amount, and matches exactly that received by the king's almsmen (or bedesmen) at Durham Cathedral.[97] These royal appointments had been instituted by Henry VIII at the refounding of a number of monastic institutions as secular cathedrals after the Dissolution.[98] They were the 'official' poor: eight poor men, nominated by the king, and often disabled soldiers or sailors. They attended cathedral services and undertook simple duties in the cathedral church in return for a quarterly pension. In his instructions regarding his own almspeople, Cosin directed that they too must attend services twice daily, processing two by two into the cathedral, and sitting in precise positions, the men 'placing themselves in ye Quire two on the south side and two on the north next and below the Almesmen of the Cathedrall Church, and the women likewise placing themselves on the upper part of the Benches before the Gentlewomens Seats'.[99] These seating arrangements indicate the respect which Cosin expected his almspeople to be accorded.

In Warwickshire in the late seventeenth century, as in the sixteenth, there was a similar contrast between establishments founded by people of very different rank and wealth. Lady Katherine Leveson, Robert Dudley's grand-daughter, founded her almshouse for twenty poor women in Temple Balsall in 1671. Her stipends, at £8 per year, were exceptionally generous.[100] But the

---

96 DRO EP/Au SA12/39(3) Auckland St Andrew's, Correspondence regarding Bishop Cosin's almshouses; H. Simpson, ed., *Antiquities of Sunderland and its Vicinity*, Sunderland Antiquarian Society 22 (Sunderland, 1960), p. 124; DRO EP/Rom 12/2 Romaldkirk Regulations for the management of the Bowes and Romaldkirk charities 1891, p. 4; DRO DU/6/1/9 *Durham Chronicle* newspaper reports on local charities 1868.

97 DULSC DCD/L/BB Cathedral Treasurer's Books 1557–1921.

98 I. Atherton, E. McGrath and A. Tomkins, '"Pressed down by want and afflicted with poverty, wounded and maimed in war or worn down with age?" Cathedral Almsmen in England 1538–1914', *Medicine, Charity and Mutual Aid: The Consumption of Health and Welfare in Britain, c.1550–1950*, ed. A. Borsay and P. Shapely (Aldershot, 2007), pp. 11–34.

99 DULSC MS/91 Mickleton and Spearman Manuscripts late 16th to early 18th centuries, f. 170.

100 HCPP, no. 18 (1828), p. 441.

small almshouses founded in Alcester by the lawyer John Bridges and his brother-in-law George Ingram in 1659 and 1680 respectively paid no stipends at all until 1702, when John's son Brooke Bridges endowed both almshouses with stipends of £2 each per year.[101] The greatest contrasts, however, are to be found in Kent, where many small almshouses paid no stipend at all, and, of those that did, the amounts ranged from 13s 4d per year at Linton Park almshouses (founded in 1610) to £6 13s 4d per year at Anthony Honywood's almshouses in Lenham (1622), while the residents of Charles Amherst's almshouses at Pembury were apparently receiving £12 per year in 1702.[102] Such variation in the value of stipends were common, and occur across the country.[103] Jordan, for instance, remarks on the disparity of stipends in the counties he examined, with his Buckinghamshire examples ranging widely 'from an almost impossible minimum of £1 p.a. each to the generous provision of ... £7 10s.'[104]

According to Jordan, the average almshouse stipend for Buckinghamshire, which he describes as an averagely prosperous county, was £4 8s 7d. This, he rather optimistically suggests, 'was sufficient to provide a maintenance probably not much less straitened than that of an agricultural labourer'.[105] In contrast, Wrightson and Levine quote a labourer's pay in Terling, Essex, as 9d per day (£11 4s per year) at the end of the sixteenth century, and 12d per day (£15 12s per year) at the end of the seventeenth, although these sums would have needed to support a family, and were dependent upon full-time work being available. Sir Richard Newdigate paid full board plus amounts from £2 to £5 10s per year for farm servants at Arbury, Warwickshire, at the end of the seventeenth century.[106] Jordan calculated that the average stipend for London foundations was £4 4s per year.[107] In Yorkshire, however, he suggests the average was much lower (as was the range, from 10s to £5 per year). Only a third of the eighteen Yorkshire almshouses he mentions paid stipends of between £4 and £5 per year, and none paid more than this. The remaining twelve paid sums ranging from 10s to £3 per year, and a further seven paid no stipends at all after the death of the founder. Jordan remarks that 'the life afforded in these institutions must, save for about a score of exceptions, have been hard and meagre'.[108] In Norfolk, he asserts that benefactors of almshouses in that county 'regarded £2 12s p.a. as adequate maintenance for

101   WRO CR 2219/13 Codicil to Brooke Bridges' will 1702.
102   HCPP, no. 30 (1837), pp. 360, 587, 505.
103   See for instance, Caffrey, *Almshouses*, p. 62.
104   W. K. Jordan, *The Charities of Rural England 1480–1660* (London, 1961), p. 48.
105   Jordan, *Rural England*, pp. 24, 48–9.
106   Wrightson and Levine, *Poverty and Piety*, pp. 40–1; Hindle, 'Work, Reward and Labour', p. 259.
107   W. K. Jordan, *The Charities of London 1480–1660* (London, 1960), p. 165.
108   Jordan, *Rural England*, pp. 252–81.

one almsperson who had his lodgings supplied'. Yet he does not discuss how this stipend might actually have been adequate, when it was so much lower than the Buckinghamshire average.[109]

In fact, on examination of Jordan's figures, it appears that some of his assumptions are questionable, and that his estimate of the average stipend received is too high. He seems to have omitted Dorothy Dayrell's almshouse in Buckingham from the bottom of his range. This was founded in 1574 for six poor women, with an annual endowment of £5 4s in total, which he claims would have given each almswoman, 'somewhat meagrely' (as he says earlier), 17s 4d per year, or 4d per week.[110] In a number of other instances he assumes an artificially high stipend, derived from a notional return on the investment of the capital sum invested or bequeathed by the founder of the almshouse. For instance, he assumes that Thomas Wedon's endowment of property in 1624 for his almshouse in Chesham actually did produce the £30 per year in income that Wedon intended, and that this gave stipends of £7 10s per year to each of the four occupants.[111] Even assuming that the capital did indeed produce the return he anticipated, this takes no account of any other expenditure such as administering the charity and keeping the almshouse in good repair. These necessary costs would have reduced the income available to pay the almspeople's stipends, but Jordan ignores them. If Jordan's Buckinghamshire average is thus too high, an average that he implied would give an almsperson a standard of living not much less than an agricultural labourer, one must conclude that the standard of living experienced by the majority of almshouse occupants would have fallen far short of this level. Jordan's methodology has been much criticised, principally for failing to take into account the steep rises in population, which doubled, and inflation, which increased fivefold, in England over the period he covers.[112] In particular, the rise in the cost of food, most marked in the years of dearth at the end of the sixteenth century, would have had severe implications for almshouse inhabitants, dependent as most of them were on their stipend for the purchase of food. In most almshouses, the price of food would have taken up the major proportion of an almsperson's stipend.

Jordan's attempt to average stipends across almost two centuries of price increases and inflation is, therefore, not helpful. It masks any ability to identify trends over time, for instance, to see whether stipends were greater in almshouses founded later in the period. Using the figures which Jordan

---

109 Jordan, *Rural England*, p. 129.
110 Jordan, *Rural England*, p. 44.
111 Jordan, *Rural England*, p. 46.
112 See, for instance, D. C. Coleman, 'Review: W. K. Jordan, Philanthropy in England', *Economic History Review* (series 2) 13 (1960–61), 113–15; J. F. Hadwin, 'Deflating Philanthropy', *Economic History Review* 31 (1978), pp. 105–17.

himself quotes, the range of known stipends in Buckinghamshire before 1600 was from 17s 4d to £4 (three examples) while between 1600 and 1660 it was from £2 12s to £7 10s (six examples). As Jordan's methodology relied largely on wills, it also does not allow for subsequent attempts by trustees and those responsible for the management of almshouse endowments to increase stipends in line with inflation. There is some evidence that, where funds were available, this did happen. For instance, the city of Coventry which took over the assets and management of both Bond's Hospital (1506) and Ford's Hospital (1509) in the mid sixteenth century, had raised the original stipends of 7½d per week in each to 2s per week at Ford's by 1636, and 3s at Bond's in 1647.[113] At other almshouses, trustees might be hampered by the terminology of the founder's will or the way the almshouse was funded. If the exact amount of the stipend was specified in the founder's will, it could be difficult for trustees to effect a change later. Where almshouses were not themselves endowed with land, a common method of providing permanent funding was for the benefactor to place a specific rent charge on lands bequeathed to their heirs to maintain their almshouse. The rent charge remained in perpetuity, to be paid by whoever subsequently owned the land, but, with inflation, declined in value over time, even though the value of the land increased. Either through inflation, or because of the abuse or misappropriation of almshouse funds, many almshouses were impoverished within a few generations. This was a problem well understood by contemporaries, and as a result many almshouses received further endowments after their initial foundation.

The great benefit of the stipend, no matter how small, was that it was a guaranteed, regular payment. There might occasionally be abuse and misappropriation of almshouse funds, preventing almspeople receiving the intended allowance, sorry examples of which can be found in many diocesan visitations and in the investigations of the commissioners for charitable uses under the late Elizabethan legislation.[114] The case study in chapter 6, for instance, details the successful suit in Chancery by the parishioners of Leamington Hastings against the heirs of almshouse founder Humphrey Davis after they had allegedly misappropriated the almshouse income. The occupants of St Stephen's Hospital, Hackington, complained at a visitation by the mayor of Canterbury in 1625 that they had not received their allowances in wood and money, and the complaints were repeated in subsequent years. It seems that the lands given by Sir Roger Manwood to support the almshouse had been sold by his son, and the mayor of Canterbury eventually had to distrain the goods of the new owner to force him to pay the almshouse occupants their

---

113   J. Cleary and M. Orton, *So Long as the World Shall Endure: The Five Hundred Year History of Ford's and Bond's Hospitals* (Coventry, 1991), pp. 54, 56.
114   39 Eliz. c. 6; 43 Eliz. c. 4.

stipends.[115] Sometimes financial problems prevented the almshouse trustees from paying the full amount of the stipend, as in 1696 when labourer William Chittam was admitted to the Leamington Hastings almshouse on a reduced stipend until the trustees could raise more revenue by revaluing their leases and increasing rental income.[116]

In some almshouses, receipt of the whole stipend might be dependent on good behaviour. Occasionally almshouse occupants were fined or had some of their allowance withheld for misdemeanours or breaches of almshouse rules, where they existed. As the previous chapter demonstrated, however, an almsperson was not readily deprived of their stipend once it had been awarded. Neither would they normally be expected to have to demonstrate their continuing need for their place once they had passed the admission criteria and started to receive the stipend. This was very different from the recipients of parish relief, who often had the amounts they received reduced or terminated on the basis of an assessment of their circumstances by an overseer of the poor. The almshouse stipend was a fixed amount, not based on an individual's needs, and usually all the occupants of the almshouse received the same stipend, regardless of their individual circumstances. There were occasionally differential rates for men and women within the same establishment, as at Thomas Stafford's almshouse in Shenley, Buckinghamshire (1615), where the four men were to receive 3d per day, and the two women only 2d per day each; and at Sir John Constable's almshouse in Halsham, Yorkshire, where the men's stipends were £4 per year, and the women's £2 per year; but these are rare examples.[117] Sometimes one or two of the almspeople received additional payments for undertaking certain duties, such as reading the prayers or nursing older residents. Sir Thomas Hesketh's almshouse in Heslington, Yorkshire (1605), for example, provided accommodation for nine poor people on stipends of £5 per year, but one of the almsmen was paid £6 13s 4d per year. He was designated master, and his duties were to read prayers each morning and evening.[118] At his hospital in Guildford, George Abbot, Archbishop of Canterbury, specified in 1617 that there should be two nurses, called 'Releevers of the Impotent', to be appointed annually from among the almswomen. They were to receive an additional 6s 8d yearly on top of their stipend.[119] Apart from exceptions such as these, most almspeople could rely on receiving the same unchanging stipend until they died.

This guaranteed, regular payment of a monetary allowance gave an

115   CCA CC S/7/1 St Stephen's Hospital Memorandum and Disbursements Book 1593–1828.
116   WRO DR43a/195 Leamington Hastings Davis/Wheler Charity records 1686–1799, 20 October 1696.
117   Jordan, *Rural England*, pp. 46, 263.
118   Jordan, *Rural England*, p. 266.
119   Taylor, *Abbot's Hospital*, p. 25.

almsperson not only considerable security in an age when most poor people's lives were characterised by chronic insecurity; it also provided a degree of autonomy and independence. An almsperson was able to choose what to spend their allowance on, unlike the recipients of parish poor relief who were often relieved in kind, and had no choice but to accept what was provided for them. This is representative of the essential ambiguity of almshouses; they were institutions that, despite being founded and run for economically dependent recipients of charity, seem designed to foster autonomy and independence. On the other hand, they also lacked the flexibility and sensitivity to changing needs that characterised the parish poor relief system. The recipients of fixed pensions and allowances fared badly in times of high inflation, fluctuating prices and food shortages. In years of high demand for poor relief, the overseers of the poor could raise an additional levy on the parish to meet demand. Parish officials and local justices could, and on occasions did, show enormous sensitivity to individual needs and circumstances when exercising their responsibilities; fine tuning what was provided on a week-by-week basis to the needs of individuals, withdrawing support when people were able to provide a little for themselves, stepping back in to fill the gaps in times of difficulty. Evidence from overseers' accounts across the country shows parishes paying for shoes and clothing, sheets and blankets, redeeming people's goods from pawn, providing extra help when people were sick, paying for medical attention and special diets, and finally meeting burial costs, even including food and drink at the wake.[120] In contrast, most almshouses provided a set stipend, regardless of individual circumstance. When additional benefits such as clothing and fuel were provided, these were also prescribed and invariable.

Some almshouses provided gowns or cloaks for their residents.[121] Clothing was both essential and expensive, and represented a valuable asset for poor people, many of whom relied on handed-down gifts or second-hand garments to clothe themselves. It was common for parishes to provide clothing for those on poor relief. The poor needed to be 'neat, clean and respectable', as rags were considered a mark of degradation.[122] But unlike the parish authorities, who paid for shoes, shirts, petticoats and shifts for adults, and would typically provide a complete suit of clothes for poor children being apprenticed, early modern almshouses generally only provided a single, outer garment. There are occasional exceptions, such as the trustees of Humphrey Davis's

---

120   Hindle, *On the Parish?*, pp. 265–71.
121   The number of almshouses providing items of clothing at any period was 'relatively small'; for instance, less than a fifth of all almshouses in Northamptonshire: B. Wood, 'Almshouse Clothing', *The British Almshouse*, ed. Goose, Caffrey and Langley (Milton Keynes, 2016), pp. 266–83 (p. 266).
122   C. Payne, 'Murillo-like Rags or Clean Pinafores?: Artistic and Social Preferences in the Representation of the Dress of the Rural Poor', *Textile History* 33/1 (2002), 48–62 (pp. 48–9).

almshouse in Leamington Hastings paying 2s 6d for a pair of shoes for Ann Tue in 1686.[123] Before her admission to the almshouse she had been on parish poor relief, and the purchase and repair of shoes for her appeared regularly in the parish overseers' accounts; it is possible that she was crippled in some way, and needed special shoes on a frequent basis. Sir Roger Manwood specified that his six almspeople should each have a gown, cap and shoes every three years.[124] The almswomen of Lady Leveson's Hospital at Temple Balsall appear to have been provided with some form of undergarment and stays as well as their expensive 'fine gray' gowns. The hospital accounts itemise expenditure on 'canvies' (fine, unbleached cloth), and on 'whalesbone, clasps and keepers' costing about 3s 6d.[125] Perhaps elsewhere it was assumed that older people entering almshouses would already possess sufficient clothing of their own. Botelho's evidence from Cratfield, Suffolk, suggests that older people were far less likely than other paupers to be provided with clothing by the overseers, although in the eighteenth century, at least, Styles believes that the emphasis in overseers' accounts on providing shirts, shifts, stockings and shoes suggests that these were garments which poor people needed to replace regularly.[126] Most almshouses seem to have been unconcerned about the possibly impover-ished state of residents' undergarments. The outer garment, when provided, undoubtedly served to keep the almsperson warm, but, perhaps more impor-tantly, it provided the wearer with a literal cloak of respectability.

Often the colour and form of the almshouse gown was specified, with distinguishing features such as a badge or the founder's initials. Thus Thomas Oken's almshouse in Warwick provided a gown every three years, made of six yards of black cloth with the letters 'TO' in white, front and back.[127] It was common for almshouses which provided gowns or cloaks to allow for replacement only every two or three years; poor people would usually have replaced their outer garments only very intermittently.[128] The much wealthier Lord Leycester Hospital provided the brethren with new gowns twice a year, a blue gown on St George's Day (23 April) and a black gown at All Hallows (1 November), which probably served as summer and winter wear. The Lord Leycester's gowns are referred to in the hospital statutes as livery, and the men had to wear them in public.[129] In the mid seventeenth century, silver badges

123   WRO DR43a/195 Leamington Hastings Davis/Wheler Charity records 1686–1799.

124   CCA CC Supp Ms/6 Alderman Gray's Notebook 1737–1780, p. 242.

125   WRO CR 1618/W15/17/7, 9, 31–32, Hospital accounts 1689–90.

126   Botelho, Old Age, p. 119; J. Styles, The Dress of the People: Everyday Fashion in Eighteenth-Century England (New Haven and London, 2007), pp. 264–5.

127   WRO CR 2758/1 Oken's Charity Accounts 1574–1596.

128   Styles, Dress, p. 217.

129   'Item that noe brother goe into the Towne without his lyverye on his Backe': WRO CR 1600/2 Founder's Statutes: Ordinances of the Hospital of Robert Earl of Leicester 26 November 1585, no. 18.

with Robert Dudley's arms of the bear and ragged staff were introduced, which each man had to purchase from his predecessor.[130] The status which these expensive badges conferred marked out the wearers as privileged dependants. As Styles remarks, 'dependency was not necessarily synonymous with humiliation. Liveries were born with pride; badges could be sought-after signs of patronage, belonging and entitlement'.[131] Yet the similar introduction of badges for the recipients of parish poor relief at the end of the seventeenth century, while marking the wearers as deserving, was also intended to stigmatise the recipients of poor relief.[132] The occurrence in almshouse rules of sometimes draconian penalties for those refusing to wear the gowns provided, suggests that not all almshouse occupants acquiesced willingly in this demonstration of their dependence. The women of Lady Leveson's Hospital, for instance, were instructed by the founder to wear their distinctive grey gowns at all times; anyone refusing to do so should lose their allowance and be 'put forth of the said House'.[133]

The other essential was fuel. Individual fireplaces, provided in most almshouses, were used both for warmth and cooking. Fuel was expensive, particularly where there was no access to firewood, either because of urbanisation and enclosure of commons, or because the almspeople were too frail to go out collecting firewood themselves. Many almshouse charities specified an allowance of coal or wood, or both, to be delivered each winter. For instance, Sir Thomas Holte's will of 1637 included 'a wain load of coals' for each occupant of his almshouses at the gates of Aston Hall. Some almshouses had a fuel supply from their own lands, for instance Jesus Hospital, Canterbury, and Queen Elizabeth Hospital, Greenwich, where William Lambarde had purchased a wood specifically to provide fuel for his almspeople.[134] The tenants of the lands owned by Leamington Hastings almshouse paid some of their rent in fuel delivered to the almshouse, but in 1696, as they were 'apt to bee slack in bringing coals and wood as they ought', the trustees made the decision that in future the whole rent would be in money, so that fuel could be purchased at the 'proper seasons'.[135] The inhabitants of the Cowden almshouse in Kent

---

130   WRO CR 1618/WA17/102 Book of admissions compiled by William Walton, Senior Steward, in 1868. In a note Walton says that the names of the men engraved on the badges were all brethren of the hospital in 1663.
131   Styles, *Dress*, p. 272.
132   8 & 9 Will. III c. 30 (1697); Styles, *Dress*, p. 274; S. Hindle, 'Dependency, Shame and Belonging: Badging the Deserving Poor, c.1550–1750', *Cultural History* 1 (2004), 29–58.
133   WRO CR 1540/6 Transcript of the Will of Lady Katherine Leveson (1671).
134   HCPP, no. 29 (1835), p. 1005; CCA U204/F1/1 Jesus Hospital Ledger 1610–1637, entry for Lady Day 1611; R. M. Warnicke, *William Lambarde, Elizabethan Antiquary* (London and Chichester, 1973), p. 44.
135   WRO DR43a/195 Leamington Hastings Davis/Wheler Charity records 1686–1799, 20 October 1696.

received a free delivery of one hundred faggots of wood each November.[136] Sometimes the value of the fuel was specified, as in the 5s in coals provided annually at Hutchinson's almshouse at Romaldkirk (founded 1674) and Morgan's almshouse at Frosterley (1641), both in County Durham. According to Jordan, Robert Butler's will of 1630 gave 3s 4d in winter to each of his four almswomen at Walpole St Peter, Norfolk, to purchase 'a chaldron of good sea coal'.[137] It is unlikely that these quantities would have enabled an almsperson to keep in a fire all winter, but they should nonetheless be seen as valuable contributions to their fuel needs. At Bishop Cosin's almshouse in Durham (1666) the almspeople each received a far more generous 15s in coals. It seems that the disparity in the status of the residents of various almshouses was demonstrated even by how warm they were able to keep themselves in winter.

Some almshouses were provided with garden plots, with the expectation that the almspeople, like poor cottagers, could provide themselves with vegetables and fruit. This would have been a useful addition to the standard of living for those almspeople still fit enough for garden work, or residents of the wealthier almshouses like the Lord Leycester which could afford to employ assistance. Even in the towns, gardens and vegetable plots were common, and provided an important supplement to the diets of those poorer people who had access to them. Other elements which could improve the quality of life for poor older people such as the provision of nursing and domestic assistance seem to have been the preserve of the better-off establishments such as Abbot's Hospital and the Lord Leycester Hospital. In less well-off almshouses, residents needing assistance would have had to rely principally on family and neighbours, as did other poor people. When the trustees of Leamington Hastings almshouse agreed to admit Widow Scotten in 1687, they gave permission for her daughter to be admitted with her. Widow Over, on her admission in 1696, asked for a particular room next to that of her brother-in-law Richard Over, so that they 'may bee helpful to each other'.[138]

These wide-ranging examples, just a handful of the many which could have been cited, demonstrate how difficult it is to arrive at any notion of an 'average' almshouse allowance, despite Jordan's pretension to statistical precision. The variations in the nature, range and value of benefits received are just too great. Quite apart from the wide range of stipends paid, some almshouses provided clothing or fuel, of different value; a very few provided food, bedding, or nursing care. Unlike the parish pension, none of this seems to have been based on the objective needs of the individual recipient, but on what the founders or trustees of almshouses could afford to provide

---

136 Barker-Read, 'Aged Poor', p. 90. A faggot was a bundle of wood. Barker-Read gives the dimensions as between three and four feet long, and twenty-four inches in girth.

137 Jordan, *Rural England*, p. 127.

138 WRO DR43a/195 Leamington Hastings Davis/Wheler Charity records 1686–1799.

or thought was adequate for the objects of their charity. On the whole this does not seem to have been affected by the gender of the intended recipients. While some of the wealthier foundations were for men only, such as the Lord Leycester, other high-status establishments such as Abbot's Hospital and Bishop Cosin's Palace Green almshouse admitted both men and women. One of the most generous foundations in Warwickshire, Lady Leveson's Hospital at Temple Balsall, was for women only.

There is, however, some suggestion of regional variation in the level and value of stipends. Steven King has identified a broad, regional difference in the level of payments of poor relief in eighteenth-century England, with lower payments in the north and west of the country than in the south and east, notwithstanding individual variations between parishes.[139] He ascribes part of this difference to cultural attitudes, and it is possible, if such variations did exist, that they might have affected attitudes to charitable giving as well. But the picture may be more complicated than this analysis would suggest. For instance, the more 'generous' culture of parish poor relief described by King for the south and east of the country might have been mirrored in greater generosity in charitable giving. Conversely, it might, as contemporary commentators feared, have reduced donors' willingness to donate to charity because of the existence of parish poor rates. Some variation might be accounted for by regional differences in the cost of living, particularly in the price and availability of food, but also in the availability of alternative resources. This would have affected not only the purchasing power of the almshouse stipend, but also local wage rates, impacting on what almshouses would need to expend on service charges and repair costs, and also local land rents, affecting almshouse income.

Recent work by Craig Muldrew on food prices, preferences and availability; the relationship between calorific intake and productivity; and the implications of this for economic development, has highlighted just how complex an area this is.[140] It is clear that the cost of living varied considerably around the country, sometimes even between villages in the same area, and was affected by patterns of food production, by custom, and also by what Muldrew terms 'non-monetary components', such as land tenure and common rights.[141] For example, Tim Wales has shown how the villagers of Cawston in Norfolk who had a cow or a cottage were described in 1601 as 'not so poor'.[142] Cawston

---

139   S. King, *Poverty and Welfare in England 1700–1850: A Regional Perspective* (Manchester, 2000).

140   C. Muldrew, *Food, Energy and the Creation of Industriousness: Work and Material Culture in Agrarian England, 1550–1780* (Cambridge, 2011).

141   Muldrew, *Food, Energy*, p. 323.

142   T. Wales, 'Poverty, Poor Relief and the Life-Cycle: Some Evidence from Seventeenth-Century Norfolk', *Land, Kinship and Life-Cycle*, ed. R. M. Smith (Cambridge, 1984), pp. 351–404 (pp. 371–2).

was a village with extensive commons, providing grazing and fuel for free; the land attached to a cottage would have enabled poor cottagers to grow food for their own consumption and even have a surplus to sell, while dairy produce from the cow could also be sold to enhance the family's income. The erosion of common rights elsewhere throughout the early modern period had a significant impact: having to pay to rent pasture for a cow, for instance, could make it uneconomical to own one.[143] The result is a series of complicated scenarios in which many factors could influence the cost of living for poor people.

The standard of living of almshouse residents

If the cost of living varied so greatly around the country, it is difficult to assess what standard of living the equally varied almshouse stipends and benefits documented above might have enabled their residents to achieve. Although this complex picture makes a nonsense of Jordan's 'average' almshouse stipend, the temptation to simplify is hard to resist if some broad-brush comparisons are to be made. Online Appendix C gives the stipends, where known, of almshouses in six English counties between 1550 and 1700: the three counties of Durham, Warwick and Kent, supplemented by information up to the 1660s from Jordan's work on wills in Buckinghamshire, Norfolk and Yorkshire. The almshouses are listed by date of foundation in three separate tables: from the 1550s to the 1590s; 1600s to 1640s; and 1650s to 1690s. The stipends paid at the time of foundation, if known, or the actual stipends paid at a later date, are entered under the appropriate decade. In a few instances, where stipends are known to have been changed, these are included again under the relevant decade.

The data is, of course, incomplete. For approximately half the establishments identified by Jordan no precise stipend is known, and these have had to be excluded. Similarly, for approximately one-third of almshouses in Warwickshire, Durham and Kent no information on stipends is available. In addition, there are very few cases where information from individual almshouses is available at more than one point in time. The evidence from wills collected by Jordan only indicates the founder's intentions; whether or not these were actually carried out is not always known. Again, many almshouse charities may have been able to adjust stipends over time to take into account changes in the cost of living, but many others paid the same fixed amount for more than a century. How establishments fared over time was often a matter of chance. Some prospered, such as the Lord Leycester

---

143 Muldrew, *Food, Energy*, pp. 253–5.

Hospital in Warwick. By the end of the seventeenth century this wealthy almshouse was reputed to be providing each brother with a share of the dividends worth more than £50 per year.[144] Many establishments attracted further endowments, but others will have declined, either through neglect, abuse, or because the income to maintain the almshouse was fixed, perhaps by a rent charge on property.[145] Often the allowances paid to almspeople were set down in the founder's will, and could not be varied. The impoverishment of many almshouses over time is evidenced by the comprehensive reports of the Brougham commissioners into charities in the 1820s and 1830s.

Particularly in the earlier part of the period covered, inflation was rapid, and any consideration of the standard of living achieved by almshouse occupants must take this into account. The index devised by Phelps Brown and Hopkins, based on the prices of a number of consumables such as food, fuel and cloth, allows historians to track inflation across any given period.[146] Appendix 4 (column a) reproduces Lynn Botelho's summary index of the price of a composite unit of foodstuffs by decade from the 1500s to 1690s.[147] Using this index, it is possible to apply a number of benchmarks with which to compare almshouse stipends over time. The earliest benchmark is the traditional 1d per day almshouse stipend of the late medieval period. This was considered an adequate, if basic, allowance and was still being specified in early-sixteenth-century foundations, such as Sir Robert Throckmorton's almshouse at Coughton, Warwickshire, in 1518. Table 5.2 shows how rapidly the value of this stipend was eroded by sixteenth-century inflation. The figures in the bottom row of the table indicate the sum that would be needed in each decade to match the value of the traditional almsman's pension at the beginning of the century. Thus, when Lawrence Sheriff's will gave his almsmen in Rugby the traditional stipend of 1d per day (£1 10s 4d per year) in 1567, the almsmen would have actually needed a stipend of £4 5s 5d per year by then if it were to match the value of that of the late medieval almsman. Sheriff, as a grocer, is unlikely to have been ignorant of the change in the value of money over his lifetime; it seems he was more concerned with upholding tradition than with genuinely meeting the needs of his poor men. By comparison with

---

144   Tibbits, 'Hospital', pp. 137–8.

145   For example, Davenport and Lilburne's separate endowments of £10 per year at their almshouse in Houghton-le-Spring, County Durham, had remained fixed, necessitating further endowments by later benefactors to maintain the income of the occupants. By the nineteenth century the bequests of subsequent rectors of Houghton had increased the stipends for the three occupants of Davenport's wing to £15 13s 4d per year, while fewer additional endowments had left the three in Lilburne's wing with a much lower £9 6s 8d: DRO EP/Ho 280 Report on Kepier School and Almshouse 1878.

146   H. Phelps Brown and S. V. Hopkins, *A Perspective of Wages and Prices* (London and New York, 1981), pp. 13–59.

147   Botelho, *Old Age*, p. 144.

Table 5.2. Traditional almsman's stipend (1d per day) increased in line with inflation

	1500s	1540s	1550s	1560s	1570s	1580s	1590s
Inflation index	106	217	315	298	341	389	530
Almsman's stipend of 1d per day	£1 10s 4d	£3 2s 2d	£4 10s 4d	£4 5s 5d	£4 17s 8d	£5 11s 6d	£7 12s 0d

the stipends of other almshouses founded in the second half of the sixteenth century (Online Appendix C), it can be seen that, apart from places like the medieval hospitals of Sherburn and Greatham where full board was provided on top of the small stipend, only three almshouse foundations come close to matching the standard of living afforded to late medieval almspeople. These were the almshouse founded in 1556 by Robert Holgate, Archbishop of York, in his home town of Hemsworth, Yorkshire, with stipends of £4 per year; William Lambe's almshouse at Sutton Valence, Kent, founded in 1574, providing the almspeople with £4 per year and half a chaldron of coal; and the Lord Leycester Hospital, Warwick, founded by Robert Dudley, Earl of Leicester, in 1571, also with stipends of £4 per year, but where the almsmen also received two gowns a year, fuel, and a share of the rental dividends. Two of these were exceptionally wealthy foundations created by high-status individuals, and not typical of the generality of almshouse foundations. Lambe's almshouse was administered by the Clothworkers' Company, which he had endowed with considerable London property. They may have been able to pay such generous stipends because Lambe's original intentions were changed when the number of almspeople was reduced from twelve to six.[148]

More interestingly, this comparison suggests that late medieval almspeople were the exceptionally privileged poor, and that later generations had lower expectations of what was considered appropriate for poor recipients of charity. Some evidence in support of this conclusion is provided by the town corporations of Stratford-upon-Avon and Gloucester. When they took over responsibility in the mid sixteenth century for town almshouses formerly run by suppressed organisations, the Guild of the Holy Cross in Stratford and St Bartholomew's Hospital in Gloucester respectively, they reduced the 1d per day allowance paid to the almspeople. Instead of receiving 7d per week, their almspeople now received only 4d per week.[149] While financial difficulties

148   Prescott, *English Medieval Hospital*, p. 137.
149   R. Savage, ed., *Minutes and Accounts of the Corporation of Stratford-Upon-Avon and Other Records 1553–1620*, vol. 1: *1553–1566*, Dugdale Society 1 (Stratford-upon-Avon, 1921), p. 151; Prescott, *English Medieval Hospital*, p. 76.

and the need for retrenchment probably drove these decisions, they may also reflect a change in assumptions about what was an appropriate standard of living for occupants of almshouses, once they had lost their intercessory function.

Another sixteenth-century benchmark can be provided by the pensions paid by the government to monks from the dissolved monasteries in the 1540s, and later to chantry and college priests. These ranged from £1 6s 8d per year to over £20 per year for a lucky few, with £5 considered 'a reasonable sum upon which a person in retirement might live'.[150] While there is no suggestion that ejected monks were expected to be poor, and the offer of adequate pensions in compensation no doubt eased the progress of the Dissolution, the sums were clearly designed to enable a single man without dependants to live reasonably well, with two-thirds of men receiving payments of at least £5 per year. This is in marked contrast to the female ex-religious, 60% of whom received less than £2 per year. Former monks would have needed to pay rent, whereas almsmen would not; even with rent taken into account, the sum of £5 in the 1540s is more than the equivalent of the traditional almsman's pay. The monk's pension remained at the same level for the remainder of his life unless he could augment it with new employment as a priest, and elderly monks living into the later years of the century would have found their circumstances much reduced.[151] Even so, only the most fortunate almshouse occupants could match £5 per year in the late sixteenth century.

An alternative comparative measure would be a notional budget requirement for an almsperson, based on assumed minimum subsistence needs and adjusted for inflation. Several historians have attempted to devise a minimum subsistence budget for poor people: Ian Archer for Elizabethan London; Wrightson and Levine for Terling in Essex at the end of the seventeenth century; and Lynn Botelho for late-seventeenth-century Suffolk.[152] All of these are in the south-east of England, where the cost of living might have been higher than in other parts of the country; unfortunately, comparative data is less readily available elsewhere.[153] The components of a poor person's budget would have comprised food, clothing, fuel and rent. The equivalent for an almsperson would have included food, some clothing, and fuel if not also provided. Food would inevitably have been the most important component.

Ian Archer has devised two budgets for a non-working widow without

---

150   G. A. J. Hodgett, ed., *The State of the Ex-Religious and Former Chantry Priests in the Diocese of Lincoln 1547–1574*, Lincoln Record Society 53 (Lincoln, 1959), p. xvii.
151   Hodgett, *Ex-Religious and Former Chantry Priests.*
152   I. Archer, *The Pursuit of Stability: Social Relations in Elizabethan London* (Cambridge, 1991), p. 194; Wrightson and Levine, *Poverty and Piety*, p. 40; Botelho, *Old Age*, p. 148.
153   The data used by Phelps Brown and Hopkins was also mainly from south-east England, so comparisons with other parts of the country may be less valid.

dependants in late-sixteenth-century London, Budget 'A', either standard or 'saver'. The food element in Archer's standard budget is based on the diet allowances of the Westminster house of correction in 1561 and the London Bridewell in 1600, together with the assessment of the York authorities in 1587 that the poor needed a minimum of 1½d per day to live on. The 'saver' budget assumes that in times of hardship it would be possible (and necessary) for a poor person to economise on food, cutting out meat and dairy products, and reducing the budget by 25%. The reduced sums Archer includes for food on this basis are £1 8s 6d per year in the mid-1580s, rising to £2 5s 9d in the late 1590s. The same 25% reduction could, Archer argues, be applied to other components of the poor person's budget. He includes the sum of 14s for clothing in his standard budget, based on the cost of providing a man with a gown, shirt and shoes in the 1590s, but acknowledges that we do not know how often this clothing would need to be replaced. Styles suggests for the eighteenth century that shirts, shifts and shoes were likely to need replacing frequently, but that replacement of outer garments would be intermittent.[154] Archer reduces the 14s for clothing by 25% for the 'saver' budget, on the basis that the poor could have reduced their expenditure on clothing by buying second hand, leaving an annual sum of 10s 6d for clothing in the 1580s and 1590s. The 10s that Archer allows for fuel in the 1580s, inflated to 12s in the 1590s, is based on the cost of the fuel allowance of a heaped bushel of coal per week to each of the beneficiaries in John Costyn's will, and the 12s paid by the Merchant Taylors' Company in the 1590s to each of the inhabitants of their new almshouses. A reduction of 25% could be achieved, Archer believes, by purchasing subsidised fuel from the London authorities. The rent element can, of course, be excluded for the purpose of comparing with an almsperson's needs, as they received rent-free accommodation. Archer's resulting subsistence budgets for a widow without dependants, excluding rent, are £2 6s 6d per year in the mid-1580s, and £3 5s 3d in the late 1590s.[155]

Wrightson and Levine arrive at the sum of £2 12s per year for an adult's food and drink in the late seventeenth century, based on sums actually paid by the overseers of the poor for the parish of Terling in the last six years of the seventeenth century. Their assumption is that the typical poor relief payment to an adult pauper of 2s per fortnight, or £2 12s per year, covered the total cost of their food and drink. Their figures are based on the needs of an adult in a family with children, and therefore presumably applied to working-age men and women. Botelho has calculated her budget for an aged person in late seventeenth-century Suffolk, and allowed £3 per year for food and drink, or 2d per day. This seems generous compared with the Terling budget, as the calorific needs of an older person would be less than those of a working

---

154 Styles, *Dress*, pp. 264–5.
155 Archer, *Stability*, pp. 190–4.

adult, but perhaps Botelho takes into account the economy of scale achieved in feeding a family of five, as in the Terling example.

With regard to clothing, Wrightson and Levine calculate that the costs of a full set of clothing for an adult in the late seventeenth century would have been 15s for a woman or 18s for a man, but that they would have been replaced only once every three years.[156] The Tonbridge workhouse in Kent provided each male inmate in the mid eighteenth century with a coat, jacket, waistcoat, hat, shoes, two shirts and two pairs of socks. The women received a gown, several caps, a waistcoat, shoes, cloak, kerchief, two petticoats, two shifts and two pairs of stockings. Each complete outfit cost around £1 and was to be replaced after three years.[157] Botelho includes 10s per year for clothing an aged poor person, though this, too, seems a little high. Her evidence from Poslingford confirms that the overseers would pay 15s to fit out a female pauper with a gown, linen, stockings and shoes, but she suggests that clothing would be frequently repaired rather than replaced.[158] Both Botelho and Wrightson and Levine include the sum of £1 per year for fuel, although Botelho does acknowledge that fuel costs could vary widely. Wood to the value of 10s was distributed each winter to the poor in Poslingford, whereas Cratfield's poor had their fuel supplied cheaply from the town lands. In Terling, the overseers spent about £1 per year on firewood for each pauper. Given the needs of the elderly for warmth and their limited ability to fetch wood for themselves, £1 to cover fuel for a year seems reasonable.

Table 5.3 summarises these estimated budgets for a single poor person without dependants. The first two columns, for the 1580s and 1590s, are derived from Archer's 'saver' budget; the third column, for the 1690s, is Botelho's budget for the aged poor; while the last column is derived from Wrightson and Levine's figures from Terling overseers' accounts. Table 5.4 adapts these estimates to construct suggested minimum subsistence budgets for an almsperson in south-east England. These reduce the clothing element of both Archer's and Botelho's budgets, on the basis that this was the area where economising would be easiest for an older person. They retain the original fuel costs from Archer's budgets, without his 25% 'saver' reduction as this only applies in London. Wrightson and Levine agree with Botelho on fuel costs of £1 per year in the late seventeenth century. An almsperson's requirement would have been similar, as most poor households of any size would usually have had only a single hearth, and the older person's need to keep warm would have been greater. The food element for the 1690s budget is based on Wrightson and Levine, rather than Botelho, as there appears to be no rationale for the higher figure that Botelho includes. These sums are

156   Wrightson and Levine, *Poverty and Piety*, p. 40.
157   Barker-Read, 'Aged Poor', p. 96.
158   Botelho, *Old Age*, p. 147.

Table 5.3. Budget per annum for single poor person without dependants

	1580s (Archer)	1590s (Archer)	1690s (Botelho)	1690s (W & L)
Food	£1 8s 6d	£2 5s 9d	£3 0s 0d	£2 12s 0d
Clothing	10s 6d	10s 6d	10s 0d	5s 0d
Fuel	7s 6d	9s 0d	£1 0s 0d	£1 0s 0d
Rent	10s 0d	10s 0d	£1 0s 0d	£1 0s 0d
Total	£2 16s 6d	£3 15s 3d	£5 10s 0d	£4 17s 0d

Source: I. Archer, *The Pursuit of Stability: Social Relations in Elizabethan London* (Cambridge, 1991), p. 194; L. A. Botelho, *Old Age and the English Poor Law, 1500–1700* (Woodbridge, 2004), p. 148; K. Wrightson and D. Levine, *Poverty and Piety in an English Village: Terling, 1525–1700* (Oxford, 1979; new edn 1995), p. 40.

Table 5.4. Suggested subsistence budget per annum for an almsperson

	1580s	1590s	1690s
Food	£1 8s 6d	£2 5s 9d	£2 12s 0d
Clothing	5s 0d	5s 0d	5s 0d
Fuel	10s 0d	12s 0d	£1 0s 0d
Rent	Free	Free	Free
Total	£2 3s 6d	£3 2s 9d	£3 17s 0d

all highly tentative estimates, of course, but, the 1690s budget adjusted for inflation, might be used to compare with the almshouse stipends of the six English counties in Online Appendix C. The first line of the tables in that appendix reproduces Botelho's inflation index from Appendix 4 (column a), while the line below gives the suggested minimum subsistence budget from the 1690s, deflated for each decade in line with the index (from Appendix 4, column b). This deflation produces slightly lower sums of £2 0s 7d for the 1580s and £2 15s 4d for the 1590s than the figures given in the suggested subsistence budgets in Table 5.4. The 1690s budget in Table 5.4 was adapted from the similar exercise undertaken by Botelho, Wrightson and Levine, who used actual payments by poor law officials in Suffolk and Essex as a guide to the cost of living. Archer's figures for the earlier periods are based on London prices, and include some payments by the London guilds and livery companies to their members, which may explain the difference.

The lower figures produced by deflating the 1690s budget back to the 1550s have been used as the *minimum subsistence budget* throughout Online

Appendix C, representing the very least sum on which an almsperson could have been expected to survive. Known almshouse stipends from any decade on the chart can then be compared with the relevant minimum subsistence budget calculated for that decade. For example, the original stipends received by the occupants of the Leamington Hastings almshouse in its early decades are not known; but when the almshouse accounts begin in 1686 each almsperson was being paid £4 per year, which was raised to £4 6s 8d a few years later. These sums, compared with the relevant minimum subsistence budget for these decades (£3 6s 6d and £3 17s respectively), show that the Leamington Hastings almspeople were relatively well off, receiving stipends above subsistence level. Much less fortunate were the occupants of the Linton almshouse in Kent, founded in 1611, who were receiving only 13s 4d in a decade when the minimum subsistence level was £3 1s.

The striking finding from these comparisons is that, throughout the period, a third of almshouses, where information on the existence of a stipend is available, provided their occupants with allowances *below* the minimum subsistence level, and a sizeable number provided no stipend at all (see Figure 5.4). This was true especially for Kent, a relatively wealthy county in the south-east, where prices and the cost of living were likely to have been closest to the prices used in estimating the minimum subsistence level (see Figure 5.5). It was also largely true across the period, with little variation (see Figure 5.6).[159]

The implication of this is that, in many establishments, the almshouse stipend was not in itself enough for a poor person to survive on; it was, instead, merely a contribution towards a poor person's maintenance, as was, in a similar way, parish poor relief. Also of note is the considerable number of almshouses where no endowment was provided to maintain a stipend at all. Online Appendix C only includes almshouses where the amount (or lack) of stipend is known; there are many other foundations in the three counties, or as recorded by Jordan, where it is not known whether or not a stipend was paid. It is impossible to judge how the information from these establishments, if known, might affect the overall pattern. The fact remains, however, that large numbers of almshouse occupants in the early modern period did not receive sufficient in stipends and allowances to maintain themselves at a basic subsistence level.

***

How then did poorer almspeople survive? This is not immediately clear. Despite a considerable amount of work by historians in recent decades, the lack of evidence for the early modern period means that much about the

---

159   Here the column for stipends paid in the 1550s includes some almshouses founded before 1550.

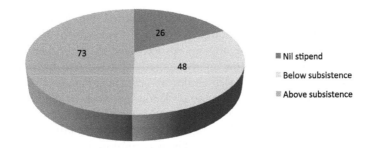

Figure 5.4. Almshouse stipends, 1550–1700
Source: Online Appendix C

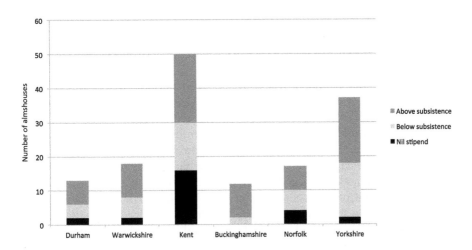

Figure 5.5. Almshouse stipends by county, 1550–1700
Source: Online Appendix C

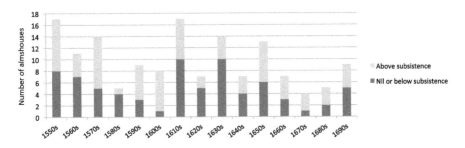

Figure 5.6. Almshouse stipends by decade, 1550–1700
Source: Online Appendix C

material lives of the poor remains essentially unknowable. It is probable that some almspeople worked, although the formal evidence for this is scanty. As shown in chapter 4, some almshouses expected their residents to work, although it is not known how many actually did so. Archbishop George Abbot's statutes for his hospital in Guildford (1622) commended 'any Brother or Sister who hath skill in any manuall Trade, do work in the same, either within the Hospitall or wthout, to gett some part of their living'.[160] William Harrison, admitted in 1660, had been the archbishop's tailor many years before, and while he was in the hospital he was employed to make the hospital gowns.[161] Goodwife Drew was given special dispensation in 1632 to live out of Hawkins' Hospital at Chatham for thirty days at a time, because she was 'a very necessary woman' who performed the duties of midwife or nurse in the parish.[162] In 1614, the almswomen of St John's Hospital in the centre of Sandwich were given 20s yearly by the town to look after poor people sent there; the following year the hospital was granted the market toll on corn, in return for which the almspeople were expected to sweep and clean the cornmarket.[163]

For most older people in the early modern period, there was no alternative but to keep working as long as they were able, in whatever capacity. The majority of almshouses, however, were intended for the poor and impotent, supposedly those who through age or disability were no longer able to work to support themselves. Indeed, the residents of St Bartholomew's Hospital, Sandwich, had to give up working their farm in 1684 and install a tenant, as it had become beyond their capacity.[164] Perhaps surprisingly, then, the seventeenth-century accounts of Sir John Boys' Jesus Hospital in Canterbury, show numerous payments to named almsmen for building and maintenance work they had undertaken around the almshouse. For instance, in 1637 Ralph Rachell was paid 1s 4d for carpentry, John Blacke 2d for scouring the gutter in the street, and Ralph Baylye 'and his man' a total of 5s 11d for brickwork, whitewashing, 'worke about the pumpe' and general repairs.[165] Boys' statutes had specified that his almspeople might engage in 'any manual trade or day labour'.[166] Less physically demanding work such as spinning, which could be undertaken in a person's own room, was the sort of occupation which almspeople, particularly women, would have been able to continue into extreme old age, although this has left no sign in the

---

160 Taylor, *Abbot's Hospital*, p. 135.
161 Taylor, *Abbot's Hospital*, p. 50.
162 MALSC CH108/21 Minute Book 1617–1691, p. 101.
163 Sandwich Local History Society, *Sandwich Almshouses 1190–1975*, Occasional Paper 2 (Sandwich, n.d.), pp. 5–6.
164 Sandwich Local History Society, *Sandwich Almshouses*, p. 12.
165 CCA U204/F/1 Jesus Hospital Ledger 1610–1637.
166 CCA U38/1 Jesus Hospital Memorandum Book.

records. Other almspeople might perform additional paid tasks within the establishment, such as caring for older residents or reading prayers. Goodman Bliss, for instance, was employed as the village schoolmaster while resident in the Leamington Hastings almshouse in the late seventeenth century, with his wife assisting him in teaching the smaller children.[167]

Others may have had private means. Some almshouses specified a maximum value of assets on admission (for instance, the £5 per year maximum allowed at the Lord Leycester Hospital), accepting that people who might be poor were not necessarily destitute.[168] One of the Lord Leycester brethren, John Stowe, was expelled in 1655 when it was discovered he had 'an estate of his owne for life' on which he could live.[169] At some of the wealthier institutions, the almspeople were entitled to a share of the dividends when leases were renewed, and in some cases this compensated for inadequate allowances. For instance, Abbot's Hospital, which paid each almsperson a generous 2s 6d per week in 1622 (£6 10s per year) continued to pay the same sum until the 1760s, by which time it was barely adequate. But the almspeople received occasional dividends which would have supplemented their stipend, for instance 4s 6d each on the renewal of a lease in 1676. William Harrison, mentioned above, was so poor at the time of his admission to Abbot's Hospital that he had to be loaned the money to equip his room, though for this to be noted in the hospital records it must have been an unusual occurrence.[170] His future income from the stipend, his employment and his share of occasional dividends, was presumably expected to be sufficient to give him a reasonable prospect of paying back this loan. At a few exceptional establishments such as the Lord Leycester Hospital, dividends could even exceed the stipend, if the founder's arrangements allowed the almspeople to share in them.

At more modest establishments, the resources which poorer people could call on to augment their stipends might well have included support from family and friends. The existence of living relatives was no bar to admission, and many almspeople would have received help from family in the same way as did other older people in the community.[171] Pat Thane suggests that the emphasis by historical demographers on the household composition of the nuclear family has resulted in an underestimate of the importance of kin networks and the contribution of non-resident family members in the lives of the elderly.[172] This is, of course, impossible to quantify. Co-residence was

167   WRO DR43a/195 Leamington Hastings Davis/Wheler Charity records 1686–1799.
168   Tibbits, 'Hospital', p. 127.
169   WRO CR 1600/19/26 Richard Nasebie's Patent 14 February 1655. Nasebie was awarded the vacancy created by the expulsion of John Stowe.
170   Taylor, Abbot's Hospital, p. 50.
171   See, for instance, Hindle, On the Parish?, pp. 48–58.
172   P. Thane, 'Old People and Their Families in the English Past', Charity, Self-Interest and Welfare in the English Past, ed. M. Daunton (London, 1996), pp. 113–38 (p. 121).

also an extremely common method of family support among poorer people. Different generations sharing a room would not have been unusual among the poor generally, and was surprisingly common in almshouses. Sometimes this was to provide practical help to an older relative, as when the aged Thomas Man had his daughter and granddaughter living with him in 1694 in his room in the Leamington Hastings almshouse, 'to nurse him & tend him' by reason of his 'great age & infirmity'.[173]

It could also be a way of pooling family income and resources. The frequent rules against co-residence in almshouses, and periodic orders to clear almshouses of strangers, suggest that sharing one's room, even with non-relatives, was attractive and not at all unusual. In the preamble to his order 'That noe strangirs lye within the Hospetall', George Abbot acknowledged the likelihood that the residents of his almshouse would 'draw their Children and kinsfolkes unto them'. But, like Archbishop Whitgift before him (see chapter 4) he absolutely forbade it, on pain of fines and expulsion.[174] The women of Lady Leveson's Hospital were criticised by the master in 1707 for entertaining their relations there.[175] Unofficial residents of the Westgate almshouses in Warwick, as revealed by the census of 1587, included Margery Watts and her two children aged twelve and eight – 'they all beg' – and Agnes Pardy and her three children. They were all ordered to be removed.[176] Similarly, Stratford Corporation had to order their almshouses 'to be clear'd of all persons except the Alm'speople, Especially Young Women and Children'.[177] While the share of a rent-free room would have been an attractive incentive for outsiders, the potential earnings of these unofficial residents and their practical assistance, for instance in collecting firewood, could have helped to augment the almsperson's income.

There is evidence that some people in early modern almshouses where stipends were low or non-existent received parish poor relief after admission. For instance, the poor women in Thomas Oken's almshouse, Warwick, founded in 1571 with stipends of only 4s per year, are unsurprisingly listed in the Warwick census of 1582 as receiving poor relief, in amounts of either 2d, 4d or 6d per week. The women in the Westgate almshouses, also in Warwick, were receiving similar amounts, although one, Agnes Twycrosse, received 8d. These variations would suggest that some of the women also had small earnings from employment.[178] Some almshouses emphasised that recipients

173   WRO DR43a/195 Leamington Hastings Davis/Wheler Charity records 1686–1799.
174   Taylor, *Abbot's Hospital*, p. 132.
175   E. Gooder, *Temple Balsall: From Hospitallers to a Caring Community, 1322 to Modern Times* (Chichester, 1999), p. 60.
176   T. Kemp, ed., *The Book of John Fisher, Town Clerk and Deputy Recorder of Warwick (1580–1588)* (Warwick, 1900), pp. 170–1.
177   SBT BRU15/15/106 Proposals for Regulating the Almshouse (late seventeenth–early eighteenth century).
178   Kemp, *John Fisher*, pp. 93, 94.

should be those who were poor through no fault of their own; being prevented from earning one's living having become incapacitated by old age or disability was considered a misfortune, to which no blame was attached. Similarly, aged recipients of parish poor relief were considered the 'deserving' poor, with no stigma attached to their receipt of alms in the earlier part of the period at least. The introduction of statutory poor relief through the Elizabethan poor laws did not at first distinguish the recipients of poor relief from other recipients of charity; all was considered charity. Even the increasing stigmatisation of parish paupers in the later seventeenth and eighteenth centuries, did not prevent the occupants of many almshouses continuing to be supported by parish poor relief, as is evidenced in the reports of the early-nineteenth-century charity commissioners.[179]

More common still was likely to have been support through informal relief, gifts and charity handouts. There is plentiful evidence from wills of donations and further endowments made to the occupants of almshouses. For instance, the sixteenth-century almshouse in the churchyard at Nuneaton, Warwickshire, is mentioned in the 1587 will of William Willoughby, who left 10s annually for fuel for the almshouses there.[180] Many casual gifts would have gone unrecorded. From the fifteenth century Yorkshire *maisons dieu* she has examined, Cullum believes that the main source of income for the poor occupants was likely to have been 'begging from door to door'.[181] Some almshouses rules specifically prohibited begging, for instance Archbishop Whitgift's rules for Eastbridge Hospital in Canterbury. Sir John Boys' statutes for the nearby Jesus Hospital, however, while outlawing begging within the city or elsewhere, yet allowed the almspeople to receive the benevolence of anybody 'willingly offering the same without craving', a nice distinction.[182] It is possible that outright begging by almshouse residents, seeking food and money door to door, did continue in practice, even if not officially condoned. Begging certainly seems to have remained culturally acceptable for poor people in the north of England.[183] In the nineteenth century, moreover, it was apparently the custom for the inhabitants of Boone's almshouse in Lee,

179   For instance, Forster's almshouse, Darlington, and Sir John Duck's almshouse, Chester-le-Street: HCPP, no. 21 (1829), p. 64; DRO DU/6/1/9 *Durham Chronicle* newspaper reports on local charities 1868.

180   HCPP, no. 29 (1835), p. 993.

181   P. Cullum, '"For Pore People Harberles": What Was the Function of the Maisondieu?', *Trade, Devotion and Governance: Papers in Late Medieval History*, ed. D. J. Clayton, R. G. Davies and P. McNiven (Stroud, 1994), pp. 36–54 (p. 46).

182   CCA CC Supp Ms/6 Alderman Gray's Notebook 1737–1780, p. 156; CCA U38/1 Jesus Hospital Memorandum Book.

183   See, for instance, the examples in J. Healey, *The First Century of Welfare: Poverty and Poor Relief in Lancashire 1620–1730* (Woodbridge, 2014), pp. 60, 176; and an example from Cumberland in 1706, Hindle, *On the Parish?*, p. 51.

Kent, to call regularly at the mansions of the wealthy families in the locality to collect 'surplus broken victuals' left out especially for them by their neighbours.[184] The location of many almshouses, beside the church (Figure 5.7), in the high street, or next to the guild hall, seems to have been purposefully designed to solicit alms from passers-by.

Abbot's Hospital in Guildford (1622) and Sandes Hospital in Kendal (founded in 1659) are both situated on the high street of their respective towns, and each had a collecting box for donations placed in the gateway. The one at Sandes is inscribed 'Remember the Poor Widows'. The location of many almshouses in the churchyard of the parish church, and the practice of distributing bread and alms at church after Sunday service, would have served as a reminder both of the almspeople's need and of their suitability as the objects of the parishioners' charity. At a time when donors were increasingly concerned about the deservingness of recipients of their charity, poor almspeople would have been an obvious choice. Almspeople were the 'approved' poor, their eligibility for largesse had already been demonstrated by their admission to the almshouse, so it was safe to donate to them.

Conclusion

It seems on the evidence presented here that not all occupants of almshouses can be regarded as the better-off poor. Tomkins has argued for a continuum of experience, 'from the comfortable to the impoverished'.[185] Their standard of living did not necessarily make almspeople a pauper elite, many of them were still obliged to adopt the same multiplicity of survival strategies as the poor in the community generally. Many aspects of their lives mirrored those of other poor people, including parish paupers. But almspeople did have some distinct advantages compared with other poor old people. The principal ones were the comfort and security of the accommodation; the permanence and regularity of the financial allowance, no matter how small; and their status as approved, deserving poor. Unlike the working poor, whose employment could be sporadic and insecure, many of the almspeople knew how much their weekly income was going to be. Unlike the recipients of parish poor relief, their allowances were dependent neither on assessed need, nor subject to the personal vagaries and possible prejudices of the parish overseers of the poor. Except in the few traditional almshouses where full board was provided and a communal existence encouraged, most residents of early modern almshouses were granted considerable independence and autonomy, freedom to spend

---

184   F. H. Hart, *History of Lee and its neighbourhood* (Greenwich, 1971), p. 10.
185   Tomkins, 'Retirement', p. 264.

Figure 5.7. Gramer's almshouses, Mancetter, Warwickshire, beside the parish church

the allowance as they chose, and live in reasonable privacy and comfort. The guaranteed nature of the stipend and the accommodation gave almspeople a measure of security which far exceeded that experienced by most poor people, whose lives were typically characterised by chronic insecurity and vulnerability. An almsperson could only be removed from their room, or lose their allowances, in clearly defined circumstances, such as a persistent breach of the establishment's rules. This is in clear contrast to the lives of most poor people, who usually had no guarantee of a regular income, particularly once they became old and frail, no guarantee of a roof over their heads and no protection against eviction by unscrupulous landlords.

Yet there were some disadvantages. Many almspeople received an inadequate stipend or none at all. For those who did receive a stipend, their income was fixed, and not responsive to individual need in the way that parish poor relief might be seen to operate. Also, almspeople may have had a more limited range of survival strategies open to them. For instance, many almshouses had rules forbidding residents to marry after admission, and sharing rooms with outsiders was generally prohibited.[186] Yet remarriage and co-residence were common strategies employed by many older people to help eke out a living in old age.[187] The occupants of almshouses had no access to land, apart from small garden plots, nor did they have common rights, giving them less opportunity to add to their income by their own efforts. In addition, their status as recipients of charity might have excluded them from undertaking less reputable forms of self-help, such as begging or pawning their clothes.

Overall, however, except for occupants of the very poorest almshouses, the advantages are likely to have outweighed the disadvantages. Admission to an almshouse was generally sought after, and Tomkins has suggested that the value placed on admission 'was higher than the material receipts alone would imply'. Tomkins proposes that the attraction was the status attached within the community to being a member of a particular institution, the confirmation of belonging, and the implied relationship with people of local standing such as patrons and trustees. Yet the benefits, particularly in terms of the accommodation, were real and tangible. Even more importantly, this status enabled almspeople to augment their income through the receipt of further donations and benefits. As a result, we cannot assume that the stated, paid allowance was their only income. Those admitted to an early modern almshouse may not necessarily have been among the ranks of the better-off

---

186   For instance, the rules of Abbot's Hospital, Guildford, chapters 5 and 11: Taylor, *Abbot's Hospital*, pp. 127, 132.

187   See, for instance, M. Pelling, 'Old Age, Poverty and Disability in Early Modern Norwich: Work, Remarriage, and Other Expedients', *Life, Death and the Elderly: Historical Perspectives*, ed. M. Pelling and R. M. Smith (London, 1991), pp. 62–84.

poor before admission, as is often assumed (and as may have become the case in later centuries), and the material benefits of an almshouse place may have differed widely, but admission placed many almshouse residents in a privileged position in relation to other groups of elderly poor.

6

Case Study: A Seventeenth-Century Welfare Republic – the Parish of Leamington Hastings and its Almshouse

> Almshouses require the attention of historians working at the local level if we are ever fully to understand their place in the history of the mixed economy of welfare.[1]

As outlined in the Introduction, there have been few attempts to place almshouses within the context of the overall range of accommodation and assistance provided for poor people in early modern England. This chapter will present a detailed study of one seventeenth-century almshouse in rural Warwickshire alongside an examination of the other welfare resources available in that parish, and will analyse the way these were utilised together for the benefit of the whole community. Leamington Hastings was chosen for this case study for two main reasons. First of all, relatively unusually for a parish of its size, it had an endowed almshouse for eight people, founded in 1607, with records and accounts surviving from 1686. Secondly, a range of other contemporary records have survived for the parish, including the overseers' accounts from 1655, the records of the Poors Plot charity from 1671, and the parish registers from 1559. Together with wills, hearth tax returns, quarter sessions orders and some manorial and settlement documents, this gave the potential to examine the almshouse alongside a number of other strands of the welfare economy in operation in this particular parish.[2]

John Broad has challenged historians to adopt 'a more holistic approach'

---

1   N. Goose, 'The English Almshouse and the Mixed Economy of Welfare: Medieval to Modern', *Local Historian* 40/1 (2010), 3–19 (p. 17).
2   The survival of this number of early documents for one parish is unusual. Steve Hindle points out that only nineteen Warwickshire parishes have surviving overseers' accounts from before 1760: S. Hindle, *The Birthpangs of Welfare: Poor Relief and Parish Governance in Seventeenth-Century Warwickshire*, Dugdale Society Occasional Paper 40 (Stratford-upon-Avon, 2000). Leamington Hastings' overseers' accounts commence a century before that; only two Warwickshire parishes' overseers' accounts are earlier. Moreover, only five other rural parishes in the county have a similar range of surviving early archival material, and none of these had an almshouse in this period.

in our attempts to understand the operation of parish relief in the time of the Old Poor Law.[3] He describes, for instance, the complementary nature of charitable funds and parish relief, which together provided a 'raft of security' for the poor, although how this operated in practice might differ from parish to parish according to local circumstances, resources and attitudes. Marjorie McIntosh, tracing the development of parish responsibilities for the poor in the sixteenth century, similarly points to the 'complementarity' and 'lack of rigid definition' in the networks of care which supported needy people, networks that were comprised of family, friends and neighbours as well as local institutions and officials.[4] The seventeenth century, however, saw the imposition and spread of formal relief beyond towns like Hadleigh, to include the whole country in a statutory system based on the parish and overseen by local justices of the peace. At the same time, the extensive deployment of commissioners for charitable uses in the early decades of the seventeenth century marked the beginning of a clearer distinction for the concept of private charity, and these developments might have been expected to disrupt the integration described by McIntosh. This case study will attempt to adopt Broad's 'holistic approach' in order to understand how the welfare system operated in this one parish, and the place of the almshouse within it.

The parish of Leamington Hastings had a range of resources available to it in the second half of the seventeenth century, most notably the almshouse. The survival of a number of different records means that an attempt can be made to examine in some detail how the parish used these resources together and in total to meet the needs of its poor. Despite its considerable endowment, the almshouse is characterised by its non-institutional nature and relatively lowly status. Unlike Trollope's stereotypical portrayal of an almshouse from this era, there was no master to supervise the almspeople; the residents wore no uniform gowns; there appear to have been no rules; and there was no obvious corporate life. Unlike the brethren of the Lord Leycester Hospital in Warwick, for example, the almspeople did not attend the parish church seated conspicuously towards the front of the nave, but on benches tucked away at the back of the church.[5] Yet evidently the almshouse was highly valued, and its survival was fought for at some considerable cost to the parish. From its records, moreover, it seems that the almshouse was fully integrated into local welfare provision, and its resources were at times used quite loosely to benefit

3 J. Broad, 'Parish Economies of Welfare, 1650–1834', *The Historical Journal* 42/4 (1999), 985–1006.

4 M. McIntosh, 'Networks of Care in Elizabethan English Towns: The Example of Hadleigh, Suffolk', *The Locus of Care: Families, Communities, Institutions and the Provision of Welfare in Antiquity*, ed. P. Horden and R. Smith (London, 1998), pp. 71–89.

5 WRO CR 1600/31 'The House Book', 10 April 1664; G. E. Wigram, 'History of Leamington Hastings' (Warwickshire County Record Office, typed, n.d.), p. 8.

the parish poor, overlapping at times with parish relief. This is in contrast with a self-governing institution such as the Lord Leycester Hospital, which had an existence completely independent of the town and parish of Warwick in which it was situated. With four-fifths of the places available allocated to men from outside the town, it could be argued that the Lord Leycester's main contribution to the relief of the town's poor was in dispensing casual relief to beggars at the almshouse gate.[6]

The Leamington Hastings almshouse is an example from a different end of the spectrum of provision than that usually presented in detailed studies.[7] It provides an opportunity to examine the role and importance in the local welfare economy of a smaller, locally run and non-stereotypical almshouse, as distinct from the more widely known, better documented and more formal institutions. This chapter will include an examination of the founding and rescue of the Humphrey Davis Hospital (as the almshouse was usually known); how the almshouse was used and managed within the parish; the availability and use of other charitable resources and of parish housing; and how the total resources of the parish were deployed to meet the needs of the poor.

Leamington Hastings is located in rural east Warwickshire, in the Felden region of mixed farming, between the market towns of Rugby to the north and Southam to the south. The parish is made up of four main settlements: the small village of Leamington Hastings itself with its church and manor house; the hamlet of Hill just outside the village; the larger settlement of Broadwell a mile and a half to the south; and the hamlet of Kites Hardwick a mile and a half to the north-east, where the road from Rugby to Southam and Banbury crosses the river Leam at Thurlaston Bridge. In the second half of the seventeenth century the parish contained around ninety households, suggesting a population of close to four hundred people.[8] Forty-eight per cent of households were assessed as exempt from paying the hearth tax in 1670, which was higher than the average for Warwickshire.[9]

---

6   For instance, the examples in chapter 4, n. 13.
7   For instance: P. Joyce, *Patronage and Poverty in Merchant Society: The History of Morden College, Blackheath 1695 to the Present* (Henley-on-Thames, 1982); S. Porter, *The London Charterhouse* (Stroud, 2009).
8   The 1670 hearth tax returns show ninety-four households, including the inhabitants of the almshouses and two empty cottages: T. Arkell and N. Alcock, eds, *Warwickshire Hearth Tax Returns: Michaelmas 1670* (Stratford-upon-Avon and London, 2010), pp. 54, 58, 281–2. Population of 396 has been calculated by multiplying ninety-two households by 4.3, as suggested in Hindle, *Birthpangs*, p. 10n. This is above the average of 271 for the Warwickshire parishes in Kineton hundred examined by Hindle, perhaps reflecting the number of separate settlements in the parish (pp. 34–5).
9   The average percentage of exempt households for Warwickshire in 1670 was 38%: Arkell and Alcock, *Warwickshire Hearth Tax*, p. 60.

The founding of the almshouse

For a parish of its size, Leamington Hastings in the seventeenth century was well endowed with charitable resources. The main benefactor had been Humphrey Davis, who in his will dated 17 December 1607 left land and property to support an almshouse for eight poor people. They were to be placed 'in my howse at Lemington which I have provided for the maintenaunce of those poore people'.[10] In his will this legacy is listed after the more detailed bequest of a fellowship and six exhibitions at Queens' College, Cambridge. It gives little indication of what sort of establishment Davis intended (or indeed may have already provided). No independent trust was established: his heirs were to be responsible for maintaining the poor inmates from the income of the lands they had inherited. Davis defined neither who the poor should be nor where they should be from; this was left to his heirs to determine.

The surviving almshouse building, next to the vicarage and close by the church and manor house, is of early-seventeenth-century origin, although considerably altered internally. It has been assumed by MacFarquhar and others, from the plaque on the front wall, that the building was erected by Sir Thomas Trevor in 1633.[11] But it is probable that this building is indeed the house provided by Humphrey Davis. Eight almspeople are named in a document relating to the court case in February 1634, which suggests that they were already in residence, and the Chancery suit judgement refers to the almshouse building as if it already existed.[12] Also, the three doors in the front of the building have apparently been cut through the walls, suggesting the adaptation of an existing domestic building to provide separate entrances to the individual apartments[13] (Figure 6.1).

Very little is known about Humphrey Davis, the founder of the almshouse. In his will of 1607 he refers to himself as a gentleman, but in their Chancery suit in the 1630s the parishioners describe him as 'schoolmaster'. He studied at Cambridge University, gaining his MA from Queens' College in 1575. He matriculated in 1567, which suggests that he was born around 1550. According to the college records he was from Warwickshire, but it is possible that he came from Wales. He was appointed rector of LLanfyllin, Montgomery in

---

10   TNA Prob/11/111 Will of Humphrey Davies (Davis) 1607.

11   G. I. MacFarquhar, *Leamington Hastings Almshouses and Poor's Plots* (Rugby, 1984), p. 5. For inscription, see opening of the 'Prologue'.

12   WRO DR43a/iii/12 Copy of Bill in Chancery relating to the hospital at Leamington Hastings; TNA C90/6 Commissioners for Charitable Uses: Confirmation in the case of Leamington Hastings charity, 7 Car. I.

13   L. F. Salzman, ed., *The Victoria History of the County of Warwick*, vol. 6: *Knightlow Hundred* (Oxford, 1951), p. 149. A similar arrangement saw separate entrances made in Lawrence Sheriff's house in Rugby, when he bequeathed his house to four poor men in 1567: W. H. D. Rouse, *A History of Rugby School* (London, 1898), p. 34.

Figure 6.1. Humphrey Davis almshouse, Leamington Hastings. The building was restored in the 1970s, at which point the three front doors were blocked up and some of the chimneys removed.

1571 while still at Cambridge, and Vicar of Darowen, also Montgomeryshire, in 1577.[14] Both parishes are in the diocese of St Asaph, and it is possible that he was related to Thomas Davis, Archdeacon and later Bishop of St Asaph, also a benefactor of Queens' College, Cambridge, who died in 1573.

Apart from his early clerical appointments, nothing further is known of Humphrey Davis's career until he was licensed schoolmaster for Leamington Hastings in 1605.[15] On his death in 1607 he left a considerable estate which the parishioners in the Chancery suit argued 'that hee had acquired by his labour'. This was presumably intended to emphasise for the purposes of the court case that his estate was not inherited family land to which his relatives might lawfully lay claim.[16] How he accumulated his wealth, what sort of man he was, and what was the motivation behind his bequest is not known. A few years before he made his own will in 1607, he witnessed that of Oliver Killingworth, described in this document as a labourer, who left the use of his money to the poor of Leamington Hastings, a sum of about £35.[17] More significantly, Davis was named as executor in the 1603 will of Thomas Squire, alias Irish, a husbandman. Most of Squire's personal bequests were in the form of debts owing to him, and he gave 5s yearly for the repair of the parish church. The rest of his goods he left for his executor to 'laye forthe to the best benefit he can', and 'the stocke beinge p[re]served' the annual profits were to be used for the poor of the parish, at the discretion of his executor.[18]

These three wills made within a few years of each other in the first decade of the seventeenth century seem to represent a departure from the previous tradition of charitable giving in the parish. Of the seventeen extant wills of Leamington Hastings parishioners from the last twenty years of the sixteenth century, four left small sums of money for the poor of the parish: George Perkins and Thomas Sedgely each left 6d 'for the poore mens boxe', John Over left 12d 'to the poore mens boxe of Lem[m]ington towurdes the Reliefe

14   J. Venn and J. A. Venn, eds, *Alumni Cantabrigienses*, part 1, vol. 2 (Cambridge, 1922), p. 15. Venn has Davis's second appointment as *Darwen*, but Darwen in Lancashire was not a parish in the sixteenth century, and it seems more likely that the place was Darowen, in the same diocese and county as Davis's first appointment.

15   LRO B/V/1/24 Liber Cleri, Lichfield and Coventry Diocese 1605. He had already been living in Leamington Hastings for some years at this point, as he was named in a land transfer of 1593: WRO DR43a/iii/5 Bond 22 February 1593. His brother Thomas lived in the neighbouring parish of Grandborough.

16   His will appears to have been the subject of an unsuccessful challenge by a group of Welsh relatives including Hugh Davis, *consanguineum* (possibly another brother), and his sisters Honoria, Grace, Ellinor and Alice, all living in the counties of Caernarvon or Denbigh: TNA Prob/11/115 Sentence of Humphrey Davies (Davis) 1610.

17   LRO cal. 1166.21 (1606); TNA C93/4/7 Commissioners for Charitable Uses: regarding the will of Oliver Killingworth.

18   LRO cal. 473.9 (1611) Will of Thomas Squier alias Fisher.

of the poore and needye', and John Pike left 5s 'to the poore of the parishe'.[19] Small one-off bequests continued into the seventeenth century; for instance, Thomas Walford (1625) left 4s 'to the poor people of Hill'; John Man (1636) 'five dozen [loaves] of white bread' to be given to the poor at his funeral; and Alexander Anstye (1655) 10s to the poor. This sort of bequest had, however, almost completely died out by the last decades of the seventeenth century.[20]

What is different about the bequests of Davis and Squire, and probably Killingworth, is that they provided permanent foundations, or stock from which the interest could be used to benefit the parish in perpetuity. As such, they fit the pattern identified by W. K. Jordan, whereby the early years of the seventeenth century, in particular, saw a marked increase in endowments for permanent charitable use. They do not, however, fit the profile of the benefactors so admired by Jordan. A labourer, a husbandman and an ordained schoolmaster were far removed in wealth and social status from the gentry and merchant aristocracy identified by Jordan as the principal actors in his philanthropic revolution. The subsequent history of Squire's and Davis's legacies emphasises, moreover, just how vulnerable testamentary bequests were to the inaction or ineptitude of executors, or to the greed and envy of relatives. Jordan's aggregated figures enumerate wishes, that is, the donor's aspirations, but they do not take into account whether those wishes actually resulted in the charitable benefits intended.[21]

In this case it seems that not only was Davis's own will subverted, resulting in costly legal proceedings for the parish, but also that Davis's inaction as executor of Squire's will caused the parish some loss. From an application by a group of parishioners to the Lichfield and Coventry Consistory Court in 1611, it is clear that, despite being named as executor, Humphrey Davis had not applied for the will to be proved after Squire's death in 1603.[22] By the terms of the will, Davis was to use Squire's legacy to benefit the poor at his discretion. It is possible that Davis had intended to do this by providing schooling in the parish, hence his application to be licensed schoolmaster in 1605. But when Davis died in 1607, the remains of Squire's legacy passed with Davis's estate into the hands of Davis's executor, his nephew Edmund Davis. By his will, Davis left his lands to his brother Thomas and Thomas's wife Katherine (Edmund's parents) for their lives, and then to be shared by Edmund and his siblings, with the profits of the lands to be used to support

19   LRO cal. 125.22 (1581), cal. 423.16 (1589), cal. 60.11 (1591), and 143.10 (1598).
20   TNA Prob/11/145 Will of Thomas Walford 1625; LRO cal. 1405.18 (1636); TNA Prob/11/248 Will of Alexander Ansttey 1655. The exception towards the end of the century was the Rev. John Allington's request to send 'charities to every poor neighbour' rather than gathering a 'multitude' at his funeral in 1683: TNA Prob/11/373 Will of John Allington 1683.
21   As such, they cannot be used as an accurate representation of the scale of charitable giving, although this should not diminish the importance of Jordan's achievement.
22   LRO cal. 473.9 (1611).

the bequests to Queens' College, Cambridge and the Leamington Hastings almshouse. But some time before 1611, Edmund Davis died intestate, leaving both Squire's and Davis's legacies in legal limbo.[23] Once Thomas and Katherine Davis had both died, the estate then passed into the hands of Edmund's brother, also called Thomas. This Thomas apparently felt under no obligation to fulfil the charitable responsibilities of the two wills.

Gaining control of the almshouse

Many charitable endowments were abused and misappropriated, and the Davis charity seemed destined to disappear, along with the remains of Squire's legacy, when Sir Thomas Trevor bought the lordship of the manor of Leamington Hastings in 1630 and immediately became actively involved in its affairs.[24] As lord of the manor, a leading government lawyer and one of the Barons of the Exchequer, Trevor assisted the parishioners in bringing a suit in Chancery in 1633 under the terms of the Statute of Charitable Uses to wrest control of the hospital's assets from Thomas Davis. He was alleged to have taken the income intended for the hospital 'to his own use without placinge any one poore person in the said house' and had 'gone about utterly to defraud, defeat and overthrow the said charitable use'.[25] According to an account written around 1685, the land Humphrey Davis had intended for the support of the hospital was 'embezled and sold away' by his nephew Thomas until the arrival of Sir Thomas Trevor, when Matthew Over 'office holder in the said p[ar]ish was imployed to begin to mannage and to sollicite a sute ... for the Recovery of the said Lands, towards w[hi]ch the freeholders and tenants did very freely lend their money'.[26]

Unravelling the facts of the case from the Chancery records, it appears that things were not as straightforward as this local memory suggests. It seems that Matthew Over, at the time one of the Overseers of the Poor for Leamington Hastings, had in 1628 accepted the sum of £110 from Thomas Davis in lieu of support for the almshouse.[27] But after Trevor had instigated the Chancery case this arrangement was deemed unacceptable by the Commissioners for

23 LRO cal. 473.9 (1611).
24 G. Jones, *History of the Law of Charity 1532–1827* (Cambridge, 1969), pp. 20, 22.
25 TNA C93/13/14 Commissioners for Charitable Uses: Inquisitions and Decrees, Leamington Hastings 1631–1632; TNA C90/6 Commissioners for Charitable Uses: Confirmation in the case of Leamington Hastings charity, 7 Car. I; WRO DR43a/iii/12 Copy of Bill in Chancery relating to the hospital at Leamington Hastings.
26 WRO DR43a/194 Leamington Hastings Records of the Poors Plot Charity.
27 TNA C90/6. Thomas Davis appears to have come to a similar agreement with the master and fellows of Queens' College, Cambridge to make them a payment of £250 in lieu of supporting the fellowship and exhibitions there, of which £100 had been paid.

Charitable Uses, and the eventual outcome was that a very aggrieved Thomas Davis was deprived of the hospital lands. Also, the parish was allowed to retain the £110 they had received from him, to cover the remainder of Squire's legacy, and for 'repairinge and further fillinge of the said Almeshouse', with any residue to be used 'toward the defraieinge and paiment' of the parishioners' 'charges and expences'.[28] Thomas Davis not only lost the lands but any involvement in the hospital, for which an independent trust was established with ten local feoffees, comprising five local gentry, including Sir Thomas Trevor and his son, and five leading parishioners.[29]

There is no mention of the original agreement between Thomas Davis and Matthew Over in subsequent parish accounts of the case, perhaps because the collusion with this attempt to alienate an endowed charity did not reflect well on the parishioners. But there was some question later of what had happened to the money Thomas Davis had paid, and to other money lent by individual parishioners to pay the costs of the court case, with Matthew Over's son John having to answer for the whereabouts of parish money after his father's death.[30] The case amply demonstrates both the vulnerability of so many early modern charitable endowments, and the necessity of the Elizabethan Statute of Charitable Uses. It also highlights the heavy responsibilities laid on quite ordinary people when they served as parish officials. Until Sir Thomas Trevor's critical intervention, the parishioners seem to have been willing to reach an accommodation with Thomas Davis. Perhaps the initial acceptance of the offer from Davis of £110 in settlement was in anticipation of the likely decades of struggle to come for Matthew Over and his successors in trying to extract payment for maintaining the almshouse from Thomas Davis and his descendants thereafter.

The success of the case not only guaranteed the survival of the almshouse, but changed its character. Without an independent body of trustees, the almshouse could either have remained a family-run charity for the benefit of those upon whom the family chose to expend their patronage or, as happened in this case, could have fallen victim to neglect and misappropriation. Through the suit in Chancery, Sir Thomas Trevor and the parish, by wresting control of

---

28   TNA C90/6.

29   The ten feoffees were: Sir Thomas Trevor, his son Thomas Trevor Esq., Sir Edward Peyto, John Sample Esq., Roland Wilcox Esq., and 'yeomen and inhabitants' Matthew Over, Richard Watson, John Mason, John Clarke and James Mason.

30   TNA C93/30/28 Chancery Inquisition 1669. The situation was complicated by another sum of £110 in parish stock which needed to be accounted for, some of which also seems to have been spent on legal fees in the Chancery suit. This £110 was made up of £50 from Thomas Squire's legacy, and £60 from a former vicar, Thomas Lever, apparently in recompense for his absence from the parish. The attempt in the court case to reconstruct how this had been spent (and how much had been lost) takes up the beginnings of the Poors Plot charity accounts: WRO DR43a/194 Records of the Poors Plot Charity.

the endowment from Davis's heirs, brought the foundation under the control of locally appointed trustees for the benefit of local people. Had Thomas Davis not misappropriated the almshouse assets, he and his heirs, like so many landed families, could have used the almshouse for their own aged retainers in perpetuity. Although this had not been specified by Humphrey Davis, the almshouse now became used solely to benefit the parish poor. There is an appropriateness about this as the costs of the legal action, which must have been considerable, seem to have been met largely from parish resources. Although this may have been a contentious decision, those involved seem to have been quite satisfied that it was acceptable to spend the parish stock in this way to win back for the community assets they described in 1685 as being worth £800.[31] This may have been an exaggeration, but what is clear, however, is the value the land provided in income. Expenditure by the almshouse in 1694, for example, was £31 12s 9d, double the average amount expended by the parish on poor relief at the time (see Table 6.1). This endowment became a benefit not just to potential almspeople, but as local control of the almshouse enabled parish paupers to be placed there, it lessened the burden on the whole community by reducing the parish rates. Using charitable resources in this way indicates a pragmatic attitude, and would have made eminent sense at a time when there were less rigid conceptual boundaries. But it was already disapproved of by some commentators, and in later years the Charity Commissioners would insist on a narrow interpretation of charitable uses, preventing charitable funds being used more generally to benefit anyone other than the direct intended recipients.[32]

It is clear that it was the intervention of Sir Thomas Trevor which enabled the case to be successfully concluded to the benefit of the parishioners.[33] He probably used his legal contacts and political influence in pursuit of the case, and is unlikely to have been motivated simply by financial considerations. Trevor was a wealthy man from a career spent accumulating public offices, and, at that point, was still at the height of his powers.[34] He was new

31   'As for and concerning the parish Stocke or money given or raised for the Releife of the poore of the parish of Leamington Hastings': WRO DR43a/194 Records of the Poors Plot Charity.

32   See the discussion in S. Hindle, *On the Parish? The Micro-Politics of Poor Relief in Rural England c.1550–1750* (Oxford, 2004), pp. 142–6. Hindle notes that in 1675 the Warwickshire bench had to remind overseers not to use bequests for the poor to reduce the rates.

33   Without Thomas Trevor to use his influence on their behalf, Queens' College, Cambridge lost Davis's fellowship and exhibitions in 1644: Venn and Venn, *Alumni Cantabrigienses*, p. 15.

34   Trevor was educated at Shrewsbury School and called to the Bar in 1603. He was appointed solicitor general to Prince Charles in 1611 and was knighted in 1619. Between 1601 and 1624 he served as a member of Parliament for various places, and in 1625 was appointed king's serjeant and one of the barons of the exchequer. In 1637 he gave judgement in favour of the Crown's right to collect ship money, for which he was impeached by Parliament in 1641. Nevertheless he accepted the authority of Parliament at the outbreak of the Civil War and refused an order from the king to attend him at Oxford. After Charles' execution he retired from public life and died at Leamington

to the role of lord of the manor, and most probably was keen to make his mark locally, unlike his predecessors, the Staffords, who had been noticeable absentees and unengaged in local affairs. Trevor was subsequently buried in the parish church where he had already commissioned a striking memorial to himself, sited in the chancel. He was typical of many of the gentry in seventeenth-century Warwickshire who were 'comparative newcomers to the shire', and who, like other minor gentry, 'were often of very insecure status'.[35] His son Thomas, born in 1612, was created a baronet in 1641, and Trevor no doubt had hopes of founding a titled dynasty.[36] In this he was not unusual. His intervention in the almshouse case ensured his name on a plaque in the centre of the village, representing his generosity, honour and virtue, these being the marks of entitlement to gentry status in the absence of birth and breeding.[37]

As this account demonstrates, those who executed donors' bequests or ensured the survival of endowments could be as important in shaping the future role and function of foundations as the original donors; as, indeed, could be the people who became involved in running such establishments. Van Leeuwen theorises that, for the elite, involvement might have a number of possible motivations but was always principally self-interested.[38] The conclusion reached by Cavallo, for instance, is that association with local hospitals enabled the Italian urban elites she studied to exercise patronage and influence in allocating valuable places.[39] The parish elite running Davis's almshouse might have been motivated by self-interest, but it was in a less obvious guise than that described by Cavallo. The trustees who attended the recorded meetings were more often the local parish representatives and the vicar, rather than the absentee gentry members who only made occasional appearances, so the opportunity did exist for the exercise of local patronage. However, there appears to be no evidence, in the seventeenth century at least,

Hastings in 1656: E. I. Carlyle, rev. W. H. Bryson, 'Trevor, Sir Thomas (c. 1573–1656)', *ODNB* (Oxford, 2004), http://www.oxforddnb.com/view/article/27735 (accessed 16 December 2013).

35   A. Hughes, *Politics, Society and Civil War in Warwickshire, 1620–1660* (Cambridge, 1987), p. 37.

36   However, the second Sir Thomas Trevor died childless in 1676 and the manor of Leamington Hastings descended to Charles Wheler, grandson of the first Sir Thomas's sister.

37   F. Heal and C. Holmes, *The Gentry in England and Wales, 1500–1700* (Basingstoke, 1994), p. 372. See also the seventeenth-century view of the traditional obligations of the lord of the manor quoted in A. Nicolson, *Earls of Paradise* (London, 2008), p. 24.

38   M. H. D. Van Leeuwen, 'Logic of Charity: Poor Relief in Preindustrial Europe', *Journal of Interdisciplinary History* 24/4 (1994), 589–613. See also the discussions in C. Jones, 'Some Recent Trends in the History of Charity', *Charity, Self-Interest and Welfare in the English Past*, ed. M. Daunton (London, 1996), pp. 51–63, and A. Kidd, 'Philanthropy and the "Social History Paradigm"', *Social History* 21 (1996), 180–92.

39   S. Cavallo, 'The Motivation of Benefactors: An Overview of Approaches to the Study of Charity', *Medicine and Charity Before the Welfare State*, ed. J. Barry and C. Jones (London, 1991), pp. 46–62 (pp. 52, 56, 60).

that admissions were influenced by personal relationships and favouritism. On the contrary, almshouse places and resources appear to have been used for the benefit of the whole parish. Nevertheless, the actions of the trustees could arguably be ascribed to a combination of altruism, self-importance, and a desire to maintain social order and economic stability in the parish.

How the parish used the almshouse

The meeting of the trustees on 18 June 1694 records a scenario entirely typical of the sort that has attracted the attention of many writers on almshouses.[40] Thomas Man was ordered to expel his unmarried daughter Jane from the almshouse because she had become pregnant.[41] Here we have a human interest story, enlivened by scandal, with named individuals making up the dramatis personae. The reaction of the trustees seems to confirm the impression that an almshouse, described in this case as a 'house dedicated to a pious use and charity', was intended to be a quasi-religious institution, and that regulating the behaviour of the poor was a prime function of these institutions. Yet the evidence does not bear out this interpretation. There is no suggestion that the Leamington Hastings almshouse inmates were expected to undertake any rigorous devotions or religious observances, and it does not appear that they were expected to attend church any more than other parishioners. The almshouse trustees may have made a point of expressing their disapproval of Jane's behaviour, but they had little option as she was committed to the house of correction for bastardy at the next quarter sessions.[42] The new rule ordered by the trustees in response to the scandal, that no one over the age of twelve or who was not born in the parish could lodge with an almshouse resident without consent, seems fairly hollow given that Jane herself had been granted permission to reside there.[43] Finally, in 1706, Jane Man was once again allowed to live in the almshouse. By this time she was forty-eight years old, still single, her parents were dead and her illegitimate child, if alive, presumably now apprenticed or in service. The fact that Jane was allowed back into the almshouse suggests that she had no other means of support, and that it was a pragmatic decision by the trustees which absolved the parishioners from having to relieve her through the poor rates.[44] As chapter 4 has demonstrated,

---

40 See, for instance, MacFarquhar, *Leamington Hastings*, p. 17.

41 WRO DR43a/195 Leamington Hastings Davis/Wheler Charity records 1686–1799.

42 WQS, vol. 9, p. 107.

43 The apparent acceptance of children under twelve in the almshouse is also interesting in view of the discussion about almshouse occupants in chapter 4.

44 This may not have been a straightforward decision, however. In the parish register a cross appears beside the entry recording her birth and baptism on 23 January 1657/8, suggesting that

only a minority of almshouses had formal rules, and this example would appear to confirm the suggestion made earlier that the importance of rules and regulations has been overemphasised in the almshouse literature.

More interesting, and possibly more typical, is the problem with which the trustees of the almshouse were grappling when they met on 20 October 1696. Despite an increase in the endowment by Dame Dorothy Wheler, and the building of an additional four rooms at the hospital, the income from the charity's lands was proving insufficient to support more than seven poor people. The trustees resolved to revalue some of the leases, and to construct additional tenements on their land to increase the rents 'by letting apartments to the parish for poor people as there shall bee occasion'. Sir William Wheler agreed to provide building materials from 'some old tenements' that stood on Bradwell Green which he wished to remove. In the meanwhile, their solution was to allocate one of the new rooms to old William Chittam as 'an eighth poor' on a reduced stipend until the matter of the rents could be resolved.[45] This was not the first time that the trustees had been forced to improvise. In 1692 they had agreed that the interest on a £10 bond should be paid to the parish overseers to give 6d per week to Richard Over of Hardwick, 'as far as it will goe in the way of ease to the parish of so much of their weekly contribution that being as much as wee can yett spare towards an eighth person to bee of the hospitall'.[46]

The continual problem of balancing the charity's books is demonstrated by the payment of £1, rather than the usual 10s, to the curate Mr Kingsborough for keeping the accounts in 1696, 'so troublesome a year for money & loss in money'.[47] The work involved in keeping this charity afloat was amply justified by the benefits it brought to the whole community. The poor benefited through the possibility of an almshouse place at the end of their lives, and the ratepayers were relieved of some of the burden of supporting their elderly poor.

Who were the almspeople?

Some of the occupants of the almshouse in the seventeenth century can be identified by name. The first listing occurs in February 1634 with eight almspeople, seven men and one woman, included in a petition to Chancery

someone had taken the trouble to check that she was indeed the parish's responsibility: WRO DR43a/1 Leamington Hastings Register of Baptisms, Marriage and Burials 1559–1704.
45   WRO DR43a/195 Leamington Hastings Davis/Wheler Charity records 1686–1799.
46   WRO DR43a/195 Leamington Hastings Davis/Wheler Charity records 1686–1799.
47   The economic situation in 1696 was particularly desperate, as the crisis resulting from the Great Recoinage compounded the impact of poor harvests and war with France.

regarding Thomas Davis's refusal to comply with the order to pass his uncle's lands to the new trustees for the hospital.[48] Some of the names on this list can be linked to individuals in the parish register, although complete assurance about identification is not always possible because of the recurrence of the same forename within families, and various gaps in the register where parts of pages have become illegible.[49] Nothing is known of Edward Eares, although the Ayres family feature regularly in parish documents of the seventeenth century, suggesting that he was a local man. A Widow Ayres was receiving parish poor relief in the 1680s.[50] Amy Gisborne, the widow, was married in the parish in 1603, suggesting she was probably born some time before 1580. Her husband John appears to have died in 1608, leaving her with three small daughters under five. Her life was, in all likelihood, hard and impoverished. In 1634, when she was in the almshouse, she would probably have been in her late fifties or early sixties.

Two of the men, John Benson and Henry Hall, also appear to have been at least in their fifties. Hall had a daughter in 1609, who died the same year, suggesting that he too was born around 1580 or earlier. John Benson was one of a large number of Bensons, making identification difficult. According to the parish register a John Benson senior died a pauper in 1608. A John junior is mentioned as having children baptised in 1603 and 1605, suggesting that he was also born before 1580.[51] Foulke Grolliver had a child baptised in 1590, which suggests that he was born around 1565 or before, making him probably in his late sixties or seventies at the time of the petition. He died in 1641. The ages of the other three almsmen can be tentatively suggested from births noted in the parish register: Richard Pedley born 1569, making him sixty-four; and Thomas Garrett and John Wilcox, both born 1564, making them sixty-nine.[52] At these ages, all these almspeople would have been considered old by contemporaries.[53]

In terms of their economic standing, the only information with which the names of these early almspeople can be compared is a list of tenants and a

---

48 WRO DR43a/iii/12 Copy of Bill in Chancery relating to the hospital at Leamington Hastings. The eight names are: Foulke Grolliver, Thomas Garrett, John Willcox, Edward Eares, Henry Hall, Aymy Gisburne, widow, John Benson and Richard Pedler (or Pedley).

49 Even where the registers are complete, the amount of accompanying information is variable, and not always sufficient to distinguish between two people of similar names, or to identify the correct generation in a family. See the discussions in E. A. Wrigley, ed., *Identifying People in the Past* (London, 1973), pp. 5–15, 64–8.

50 WRO DR43a/20 Leamington Hastings Overseers' Accounts 1681–1704.

51 However, after John's wife died in 1606, further children are born to a John junior (in 1611 and 1612) suggesting either that he had remarried or that the epithet had been passed to another John Benson.

52 WRO DR43/1 Leamington Hastings Register of Baptisms, Marriage and Burials 1559–1704.

53 L. Botelho, 'The Seventeenth Century', *The Long History of Old Age*, ed. P. Thane (London, 2005), pp. 113–74 (pp. 115–17).

valuation of their property, compiled in 1629 for the sale of the manor to Sir Thomas Trevor. None of the almspeople appears as a tenant in 1629, which would suggest that most, if not all of them, were already inmates of the almshouse by that time. This lends weight to the possibility that the almshouse was already operational in some form before Sir Thomas Trevor's intervention. Alternatively, if they were the poorest and oldest parishioners, they might have been illegal cottagers or inmates in other people's houses. Without the information from a household census or something similar, it is hard to be certain. Some people appearing on the tenants' list share a surname with one of the almshouse residents, and were probably from the same family, but it is not possible to say how closely related they were. For instance, Jeffrey Hall is listed as renting a cottage in Leamington worth 10s per year, William Pedley has one messuage worth £3, Jeffrey (or Nicholas) Wilcox has a cottage in Bradwell valued at £1.[54] More substantial tenants were a Gisborne lately holding a farm at Hill worth £13, and Thomas and William Benson, holding farms worth £6 10s and £8 respectively. These were relatively modest sums for farms on this manor. The valuations of the thirty farms listed ranged from £6 to £30, with the average at £12 10s; typical rents for a cottage were from 10s to 30s. Taken together, this information suggests that the early residents of the almshouse were local people, generally elderly, and drawn from the less well-off strata of parish society.

After this early listing, there is a gap until the next mention of probable almshouse residents in the parish register. Widow Cleaver of Hill, for instance, described in the parish register as *ex Eleemosinariis una*, was buried in 1670, followed the same day by Widow Johnson *ex Eleemosinariis altera*. Isabella Canning *ex Eleemosinary* was buried in 1674, and Alice Blythe 'one of ye Hospitall' in 1679.[55] From 1682, annual lists of burials in woollen were being recorded in the overseers' accounts and, either here or in the parish register, some people would be noted as 'beadswoman' or 'a member of the Hospitall'. After the almshouse accounts and minutes begin in 1686, individual residents are often named; Thomas Man, for instance, had a door lock fitted in 1690. When admissions are recorded they often note whose place had become vacant, giving further names. A review of the hospital seems to have been undertaken in 1698, when the names of all current residents were listed, the first such complete list since 1634. At this point there were ten

---

54   WRO CR 1319/95 Manor of Leamington Hastings list of tenants 1629. The valuations are usually described as 'will be at the end of the aforesaid lease worth per annum …'.
55   WRO DR43a/1 Leamington Hastings Register of Baptisms, Marriage and Burials 1559–1704. It is probable, although not absolutely certain, that the term *ex eleemosinary* refers to a resident of the almshouse rather than a recipient of parish relief. Widow Cleaver had received poor relief in 1667, but Widow Johnson does not appear at all in the overseers' accounts.

residents occupying the eight places: one man, two couples, and five widows, a noticeable gender shift from the earlier listing.[56]

In total, thirty-three named individuals can be identified as having been resident in the hospital at some time between 1674 and 1720 (and a further three were supported elsewhere from hospital funds). The great majority of these names also appear in the 1674 hearth tax assessment, and appear to be identifiable as the same individuals, or, if not, members of the same family.[57] For instance, William Chittam, a labourer, was admitted to one of the almshouse rooms in 1696, where he died in 1698. The following year his son John was also allocated a place, dying shortly afterwards. William had appeared in the hearth tax returns in 1674 as exempt. An Adam Oakley was exempted from the tax in 1674 and in 1686 his widow Jane died in the almshouse. Eleanor Blythe, dying in the almshouse in 1720 aged ninety-six, was the widow of Thomas Blythe, exempted from the hearth tax in 1674. Of the twenty-two almshouse residents who can be identified in the hearth tax returns, eighteen were assessed as exempt, or appear to be relatives of those who had been assessed as exempt. Of those paying the tax, Thomas Man, who died in the almshouse in 1696, had been assessed on one hearth, as had Thomas Isaacson, whose daughter Susannah was given a place in the almshouse in 1703.

Hearth tax assessments and the exempt category cannot be absolutely relied on as an indicator of who was poor. According to Arkell, 'not all the exempt were living in poverty'.[58] But while the poverty of some of those exempt may have been 'relative' rather than absolute, this still confirms the picture suggested earlier in the century, that the majority of the almspeople were of lowly economic status. The exceptions were two widows, Jane Twiggar who died in the almshouse in 1708 aged ninety-two, and Faith Mathews who was a member of the almshouse but who died at Coventry in 1713. Jane's husband Richard Twiggar, a tailor, had been assessed on one hearth in 1670, and two hearths in 1674. His home was often mentioned in the overseers' accounts as the place where they met, and it may have been an inn or alehouse.[59] Faith was the widow of Thomas Mathews, Sir Thomas

---

56 See the discussion in chapter 4. The ten residents were: Schoolmaster Henry Bliss and his wife, Widow Scotten, Widow Turner, Widow Hawten, Widow Russell, Widow Over, Matthew (Richard?) Over, and Richard Wheeler and his wife.

57 WRO QS 11/56 Hearth Tax Assessment Book 1674, Knightlow Hundred, Southam Division. The 1674 assessment was chosen for this exercise because it is the one closest in date to the commencement of the surviving almshouse records. It is not known whether the assessment includes among the exempt those people already resident in the almshouse.

58 T. Arkell, 'The Incidence of Poverty in England in the Later Seventeenth Century', *Social History* 12 (1987), 23–47 (p. 33).

59 'It. Spent at Twiggers when wee made a levy and taken the constables accounts 4s 6d': WRO DR43a/19 Leamington Hastings Overseers' Accounts 1676.

Trevor's agent and probable tenant of the manor house, who had paid tax on eleven chimneys. The presence of these two widows suggests it is possible that, by the early eighteenth century, a shift might have been occurring in who was regarded as eligible, with some better-off people beginning to be admitted into the almshouse. This is reflected in the evidence of wills left by Leamington Hastings parishioners. None of the seventeenth-century almshouse residents left a will, which is not surprising, but does contrast with the evidence from other Warwickshire almshouses such as Stoneleigh, Stratford and Temple Balsall. Here, a few extant wills left by inmates suggest that these almshouses included people who were not the very poor.[60] Jane Twiggar did not leave a will, but letters of administration were granted to her son Nicholas after her death in 1708, suggesting there was some property at stake. Faith Mathews' husband Thomas died in 1685, leaving an estate worth £180 1s 5d to his wife and children. Similarly, Elizabeth Mathews, who died in the almshouse in 1723, was most probably the widow of John Mathews whose inventory in 1708 totalled £144 12s 2d. A John Mathews, probably brother to Thomas, had been assessed on five hearths in 1674. These three widows appear to come from relatively, if not very well-off families.

Until this point, the almshouse inhabitants had been identifiable as among the poorest in the parish, with no evidence to suggest that particular families were privileged. Many of the seventeenth-century almspeople had, in fact, been parish paupers prior to admission, as the following examples demonstrate. Ann Tue, 'maiden', who was buried 'out of the hospital' in 1687, aged seventy-eight, was on parish relief for years. It is possible that she was crippled in some way, as the overseers' accounts mention not only several purchases of shoes or boots for her (for instance, in 1658, 1667, 1669, and 1675) but also record that, in 1674, 2s was 'payd to Mary Scotton for cuareing Ann Tewes lege'. From 1665 the parish paid for her to be boarded with various parishioners.[61] When the almshouse accounts begin in 1686 she was an almshouse resident; one of the first items of expenditure recorded is 'pd for a pare of shoose for Ann Tew 2s 6d'. The hospital paid 1s for her burial in 1687, and a meeting of the trustees in 1688 noted 'Widow Horton is chosen to succeed Ann Tue in the hospitall'.[62] Margery Guilliams 'a diseased person' and her 80-year-old widowed mother were ordered to receive 12d weekly from the parish by the Warwick quarter

60   Stoneleigh: N. W. Alcock, *People at Home: Living in a Warwickshire Village, 1500–1800* (Chichester, 1993), p. 143; Stratford: J. Jones, ed., *Stratford-upon-Avon Inventories*, vol. 1: *1538–1625*, Dugdale Society 39 (Stratford-upon-Avon, 2002), pp. 55, 171; Temple Balsall: WRO CR 112/Ba65/47 Inventory of Bridget Phipps 9 March 1713/4, CR 112/Ba45 Will of Bridget Phipps 16 November 1713, and CR 112/Ba55/2 Will of Dorothy Clarke 30 March 1729.
61   WRO DR43a/19 Leamington Hastings Overseers' Accounts 1655–1679: 'Paid to Thomas Mathewes for ye keeping of Ann Tue and for providing hir thinges necessary for hir – £1 8s od' (1665); 'Paid to John Mathews for Ann Tues board at 12d a week' (1672).
62   WRO DR43a/195 Leamington Hastings Davis/Wheler Charity records 1686–1799.

sessions in 1661.[63] There is no record of this maintenance in the overseers' accounts, but the overseers paid 11s 2d for repairs to their house in 1662 and 3s for burying Widow Guilliams in 1665.[64] That same year Margery was indicted for stealing three pecks of wheat and barley, to the value of 10d. She confessed and was sentenced to be whipped.[65] How she supported herself for the next nine years is not known but, along with others, she received a dole of 1s 6d from the executors of John Masters' will in 1669.[66] Margery appears in the 1670 hearth tax records as exempt, and in 1674 Mary Scotten was paid 9s by the overseers for lodging her for six months.[67] It is not known when Margery was admitted to the hospital, but she died there in 1686.

Willam Chittam was admitted to the almshouse on a part stipend in 1696. He was a poor labourer, and had previously made many appearances in the overseers' accounts prior to his admission to the hospital, receiving payments for work done rather than relief. Examples include: 'It. payd to William Chitom for catchin the burds 1s 6d' (1676); 'William Chittom for catching the birds 2s 6d' (1676); 'Item paide to William Chitham for chasen of sparras 4s 8d' (1678); 'paid to William Chetam for killen of sparrows 1s' (1683), and so forth.[68] It was the churchwardens' responsibility to get rid of sparrows, but here the expenditure is clearly being borne by the overseers, probably as a pragmatic alternative to supporting Chittam through poor relief. Other almshouse residents had previously been paid by the overseers to lodge or look after other poor people, for instance when they were sick. Mary Scotten, mentioned above, had lodged Ann Tue; Mary Rushall was paid a shilling in 1682 'for locken to ye widdow Cooks when she was sick'.[69] Henry Bliss, living in the almshouse with his wife Alice, was paid from the Poors Plot charity accounts to teach the village children. He was probably the Henry Bliss of Kites Hardwick listed as exempt from the hearth tax in 1670, who had been in gaol for debt some years earlier. If so, he had 'a great charge of children to provide for', and he and Alice were frequently in receipt of poor relief in the 1660s and 1670s.[70]

63 WQS, vol. 4, p. 158.
64 WRO DR43a/19 Leamington Hastings Overseers' Accounts 1655–1679.
65 WQS, vol. 6, p. 159.
66 WRO DR43a/19 Leamington Hastings Overseers' Accounts 1655–1679.
67 (Margr Gilly), Arkell and Alcock, Warwickshire Hearth Tax, p. 282.
68 WRO DR43a/19 Leamington Hastings Overseers' Accounts 1655–1679, and DR43a/20 Overseers' Accounts 1681–1704.
69 Paying the poor to look after the poor was a common strategy, as noted elsewhere in, for example, Hindle, On the Parish?, p. 266; M. Barker-Read, 'The Treatment of the Aged Poor in Five Selected West Kent Parishes from Settlement to Speenhamland (1662–1797)' (PhD thesis, Open University, 1988), pp. 104–5.
70 WRO DR43a/194 Leamington Hastings Records of the Poors Plot Charity, 28 September 1689; Arkell and Alcock, Warwickshire Hearth Tax, p. 282; WRO DR43a/19 Leamington Hastings Overseers' Accounts 1655–1679.

Nicholas Jelly was never an inmate of the hospital, though he was supported by the almshouse charity for the last years of his life. He was in receipt of poor relief for many years, beginning when he and his wife had young children. They received regular payments for a time in 1655, and then again, in 1664, 6d per week for eleven weeks. He was given 2s 6d in 1669, 'being very poore and sicke'; his wife was helped in 1672 when she was sick; and the same year the overseers paid £6 10s 3d for repairs to his house and for a suit of clothes for his son when he was placed apprentice. By 1674 Jelly was receiving regular relief again, and that year the overseer added an extra 9s 4d 'for dyet'. The overseers' accounts suggest he and his wife were living in some misery; they record expenditure on a sheet and a blanket 'to lay one them'. Jelly's wife Catherine died in 1681, by which time their regular relief had risen from 6d per week to 1s 6d. When the almshouse accounts commence in 1686, the hospital appears to have taken over responsibility for supporting the widower Jelly. He was receiving 1s per week from them, and Goody Twiggar was being paid 10s per year for his lodging. This arrangement continued until Jelly's death in 1694, when the almshouse accounts record after his last payment: 'Extraordinary Expenses about him for lodging & nursing some months before he dyed 19s 4d', and 'Charges in the burying him more than his clothes sold for 10s 1d'.

Nicholas Jelly's case raises several interesting questions. Why was responsibility for supporting him transferred from the overseers to the almshouse trustees? Why did the almshouse pay his maintenance but not offer him a place? After his wife died and he was no longer able to maintain a home, a place in the almshouse might have seemed the logical progression. He was probably in his fifties or sixties by this time, and had passed into a notional category of eligibility as an elderly widower. Perhaps no place was available, although it is difficult to believe that not one vacancy arose in the eight years he lodged with Widow Twiggar. Was his long career as a parish pauper considered a bar to the respectability required of almshouse residents, or was keeping him at Goody Twiggar's merely a purely practical decision based on the amount of care he needed? Other almshouse residents such as Thomas Man had relatives living with them to look after them, and it is possible that Jelly had no one.[71] There is also the possibility that the almshouse had insufficient accommodation for all its eight members. The hearth tax listing records only six hearths for the almshouse, which means that either some of the eight almshouse residents had to share rooms, or had to be accommodated in

---

71   This was a common consequence of parishes apprenticing out pauper children, and may have added to poor people's vulnerability in old age. In addition, many people who reached sixty-five had no surviving children: Thane, 'Old People and Their Families in the English Past', *Charity, Self-Interest and Welfare in the English Past*, ed. M. Daunton (London, 1996), pp. 113–38 (p. 131).

unheated rooms, or even had to live elsewhere, like Jelly. This is borne out by the extension to the almshouse funded by the will of Dame Dorothy Wheler in 1696, whereby two extra places for the almshouse were endowed, but four new rooms were built.[72]

Another person who was supported by the almshouse charity but not admitted to a room was Widow Benson. In 1707 the trustees ordered that 40s be paid to John Benson, who had been keeping his mother for some time past, 'as she is now grown very Old & hath been tenant to the hospital land above these forty years'.[73] They went on to order that 30s should be paid every half year towards her maintenance from this account, over and above the 10s she received twice a year out of the Poors Plot charity. Her total maintenance from charitable funds of £4 per year was only a little less than she would have received in the almshouse (at that time £4 6s 8d per year plus fuel) and suggests that her son was expected to provide little more for her than a roof over her head.[74] The almshouse clearly had additional funds at this time, in contrast to the situation five years earlier, when they had had to keep a place empty after Matthew Over's death 'until the arrears due to the accountant are paid'.[75] The noting of Widow Benson's status as a tenant of the hospital, and the weight this seems to have carried, is typical of many almshouses of the time which favoured particular categories of tenants and retainers (usually connected to the patron's family, but in this case connected to the almshouse itself). Once again, this indicates the possibility that the early eighteenth century was a period of change in the way the almshouse was regarded and utilised, with less emphasis being placed on supporting the poorest and neediest, to be replaced by more conventional ties of patronage and influence.

The parish elite

The people who ran the parish were a relatively small group of better-off parishioners. Of the eighty-five householders recorded for the 1670 hearth tax assessment, just thirteen, plus the vicar, were freeholders identified in

---

72   MacFarquhar, *Leamington Hastings*, p. 7.
73   WRO DR43a/195 Leamington Hastings Davis/Wheler Charity records 1686–1799, 23 October 1707.
74   There were a number of Bensons in the parish over the period, of quite different economic status (who were possibly only distantly related, if at all). Two Bensons are listed in the hearth tax returns for 1674: George, a labourer, paid tax on one hearth; Henry, a yeoman, paid on two.
75   WRO DR43a/195 Leamington Hastings Davis/Wheler Charity records 1686–1799, Accounts 1701–1702. This is not the same Matthew Over as the parish official earlier in the century. There were six households of Overs in the 1674 hearth tax, of varying economic status. Two were exempt, including a Matthew Over; three paid tax on two hearths; and another Matthew Over, a yeoman, paid tax on four.

the enclosure agreement of 1665.[76] Yet these thirteen dominated the office of overseer of the poor for the parish between 1664 and 1684, with at least one of them, and frequently two, occupying the position in all but four of these twenty years. For the years 1664 to 1684, twenty-one people who served as overseer can be positively identified from the 1674 hearth tax assessment. Of these, eighteen were assessed on two or more hearths, with three being assessed on four hearths. This is not surprising, as overseers were expected to be men of 'substantial' means who could be trusted with the parish stock.[77] If one includes the vicarage with four hearths, the manor house with eleven, and the five-hearth home of John Mathews, brother to the lord's bailiff, it appears that membership of the parish elite, those who were involved in the business of parish government, would be amply demonstrated by the size of one's house.

In later years, with the survival of more records, it is possible to see at any one time a handful of the same names rotating through the offices of overseer, constable, churchwarden and charity trustee. For instance, one of the more substantial freeholders, William Cleaver, was overseer in 1667 and also appointed as one of the original trustees of the Poors Plot charity in 1669. His son Samuel became a trustee of the almshouse in 1693, was constable in 1695, overseer in 1698 and 1705, and churchwarden in 1711 and 1712. Thomas Watson, another trustee of the almshouse, was constable in 1678, overseer in 1683, 1684 and 1696, and churchwarden in 1684. Edmund Clarke was also a substantial freeholder and another of the original trustees of the Poors Plot charity. He also served as a trustee of the almshouse from the start of the surviving accounts in 1686 until his death in 1693. He was overseer in 1664 and 1677, and constable in 1691. He does not appear to have served as churchwarden, unsurprisingly, as he was fined for not attending church at the Easter quarter sessions in 1683, and in 1689 was granted a licence for his house to be used as a place of congregation for religious worship and a Presbyterian meeting.[78]

Edmund Clarke was clearly a respected individual who appears to have been able to work constructively alongside people of very different religious persuasion in running the affairs of the parish.[79] The vicar of the parish from 1662 until his death in 1682, for instance, was the loyal Anglican John Allington, who had been sequestered from two parishes during the Civil War and Commonwealth for using the Book of Common Prayer.[80] At the

---

76   Arkell and Alcock, *Warwickshire Hearth Tax*, pp. 281–2; WRO DR43a/193 Leamington Hastings Enclosure agreement 1665.

77   Hindle, *On the Parish?*, p. 257.

78   WQS, vol. 8, pp. 31, 43, 78, 252.

79   He was described as 'Mr' in the hearth tax assessment, and paid tax on four hearths: Arkell and Alcock, *Warwickshire Hearth Tax*, p. 282.

80   Allington, sequestered from Uppingham in 1646 and Oakham in 1655, called himself 'A Suffering Son of the Church of England'. He published several sermons and tracts in support of

Restoration he was made a prebendary of Lincoln Cathedral, together with his appointment to Leamington Hastings.[81] His successor at Leamington Hastings, William Binckes D.D., was a high churchman and nephew of the lord of the manor.[82] As well as being the parish priest, Dr Binckes was also Dean of Lichfield from 1703 until his death in 1712. He chaired the Lower House of Convocation from 1704 until 1707, and was vocal in defending the church from dissent and heresy, though also appealing for church unity.[83] Despite his high position in the church he seems to have been actively involved in the affairs of Leamington Hastings, and was buried there. The surviving records of both the Poors Plot charity and the Davis almshouse date from shortly after his appointment, and it would appear that he initiated a review of both charities soon after his arrival and put their affairs in order. He and Edmund Clarke appear to have had a relationship of mutual respect. As Clarke was dying in 1693, Binckes visited him and took down the testament he dictated as a codicil to his will.[84]

Clarke was not the only parishioner brought before the justices for not attending church. Alongside him and his wife Mary in 1683 were another freeholder, David Ryland and his wife Mary; husbandman Thomas Isaacson and his wife Anne; and a poor man, Henry Smith. In 1686 a further group was indicted for non-attendance, including carpenter Richard Russell, and pauper Nicholas Jelly, mentioned above.[85] Clarke's licence for a Presbyterian meeting house in Broadwell suggests that there were a number of dissenters in the parish. In addition, one of the many John Overs in the parish was a Catholic recusant, known as John Over Papist to distinguish him from, among others, John Over Carpenter. He was gaoled in 1679 'being formerly indicted for refusing to take the oath of Supremacy', and was presented as a 'popish recusant' at the Easter quarter sessions in 1680.[86] He seems to have had some support in the parish, however, for John Over Carpenter, serving as constable in 1690, was himself indicted at the quarter sessions for failing to present the other John Over for being a papist.[87] Despite the orthodox Anglican

the king and the sequestered clergy, including *The Grand Conspiracy of the Members Against the Mind of Jews Against their King* (series of four sermons, 1644–49); *A Brief Apologie for the Sequestered Clergie* (1648); *A Continuation of the Grand Conspiracy by the Impudent Usurper and the Royal Intrudere* (two sermons, 1654–55).

81   J. Stevinson, ed., 'Leamington Hastings in an Age of Revolution' (Warwickshire County Record Office, 1993), unpaginated.

82   His mother was the sister of Sir Charles Wheler, who inherited the lordship from the Trevors in 1676.

83   T. Claydon, 'Binckes, William (bap.1653, d.1712)', *ODNB* (Oxford, 2004; online edn, Jan. 2008), http://www.oxforddnb.com/view/article/2402 (accessed 4 February 2009).

84   LRO cal. 176.31 (1693).

85   WQS, vol. 8, pp. 31, 43, 159.

86   WQS, vol. 7, pp. 132, 180.

87   WQS, vol. 9, p. 2.

credentials of the two clergymen who served the parish in the second half of the seventeenth century, it seems that among some parishioners at least, religious dissent in various forms was tolerated, and was apparently no bar to admission to the almshouse.[88] In the late seventeenth century more leading parishioners were involved in the office of overseer than as churchwarden, and it may be that after the bitter religious and political divisions of earlier years, managing the resources of the parish for the benefit of all parishioners was a unifying activity that involvement with the established church was no longer able to provide.[89]

The Poors Plot Charity

The parish elite in the late seventeenth century not only controlled Humphrey Davis's almshouse, but another major parish resource, the Poors Plot charity, established as part of the enclosure agreement of 1665. This was initiated by Sir Thomas Trevor II and confirmed in a Chancery decree of 1669. In this document, the twenty-seven freeholders, only half of whom lived in the parish, agreed that one acre in every yardland enclosed should be set aside for the relief of the poor.[90] This eventually provided 108 acres in two plots, which were to be free of tithes and held in trust for the relief of the poor of the parish and for other charitable uses.[91] The trustees were to be the lord of the manor and the vicar, four local gentry and four principal freeholders. The uses of the Poors Plot charity were specified in the final agreement of 1669 as being the relief of the poor, the repair of the church, the apprenticing of poor children and the maintenance of a schoolmaster.[92]

   The Poors Plot charity also absorbed the remains of the parish stock. This consisted in principle of £50 from the bequest of Thomas Squire and about

88   Unlike the situation dictated by Rev. Nicholas Chamberlaine at another Warwickshire parish. His almshouse at Bedworth excluded nonconformists (see chapters 3 and 4).
89   As suggested by McIntosh for post-Reformation Hadleigh: McIntosh, 'Networks of Care', p. 76. Interestingly, although repair of the parish church was one of the permitted uses set down for the Poors Plot charity, there is no evidence that its funds were ever used for this purpose.
90   WRO DR43a/193 Leamington Hastings Enclosure agreement 1665.
91   This seems a very sizeable allocation, exceeding the later examples given by Sylvia Pinches for other Warwickshire charities created as a result of enclosure: S. Pinches, 'From Common Rights to Cold Charity: Enclosure and Poor Allotments in the Eighteenth and Nineteenth Centuries', ed. A. Borsay and P. Shapely, *Medicine, Charity and Mutual Aid: The Consumption of Health and Welfare in Britain, c.1550–1950* (Aldershot, 2007), pp. 35–53. Pinches quotes J. M. Martin's finding that there was a decline in the generosity of compensation awarded by the enclosure commissioners to the poor over time.
92   The original agreement drawn up in 1665 at the start of the enclosure negotiations had specified a wider range of uses, including repairs to highways and bridges, the marriage of poor maids, and the payment of Fifteenths and setting out soldiers.

£60 owed and recovered from a previous vicar, Thomas Lever.[93] However, most of this money had either been spent on the costs of bringing the suit in Chancery to recover the Davis Hospital lands, or had been lost through being lent out to parishioners who had subsequently died insolvent (a common occurrence for such loan charities).[94] Between 1677 and 1680 the trustees of the Poors Plot lands experimented by letting out one of the two plots to ten labourers from Broadwell 'to make the best of itt to their owne benefitt', but this had not been a success. The labourers were supposed to pay rent for each animal they grazed there, but the men 'broke their words' and failed to pay the charges. After this experiment the plots were let conventionally and the rents distributed by the trustees. At Christmas 1681 the trustees recorded that they had distributed £31 over the previous three years to 'severall widdowes children and day labourers'.[95]

In 1683 the trustees decided that the Poors Plot and the Hospital should have the same trustees, although separate accounts would be kept. From the Poors Plot records it seems that the trustees met once or twice a year to make decisions about the distribution of the proceeds. Frequently this involved paying for apprenticeships for poor children, usually the children of widows, but not necessarily those on parish relief.[96] In addition, as well as making occasional payments to people in need, each year an agreed sum was given to the overseers of the poor to distribute to a number of poor parishioners specified on a list drawn up for the purpose. In some years the local trustees (that is, the leading parishioners rather than the gentry trustees) were also authorised to make emergency payments if circumstances were 'particularly necessitous', or the curate was authorised to purchase coal for distribution to poor people in the winter. The purchase of wool, hemp, flax and wheels was also made in some years to assist the poor who would otherwise be unable to work. The regular disbursements were made by the overseers, demonstrating how enmeshed parish resources were at this time.

In most years the distribution was made just twice a year, for example in

93   Thomas Lever was vicar of Leamington Hastings from 1619 to 1639. From 1628 he was also rector of the neighbouring parish of Stockton. According to the Chancery Confirmation Order in the Davis case, at the time of that inquisition (1633) Thomas Lever was in possession of £40 due to the poor of Leamington Hastings which he had been ordered to pay by the Diocesan Court because of non-residence. The Chancery decree included the recovery of this money with interest: TNA C90/6 Commissioners for Charitable Uses: Confirmation in the case of Leamington Hastings charity, 7 Car. I.

94   Opening statement, 'As for and concerning the parish stocke ...', in WRO DR43a/194 Leamington Hastings Records of the Poors Plot Charity. The remaining money was let out at interest as bonds.

95   WRO DR43a/194 Leamington Hastings Records of the Poors Plot Charity.

96   John Allington, vicar, also left £10 in his will of 1683 to add 20s a time to each 40s laid out by the Poors Plot in apprenticeships until the sum was used up: TNA Prob/11/373 Will of John Allington 1683.

1688 on 17 July and on St Thomas's Day (21 December). In 1683, however, the trustees had decided that on every Sunday between All Saints Day and Easter Day, 20s would be distributed at church 'by sixpences and shillings' to those whose names appeared on a list prepared beforehand. Those not at church to receive it, without reasonable excuse, would lose their payment.[97] It is possible that the lists of named individuals were selected by the trustees; if this were the case it appears to have been a contentious decision. A curious note by the curate in the accounts seems to indicate some independence on the part of the local parish officials, as it suggested that the trustees (half of whom were neighbouring gentry rather than residents of the parish) were only responsible for managing the charity's assets, not the disbursements.[98]

The overseers were expected to account for the expenditure and enter 'into their bookes' the names of those receiving assistance and the respective amounts.[99] For two years (1686/7 and 1687/8) the actual list of names appears in the overseers' accounts for that year, but after this they merely record the total sum given by the trustees and the amount disbursed, for instance in 1690/1, 'received and distributed by order of the Trustees £10 7s'.[100] A total of thirty-two people appear on the list for 1686/7, receiving amounts varying from 15s down to just 2s. Twelve recipients were widows; the remainder were probably poor labourers such as William Chittam (mentioned above), who received 3s 6d. Three people on the list that year were also in receipt of parish poor relief: Widow Over was given 2s 6d, Joseph Turner 6s and Nicholas Jelly received 5s, with Jelly's payment specified as being for fuel. The following year the list contains the same names, minus Nicholas Jelly, and seven additional names, including at least two more who were on regular parish relief. As with the names of those exempt from the hearth tax, it is impossible to know just how poor the recipients of the annual disbursements were; many were probably on the margins of poverty, getting by through a variety of means. Also, one cannot tell what particular circumstances prompted the trustees to authorise a payment of 15s to Nicholas Twiggar and 10s each to the widows Whitehead and Hawten, when most recipients were awarded much smaller

97   TNA Prob/11/373 Will of John Allington 1683.
98   The note inserted in the minutes of 8 April 1685 by the curate John Garrett, seemingly on his own initiative, states: 'Memorandum that the Trustees for the charitable use named on the Preceedent page, take care only of the Land given to the Maintenance of Mr Davis's Hospitall & the two plots of Ground ... given to charitable uses. The charitable stock in money for the said parishe is under the care & management of the Overseers of the poor of Leamington aforesaid for the Time Being. This memorandum without order from or Privity [?] of the Trustees aforesaid was intred by me John Garrett, thereby hoping to Prevent Mistake and Differences for the time to come': WRO DR43a/194 Leamington Hastings Records of the Poors Plot Charity.
99   WRO DR43a/194 Leamington Hastings Records of the Poors Plot Charity, Minute of 18 March 1687.
100   WRO DR43a/20 Leamington Hastings Overseers' Accounts 1681–1704.

amounts.[101] But it seems clear at least that in the early years of the charity there was no discrimination against those in receipt of parish relief. In fact it seems that the charitable funds were used to assist a wide range of poor people, variously including almshouse residents, parish paupers, and those not on relief.

As well as the disbursements given to the overseers, the Poors Plot accounts record the occasional payments made to those in need. In 1688, for example, Joseph Turner received a further 7s 'when sick', and Mary Cox received 6s 'for cloaths'. Turner had already received a payment of 10s in 1685, and was on the lists as receiving 6s in 1686/7 and 6s 6d in 1687/8. In 1687 Turner started to receive regular parish relief. He died in 1688, so it is possible that the additional payment from the Poors Plot charity that year, on top of his poor relief, was for additional expenses in his final illness. Paying for additional care for people when ill occurs frequently in the records. Goody Rushall, for example, one of the almshouse inhabitants, had an additional 1s per week allocated from the Poors Plot in 1698 on top of her hospital stipend until her death in 1699: 'as expended on the looking after Goody Rushall during her lunacy more than her hospital pay'. When her goods were sold after her death, it was the Poors Plot rather than the almshouse which received the partial reimbursement.[102] In 1708, Ann Dury was granted 10s, and a further £1 in 1709, 'for [th]e care of her mother by reason of her great age'. Also in 1708 Goody Man, described as a 'member' of the almshouse, was paid 6d per week out of the Poors Plot 'for nursing Old Goody Hawten' (another almshouse resident), 'the same to be repaid out of Hawten's goods when she dyes'.[103]

Specialist nursing care or accommodation beyond what was available in the village also seems to have been purchased using the Poors Plot resources. As well as paying Mr Chebsey of Rugby 'for his care of Sam. Benson & that he may be encouraged to make a cure' (1708), John Benson of the neighbouring parish of Bourton-on-Dunsmore was paid in 1709 to look after not only his own mother but also Widow Mathews. By 1712 Widow Mathewes was being lodged with a person by the name of Shaw in Coventry, where she died the following year. The Poors Plot paid £3 7s 6d for her lodgings there for two and a quarter years, and £1 5s 'to buy her fewel & for other necessarys when she was sick'.[104] This was Faith Mathews, widow of Thomas Mathews, who had been Sir Thomas Trevor's agent. She was listed in the

101   Widow Hawten was admitted to the almshouse in place of Ann Tue in 1688: WRO DR43a/195 Leamington Hastings Davis/Wheler Charity records 1686–1799.

102   WRO DR43a/194 Leamington Hastings Records of the Poors Plot Charity.

103   Jane Man appears to have achieved respectability at last, with the epithet 'Goody'. She was now aged fifty, and clearly making herself useful in the almshouse.

104   WRO DR43a/194 Leamington Hastings Records of the Poors Plot Charity, 1712–13.

parish register as a member of the almshouse when she died, although not living there and presumably received the hospital stipend in addition to the Poors Plot funding. Similarly, a payment of 10s was made in 1712 by the Poors Plot trustees to Griffin Fennel, with whom Susannah Isaacson was lodged, to buy her some clothes. Susannah's lodgings with Griffin Fennel had been paid by the overseers out of parish poor relief since 1694, and the expense was considerable. In 1694/5 the overseers had paid £5 for her keep and £1 7s 7d for clothing; in 1696/7 the overseer claimed a shilling 'spent when I did bargain with Griffin Fennel' for £5 for the coming year.[105] This suggests a more professional, commercial transaction, different from the usual boarding out of paupers in the parish with poor widows glad of the additional income. In fact, 'farmer' Griffin Fennel of Harbury was Susannah's brother-in-law.[106] It is possible that Susannah was disabled, and that Fennel made his living by taking in people requiring care. In 1703 Susannah was 'admitted' to the almshouse, although remaining with Griffin Fennel, presumably to take advantage of the hospital stipend and relieve the burden on the parish.[107]

   These examples show the Poors Plot charity funds being used in a very flexible way to meet exceptional needs, with the funding often being used in tandem with parish poor relief or almshouse resources for particular individuals. Table 6.1 shows the amounts between 1690 and 1693 given to the overseers by the trustees for distribution to the poor, compared with the amounts raised in those years by parish relief. It is clear from the table that the Poors Plot charity made a significant contribution each year, in some cases equalling or exceeding the amounts paid in parish relief.[108] Both the regular and exceptional disbursements would have made a considerable difference to those poor people who received them, and most probably relieved the parish of a substantial amount in poor relief payments. Whether the sums received actually compensated individual cottagers for their loss of access to common rights at enclosure is impossible to calculate. What the charity did do, as Buchanan Sharp has suggested, was provide another arena for better-off householders in Leamington Hastings to be involved in the administration of parish affairs, and to control aspects of the lives of their poorer neighbours, however benevolent their intentions.[109] The payments from the Poors Plot charity were

105   WRO DR43a/20 Leamington Hastings Overseers' Accounts 1681–1704.
106   Fennel's wife Ursula was granted letters of administration in 1692 when her father Thomas Isaac(son) died intestate: LRO cal.364.18 (1692).
107   WRO DR43a/195 Leamington Hastings Davis/Wheler Charity records 1686–1799, Davis Hospital minutes, 1703: Susannah Isaacson 'to succeed Mathew Over'.
108   Yet both were dwarfed by the resources of the almshouse. Expenditure by the almshouse in 1694 on six residents and Nicholas Jelly came to £31 12s 9d.
109   B. Sharp, 'Common Rights, Charities and the Disorderly Poor', *Reviving the English Revolution: Reflections and Elaborations on the Work of Christopher Hill*, ed. G. Eley and W. Hunt (London and New York, 1988), pp. 107–37.

Table 6.1. Expenditure on the poor in Leamington Hastings

Year	Poors Plot	Parish Relief	Total
1690–91	£15 3s 6d	£11 18s 0d (2 levies)	£27 1s 6d
1691–92	£13 3s 0d	£17 17s 0d (3 levies)	£31 0s 0d
1692–93	£13 6s 0d	£12 5s 4d (2 levies)	£25 11s 4d

Source: WRO DR43a/194 Records of the Poors Plot Charity, and DR43a/20 Overseers' Accounts 1681–1704

not a right, and recipients could not rely on receiving them. The trustees had to ensure the receipt of the rents before disbursements could be made, and sometimes tenants of the plots were in arrears, as in 1718 when the tenant owed two years' rent. In the financial crisis of 1696, the trustees acknowledged that they were not able to make the usual distribution, but guaranteed instead to arrange for 'coal or wood or credit for bread'.[110] An individual's lack of deference could, moreover, result in the loss of a payment, as in 1719 when the trustees ordered £10 to be distributed on New Year's Day 'excepting only that John Over of Bradwell shall have no share of this mony as well because he very unthankfully refus'd wt was offord him in [th]e last distribution as because he has of late behav'd himself very ill in other respects'.[111]

Eligibility could be determined and, more importantly, changed by the trustees. Whereas the early disbursements appear to have been made to a range of poor people, including those receiving parish relief, the minutes in 1696 state that the purpose of the charity was 'to keep persons from coming upon the parish', although this was not specified in the founding agreement. Later pronouncements, for example in 1717, reserve the distribution for those 'as do not receive Collection'.[112] Although it is impossible to ascertain to what degree this was implemented, as subsequent lists of recipients have not survived, this pronouncement does mark a clear change in policy. The distinction in the minds of the governing elite between charity and poor relief developed during the course of the seventeenth century, as central government, local magistrates and commissioners for charitable uses all emphasised that charitable endowments were distinct from, and should not be used to subsidise, the poor rates.[113] This proposed discrimination by the trustees of the Poors Plot represented a newly prejudicial attitude in this

110 WRO DR43a/194 Leamington Hastings Records of the Poors Plot Charity, 23 June 1696.
111 WRO DR43a/194 Leamington Hastings Records of the Poors Plot Charity, 23 December 1719. Cf. Hindle, On the Parish?, pp. 387–90.
112 WRO DR43a/194 Leamington Hastings Records of the Poors Plot Charity, October 1717.
113 See the discussion in Hindle, On the Parish?, pp. 142–6.

parish towards those on poor relief, but one which was entirely typical of the condemnatory rhetoric of the time.

Parish housing

A final major resource used to assist the poor in Leamington Hastings was housing provided by the parish. The national framework of parish poor relief established by the Elizabethan poor laws of 1597 and 1601 included the responsibility of parishes to provide accommodation for poor people, and oversight by justices of the peace to ensure that parishes were exercising their responsibilities appropriately (see chapter 1). Surviving quarter sessions records of the seventeenth century provide many examples of justices intervening in contested poor relief cases and settlement disputes. The Warwickshire Quarter Sessions Order Books survive from 1625 and include hundreds of examples of the justices making habitation orders, requiring the overseers in a particular parish to provide a 'house habitable and fit for a Christian'.[114] There are several entries for Leamington Hastings which pre-date the commencement of the surviving overseers' accounts in 1655. In 1630, for instance, Joan Biddle, by agreement with the parish, offered her goods to the overseers in return for habitation and maintenance.[115] Other cases give an indication of how this parish, like many others of the time, attempted to rid itself of inhabitants likely to become a burden on the poor rates. In 1649 two widows, Joan Andrews and Eleanor Thompson, were indicted for keeping inmates.[116] Joan Andrews had her daughter living with her while her son-in-law, Thomas Hawten (or Horten), was away as a Parliamentary soldier. When he returned to live with Joan the parish tried to eject him and his wife. The justices supported Hawten against the overseers, and ordered that he be permitted to remain.[117] He worked as a slaymaker, but appears to have been always poor.[118] He was exempt from the hearth tax in 1674. Joan Andrews received regular poor relief from 1655 until 1662, the date she was possibly admitted to the almshouse, where she died in 1683. Hawten also died in 1683. His widow was herself admitted to the almshouse five years later, and died there 'aged 94' in 1708.[119]

114   WQS, vol. 1, p. 81.
115   WQS, vol. 1, p. 100.
116   WQS, vol. 6, p. 90.
117   WQS, vol. 2, p. 255.
118   A slaymaker worked in the textile industry, making tools for weaving: L. Newman, 'Deserted Medieval Villages', paper given to Warmington Heritage Group, Warwickshire, 10 May 2010. http://www.warmingtonheritage.com/publications/research-projects/deserted-medieval-villages/ (accessed 16 December 2013).
119   WRO DR43a/195 Leamington Hastings Davis/Wheler Charity records 1686–1799, Davis Hospital accounts.

The justices went further with Eleanor Thompson. Her son William and his family were initially ordered to be sent back to the neighbouring parish of Birdingbury, but this was reversed at Easter 1650 when his settlement was ordered in Leamington Hastings. At Trinity 1650 the justices ordered the overseers 'forthwith' to provide him with 'an house wherein he may live and follow his trade'. The order was repeated at Michaelmas, with the threat that the overseers would be bound over if they did not comply.[120] Nothing further is heard of William Thompson, but a Widow Tompson, possibly his mother or his wife, began to receive poor relief in 1672 and was exempt from the hearth tax in 1674.[121]

It is not possible to determine how the overseers met their obligation to house Thompson, but a little more information is available in the case of Joseph Turner, a labourer. At Epiphany 1652 the overseers were ordered to provide habitation for Turner, described as an inhabitant but 'destitute of an habitation'; he was to pay 'a moderate rent'. At Michaelmas he was recorded as being provided with a house, for which he was paying 40s per year. The overseers were demanding security for the rent, but this was refused by the justices. The demand for security suggests that the parish owned or had taken on the lease of the property he had been assigned.[122] Despite the overseers' misgivings, Turner seems to have just about managed with this arrangement for many years. But he needed poor relief in 1672, was exempt from the hearth tax in 1674, and appeared among the people paid by the overseers for boarding Ann Tue that year. In October 1687 he started to receive regular poor relief of 2s 6d per week, as well as grants from the Poors Plot charity (see previous section). The overseers also paid £1 3s 4d to repair his house; again, this suggests that it was probably parish property.[123] Turner died the following year, and his widow was given leave to live in the almshouse 'till a place shall fall' (in other words without the stipend). This arrangement would have freed up their house for another parish pauper. On the death in 1689 of Widow Dury, one of the almshouse inhabitants, Widow Turner was 'admitted to her whole pay'.[124]

How the Leamington Hastings overseers acquired the property to house parish paupers, or what form it took, cannot be ascertained from the records, although there is evidence available from parishes elsewhere. For instance, in the Essex Quarter Sessions Order Book for 1652 to 1661 there

120   WQS, vol. 3, pp. 2, 25, 36.
121   WRO DR43a/19 Leamington Hastings Overseers' Accounts 1655–1679, and QS 11/56 Hearth Tax Assessment Book 1674, Knightlow Hundred, Southam Division.
122   WQS, vol. 3, pp. 98, 131.
123   WRO DR43a/19 Leamington Hastings Overseers' Accounts 1655–1679, DR43a/20 Leamington Hastings Overseers' Accounts 1681–1704, and QS 11/56 Hearth Tax Assessment Book 1674, Knightlow Hundred, Southam Division.
124   WRO DR43a/195 Leamington Hastings Davis/Wheler Charity records 1686–1799.

are a number of examples of the overseers contracting with owners to rent houses and tenements in which to place the parish poor.[125] No rent payments are recorded in the surviving Leamington Hastings overseers' accounts, but from 1655 onwards there are many records of payments for repairs to houses. Sometimes the people living in them, like Joseph Turner, were not on regular relief. John Man, for example, had his house repaired in 1660 at a cost of 14s, and the repairs to the house of the Guilliams, mother and daughter, cost 11s 2d in 1663. It is probable that Widow Joan Guilliams is Joan Gill, listed as one of the freeholders in the enclosure agreement of 1665, in which case the overseers' contribution towards repairing the house is an indication of how poor she and her daughter were. Joan's daughter Margery is listed as an exempt householder in the hearth tax assessment of 1670, suggesting she had inherited the house on her mother's death.[126] In some cases, however, the sums expended were quite considerable, which would seem to indicate that the parish owned and was prepared to invest in the property. For instance, the overseers paid out £5 9s 5d for repairing Nicholas Jelly's house in 1672. Widow Anne Tarsey, who, like Jelly, was on regular relief, had her house repaired at a cost of £4 4s 0d in 1661; another 16s was spent on repairs in 1664; and again £1 3s 6d in 1669.[127] Set against the usual amounts paid for weekly relief (6d per week rising to 1s 6d per week in the 1660s for Widow Tarsey, shillings and sixpences in the 1670s to Nicholas Jelly), these sums are considerable, and indicate the importance the parish accorded its investment. Economic historians have calculated that property owners of the seventeenth century needed to allow an annual sum of 10–11% of the value of the property to maintain small farms in good repair.[128] This does not necessarily imply that vernacular architecture was essentially flimsy, but the timber, mud and thatch construction of most rural buildings, while perfectly serviceable, required regular maintenance to keep it weatherproof.[129]

125   D. H. Allen, ed., *Essex Quarter Sessions Order Book 1652–1661*, Essex Edited Texts 1 (Chelmsford, 1974), p. 27 (Coe); p. 94 (Tarling); p. 144 (Blakemore). I am grateful to Bernard Capp for bringing these references to my attention.
126   WRO DR43a/19 Leamington Hastings Overseers' Accounts 1655–1679, and DR43a/193 Leamington Hastings Enclosure agreement 1665; Arkell and Alcock, *Warwickshire Hearth Tax*, p. 282.
127   WRO DR43a/19 Leamington Hastings Overseers' Accounts 1655–1679.
128   C. Clay, 'Landlords and Estate Management in England', *The Agrarian History of England and Wales*, vol. 5(2), ed. J. Thirsk (Cambridge, 1985), pp. 119–251 (p. 247). According to archaeologists, medieval peasants' homes required rebuilding at least once a generation: M. Beresford and J. G. Hurst, *Deserted Medieval Villages*, 3rd edn (Gloucester 1989), p. 77. The consequence of inadequate building and repairs was demonstrated when the end room of South Ormsby's poor house 'fell down in the winter of 1672–3': M. W. Barley, *The English Farmhouse and Cottage* (London, 1961), p. 208.
129   D. Tankard, 'The Regulation of Cottage Building in Seventeenth-Century Sussex', *Agricultural History Review* 59 (2011), 18–35 (p. 32).

From the examples above it appears that the parish of Leamington Hastings had built up a stock of housing by the time the overseers' accounts begin in 1655. There are no recorded habitation orders for the parish after 1652, perhaps because by this stage the parish could anticipate the line the justices were likely to take and had the resources available to meet their obligations. Certainly with Alice Pedley, 'a poor inhabitant, sick, with four small children', the overseers exceeded the order of the justices in 1660 to pay her maintenance of 10d per week, by providing her with a house as well.[130] Alice's husband William had died in 1656, leaving her with four daughters, the youngest only two years old. Why the matter of her support should have come before the justices is not known, but once the maintenance order was made the parish mobilised to care for her. The overseers paid for her to be lodged, first with Adam Oakley, then with Thomas Hincks. Meanwhile, a house was 'built' for her. Nathaniel Pedley and other workmen were paid a total of £1 7s 2d in 1661 for 'building the Widdow Pedley houes'. Other items of expenditure included 4s for 'four tunne of winding and tooe tunne of lath', 5s 6d for 'carridge for wood and earth and for three bunches of windinges', and 1s for 'drawing a leaisee'.[131] This relatively small expenditure suggests that the accommodation was not a cottage built from scratch, but perhaps the conversion of an outbuilding. In 1662 the overseers paid John Mathews 10s 'for Widow Pedler cowes graseing' indicating that she had previously had a smallholding (and had perhaps become too ill to keep it on or had been evicted), and was now in accommodation with no access to land or common.[132]

Her lease for the new house has not survived, but may well have included not only the conditions of the tenancy but also the agreement for her maintenance. When she died in 1663 all her possessions were sold by the overseers. They came to £4 11s 7d in total. The annual accounts for 1663 refer to 13s 6d 'laid out more than the goods of the Widow Pedler did amount two'. Her possessions suggest that Widow Pedley had known slightly better times, and this may have been the reason the overseers had been initially reluctant to support her. As well as two small bonnets sold for 2s 6d, the items included a bed sold for 13s, sheets, blankets and pillows, including two feather pillows and a feather bolster sold for 13s, but also more meagre items such as an old chair sold for 6d, an old churn and a chest without a lid.[133]

---

130   WQS, vol. 4, Trinity 1660, p. 127.

131   WRO DR43a/19 Leamington Hastings Overseers' Accounts 1655–1679, pp. 11, 12 (1661).

132   The importance of owning a cow or smallholding for the survival of poor widows has been ably demonstrated by Tim Wales' examination of the poor lists for the Norfolk town of Cawston in 1601: T. Wales, 'Poverty, Poor Relief and the Life-Cycle: Some Evidence from Seventeenth-Century Norfolk', *Land, Kinship and Life-Cycle*, ed. R. M. Smith (Cambridge, 1984), pp. 351–404 (pp. 370–1).

133   Apart from the bonnets, no clothes are mentioned. Presumably Widow Pedley's clothes were kept and passed on to her daughters. See P. King, 'Pauper Inventories and the Material

Unlike many other parishes, the Leamington Hastings overseers' accounts do not include any evidence of rents paid, which suggests that the houses in which they placed paupers were either owned by the parish, or being provided by a landowner rent free, perhaps in return for the parish maintaining the property. From the simultaneous repairs listed for several properties in some years it would appear that the parish had more than one property at its disposal.[134] The parish not only seems to have owned its own property portfolio, but to have been involved in managing where poor people lived. For instance, the overseers had paid 14s to repair John Man's house in 1660 when he was not on regular relief. He had occasional relief owing to sickness in 1669, and in 1673 the overseers paid Thomas Mathews (Sir Thomas Trevor's agent) 12s 6d 'for letting John Man remove his house'. They also gave John Man 3s 'when his house was building'. From 1674 he appears to have received regular relief for at least the next ten years. Why he should have wanted, or needed, to move is not known, but the assistance of the parish in the arrangement suggests it was not a frivolous move and may have resulted in a more suitable property being released for someone else.

Managing the placement of poor people in suitable properties is also evident in the request recorded at the Trinity quarter sessions in 1696 for Mary Makepeace, 'a poor widow', to be placed in a cottage formerly erected on the waste at Hardwick Green, 'late in the occupation of Elizabeth Over, widow'. Mr Mathews, bailiff to the lord of the manor, confirmed Sir Thomas's consent to this arrangement at the Michaelmas session.[135] This cottage appears to have been maintained by the parish during Elizabeth Over's tenancy, even possibly built at parish expense. The two loads of earth required for repairs in 1687 suggest it had been simply built of mud construction, as was common at the time in rural areas. When Widow Over vacated the cottage in 1696 to move into the almshouse, the overseers expended £7 3s 9d on considerable improvements to the property, including the use of timber, bricks and glazing, before paying a shilling to have Widow Makepeace's possessions conveyed there.[136] Improving the cottage in this way was presumably a more secure investment for the parish once its existence had been regularised by the court.

While some houses appear to have been built with the assistance of the

Lives of the Poor in the Eighteenth and Early Nineteenth Centuries', *Chronicling Poverty: The Voices and Strategies of the English Poor, 1640–1840*, ed. T. Hitchcock, P. King and P. Sharpe (Basingstoke, 1997), pp. 155–91.

134 For instance, 1661, Widow Tarsey and Widow Pedley's houses (WRO DR43a/19 Leamington Hastings Overseers' Accounts 1655–1679); 1687, William Turner's house, Benson's house and Widow Over's house; 1700, repairs to houses of John Benson, Mary Mann, William Turner and Mary Tarsey (WRO DR43a/20 Leamington Hastings Overseers' Accounts 1681–1704).

135 WQS, vol. 9, pp. 133, 141.

136 WRO DR43a/20 Leamington Hastings Overseers' Accounts 1681–1704.

parish, others may have been pulled down, as landowners took steps to control poor people's access to housing (and also, by implication, settlement).[137] In 1635, a group of men were fined in the manorial court for breaking in the door one Sunday of a house erected on the waste, and putting Thomas Garrett in possession of it.[138] John Over of Broadwell was presented at the Epiphany quarter sessions in 1662 for erecting a cottage without the requisite four acres.[139] The overseers' accounts for 1661–62 include expenditure of 1s 6d 'for going to the Justices with the witness conserninge pluckeng downe the house', which may relate to this episode.[140] Sir William Wheler, the lord of the manor, demolished some tenements in Broadwell in 1696 and gave the building materials to the almshouse to build new tenements on their land. It was not, therefore, only through the settlement legislation that the parish elite could determine where and how the poor should live.

Conclusion

The purpose of this case study was to use the evidence from one Warwickshire parish to explore the context within which a single almshouse was founded and managed, including what other resources were available to the parish and how these were utilised. By bringing together and examining information from a range of seventeenth-century records, it has been possible to build up a suggestive picture of how, in this parish, the housing needs of some of the poor were met, and how the operation of the almshouse fitted within this overall perspective. The survival of both the overseers' accounts and the minutes of the almshouse trustees shows how the same individual might be housed at different times in their life in lodgings, then provided with a parish house, and ultimately a room in the almshouse. For some there might even be a stage beyond the almshouse, receiving specialist nursing care in someone's home.

The parish elite, in the second half of the seventeenth century, appear to have managed the resources of the parish in a fairly pragmatic way, drawing upon whatever was available regardless of technical responsibilities. For instance, the overseers used parish relief to pay for catching sparrows, which was the responsibility of the churchwardens; the almshouse paid for people not actually in the almshouse, reducing their need for parish relief; and the Poors Plot charity provided additional assistance to those on relief or in the

---

137 As described by J. Broad, 'Housing the Rural Poor in Southern England, 1650–1850', *The Agricultural History Review* 48/2 (2000), 151–70.
138 WRO CR 1319/119 Copy of entries in the manorial court rolls c.1900.
139 WQS, vol. 6, p. 139.
140 WRO DR43a/19 Leamington Hastings Overseers' Accounts 1655–1679.

almshouse, as well as supporting those not on relief. As the source of all their resources was the parishioners themselves, or previous generations of them, this must have seemed perfectly reasonable. Local decisions were overseen by the justices of the peace who signed off the overseers' accounts, and by the local gentry who occasionally attended meetings as charity trustees. There were periodic interventions by order of quarter sessions, but on the whole the local officials acted with a great deal of autonomy in managing the affairs of this small, self-sufficient, 'welfare republic'.[141] In fact, the officials may have tried to ensure that there was as little outside intervention as possible: the overseers gave William Rushall an extra 5s in 1673 'to keepe him from going for more colection'.[142] The limitation of the records, of course, is that only those who were assisted appear in the accounts; it is usually not possible to see what claims were rejected or whose needs were not met. There is also a suggestion that the end of the period might have seen the beginnings of a distinction between the recipients of private charity and poor relief, for instance by the restriction of the Poors Plot charity to those not on poor relief, and the admission of better-off people to the almshouse. Yet, even with these caveats, the picture that emerges is a fairly inclusive one, with little evidence of decisions being made on the basis of patronage or discrimination. For example, a range of very different people seem to have been accepted into the almshouse: William Chittam the bird catcher; Goody Twiggar the innkeeper's widow; Jane Man the unmarried mother; and even the troublesome William Rushall.

The evidence obtained has thus shown the benefits of adopting Broad's 'holistic approach'. Examining the records together rather than in isolation has revealed not only the links between the ways the different types of provision were used, but also the networks and overlap between the people making the decisions. There was evidence of conflict and dissent at times, but generally this seems to have been outweighed by a commitment to work together for the overall benefit of the parish. Perhaps, as McIntosh suggested for Hadleigh, implementing a policy of parish welfare itself promoted a sense of community.[143] This is not to underestimate, however, the deeply paternalistic nature of that community. The decisions made on behalf of the poor by the parish elite were by no means altruistic, and much of the 'management' of the parish resources entailed management of the poor also. The generous disbursements from the Poors Plot charity were no doubt of great help to the poor and those at the margins of poverty, so long as they, unlike the John Over mentioned earlier, showed due deference and gratitude. The pragmatic

---

141   The term 'welfare republic' is used by Steve Hindle to describe the administrative unit of the parish in *Birthpangs*, p. 2.
142   WRO DR43a/19 Leamington Hastings Overseers' Accounts 1655–1679.
143   McIntosh, 'Networks of care', p. 76.

decisions about the use of resources not only benefited poorer parishioners but ratepayers as well, who could be confident that the needs of the poor would be met without overburdening their better-off neighbours. The cooperation among the freeholders which had resulted in the enclosure of the open fields in 1665 was itself the act which had simultaneously deprived the poor of their ancient rights and placed the resulting charitable funds, through the creation of the Poors Plot charity, into the hands of the parish elite, to be controlled by them and dispensed at their pleasure.

Humphrey Davis's almshouse, too, was a part of the support network controlled by the better-off parishioners. The almshouse made a genuine contribution within the range of resources available for the poor in the locality, and, at least in the second half of the seventeenth century, the trustees appear to have operated a surprisingly inclusive admissions policy in a model of benevolence which may well have been replicated elsewhere. This benevolence, however, was not guaranteed, and there are suggestions in the records by the end of the period that attitudes towards the poor in Leamington Hastings might have been hardening in line with contemporary public opinion.

Conclusion

'An unsatisfactory form of charity', or 'a touchstone of concern for life-cycle poverty'?[1]

This book set out to examine early modern almshouses within the wider context of the range of welfare provision available in early modern England. Although historians of the late medieval period have lately included almshouses as part of the range of provision available to meet the needs of the poor, post-Reformation almshouses have generally been viewed as operating outside the framework of statutory poor relief in England, making little contribution towards the support of the genuinely poor and needy.[2] The standard portrayal of the almshouse is thus of a quaint but largely irrelevant institution, providing care and shelter for a small number of respectable, privileged elderly people, participants in a living tableau of traditional beneficence among attractive heritage buildings. This cosy image proved to be remarkably enduring, and is only very recently becoming subject to challenge.[3] Many of the examples in this book, nevertheless, demonstrate the remarkable diversity of early modern almshouses, and how far removed from the conventional portrayal the majority of them were.

The 'comfortable and positive image' of almshouse life has recently been revised by Tomkins, and the continuum of experience she describes in relation to eighteenth-century almshouse life applies equally to other features of early modern almshouses.[4] These include, for instance, the many variations

---

1 Walter Sherburne Prideaux, clerk of the Goldsmith's Company, recommending in 1890 that the Bowes almshouses in Woolwich should not be rebuilt, cited by C. MacKeith, 'The Christopher Boone Almshouse Charity in Lee: A Study of Poor Relief and Almshouse Traditions in the Blackheath Hundred', paper given at the Almshouses in Europe conference, Haarlem, the Netherlands, 8 September 2011; M. McIntosh, 'Local Responses to the Poor in Late Medieval and Tudor England', *Continuity and Change* 3/2 (1988), 209–45 (p. 221).

2 M. K. McIntosh, *Poor Relief in England 1350–1600* (Cambridge, 2012), pp. 59–94, 186–224; C. Dyer, 'Poverty and its Relief in Late Medieval England', *Past and Present* 216 (2012), 41–78 (pp. 45–6, 62).

3 See, for instance, the title and content of Mary Raphael's travelogue, *The Romance of English Almshouses*, published (appropriately) by Mills and Boon (London, 1926).

4 A. Tomkins, 'Retirement from the Noise and Hurry of the World? The Experience of Almshouse Life', *Accommodating Poverty: The Housing and Living Arrangements of the English Poor, c.1600–1850*, ed. J. McEwan and P. Sharpe (Basingstoke, 2011), pp. 263–83 (p. 264).

in the form and function of foundations; in the governance arrangements; and in the social and economic standing of the occupants. At one end of this continuum sit the stereotypical foundations described above: the well-known, wealthy institutions such as the Lord Leycester Hospital at Warwick or Trinity Hospital, Greenwich, established by high-status individuals in grand or interesting buildings, providing a comfortable, well-ordered existence for a carefully selected group of privileged almspeople. Often such institutions were incorporated and largely self-governing, admitting almspeople who were not necessarily destitute, or those who came from outside the immediate locality, and operating independently of the statutory welfare framework. At the opposite end of the continuum would be found simple, unendowed rows of cottages, such as the Bleachfield and Priory almshouses in Alcester, Warwickshire that were donated by better-off parishioners and townspeople, managed by the parish officers, inhabited rent free by a small number of local poor people and with no overt rules or communal life. Sometimes the only feature which appears to distinguish these unendowed almshouses from other parish or town housing is in their origin as the specific gift of a named individual. The hundreds of other early modern almshouses which ranged along the continuum between these two extremes, exhibit a variety of features in different combinations. Some were wholly under the control of the founder's heirs, some were managed by a body of independent trustees, and others by town officials or the minister and churchwardens. Some gave their occupants a comfortable existence, with servants, stipends, clothing and fuel provided, while others had small or non-existent stipends and no additional benefits. At some almshouses the occupants were expected to work, but others were intended for those who were incapable of work. Some almspeople were subject to onerous rules and on-site supervision, while others led unrestricted lives in comparative freedom. At some almshouses spouses and children were permitted, at others they were prohibited. People in receipt of parish relief might be supported in some establishments, while at others they were refused admission. Almost any attempt at categorisation seems destined to fail in the face of such diversity.

This diversity in itself was one of the factors contributing to the continuing popularity of almshouses as a form of philanthropy, despite the considerable resources required of benefactors. The flexibility of the form lent itself to a number of different models, and could usefully combine the resources of public and private charity in a way which at the time felt completely natural. Donors were able to personalise the provision if they wished, by specifying for whom their almshouse was intended, what would be provided there, and even the exact specification of the building itself.[5] In the many almshouses where the donor had not specified the form the institution was to take, those running and

---

5 For example, Lady Katherine Leveson's very detailed instructions for the building of her hospital at Temple Balsall, Warwickshire: WRO CR 112/Ba177/1 Agreement for Building the first Hospital.

using the almshouse were able continually to shape and reshape the provision according to their own needs and priorities, as these changed over time.[6] The people who founded and administered almshouses were a more diverse group than the merchant aristocracy and landowning nobility and gentry described by Jordan, and the motives which inspired them seem to have been equally various. Many founders were pursuing an agenda which was principally about personal reputation and memorialisation; others were attempting to respond to social need, in response to contemporary anxieties and debate. For some, however, the motivation appears to have been the creation of an idealised model community which went beyond the practical manifestation of private benevolence for a few carefully selected individuals, and reflected instead a more abstract but still powerful concept of an imagined, ordered and disciplined Christian society.

Although emphasis has been placed throughout on the central position of philanthropy, it is equally clear that private charity and poor relief were necessarily enmeshed. Almshouses in this period were not just interesting yet isolated institutions, but were deeply embedded, both conceptually and in practice, in the welfare systems of the time. Initially at least, at a policy level it seems that almshouses were viewed as an essential part of a national system of institutional relief, as indicated in the Elizabethan legislation discussed in chapter 1. A number of early benefactors such as Sir Roger Manwood and William Lambarde appear to have been consciously following the contemporary policy agenda with their foundations, and this motivation can too easily be overlooked when the emphasis is placed on personal memorialisation. Robert Dudley's foundation at Warwick was not only an opportunity to impress the queen and his rivals, but to show the lead in meeting the needs of disabled soldiers, who were considered to contribute to the problem of vagrancy in Elizabethan England. It may even have been the forerunner of a conscious attempt to create a national network of such establishments, as an inquiry by Lord Burghley in 1593 demonstrated the inadequacy of the existing provision for disabled soldiers.[7] Although neither Elizabeth nor the early Stuarts founded almshouses themselves, both she and James I authorised the refounding of many medieval almshouses, such as Sherburn Hospital in County Durham and St Edmund's Hospital in Gateshead, which ensured their survival. Again, under Charles II there was a further, although ineffectual, government attempt to commandeer places in almshouses

---

6   Sir William Pritchard's bequest to the parish in 1697 of the Old Market House in Rope Yard, Woolwich, for example, which was originally used as an almshouse for eight aged and impotent poor, was transformed into a workhouse in 1731: MacKeith, 'Boone Almshouse Charity', p. 6.
7   P. Slack, *From Reformation to Improvement: Public Welfare in Early Modern England* (Oxford, 1999), p. 56. As examples, Christ's Hospital, Buckingham, was founded by royal charter in 1598 for thirty-six maimed and unmarried soldiers, to be followed by Coningsby's Company of Old Servitors in Hereford in 1612: B. Willis, *The History and Antiquities of the Town, Hundred and Deanery of Buckingham* (London, 1755), p. 86, n. 413; E. Prescott, *The English Medieval Hospital 1050–1640* (Melksham, 1992), p. 128.

for disabled soldiers and seamen. This failed because the management of most almshouses lay outside government control, although Bishop Cosin did try to order the almshouses in his diocese to respond to the government initiative.[8] The solution in the end was the creation of the two large royal hospitals, Chelsea for disabled soldiers later in Charles' reign and the Royal Hospital for Seamen at Greenwich founded by William and Mary. There were no further attempts at government control of independent almshouses. They were generally too small to be a useful part of a national programme; they were not necessarily located in the places of greatest need; and they had too much legal autonomy for the authorities easily to appropriate their resources.

At a local rather than a national level, however, almshouses were often integrated within the range of available welfare provision, particularly if their administration and the allocation of places were effectively under the control of those same local officials who exercised responsibility for poor relief. Many community-spirited small benefactors made a contribution in their local area, in line with a long tradition of practical philanthropy stretching back to medieval times, by leaving their own house or other property to the parish to be used as almshouses for the poor, Where there were independent trustees, such as at Leamington Hastings, and at Oken's and Eyffler's in Warwick, these trustees might be the very same people who served as the parish officers, and their decisions might well be influenced by their dual responsibilities for poor relief, as shown in chapter 6. The distribution of almshouses, however, was generally too random for them to have a major practical impact on meeting the needs of the poor nationally; most villages and many towns would not have had access to an almshouse, and after the early decades of the eighteenth century the rate of new foundations declined sharply. According to one historian, they were 'popular and numerous, but not numerous enough'.[9] Their impact, nonetheless, was greater than their numbers might suggest, with the ideal of the almshouse as an appropriate means of caring for the poor continuing to be influential in shaping the expectations and sense of entitlement to accommodation of both the poor and those in authority.[10]

---

8   According to Bishop Cosin's instruction to John Machin, Master of Sherburn Hospital, the king and Council on 7 August 1666 ordered any vacancies in 'the Alms Mens Places in all the Hospitals within this Kingdom' should be reserved for soldiers and sailors disabled in the service of the king: G. Allan, *Collectanea Dunelmensis: Collections Relating Sherburn Hospital in the County Palatine of Durham* (1771), p. 251. At the time of Charles' order, Christ's Hospital, Buckingham, was found to be occupied by seven ancient women, rather than the thirty-six maimed soldiers for whom it was intended: Willis, *Buckingham*, p. 86, n. 414.

9   B. K. Gray, *A History of English Philanthropy from the Dissolution of the Monasteries to the Taking of the First Census* (London, 1905), p. 15.

10   See, for instance, the discussion about the virtues of cottages and the labouring poor in S. Lloyd, 'Cottage Conversations: Poverty and Manly Independence in Eighteenth-Century England', *Past and Present* 184 (2004), 69–108.

The evidence set out in chapters 4 and 5 on almshouse occupants, on the benefits they received and on their experience of almshouse life, challenges the accepted stereotype of almshouses as exclusive places for the respectable elderly poor. The in-depth exploration in chapter 6 of a single institution, through the example of the Humphrey Davis almshouse in Leamington Hastings, gives a rare opportunity to see how a seventeenth-century almshouse operated in practice, in particular the pragmatic way the local trustees used the almshouse resources in tandem with parish poor rates and other charitable funds to meet the needs of the parish. This endowed almshouse was used to house a range of people who would not appear to fit the usual model of the deserving poor, including, as it did at the end of the seventeenth century, an unmarried mother who had been sent to the house of correction for bastardy, a woman convicted and whipped for theft, and a schoolmaster who had apparently once been in prison for debt.[11] It is commonplace to talk of a distinction in the early modern period between the deserving and the undeserving poor, but these examples suggest that our idea of *deservingness* needs revising. In effect, anyone who received alms or a benefit of some kind had been categorised as deserving by the very act of donation, and this did not necessarily imply a moral judgement. It may be more helpful to think in terms of categories of belonging, which led to acceptance of a person's need regardless of their moral worth. Poor people accepted into an almshouse, or those provided with parish relief, even if reluctantly, had all been approved in some way. They were neither vagrants nor outcasts (both categories which were, in this respect, genuinely undeserving). Recipients of poor relief had shown they were entitled to settlement and therefore support in the parish; almshouse occupants had met the founder's criteria for admission, or were part of a network of obligation which ensured their admission through patronage. Respectability and impeccable behaviour were not essential for this entitlement. The frequent patents or certificates declaring that a person seeking admission to an almshouse place was of 'good life and conversation' were often no more than formulaic. They were not necessarily any more truthful than statements such as that the applicant was 'desirous to spend the rest of his tyme in the service of God'.[12] What was important was that the applicant had sufficient credit, for whatever reason, to persuade someone to certify this on their behalf.

There were surprising similarities, particularly in the less wealthy almshouses, between almshouse residents and the recipients of parish relief.

---

11 Jane Man, Margery Guilliams and Henry Bliss (see chapter 6).
12 For instance, the patents of admission for the Lord Leycester Hospital, Warwick, for Francis Whetstone (1625), John Terry (1632), Edward Moore (1638), William Barrett and John Woodgate (1643), Leonard Harrison (1646), John Myles (1647), John Duglas (1658), Robert Sydney (1663), William Colson (1673), Richard Welch (1696), Matthew Crew (1705), Richard Bolton (1708): WRO CR 1600/19/2, 3, 6, 8, 11, 15, 17, 33, 36, 46, 68, and CR 1600/20/41, 59.

One of the key findings in chapter 5 is that in a large number of almshouses the stipend was either non-existent or insufficient to provide the almsperson with a basic subsistence; in many places where there was one, the stipend was merely a contribution to a poor person's living costs, operating in the same way as poor relief. This suggests that many almspeople, just like other poor people in the community, had to 'make shift', employing a multiplicity of strategies in order to survive. There were, however, some crucial differences between people on poor relief and the occupants of almshouses; for instance, almspeople were more likely than parish paupers to be able to attract additional forms of support. One of the most important differences was the security of the almsperson's position. Any benefits they received, including their accommodation, were more or less guaranteed, unlike the recipients of poor relief, who were always subject to the sometimes arbitrary decisions of individual overseers.

There has been considerable interest in the rules that prevailed in some almshouses, but their importance has probably been overemphasised.[13] Where rules existed, they laid down the expected behaviour of almspeople, such as requiring church attendance or prohibiting drunkenness. There was usually a scale of fines or penalties, with expulsion for persistent breaches. In practice, there is little evidence of the rules being rigorously applied, and expulsions seem to have been rare. A place in an almshouse was usually granted for life, and the rules can be viewed principally as a form of contract, rather than a set of onerous restrictions on the almsperson's behaviour. This contract not only protected the gift of a place and the resources of the almshouse from abuse, but it also functioned as a protection of the rights of the occupant against arbitrary punishment and loss of their place. Indeed, some almshouse residents appear to have been very well aware of their rights. Samuel Jemmat, Master of the Lord Leycester Hospital in 1700, complained that when he tried to fine the brethren for offences such as answering him back and not attending church, they threatened to call for a Visitation (the official Visitors were the Bishop, Dean and Archdeacon of Worcester).[14] Poor people on relief and in parish housing almost invariably enjoyed less protection. They might appeal to the magistrates, as did Jude Atkins when he tried to prevent the overseers of Baginton, Warwickshire, from placing another family in his cottage, but there was no guarantee of success. In this instance, the parish argued that Atkins and his family were in their cottage 'upon charity', and he lost his appeal. He was ordered to accept William Brookes and his family into his cottage and not 'make any disturbance'.[15]

---

13 For example, C. Richmond, 'Victorian Values in Fifteenth-Century England: The Ewelme Almshouse Statutes', *Pragmatic Utopias: Ideals and Communities, 1200–1630*, ed. R. Horrox and S. Rees Jones (Cambridge, 2001), pp. 224–41.
14 WRO CR 1741/57 Philip Styles' Notebook, p. 13.
15 WQS, vol. 8, Michaelmas 1687, p. 223.

In most almshouses, occupants seem to have been entitled to private space. Usually this consisted of one or two rooms, or even a small house of their own, with their own fireplace and often their own front door. While little direct evidence survives to compare this with the standard of accommodation in ordinary poor people's housing at the time, appeals to quarter sessions by parish paupers suggest that poor people aspired to the same attributes in publicly provided housing as were available in most almshouses.[16] The support they often received from magistrates, who were themselves part of a propertied class involved in founding or running almshouses, suggests that those in authority often agreed their aspirations were reasonable. Private space and separate doors and hearths were important both practically and symbolically. They enabled the occupants to live independently, despite their economic dependence, and to adopt the appearance if not the reality of autonomous householders.[17] In one of the many paradoxes presented by the evidence, residents in the minority of higher status almshouses appear to have enjoyed less autonomy and independence than the majority of almshouse residents. Occupants living in one of the grander almshouses protected by a gatehouse might have had less direct access to the outside world than those in humbler accommodation. In higher status almshouses with communal facilities, the residents may have been expected to eat together, and spend time with other residents rather than on their own. They were more likely to have been expected to conform to intrusive rules, such as, for example, restricting the amount of time they could be absent from the almshouse; and they may have been subject to on-site supervision and surveillance from a master or warden. In other words, the economic benefits of a place in a wealthier establishment came at a price. The position of these residents was not analogous to that of independent householders, but to that of fairly lowly members of an elite household, where, within a clearly hierarchical establishment, their personal independence was sacrificed in return for the status and material benefits that came with the livery.

The position of women in almshouses is especially interesting, even ambiguous; they were clearly seen as problematic in many establishments, yet women were likely to have benefited most from an almshouse place. Economic discrimination against women was commonplace in early modern England. Women's wages were usually lower than men's, and women often received less in poor relief than male paupers.[18] In some almshouses women had to share

---

16 See, for instance, the discussion in A. Nicholls, '"A convenient habitation fit for Christians to dwell in": Parish Housing for the Poor in Seventeenth-Century Rural Warwickshire', *Warwickshire History* 16/4 (2015/16), 156–69.

17 Rexroth suggests that the importance of the hearth was that it allowed a person to 'keep house': F. Rexroth, *Deviance and Power in Late Medieval London*, trans. P. E. Selwyn (Cambridge, 2007), p. 254.

18 J. Healey, *The First Century of Welfare: Poverty and Poor Relief in Lancashire 1620–1730* (Woodbridge, 2014), p. 193; P. Slack, ed., *Poverty in Early-Stuart Salisbury* (Devizes, 1975),

their accommodation, whereas men rarely did, and some almswomen were expected to take care of other residents. It is nonetheless striking that almshouse stipends rarely discriminated against women, and the material benefits almswomen received were a significant improvement on the circumstances of most poor women. In particular, becoming the occupant of an almshouse may have afforded some poor women an opportunity which they would otherwise have been unable to achieve, that of increased independence and autonomy in old age.[19] Despite the anxiety about the inclusion of women in some establishments, women residents came to predominate in many almshouses where they were eligible for admission, unless their numbers were specifically restricted. This may have been partly a consequence of the apparent shift towards an older population in almshouses over the period of the study. Elderly women outlived men, then as now, and their needs may have been greater than men's if they had fewer alternative means of support available to them.

This predominance may also, however, have been a reflection of a gradual shift in accepted ideas about who were the most appropriate recipients of an almshouse place. There are hints that, by the early eighteenth century, almshouses were beginning to conform to a more restricted model, as trustees of existing almshouses and founders of new ones admitted a less diverse population of resident poor. Travellers, families, and those on parish poor relief were less likely to be included, and specific age requirements became more common in admissions criteria. Elderly widows may increasingly have been seen as a safe choice, people whose circumstances meant that they were in need through no fault of their own. Slack's 'increasing fastidiousness' in who was considered suitable for an almshouse place seems apt, although he was applying it mainly to the earlier exclusion of people such as lepers and lunatics.[20] Slack suggests, moreover, that it was the parallel development of parish poor relief through the seventeenth century that allowed almshouses to become more exclusive: 'A publicly funded system of relief was the foundation … which permitted [Englishmen] to indulge their benevolence in ways which did not need to embrace the disadvantaged and the dispossessed'.[21] By the early eighteenth century pressure of numbers, rising poor rates and hardening

---

pp. 75–82. As a further example, at the Dissolution former nuns received far less compensation than monks and chantry priests: G. A. J. Hodgett, ed., *The State of the Ex-Religious and Former Chantry Priests in the Diocese of Lincoln 1547–1574*, Lincoln Record Society 53 (Lincoln, 1959), p. xvii.

19 Similar, perhaps, to the increased independence experienced by older women of the middling sort in early modern Southampton, as described by A. M. Froide, 'Old Maids: The Lifecycle of Single Women in Early Modern England', *Women and Ageing in British Society Since 1500*, ed. L. Botelho and P. Thane (Harlow, 2001), pp. 89–110.

20 P. Slack, *From Reformation to Improvement: Public Welfare in Early Modern England* (Oxford, 1999), p. 25.

21 Slack, *Reformation*, p. 164.

attitudes meant that public provision for the poor increasingly adopted different characteristics from almshouses.

This is shown most clearly in the development of residential parish workhouses after the 1723 legislation, where the buildings exhibit none of the domestic touches associated with almshouses. For instance, the Chatham workhouse in Kent, built in 1725, was a large, four-storey building with wings at either end, rows of windows but only one door, and two chimney-stacks, one at either end of the building. A plan of the ground floor shows the only fireplaces to have been in the side wings, one of which was the master's accommodation and the other the kitchen and dining room. The central working area, fifty-nine feet in length, was undivided and unheated.[22] There are no surviving plans to show the upper floors, so it is impossible to be sure how the accommodation was arranged, but from the layout of the ground floor it seems likely that the workhouse residents lived in large unheated dormitories with no private space.[23] This was certainly the arrangement at the Framlingham Poor House, built in 1729 within the walls of Framlingham Castle on the site of the castle's great hall (Figure 7.1). This institutional building replaced the seventeenth-century Red House, which had been used as an earlier, more domestic poor house (seen on the left in the photograph).[24] Both the examples at Framlingham and Chatham are in marked contrast to the image of Sir John Banks's six almshouses at Maidstone (shown in Figure 7.2), which were built around 1700 in a superficially similar architectural style. Here, there is no main entrance nor any communal areas. Instead, each of the six almshouses has its own front door and double chimney-stack, indicating at least two heated rooms for each occupant. This would have afforded the fortunate residents considerable independence and comfort.

Reading history backwards from a time when almshouses were juxtaposed with workhouses, it is easy to see that they were distinct institutions, intended for very different categories of poor people, yet it seems that this had not always been the case. The degree of variation in early modern almshouses, particularly in the earlier part of the period under examination, is marked. It is clear that the definitions applied in the sixteenth and seventeenth centuries were much looser than our modern understanding of an almshouse as a charitable foundation with a permanent endowment and independent existence, providing accommodation primarily for old people. It

22   MALSC U480/P17 Plan and Elevation of Workhouse at Chatham c.1725.
23   In the first six years after it was built in 1725, there were on average seventy-three people accommodated in the new workhouse at Chatham: S.P.C.K., *An Account of Several Work-houses*, 1732 edn, http://www.workhouses.org.uk/parishes/index.shtml#Account (accessed 3 November 2016).
24   The Red House had three rooms on each floor: N. Stacey, *Framlingham Castle* (London, 2009), pp. 7, 10, 38.

Figure 7.1. Framlingham Poor House, Suffolk, built in 1729

Figure 7.2. Sir John Banks's Almshouses, Maidstone

is interesting to note that the concept of an almshouse which was exported to the American colonies in the seventeenth century appears to have conformed to an earlier and broader definition, for the characteristic institution known as an almshouse in North America in the eighteenth and nineteenth centuries provided accommodation for orphans, the old, the sick and the deranged. It was based, moreover, around a regime of compulsory work, and was usually supported from public funds.[25]

The early diversity in almshouse provision has been obscured by the subsequent separate trajectories of almshouses and statutory poor relief. This divergence was partly a result of the introduction of workhouses, a very different form of provision, but it was also caused by the gradual separation of the concepts of voluntary charity and statutory responsibility. Seventeenth-century justices of the peace advising parish officers, and commissioners for charitable uses investigating abuses, increasingly argued that charitable bequests should not be used to reduce the poor rates. Once applied, this had the paradoxical effect that gifts left to meet the needs of 'the poor' could no longer be used for the benefit of those poor people, often the very poorest, whose support had become the responsibility of a statutory authority.[26] In this way, parish paupers became increasingly excluded from those groups which benefited from charitable funds, while these in turn became the preserve of the less poor. This can be seen, for instance, in the decision made by the trustees of the Leamington Hastings Poors Plot Charity in 1717 to restrict payments to those parishioners who 'do not receive Collection'. It would be logical to assume that many almshouses also became subject to the same restrictive attitudes, and there are suggestions of this in the evidence discussed in chapters 4 and 6.[27] These changes, like the withdrawal of out-relief and its replacement by workhouses, may have progressed slowly or hardly at all in some places, as argued by Broad in relation to parish housing, but the final separation of charitable funds and statutory responsibilities was legally enforced in the early nineteenth century through municipal reform.[28]

---

25 P. R. Huey, 'The Almshouse in Dutch and English Colonial North America and its Precedent in the Old World: Historical and Archaeological Evidence', *International Journal of Historical Archaeology* 5/2 (2001), 123–54 (p. 144); A. Tobriner, 'Almshouses in Sixteenth-Century England: Housing for the Poor Elderly', *Journal of Religion and Aging* 1/4 (1985), 13–41 (p. 37).

26 The same law of charitable uses controversially excludes state school pupils today from the benefits of many ancient educational charities.

27 WRO DR43a/194 Leamington Hastings Records of the Poors Plot Charity, October 1717.

28 J. Broad, 'Housing the Rural Poor in Southern England, 1650–1850', *The Agricultural History Review* 48/2 (2000), 151–70. The Municipal Reform Act of 1835 removed charitable funds from town corporations which, like Faversham and Warwick, had used them, together with the proceeds of local taxation, in an undifferentiated fashion to meet the needs of their local population. Towns were required instead to establish separate and wholly independent municipal charities to administer any charitable funds previously under their control.

However great the degree of variation in early modern almshouses and however distorted the modern perceptions of comfortable almshouse life, the concept of the almshouse that survived in England was nevertheless that of an institution of benevolence. This had deep roots in medieval England, where the recurring demand for the 'hundred hospitals' represented a rallying cry for reform and concern for the plight of the poor. Almshouses may have failed to address the national problems of poverty and vagrancy, and they may have been overtaken by workhouses as the standard means by which the poor came to be accommodated. Yet, at the local level, they could still provide a model of tangible philanthropy and, through their portrayal of homely independence, an idealised articulation of how the poor should live. The reality of a local almshouse, such as Humphrey Davis's at Leamington Hastings, may not have matched the grandeur and comfort of more famous institutions, nor even the imagined respectability of popular perception, but it was a more typical representation of the early modern almshouse than that usually portrayed. Occupied by the poor of the parish and managed by local trustees, its continued contribution to housing the poor over four centuries remains a tribute to the efforts of men such as Humphrey Davis, Thomas Trevor, Matthew Over and their neighbours.

Appendix 1: Almshouse Foundations by County, 1550–1870

County	[a] Almshouses founded 1550–1599[1]	[b] Number of Almshouses by 1600[1]	[c] Localities with Almshouses c.1870[2]
Bedfordshire	0	1	15
Berkshire	6	19	28
Buckinghamshire	3	7	32
Cambridgeshire	8	15	16
Cheshire	0	3	10
Cornwall	0	3	13
Cumberland	0	1	7
Derbyshire	2	2	29
Devon	10	26	44
Dorset	3	8	22
Durham	0	6	15
Essex	12	27	38
Gloucester (incl. Bristol)	7	31	27
Hampshire	4	11	18
Herefordshire	1	5	18
Hertfordshire	4	5	26
Huntingdonshire	0	0	9
Kent	15	26	58
Lancashire	1	4	17
Leicestershire	1	3	26
Lincolnshire	3	8	59
Middlesex and London	12	44	44
Norfolk	5	21	22

County	[a] Almshouses founded 1550–1599[1]	[b] Number of Almshouses by 1600[1]	[c] Localities with Almshouses c.1870[2]
Northamptonshire	3	11	34
Northumberland	0	7	5
Nottinghamshire	1	11	20
Oxfordshire	1	6	21
Rutland	2	3	7
Shropshire	2	13	17
Somerset	7	20	36
Staffordshire	1	4	19
Suffolk	10	23	32
Surrey	2	5	31
Sussex	2	9	23
Warwickshire	6	11	16
Westmorland	0	0	3
Wiltshire	3	18	28
Worcestershire	3	5	13
Yorkshire, East Riding of	7	21	14
Yorkshire, North Riding of	2	14	19
Yorkshire, West Riding of	8	15	69

1   Figures from Marjorie McIntosh database.
2   Figures from N. Goose and M. Yates, 'Charity and Commemoration: A Berkshire Family and their Almshouse, 1675–1763', *Population, Welfare and Economic Change in Britain 1290–1834*, ed. C. Briggs, P. M. Kitson and S. J. Thompson (Woodbridge, 2014), pp. 227–48 (pp. 234–6).

Appendix 2: Size of Almshouses in Eight English Counties, 1550–1725

County	Number of almshouses	Total places[1]	Average size[2]	Range	Median	Almshouses with 12 or more residents	Percentage of almshouses with 12 or more residents
Durham	19	139	7.5	3–15	6	5	26%
Warwickshire	32	241	7.7	2–24	6	5	16%
Kent[3]	75	610	8.4	2–40	6	15	20%
Nottinghamshire	30	228	7.6	2–24	6	7	23%
Dorset	27	199	7.4	2–16	6	3	11%
Yorkshire, West Riding of	60	471	7.9	2–20	6	15	25%
Lincolnshire	54	343	6.4	2–16	6	6	11%
Shropshire	20	171	8.6	4–33	6	8	40%
Total	317	2402	7.6	2–40	6	64	20%

1 Where the number of places in an almshouse is not known, the median has been assumed. Out-pensioners have been excluded.

2 Only almshouses where the number of places is known have been used to calculate the average size.

3 The more than one hundred residents of the Royal Naval Hospital at Greenwich have been excluded from all calculations for Kent.

Appendix 3: Almshouse Numbers and Places in Three Counties, 1550–1800

County	Almshouses c.1550		Almshouses in 1600		Almshouses in 1670			Almshouses in 1725		Almshouses in 1800		
	No.	Places	No.	Places	No.	Places	Places as % of over-sixty population	No.	Places	No.	Places	Places as % of over-sixty population
Durham	5	40	5	40	12	73	1.39%	19	139	20	145	1.27%
Warwickshire	7	64	14	109	21	148	1.82%	32	236	32	236	1.95%
Kent	17	198	36	331	60	480	3.23%	75	590	81	615	2.60%
Total	29	302	55	480	93	701		126	965	133	996	

Source: Online Appendix A.

Appendix 4: Minimum Subsistence Budget in 1690s Adjusted for Inflation

Year	[a] Inflation index	[b] Minimum subsistence budget	Year	[a] Inflation index	[b] Minimum subsistence budget
1500s	106		1600s	527	£2 15s 0d
1510s	116		1610s	583	£3 1s 0d
1520s	159		1620s	585	£3 1s 2d
1530s	161		1630s	687	£3 11s 8d
1540s	217		1640s	723	£3 15s 6d
1550s	315	£1 13s 0d	1650s	687	£3 11s 8d
1560s	298	£1 11s 2d	1660s	702	£3 13s 4d
1570s	241[1]	£1 15s 6d[1]	1670s	675	£3 10s 6d
1580s	389	£2 0s 7d	1680s	631	£3 6s 6d
1590s	530	£2 15s 4d	1690s	737	£3 17s 0d

[a] Inflation index, based on a composite unit of foodstuffs (1451–1470 = 100), reproduced from L. A. Botelho, *Old Age and the English Poor Law, 1500–1700* (Woodbridge, 2004), p. 144.
[b] Minimum subsistence budget from 1690s adjusted for inflation

1 The figure of 241 seems surprising and does not accord with the movement in prices shown in Keith Wrightson's similar table, where the respective figures for the 1560s and 1570s are 278 and 315: K. Wrightson, *Earthly Necessities: Economic Lives in Early Modern Britain, 1470–1750* (London, 2002), p. 117. Assuming this is a misprint, the figure of 341 is used to calculate the minimum subsistence budget for the 1570s.

Bibliography

Manuscript sources

CCA Canterbury Cathedral Archives
CC/S/7/1 St Stephen's Hospital Memorandum and Disbursements Book 1593–1828
CC/S/8/1 Maynard and Cotton Almshouses, Accounts 1599–1653 and Admissions 1630–1795
CC/S/24/1 Alderman Bunce's Register of Loans and Charitable Donations to the City of Canterbury (1798)
CC Supp Ms/6 Alderman Gray's Notebook 1737–1780
U3/39/28/13 Hackington Churchwardens' Accounts 1588–1601 (typed transcripts)
U3/173/25/6 Fulnetby's Charity, Sandwich
U13 Records of St John's Hospital, Canterbury
U38/1 Jesus Hospital Memorandum Book
U204 Records of Jesus Hospital, Canterbury (Sir John Boys' Hospital)

CHC Coventry History Centre
BA/H/3/17/1 Coventry Council Minute Book 1557–1640

CKS Kent History and Library Centre, Maidstone (formerly the Centre for Kentish Studies)
Ch147/A2 Thomas Dunk's Charity Register
Ch147/A10 Copy of will of Sir Thomas Dunk
Ch153/F1 Thomas Iddenden's Charity Accounts
Fa/Ac4/1 Faversham Wardmote Minutes 1633–1740 part 1
Fa/Ac5/1 Faversham Wardmote Minutes 1741–1820 part 1
P12/12/3 Aylesford Overseers' accounts 1713–1746
P142/12/1 East Farleigh Overseers' Accounts 1715–1751
P178/5/9 Hawkhurst Churchwardens' Accounts 1717–1759
P178/11/1 Hawkhurst Overseers' Poor Book 1711–1726
P178/13/315 Hawkhurst warrant 1723
P178/13/316 Hawkhurst order 1726
P206/12/1 Kenardington Churchwardens' and Overseers' Accounts 1642–1707

P223/5/1 Leigh Churchwardens' and Overseers' Accounts 1631–1683
P241/11/1 Maidstone Poor Book 1668–1677
P243/18/164 West Malling Overseers' records, Sale of household goods of Dorothy Harding to the Overseers 1687
P309/11/1 New Romney Overseers' Accounts 1653–1710
U187/7/1 St Thomas's Hospital Sandwich, 1725 hospital rules

DCL Durham Cathedral Library
Add MS 375/1 Transcription (1898) of Chapter Act Book vol. 1, 1578–1726

DRO Durham County Record Office
D/HH 10/17/170 St John's Hospital, Barnard Castle 1592–1593
DU/6/1/6 Charity Commissioners, Further Report 30 January 1830
DU/6/1/9 *Durham Chronicle* newspaper reports on local charities 1868
EP/Au SA12/39(3) Auckland St Andrew's, Correspondence regarding Bishop Cosin's almshouses
EP/CS 4/92 and 4/93 Churchwardens and Overseers Account Books 1606–1666 (three volumes) and 1670–1702
EP/CS 4/104 Chester-le-Street Memorandum Book of Charities 1626–1919
EP/Du.MB 10 St Mary-le-Bow Durham Parish Book 1678–1760
EP/Du.SO 203–4 St Oswald's Durham Churchwardens' Accounts 1580–1656, 1658–1822
EP/Ga.SM 5/1 Gateshead St Mary's Resolutions of Vestry Meetings 1681–1807
EP/Ho 280 Report on Kepier School and Almshouse 1878
EP/Ho 300 Letter from Jane Tooley, daughter of George Lilburne of Sunderland, 11 June 1697
EP/Ho 559 Foundation Document of Kepier School and Almshouse 1570–1571
EP/Ho 613 Thomas Delaval's Notebook 1657–1663
EP/Pi 22 Pittington parish records
EP/Rom 12/2 Romaldkirk Regulations for the management of the Bowes and Romaldkirk charities 1891
EP/Wi 18 Winston Overseers' books 1632–1728
Q/S/OB5 Quarter Sessions Order Book 1660–1668
Q/S/OB6 Quarter Sessions Order Book January 1668–January 1681

DULSC Durham University Library Special Collections
DCD/L/BB Cathedral Treasurer's Books 1557–1921
DCD/T/YB York Book 1567–1599
MS/91 Mickleton and Spearman Manuscripts late 16th to early 18th centuries
MSP 25 Mickleton and Spearman Manuscripts 1635–1691

LRO Lichfield Record Office
B/V/1/24 Leber Cleri, Lichfield and Coventry Diocese 1605
Calendar of wills: cal. 125.22 (1581); cal. 423.16 (1589); cal. 60.11 (1591);
    143.10 (1598); cal. 1166.21 (1606); cal. 473.9 (1611); cal. 1405.18 (1636);
    cal.364.18 (1692); cal. 176.31 (1693)

MALSC Medway Archives and Local Studies Centre, Strood
CH108 Records of Sir John Hawkins's Hospital 1500–1984
P85/5/2 Chatham St Mary's Churchwardens' Accounts 1673–1686
P85/8/2 Chatham St Mary's Vestry Minutes 1715–1739
P188/12 Hoo Overseers' Accounts 1601–1760
P336/5/1 Shorne Churchwardens' accounts 1630–1681
RCA/A1 Rochester City Corporation records 1227–1974
U480/P17 Plan and Elevation of Workhouse at Chatham c.1725
VF COB 726.709 Rules and Ordinances made for the New College of Cobham
    in the Countie of Kent [undated]

NRO Northumberland Record Office, Woodhorn
309/A/2 Virgin Mary Hospital, Newcastle, Account Book no. 2, 1686–1699

SANT Society of Antiquaries of Newcastle upon Tyne:
SANT/BEQ/5/1/3 Thomas Bell's Collections re King James' Hospital
SANT/DEE/3/20/9 Keelmen's Hospital Indenture 1700
SANT/GUI/NCL/6/6/2 St Mary Magdalene Hospital Act (1867)

SBT Shakespeare Birthplace Trust Record Office, Stratford-upon-Avon
BRU15/15/106 Proposals for Regulating the Almshouse (late seventeenth–early
    eighteenth century)
DR18/13/9/1 Will of Sir Thomas Leigh

TNA National Archives, Kew
C90/6 Commissioners for Charitable Uses: Confirmation in the case of
    Leamington Hastings charity, 7 Car. I
C93/13/14 Commissioners for Charitable Uses: Inquisitions and Decrees,
    Leamington Hastings 1631–1632
C93/4/7 Commissioners for Charitable Uses: regarding the will of Oliver
    Killingworth
C93/30/28 Chancery Inquisition 1669
Prob/11/111 Will of Humphrey Davies (Davis) 1607
Prob/11/115 Sentence of Humphrey Davies (Davis) 1610
Prob/11/145 Will of Thomas Walford 1625
Prob/11/248 Will of Alexander Ansttey 1655
Prob/11/373 Will of John Allington 1683

Prob/11/548/170 Will of Nicholas Chamberlaine, Clerk of Bedworth Warwickshire, 24 June 1715

WRO Warwickshire County Record Office, Warwick
CR 112 Manorial records of Temple Balsall, including Lady Leveson's Hospital
CR 136/M14 Map of the three common fields of Chilvers Coton 1684
CR 556/164 Correspondence between Matthew Wise and Warwick Corporation 1747–1755, 1781
CR 1319 Manorial records of Leamington Hastings
CR 1540/6 Transcript of the Will of Lady Katherine Leveson (1671)
CR 1600 Records of the Hospital of Robert Earl of Leicester
CR 1618/W15/17/7, 9, 31–32, Hospital accounts 1689–90
CR 1618/WA3/84 Nineteenth-century copy of Thomas Oken's will 1570
CR 1618/WA3/89 Review of Puckering's Charity [undated, post-1809]
CR 1618/WA12 Warwick town records of charities, including records of Oken's and Eyffler's almshouses, and the Lord Leycester Hospital
CR 1618/WA17/102 Book of admissions compiled by William Walton, Senior Steward, in 1868
CR 1741/28 Ipsley Overseers' Accounts 1661–1730
CR 1741/57 Philip Styles' notebook
CR 2219/13 Codicil to Brooke Bridges' will 1702
CR 2758/1 Oken's Charity Accounts 1574–1596
DR18/15/3 Temple Balsall lawsuit by the overseers of the poor regarding the administration of the hospital, 1685–1700
DR43/1 Leamington Hastings Register of Baptisms, Marriage and Burials 1559–1704
DR43a/iii/5 Bond 22 February 1593
DR43a/iii/12 Copy of Bill in Chancery relating to the hospital at Leamington Hastings
DR43a/19 Leamington Hastings Overseers' Accounts 1655–1679
DR43a/20 Leamington Hastings Overseers' Accounts 1681–1704
DR43a/193 Leamington Hastings Enclosure agreement 1665
DR43a/194 Leamington Hastings Records of the Poors Plot Charity
DR43a/195 Leamington Hastings Davis/Wheler Charity records 1686–1799
DRB36/5 Temple Balsall Register of Admissions 1678–1890
M287 'The Estemat of Sam Dunckley for the Almseshowes upon the backhills' (microfiche of original documents in the Folger Shakespeare Library, Washington DC)
QS 11/56 Hearth Tax Assessment Book 1674, Knightlow Hundred, Southam Division
Z725/5 Correspondence relating to the Lord Leycester Hospital, 1689–1775

Government publications
Online at: http://parlipapers.proquest.com/parlipapers

HCPP (House of Commons Parliamentary Papers), *Reports of the Commissioners Appointed to Inquire Concerning Charities in England and Wales*, no. 7 (1822); no. 8 (1823); no. 12 (1825); no. 15 (1826); no. 18 (1828); no. 21 (1829); no. 23 (1830); no. 28 (1834); no. 29 (1835); no. 30 (1837); no. 32, part 2 (1837–38)

———, *Report from the Committee on Certain Returns, Relative to the State of the Poor, and to Charitable Donations; &c. Reported by Thomas Gilbert, Esq.* (23 May 1787)

Printed primary sources

Allan, G., *Collectanea Dunelmensis: Collections Relating Sherburn Hospital in the County Palatine of Durham* (1771)

Allen, D. H., ed., *Essex Quarter Sessions Order Book 1652–1661*, Essex Edited Texts 1 (Chelmsford, 1974)

Anon., *A Brief History of Sherburn Hospital in the County of Durham, with Observations on the 'Scheme' Proposed by the Charity Commissioners 'for the Application and Management and the Estates and Possessions Thereof'* (London and Oxford, 1855)

Anon., *Churchwardens' Accounts of Pittington and Other Parishes in the Diocese of Durham from AD 1580 to 1700*, Surtees Society 84 (Durham, 1888)

Anon., *The Compleat Parish Officer*, 7th edn (1734)

Anon., *An Ease for Overseers of the Poore, Abstracted from the Statutes, Allowed by Practice, and Now Reduced Into Forme, as a Necessarie Directorie for Imploying, Releeving, and Ordering of the Poore* (1601)

Anon., *The Foundation Deeds and Other Documents Relating to Dame Sarah Hewley's Charity* (London, 1849)

Anon., *A Supplication of the Poor Commons* (1546)

Arkell, T. and N. Alcock, eds, *Warwickshire Hearth Tax Returns: Michaelmas 1670* (Stratford-upon-Avon and London, 2010)

Bavington Jones, J., ed., *The Records of Dover* (Dover, 1920)

Dalton, M., *The Countrey Justice* (1630)

Farr, M., ed., *The Great Fire of Warwick 1694*, Dugdale Society 36 (Stratford-upon-Avon, 1992)

Fox, L., ed., *Minutes and Accounts of the Corporation of Stratford-Upon-Avon and Other Records*, vol. 5: *1593–1598*, Dugdale Society 35 (Stratford-upon-Avon, 1990)

Green, A., E. Parkinson and M. Spufford, eds, *Durham Hearth Tax Assessment Lady Day 1666* (London, 2006)

Hale, M., *A Discourse Touching Provision for the Poor* (1683)

Harrington, D. and P. Hyde, eds, *The Early Town Books of Faversham, c.1251 to 1581* (Folkestone, 2008)

Harrington, D., S. Pearson and S. Rose, eds, *Kent Hearth Tax Assessment Lady Day 1664* (London and Maidstone, 2000)

Hartley, T. E., ed., *Proceedings in the Parliaments of Elizabeth I*, vol. 1: *1558–1581* (Leicester, 1981)

Hasted, E., *The History and Topographical Survey of the County of Kent*, vol. 3 (1797); vol. 4 (1798)

Hodgett, G. A. J., ed., *The State of the Ex-Religious and Former Chantry Priests in the Diocese of Lincoln 1547–1574*, Lincoln Record Society 53 (Lincoln, 1959)

Hughes, P. L. and J. F. Larkin, eds, *Tudor Royal Proclamations*, vol. 2: *The Later Tudors (1553–1587)* (New Haven and London, 1969)

Johnson, H. C., ed., *Warwick County Records*, vol. 8: *Quarter Sessions Records, Trinity 1682 to Epiphany 1690* (Warwick, 1953)

Johnson, H. C. and N. J. Williams, eds, *Warwick County Records*, vol. 9: *Quarter Sessions Records, Easter 1690 to Michaelmas 1696* (Warwick, 1964)

Jones, J., ed., *Stratford-upon-Avon Inventories*, vol. 1: *1538–1625*, Dugdale Society 39 (Stratford-upon-Avon, 2002)

Kemp, T., ed., *The Black Book of Warwick* (Warwick, 1898)

———, ed., *The Book of John Fisher, Town Clerk and Deputy Recorder of Warwick (1580–1588)* (Warwick, 1900)

Merry, M. and C. Richardson, eds, *The Household Account Book of Sir Thomas Puckering of Warwick 1620*, Dugdale Society 45 (Warwick, 2012)

Ornsby, G., ed., *The Correspondence of John Cosin D.D. Lord Bishop of Durham: Together with Other Papers Illustrative of his Life and Times, Part I*, Surtees Society 52 (Durham, 1869)

———, ed., *The Correspondence of John Cosin D.D. Lord Bishop of Durham: Together with Other Papers Illustrative of his Life and Times, Part II*, Surtees Society 55 (Durham, 1872)

———, ed., *Miscellanea*, Surtees Society 37 (Durham, 1861)

Ratcliff, S. C. and H. C. Johnson, eds, *Warwick County Records*, vol. 1: *Quarter Sessions Order Book, Easter 1625 to Trinity 1637* (Warwick, 1935)

———, eds, *Warwick County Records*, vol. 2: *Quarter Sessions Order Book, Michaelmas 1637 to Epiphany 1650* (Warwick, 1936)

———, eds, *Warwick County Records*, vol. 3: *Quarter Sessions Order Book, Easter 1650 to Epiphany 1657* (Warwick, 1937)

———, eds, *Warwick County Records*, vol. 4: *Quarter Sessions Order Book, Easter 1657 to Epiphany 1665* (Warwick, 1938)

————, eds, *Warwick County Records*, vol. 5: *Quarter Sessions Order Book, Easter 1665 to Epiphany 1674* (Warwick, 1939)

————, eds, *Warwick County Records*, vol. 6: *Quarter Sessions Indictment Book, Easter 1631 to Epiphany 1674* (Warwick, 1941)

————, eds, *Warwick County Records*, vol. 7: *Quarter Sessions Records, Easter 1674 to Easter 1682* (Warwick, 1946)

Savage, R., ed., *Minutes and Accounts of the Corporation of Stratford-Upon-Avon and Other Records 1553–1620*, vol. 1: *1553–1566*, Dugdale Society 1 (Stratford-upon-Avon, 1921)

Tawney, R. H. and E. Power, eds, *Tudor Economic Documents*, vol. 2 (London, 1924)

Thomas, A. H. and I. D. Thornley, eds, *The Great Chronicle of London* (London, 1983)

Vives, J. L., 'De subventione pauperum' (1526), *Some Early Tracts on Poor Relief*, ed. F. R. Salter (London, 1926), pp. 4–31

Secondary sources

Adams, M. and C. MacKeith, *Boone's Chapel: History in the Making* (London, 2010)

Alcock, N. W., *People at Home: Living in a Warwickshire Village, 1500–1800* (Chichester, 1993)

Archer, I. W., 'The Charity of Early Modern Londoners', *Transactions of the Royal Historical Society* 12 (2002), 223–44

————, *The Pursuit of Stability: Social Relations in Elizabethan London* (Cambridge, 1991)

Arkell, T., 'The Incidence of Poverty in England in the Later Seventeenth Century', *Social History* 12 (1987), 23–47

————, 'Multiplying Factors for Estimating Population Totals from the Hearth Tax', *Local Population Studies* 28 (1982), 52–7

Arnold, A. A., *Cobham College* (London, 1905)

Aston, M., '"Caim's Castles": Poverty, Politics and Disendowment', *The Church, Politics and Patronage in the Fifteenth Century*, ed. B. Dobson (Gloucester, 1984), pp. 45–81

Atherton, I., E. McGrath and A. Tomkins, '"Pressed down by want and afflicted with poverty, wounded and maimed in war or worn down with age?" Cathedral Almsmen in England 1538–1914', *Medicine, Charity and Mutual Aid: The Consumption of Health and Welfare in Britain, c.1550–1950*, ed. A. Borsay and P. Shapely (Aldershot, 2007), pp. 11–34

Baer, W. C., 'Housing the Poor and Mechanick Class in Seventeenth-Century London', *The London Journal* 25/2 (2000), 13–39

Bailey, B., *Almshouses* (London, 1988)

Barley, M. W., *The English Farmhouse and Cottage* (London, 1961)

Barnes, T. G., 'The Prerogative and Environmental Control of London Building in the Early Seventeenth Century: The Lost Opportunity', *California Law Review* 58 (1970), 1332–63

Beier, A. L., *The Problem of the Poor in Tudor and Early Stuart England* (London, 1983)

———, 'The Social Problems of an Elizabethan Country Town: Warwick, 1580–90', *Country Towns in Pre-Industrial England*, ed. P. Clark (Leicester, 1981), pp. 46–79

Beresford, M. and J. G. Hurst, *Deserted Medieval Villages*, 3rd edn (Gloucester 1989)

Bettey, J., ed., *Wiltshire Farming in the Seventeenth Century* (Trowbridge, 2005)

Blaydon, A., 'Almshouse Rules and Regulations for Trustees and Almspeople with Particular Reference to Surrey', *The British Almshouse: New Perspectives on Philanthropy ca. 1400–1914*, ed. N. Goose, H. Caffrey and A. Langley (Milton Keynes, 2016), pp. 211–31

Bolitho, P., *Warwick's Most Famous Son: The Story of Thomas Oken and his Charity* (Warwick, 2003)

Botelho, L. A., *Old Age and the English Poor Law, 1500–1700* (Woodbridge, 2004)

———, 'The Seventeenth Century', *The Long History of Old Age*, ed. P. Thane (London, 2005), pp. 113–74

Botelho, L. and P. Thane, *Women and Ageing in British Society Since 1500* (Harlow, 2001)

Boulton, J. and L. Schwarz, '"The Comforts of a Private Fireside"? The Workhouse, the Elderly and the Poor Law in Georgian Westminster: St Martin-in-the-Fields, 1725–1824', *Accommodating Poverty: The Housing and Living Arrangements of the English Poor, c.1600–1850*, ed. J. McEwan and P. Sharpe (Basingstoke, 2011), pp. 221–45

Broad, J., 'Housing the Rural Poor in Southern England, 1650–1850', *The Agricultural History Review* 48/2 (2000), 151–70

———, 'Parish Economies of Welfare, 1650–1834', *The Historical Journal* 42/4 (1999), 985–1006

———, 'The Parish Poor House in the Long Eighteenth Century', *Accommodating Poverty: The Housing and Living Arrangements of the English Poor, c.1600–1850*, ed. J. McEwan and P. Sharpe (Basingstoke, 2011), pp. 246–62

Burgess, C., '"A fond thing vainly invented": An Essay on Purgatory and Pious Motive in Later Medieval England', *Parish, Church and People: Local Studies in Lay Religion 1350–1750*, ed. S. Wright (London, 1988), pp. 56–84

Burton, N., *The Geffrye Almshouses* (London, 1979)

Caffrey, H., 'Almshouse Buildings: Form, Function and Meaning', *The British Almshouse: New Perspectives on Philanthropy ca. 1400–1914*, ed. N. Goose, H. Caffrey and A. Langley (Milton Keynes, 2016), pp. 22–45

———, *Almshouses in the West Riding of Yorkshire 1600–1900* (King's Lynn, 2006)

Carpenter, C., *Locality and Polity: A Study of Warwickshire Landed Society, 1401–1499* (Cambridge, 1992)

Carter, J. and J. Smith, *Give and Take: Scenes from the History of Christ's Hospital, Abingdon, 1553–1900* (Abingdon, 1981)

Cavallo, S., 'The Motivation of Benefactors: An Overview of Approaches to the Study of Charity', *Medicine and Charity Before the Welfare State*, ed. J. Barry and C. Jones (London, 1991), pp. 46–62

Chalkin, C. W., *Seventeenth-Century Kent* (London, 1965)

Chatwin, P. B., 'The Hospital of Lord Leycester, Formerly the Hall and Other Buildings of the Medieval Guilds in Warwick', *Birmingham Archaeological Society: Transactions and Proceedings* 70 (1952), 37–47

Clark, E., 'Social Welfare and Mutual Aid in the Medieval Countryside', *Journal of British Studies* 33 (1994), 381–406

Clark, P. and L. Murfin, *The History of Maidstone: The Making of a Modern County Town* (Stroud, 1995)

Clarke, H., S. Pearson, M. Mate and K. Parfitt, *Sandwich, 'the completest medieval town in England': A Study of the Town and Port from its Origins to 1600* (Oxford, 2010)

Clay, C., 'Landlords and Estate Management in England', *The Agrarian History of England and Wales*, vol. 5(2), ed. J. Thirsk (Cambridge, 1985), pp. 119–251

Clay, R. M., *The Medieval Hospitals of England* (London, 1909)

Cleary, J. and M. Orton, *So Long as the World Shall Endure: The Five Hundred Year History of Ford's and Bond's Hospitals* (Coventry, 1991)

Cockburn, E. O., *The Almshouses of Dorset* (Dorchester, 1970)

Coleman, D. C., 'Review: W. K. Jordan, Philanthropy in England', *Economic History Review* (series 2) 13 (1960–61), 113–15

Cooper, C., *Maidstone, A History* (Chichester, 2008)

Cowley, P., *The Church Houses* (London, 1970)

Croft, P., 'The Catholic Gentry: The Earl of Salisbury and the Baronets of 1611', *Conformity and Orthodoxy in the English Church, c.1560–1660*, ed. P. Lake and M. Questier (Woodbridge, 2000), pp. 262–81

Cronin, H. S., 'The Twelve Conclusions of the Lollards', *The English Historical Review* 22/86 (1907), 292–304

Crust, L., *Lincolnshire Almshouses: Nine Centuries of Charitable Housing* (Sleaford, 2002)

Cullum, P., '"For Pore People Harberles": What Was the Function of the

Maisondieu?', *Trade, Devotion and Governance: Papers in Late Medieval History*, ed. D. J. Clayton, R. G. Davies and P. McNiven (Stroud, 1994), pp. 36–54

Davidson, A., *A History of the Holtes of Aston, Baronets; with a Description of the Family Mansion, Aston Hall, Warwickshire* (Birmingham, 1854)

Dollman, F. T., *Examples of Ancient Domestic Architecture: Illustrating the Hospitals, Bede-Houses, Schools, Almshouses, etc. of the Middle Ages in England* (London, 1858)

Dyer, C., 'Poverty and its Relief in Late Medieval England', *Past and Present* 216 (2012), 41–78

———, *Standards of Living in the Later Middle Ages: Social Change in England, c.1200–1520* (Cambridge, 1989)

Earl, E. A., *Nottinghamshire Almshouses, from Early Times to 1919* (self-published, 2011)

Elton, G. R., *The Parliament of England 1559–1581* (Cambridge, 1986)

Fewster, J. M., *The Keelmen of Tyneside: Labour Organisation and Conflict in the North-East Coal Industry, 1600–1830* (Woodbridge, 2011)

Froide, A. M., 'Old Maids: The Lifecycle of Single Women in Early Modern England', *Women and Ageing in British Society Since 1500*, ed. L. Botelho and P. Thane (Harlow, 2001), pp. 89–110

Godfrey, W. H., *The English Almshouse, with Some Account of its Predecessor, the Medieval Hospital* (London, 1955)

Goodall, J., *God's House at Ewelme: Life, Devotion and Architecture in a Fifteenth-Century Almshouse* (Aldershot, 2001)

Gooder, E., *Temple Balsall: From Hospitallers to a Caring Community, 1322 to Modern Times* (Chichester, 1999)

Goose, N., 'The English Almshouse and the Mixed Economy of Welfare: Medieval to Modern', *Local Historian* 40/1 (2010), 3–19

Goose, N. and S. Basten, 'Almshouse Residency in Nineteenth-Century England: An Interim Report', *Family and Community History* 12/1 (2009), 65–76

Goose, N., H. Caffrey and A. Langley, eds, *The British Almshouse: New Perspectives on Philanthropy ca. 1400–1914* (Milton Keynes, 2016)

Goose, N. and H. Looijesteijn, 'Almshouses in England and the Dutch Republic *circa* 1350–1800: A Comparative Perspective', *Journal of Social History* 45/4 (2012), 1049–73

Goose, N. and L. Moden, *A History of Doughty's Hospital, Norwich, 1687–2009* (Hatfield, 2010)

Goose, N. and M. Yates, 'Charity and Commemoration: A Berkshire Family and their Almshouse, 1675–1763', *Population, Welfare and Economic Change in Britain 1290–1834*, ed. C. Briggs, P. M. Kitson and S. J. Thompson (Woodbridge, 2014), pp. 227–48

Gray, B. K., *A History of English Philanthropy from the Dissolution of the Monasteries to the Taking of the First Census* (London, 1905)

Green, A., 'Heartless and Unhomely? Dwellings of the Poor in East Anglia and North-East England', *Accommodating Poverty: The Housing and Living Arrangements of the English Poor, c.1600–1850*, ed. J. McEwan and P. Sharpe (Basingstoke, 2011), pp. 69–101

Hadwin, J. F., 'Deflating Philanthropy', *Economic History Review* 31 (1978), 105–17

Hallett, A., *Almshouses* (Princes Risborough, 2004)

Hare, S., 'Almshouse Gardens with Particular Reference to Somerset', *The British Almshouse: New Perspectives on Philanthropy ca. 1400–1914*, ed. N. Goose, H. Caffrey and A. Langley (Milton Keynes, 2016), pp. 298–314

Hart, F. H., *History of Lee and its Neighbourhood* (Greenwich, 1971)

Harvey, M., *Lay Religious Life in Late Medieval Durham* (Woodbridge, 2006)

Heal, F., 'The Idea of Hospitality in Early Modern England', *Past and Present* 102 (1984), 66–93

Heal, F. and C. Holmes, *The Gentry in England and Wales, 1500–1700* (Basingstoke, 1994)

Healey, J., *The First Century of Welfare: Poverty and Poor Relief in Lancashire 1620–1730* (Woodbridge, 2014)

Heath, S., *Old English Houses of Alms: A Pictorial Record with Architectural and Historical Notes* (London, 1910)

Hill, D. I., *The Ancient Hospitals and Almshouses of Canterbury* (Canterbury, 2004)

Hindle, S., *The Birthpangs of Welfare: Poor Relief and Parish Governance in Seventeenth-Century Warwickshire*, Dugdale Society Occasional Paper 40 (Stratford-upon-Avon, 2000)

———, 'Dependency, Shame and Belonging: Badging the Deserving Poor, c.1550–1750', *Cultural History* 1 (2004), 29–58

———, *On the Parish? The Micro-Politics of Poor Relief in Rural England c.1550–1750* (Oxford, 2004)

———, '"Without the cry of any neighbours": A Cumbrian Family and the Poor Law Authorities, c.1690–1730', *The Family in Early Modern England*, ed. H. Berry and E. Foyster (Cambridge, 2007), pp. 126–57

———, 'Work, Reward and Labour Discipline in Late Seventeenth-Century England', *Remaking English Society: Social Relations and Social Change in Early Modern England*, ed. S. Hindle, A. Shepard and J. Walter (Woodbridge, 2013), pp. 255–80

Hinkley, E. J. F., *A History of the Richard Watts Charity* (Rochester, 1979)

Hiscock, R. H., *A History of Gravesend* (Chichester, 1976)

Hitchcock, T., *Down and Out in Eighteenth-Century London* (London, 2004)

Hitchcock, T., P. King and P. Sharpe, eds, *Chronicling Poverty: The Voices and Strategies of the English Poor, 1640–1840* (Basingstoke, 1997)

Horden, P., 'Small Beer? The Parish and the Poor and Sick in Later Medieval England', *The Parish in Late Medieval England*, ed. C. Burgess and E. Duffy (Donington, 2006), pp. 339–64

Hoskins, W. G., 'The Rebuilding of Rural England, 1570–1640', *Past and Present* 4 (1953), 44–59

Howson, B., *Almshouses: A Social and Architectural History* (Stroud, 2008)

———, *Houses of Noble Poverty: A History of the English Almshouse* (Sunbury-on-Thames, 1993)

Huey, P. R., 'The Almshouse in Dutch and English Colonial North America and its Precedent in the Old World: Historical and Archaeological Evidence', *International Journal of Historical Archaeology* 5/2 (2001), 123–54

Hufton, O., *The Poor of Eighteenth-Century France, 1750–1789* (Oxford, 1974)

Hughes, A., *Politics, Society and Civil War in Warwickshire, 1620–1660* (Cambridge, 1987)

Hutchinson, W., *The History and Antiquities of the County Palatine of Durham*, vol. 2 (Newcastle, 1785)

Imray, J., *The Charity of Richard Whittington: A History of the Trust Administered by the Mercers' Company, 1424–1966* (London, 1968)

———, 'The Early Days of Trinity Hospital', *Transactions of the Greenwich and Lewisham Antiquarian Society* 9/3 (1981), 117–36

Innes, J., 'Prisons for the Poor: English Bridewells, 1555–1800', *Labour, Law and Crime: An Historical Perspective*, ed. F. Snyder and D. Hay (London, 1987), pp. 42–122

Jackson, N. G., *Southlands 1610–1960* (Nottingham, 1960)

Jacob, E., *History of Faversham* (1774; new edn, Sheerness, 1974)

Johnson, M., *Housing Culture: Traditional Architecture in an English Landscape* (London, 1993)

Jones, C., 'Some Recent Trends in the History of Charity', *Charity, Self-Interest and Welfare in the English Past*, ed. M. Daunton (London, 1996), pp. 51–63

Jones, G., *History of the Law of Charity 1532–1827* (Cambridge, 1969)

Jones, J., *Family Life in Shakespeare's England: Stratford-upon-Avon 1570–1630* (Stroud, 1996)

Jordan, W. K., *The Charities of London 1480–1660* (London, 1960)

———, *The Charities of Rural England 1480–1660* (London, 1961)

———, 'The Forming of the Charitable Institutions of the West of England: A Study of the Changing Pattern of Social Aspirations in Bristol and Somerset, 1480–1660', *Transactions of the American Philosophical Society* (new series) 50/8 (1960), 29–58

———, *Philanthropy in England 1480–1660: A Study of the Changing Pattern of English Social Aspirations* (London, 1959)

————, *Social Institutions in Kent: A Study of the Changing Pattern of Social Aspirations*, Archaeologia Cantiana 75 (Maidstone, 1961)

————, *The Social Institutions of Lancashire: A Study of the Changing Patterns of Aspirations in Lancashire, 1480–1660*, Chetham Society (3rd series) 11 (Manchester, 1962)

Joyce, P., *Patronage and Poverty in Merchant Society: The History of Morden College, Blackheath 1695 to the Present* (Henley-on-Thames, 1982)

Jütte, R., *Poverty and Deviance in Early Modern Europe* (Cambridge, 1994)

Kennett, J., *Thomas Philipot's Almshouse Charity of Eltham and Chislehurst* (Eltham, 1997)

Kidd, A., 'Philanthropy and the "Social History Paradigm"', *Social History* 21 (1996), 180–92

King, P., 'Pauper Inventories and the Material Lives of the Poor in the Eighteenth and Early Nineteenth Centuries', *Chronicling Poverty: The Voices and Strategies of the English Poor, 1640–1840*, ed. T. Hitchcock, P. King and P. Sharpe (Basingstoke, 1997), pp. 155–91

King, S., *Poverty and Welfare in England 1700–1850: A Regional Perspective* (Manchester, 2000)

King, S. and A. Tomkins, eds, *The Poor in England 1700–1850: An Economy of Makeshifts* (Manchester, 2003)

Kipps, P. K., 'Trinity Hospital, Greenwich', *Transactions of the Greenwich and Lewisham Antiquarian Society* 3/6 (1935), 294–301

Knighton, C. S., 'The Reformed Chapter, 1540–1660', *Faith and Fabric: A History of Rochester Cathedral, 604–1994*, ed. N. Yates and P. A. Welsey (Woodbridge, 1996), pp. 57–76

Kreider, A., *English Chantries: The Road to Dissolution* (Cambridge, MA and London, 1979)

Langley, A., 'Warwickshire Almshouses, 1400 to 1900: "Affording comfortable asylums to the aged and respectable poor"', *Warwickshire History* 14/4 (2009/10), 139–55

————, 'Warwickshire Almshouses: To What Extent Were They "affording comfortable asylums to the aged and respectable poor"?', *The British Almshouse: New Perspectives on Philanthropy ca. 1400–1914*, ed. N. Goose, H. Caffrey and A. Langley (Milton Keynes, 2016), pp. 121–37

Lawrence, A. H., *The Rev. Nicholas Chamberlaine Rector of Bedworth: His Times and his Charity 1715–1965* (Nuneaton, n.d.)

Leonard, E. M., *The Early History of English Poor Relief* (Cambridge, 1900)

Lloyd, S., 'Cottage Conversations: Poverty and Manly Independence in Eighteenth-Century England', *Past and Present* 184 (2004), 69–108

Lutton, R., *Lollardy and Orthodox Religion in Pre-Reformation England: Reconstituting Piety* (Woodbridge, 2006)

MacFarquhar, G. I., *Leamington Hastings Almshouses and Poor's Plots* (Rugby, 1984)

Manco, J., *The Spirit of Care: The Eight Hundred Year Story of St John's Hospital, Bath* (Bath, 1998)

Markus, T. A., *Buildings and Power* (London, 1993)

Marshall, D., *The English Poor in the Eighteenth Century: A Study in Social and Administrative History* (London, 1926)

Marshall, P., *Beliefs and the Dead in Reformation England* (Oxford, 2002)

Mauss, M., *The Gift: Forms and Functions of Exchange in Archaic Societies*, trans. Ian Cunnison (originally *Essai sur le don*, 1925; London, 1966)

May, T., *The Victorian Workhouse* (Princes Risborough, 1997)

McEwan, J. and P. Sharpe, eds, *Accommodating Poverty: The Housing and Living Arrangements of the English Poor, c.1600–1850* (Basingstoke, 2011)

McIlwain, J., *The Hospital of St Cross and St Cross Church* (Andover, 1993)

McIntosh, M., *A Community Transformed: The Manor and Liberty of Havering, 1500–1620* (Cambridge, 1991)

———, 'Local Responses to the Poor in Late Medieval and Tudor England', *Continuity and Change* 3/2 (1988), 209–45

———, 'Negligence, Greed and the Operation of English Charities, 1350–1603', *Continuity and Change* 27 (2012), 53–81

———, 'Networks of Care in Elizabethan English Towns: The Example of Hadleigh, Suffolk', *The Locus of Care: Families, Communities, Institutions and the Provision of Welfare in Antiquity*, ed. P. Horden and R. Smith (London, 1998), pp. 71–89

———, *Poor Relief and Community in Hadleigh, Suffolk 1547–1600* (Hatfield, 2013)

———, *Poor Relief in England 1350–1600* (Cambridge, 2012)

———, 'Poverty, Charity and Coercion in Elizabethan England', *Journal of Interdisciplinary History* 35/3 (2005), 457–79

Muldrew, C., *Food, Energy and the Creation of Industriousness: Work and Material Culture in Agrarian England, 1550–1780* (Cambridge, 2011)

Mulryne, J. R., ed., *The Guild and Guild Buildings of Shakespeare's Stratford: Society, Religion, School and Stage* (Farnham, 2012)

Neale, J. E., *The Elizabethan House of Commons* (London, 1949)

Nicholls, A., '"A convenient habitation fit for Christians to dwell in": Parish Housing for the Poor in Seventeenth-Century Rural Warwickshire', *Warwickshire History* 16/4 (2015/16), 156–69

Nicolson, A., *Earls of Paradise* (London, 2008)

Orme, N. and M. Webster, *The English Hospital 1070–1570* (New Haven and London, 1995)

Ottaway, S., *The Decline of Life: Old Age in Eighteenth Century England* (Cambridge, 2004)

Owen, D., *English Philanthropy 1660–1960* (Oxford, 1965)

Page, W., ed., *A History of the County of Warwick* (Victoria County History), vol. 2 (London, 1909)

Payne, C., 'Murillo-like Rags or Clean Pinafores?: Artistic and Social Preferences in the Representation of the Dress of the Rural Poor', *Textile History* 33/1 (2002), 48–62

Pears, S. A., 'The Lord Leycester Hospital, Warwick', *Transactions of the Ancient Monuments Society* (new series) 13 (1965/6), 35–41

Peck, L. L., *Northampton: Patronage and Policy at the Court of James I* (London, 1982)

Pelling, M., *The Common Lot: Sickness, Medical Occupations and the Urban Poor in Early Modern England* (Harlow, 1998)

——, 'Old Age, Poverty and Disability in Early Modern Norwich: Work, Remarriage, and Other Expedients', *Life, Death and the Elderly: Historical Perspectives*, ed. M. Pelling and R. M. Smith (London, 1991), pp. 62–84

——, 'Who Most Needs to Marry?', *Women and Ageing in British Society Since 1500*, ed. L. Botelho and P. Thane (Harlow, 2001), pp. 31–42

Phelps Brown, H. and S. V. Hopkins, *A Perspective of Wages and Prices* (London and New York, 1981)

Pinches, S., 'From Common Rights to Cold Charity: Enclosure and Poor Allotments in the Eighteenth and Nineteenth Centuries', ed. A. Borsay and P. Shapely, *Medicine, Charity and Mutual Aid: The Consumption of Health and Welfare in Britain, c.1550–1950* (Aldershot, 2007), pp. 35–53

Platt, C., *The Great Rebuildings of Tudor and Stuart England: Revolutions in Architectural Taste* (London, 1994)

Porter, S., *The London Charterhouse* (Stroud, 2009)

——, 'Order and Disorder in the Early Modern Almshouse: The Charterhouse Example', *The London Journal* 23/1 (1998), 1–14

Prescott, E., *The English Medieval Hospital 1050–1640* (Melksham, 1992)

Pugh, R. B., *The Victoria History of Wiltshire*, vol. 7 (London, 1953)

Questier, M. C., *Catholicism and Community in Early Modern England: Politics, Aristocratic Patronage and Religion, c.1550–1640* (Cambridge, 2006)

Raphael, M., *The Romance of English Almshouses* (London, 1926)

Rexroth, F., *Deviance and Power in Late Medieval London*, trans. P. E. Selwyn (Cambridge, 2007)

Richardson, W. C., *History of the Court of Augmentations, 1536–1554* (Baton Rouge, 1961)

Richmond, C., 'Religion', *Fifteenth-Century Attitudes: Perceptions of Society in Late Medieval England*, ed. R. Horrox (Cambridge, 1994), pp. 183–201

——, 'Religion and the Fifteenth-Century English Gentleman', *The Church, Politics and Patronage in the Fifteenth Century*, ed. B. Dobson (Gloucester, 1984), pp. 193–208

——, 'Victorian Values in Fifteenth-Century England: The Ewelme Almshouse Statutes', *Pragmatic Utopias: Ideals and Communities, 1200–1630*, ed. R. Horrox and S. Rees Jones (Cambridge, 2001), pp. 224–41

Roberts, P., 'Elizabethan Players and Minstrels and the Legislation of 1572 Against Retainers and Vagabonds', *Religion, Culture and Society in Early Modern Britain*, ed. A. Fletcher and P. Roberts (Cambridge, 1994), pp. 29–55

Robson, H. L., 'George Lilburne, Mayor of Sunderland', *Antiquities of Sunderland and its Vicinity*, ed. H. Simpson, Sunderland Antiquarian Society 22 (Sunderland, 1960), pp. 92–102

———, 'The Medieval Hospitals of Durham: Paper Read to the Sunderland Antiquarian Society 17 November 1953', *Antiquities of Sunderland and its Vicinity*, ed. H. Simpson, Sunderland Antiquarian Society 22 (Sunderland, 1960), pp. 33–56

Roome, K. M., *Styleman's Almshouses* (Bexley, 1985)

Rosenthal, J. T., *The Purchase of Paradise: Gift Giving and the Aristocracy, 1307–1485* (London, 1972)

Rouse, W. H. D., *A History of Rugby School* (London, 1898)

Royal Commission on Historical Monuments, *An Inventory of Historical Monuments: The Town of Stamford* (London, 1977)

Rubin, M., *Charity and Community in Medieval Cambridge* (Cambridge, 1987)

———, 'Development and Change in English Hospitals, 1100–1500', *The Hospital in History*, ed. L. Granshaw and R. Porter (London and New York, 1989), pp. 41–59

———, 'Imagining Medieval Hospitals: Considerations on the Cultural Meaning of Institutional Change', *Medicine and Charity Before the Welfare State*, ed. J. Barry and C. Jones (London, 1991), pp. 14–25

Ruddock, A. A., 'The Trinity House at Deptford in the Sixteenth Century', *English Historical Review* 65/257 (1950), 458–76

Rushton, N. S., 'Monastic Charitable Provision in Tudor England: Quantifying and Qualifying Poor Relief in the Early Sixteenth Century', *Continuity and Change* 16/1 (2001), 9–44

Salzman, L. F., ed., *The Victoria History of the County of Warwick*, vol. 6: *Knightlow Hundred* (Oxford, 1951)

Sandwich Local History Society, *Sandwich Almshouses 1190–1975*, Occasional Paper 2 (Sandwich, n.d.)

Saville, G. E., *Bleachfield and Swan Streets and Stratford Road*, Alcester and District Local History Society Occasional Paper 35 (Alcester, 1985)

Sharp, B., 'Common Rights, Charities and the Disorderly Poor', *Reviving the English Revolution: Reflections and Elaborations on the Work of Christopher Hill*, ed. G. Eley and W. Hunt (London and New York, 1988), pp. 107–37

Shepard, A., *Meanings of Manhood in Early Modern England* (Oxford, 2003)

Simpson, H., ed., *Antiquities of Sunderland and its Vicinity*, Sunderland Antiquarian Society 22 (Sunderland, 1960)

Slack, P., *From Reformation to Improvement: Public Welfare in Early Modern England* (Oxford, 1999)

——, 'Hospitals, Workhouses and the Relief of the Poor in Early Modern London', *Health Care and Poor Relief in Protestant Europe 1500–1700*, ed. O. P. Grell and A. Cunningham (London, 1997), pp. 234–51

——, ed., *Poverty in Early-Stuart Salisbury* (Devizes, 1975)

——, *Poverty and Policy in Tudor and Stuart England* (London, 1988)

Smith, C., *The Almshouses of York* (York, 2010)

Smith, R. M., 'Ageing and Well-Being in Early Modern England: Pension Trends and Gender Preferences Under the English Old Poor Law c.1650–1800', *Old Age from Antiquity to Post-Modernity*, ed. P. Johnson and P. Thane (London and New York, 1998), pp. 64–95

Somerville, R., *The Savoy, Manor: Hospital: Chapel* (London, 1960)

Stacey, N., *Framlingham Castle* (London, 2009)

Stephens, W. B., ed., *A History of the County of Warwick*, vol. 8: *The City of Coventry and Borough of Warwick* (London, 1969)

Styles, J., *The Dress of the People: Everyday Fashion in Eighteenth-Century England* (New Haven and London, 2007)

Styles, P., 'The Evolution of the Law of Settlement', *Studies in Seventeenth-Century West Midlands History* (Kineton, 1978), pp. 175–204

Surtees, R., *The History and Antiquities of the County Palatine of Durham*, vol. 1 (London, 1816)

Sweetinburgh, S., *The Role of the Hospital in Medieval England: Gift-Giving and the Spiritual Economy* (Dublin, 2004)

Tankard, D., 'The Regulation of Cottage Building in Seventeenth-Century Sussex', *Agricultural History Review* 59 (2011), 18–35

Taylor, B., *Abbot's Hospital, Guildford* (Guildford, 1999)

Tennant, A., 'The Property and Landholding Survey of 1607', *Brailes History: Episodes from a Forgotten Past* 4 (2005), 1–28

Thane, P., *The Long History of Old Age* (London, 2006)

——, *Old Age in English History: Past Experiences, Present Issues* (Oxford, 2000)

——, 'Old People and Their Families in the English Past', *Charity, Self-Interest and Welfare in the English Past*, ed. M. Daunton (London, 1996), pp. 113–38

Thirsk, J., *Food in Early Modern England: Phases, Fads, Fashions, 1500–1760* (London, 2007)

Thomson, J. A. F., 'Piety and Charity in Late Medieval London', *Journal of Ecclesiastical History* 16 (1965), 178–95

Tibbits, E. G., 'The Hospital of Robert, Earl of Leicester, in Warwick', *Birmingham Archaeological Society: Transactions and Proceedings* 60 (1936), 112–44

Tobriner, A., 'Almshouses in Sixteenth-Century England: Housing for the Poor Elderly', *Journal of Religion and Aging* 1/4 (1985), 13–41

Tomkins, A., *The Experience of Urban Poverty 1723–82: Parish, Charity and Credit* (Manchester, 2006)

———, 'Retirement from the Noise and Hurry of the World? The Experience of Almshouse Life', *Accommodating Poverty: The Housing and Living Arrangements of the English Poor, c.1600–1850*, ed. J. McEwan and P. Sharpe (Basingstoke, 2011), pp. 263–83

Tyack, G., *The Making of the Warwickshire Country House 1500–1650*, Warwickshire Local History Society Occasional Paper 4 (Warwick, 1982)

van der Slice, A., 'Elizabethan Houses of Correction', *Journal of Criminal Law and Criminology* 27/1 (1936), 45–67

Van Leeuwen, M. H. D., 'Logic of Charity: Poor Relief in Preindustrial Europe', *Journal of Interdisciplinary History* 24/4 (1994), 589–613

Venn, J. and J. A. Venn, eds, *Alumni Cantabrigienses*, part 1, vol. 2 (Cambridge, 1922)

Wales, T., 'Poverty, Poor Relief and the Life-Cycle: Some Evidence from Seventeenth-Century Norfolk', *Land, Kinship and Life-Cycle*, ed. R. M. Smith (Cambridge, 1984), pp. 351–404

Walsham, A., *The Reformation of the Landscape: Religion, Identity, and Memory in Early Modern Britain and Ireland* (Oxford, 2011)

Warnicke, R. M., *William Lambarde, Elizabethan Antiquary* (London and Chichester, 1973)

Watts, S., *Shropshire Almshouses* (Woonton Almeley, 2010)

Webb, J., *Great Tooley of Ipswich: Portrait of an Early Tudor Merchant* (Ipswich, 1962)

———, *Poor Relief in Elizabethan Ipswich*, Suffolk Records Society 9 (Ipswich, 1966)

Webb, S. and B. Webb, *English Local Government*, vol. 7: *English Poor Law History, Part I: The Old Poor Law* (London, 1927)

White, J., 'The Laboring-Class Domestic Sphere in Eighteenth-Century British Social Thought', *Gender, Taste, and Material Culture in Britain and North America 1700–1830*, ed. J. Styles and A. Vickery (New Haven and London, 2006), pp. 247–63

Whyte, W., 'How Do Buildings Mean? Some Interpretations in the History of Architecture', *History and Theory* 45/2 (2006), 153–77

Williams, E. H. D., 'Church Houses in Somerset', *Vernacular Architecture* 23 (1992), 15–23

Willis, B., *The History and Antiquities of the Town, Hundred and Deanery of Buckingham* (London, 1755)

Wood, B., 'Almshouse Clothing', *The British Almshouse: New Perspectives on Philanthropy ca. 1400–1914*, ed. N. Goose, H. Caffrey and A. Langley (Milton Keynes, 2016), pp. 266–83

Woodfield, C. and P. Woodfield, *Lyddington Bede House Rutland* (London, 1988)

Wrightson, K., *Earthly Necessities: Economic Lives in Early Modern Britain, 1470–1750* (London, 2002)
———, *English Society 1580–1680*, 2nd edn (London, 2003)
Wrightson, K. and D. Levine, *Poverty and Piety in an English Village: Terling, 1525–1700* (Oxford, 1979; new edn 1995)
Wrigley, E. A., ed., *Identifying People in the Past* (London, 1973)
Wrigley, E. A. and R. S. Schofield, *The Population History of England 1541–1871: A Reconstruction* (Cambridge, 1989)
WRO (Warwickshire County Record Office), *'To Divers Good Uses': A Directory of the Warwick Charities Past and Present* (Warwick, 1993)

Unpublished sources

Barker-Read, M., 'The Treatment of the Aged Poor in Five Selected West Kent Parishes from Settlement to Speenhamland (1662–1797)' (PhD thesis, Open University, 1988)
Boulton, J., 'The Almshouses and Almswomen of St Martin-in-the-Fields, 1614–1818', paper given at the Almshouses in Europe conference, Haarlem, the Netherlands, 7 September 2011
Fox, C. M., 'The Royal Almshouse at Westminster c.1500–c.1600' (PhD thesis, Royal Holloway, University of London, 2012)
MacKeith, C., 'The Christopher Boone Almshouse Charity in Lee: A Study of Poor Relief and Almshouse Traditions in the Blackheath Hundred', paper given at the Almshouses in Europe conference, Haarlem, the Netherlands, 8 September 2011
Newman, L., 'Deserted Medieval Villages', paper given to Warmington Heritage Group, Warwickshire, 10 May 2010, http://www.warmingtonheritage.com/publications/research-projects/deserted-medieval-villages/ (accessed 16 December 2013)
Stevinson, J., ed., 'Leamington Hastings in an Age of Revolution' (Warwickshire County Record Office, 1993)
Wigram, G. E., 'History of Leamington Hastings' (Warwickshire County Record Office, typed, n.d.)

Websites

Almshouse Association, http://www.almshouses.org
Oxford Dictionary of National Biography, http://www.oxforddnb.com
S.P.C.K., *An Account of Several Work-houses*, 1732 edn, http://www.workhouses.org.uk/parishes/index.shtml#Account

Index

A Supplication of the Poor Commons   37

Abbot, George, Archbishop of Canterbury
30, 59, 67, 87, 165, 180, 182

Abbot's Hospital, Guildford   30, 67,
139n, 143, 144, 148, 169, 170, 180, 181,
182, 184

Abiding places   23, 24, 25, 26, 36

Abingdon, Oxfordshire (formerly
Berkshire)   70, 80

Accommodation in almshouses   10, 17,
62, 72, 91, 92, 119, 138, 139–46, 147,
151, 156, 157, 158, 186
  compared with parish housing   154,
155, 157, 230
  cubicles   140, 146, 149, 150
  geographical differences   149–50
  hearths and chimneys   139, 140, 141,
143, 148, 149, 158, 168, 206, 230, 232
  individual front doors   139, 142, 143,
191, 230, 232
  individual rooms   140, 150, 230
  number of rooms   132, 147, 149, 150,
151, 232
  privacy   140, 141, 143, 156, 158, 186,
230
  sharing rooms   115, 143, 150, 151, 153,
206, 230
  size of rooms   151

Acts of Parliament
  1536 Act for Punishment of
Sturdy Vagabonds and Beggars
(27 Hen. VIII c. 25)   22
  1547 Act for the Punishment of
Vagabonds and for the Relief of
the Poor and Impotent Persons
(1 Edw. VI c. 3)   21, 22
  1552 Act for the Provision and Relief of
the Poor (5 & 6 Edw. VI c. 2)   22
  1563 Act for the Relief of the Poor
(5 Eliz. c. 3)   22, 23, 28

1571 Earl of Leicester's Hospital Act
(13 Eliz. c. 17)   28

1572 Act for the Punishment of
Vagabonds and for Relief of the
Poor and Impotent (14 Eliz. c. 5)
22, 23, 24, 25, 27, 28, 29, 30, 31, 36,
43

1576 Act for the Setting of the Poor
on Work, and for the Avoiding of
Idleness (18 Eliz. c. 3)   23, 25, 27,
28, 30, 43

1589 Act against Erecting and
Maintaining of Cottages (31 Eliz.
c. 7)   32

1598 Act for the Relief of the Poor
(39 Eliz. c. 3)   22, 27, 29, 36

1598 Act for the Punishment of Rogues,
Vagabonds and Sturdy Beggars
(39 Eliz. c. 4)   28

1598 Act for Erecting of Hospitals or
Abiding and Working Houses for
the Poor (39 Eliz. c. 5)   26–7, 28,
30, 42, 43

1598 Act to Reform Deceits and
Breaches of Trust, touching Lands
given to Charitable Uses (39 Eliz.
c. 6)   31, 42, 43

1601 Act for the Relief of the Poor
(43 Eliz. c. 2)   22, 27, 36

1601 Act to Redress the
Misemployment of Lands, Goods
and Stocks of Money given to
Charitable Uses (43 Eliz. c. 4)   31

1610 Act for the due execution of divers
Laws and Statutes heretofore made
against Rogues Vagabonds and
Sturdy Beggars and other lewd and
idle persons (7 Jac. I c. 4)   27

1662 Act for the Better Relief of the Poor of this Kingdom (14 Car. II c. 12)   32

1697 Act for supplying some Defects in the Laws for the Relief of the Poor of this Kingdom (8 & 9 Will. III c. 30)   34

1723 Act for Amending the Laws relating to the Settlement, Employment and Relief of the Poor (Workhouse Test Act, Knatchbull's Act) (9 Geo. I c. 7)   14, 34, 35, 54, 232

1736 The Mortmain Act (9 Geo. II c. 36)   54

1835 The Municipal Corporations Act (Municipal Reform Act) (5 & 6 Wm IV c. 76)   235n

Administration of almshouses   15, 58, 78, 79, 80, 82, 83, 86, 89, 91, 95, 99, 115, 121, 129, 130, 131, 163, 196, 197, 224, 227
   by Town Corporations   56, 58, 78, 80
Admission fee   119, 120, 121
Admissions criteria for almshouses   29, 33, 71, 90, 91, 100, 101, 103, 106, 110, 114, 117, 118, 125, 136, 181, 223, 228, 231
   abuse of   110, 121
   changes, restrictions   204, 207, 231
Age of almshouse occupants   91, 103, 106, 107, 108, 111, 116, 201, 231
Alcester, Warwickshire   60, 86, 162, 225
Alcock, Nat   151
Aldrich, John, Mayor of Norwich   25n
Allen, Robert, Mayor of Faversham   80
Allesley, Warwickshire   135
Allington, Rev. John   208, 211n
Almshouse buildings   10, 13, 84, 89, 146, 156, 159, 232
   architecture   9, 10, 13, 67, 139, 143, 144, 146, 159
   chapel   10, 128, 132, 139, 144
   communal facilities   148, 230
   cottage row   10, 72, 139, 143, 144, 146, 148, 225
   courtyard, quadrangle   10, 132, 139, 143
   domestic house   72, 142, 191, 227
   garde robes   140, 147
   gates, gatehouse   133, 143, 190, 230

infirmary hall   139, 148
   location   51, 55, 61, 73, 75, 78, 135, 143, 184, 227
   repairs   120, 146, 156, 163, 170, 180, 196
Almshouse definition   3, 6, 17, 91
   distinction between almshouses and hospitals   6, 7, 91
   other names for   6
Almshouse numbers   17, 39, 44, 45, 47, 53, 54, 57, 86
   increase in   30, 37, 42, 44, 46, 53
   regional difference in   40, 46, 47, 51, 55, 79
Almshouse size   71–2, 139, 227
Almshouses, joint foundations with schools   70, 95, 110, 134
Almshouses, social significance of   2, 13, 29, 41, 71, 224, 227, 236
Almshouses and poor relief   4, 126, 138, 165, 166, 168, 169, 178, 184, 186, 190, 228, 229, 235
Almshouses as a response to social need   12, 18, 37, 41, 42, 43, 49, 51, 54, 55, 88, 224, 226, 227
Almshouses as places of privilege   28, 117, 173, 187, 224, 225, 228
Almshouses for founder's tenants, servants and dependants   51, 56, 74, 89, 100, 102
Almshouses for occupational groups
   clergy widows   88, 100
   merchants   99, 132
   seamen   7, 79, 99
   soldiers   28, 29, 39, 67, 101, 108, 226n, 227
   tradesmen   77, 98, 99, 100
   weavers   98
Almshouses for specific religious denominations   100
Almshouses for the poor   39, 60, 117, 180, 197
Almshouses for the sick   90, 91, 93, 94, 235
Almshouses for travellers   29, 38, 61, 70, 90, 91, 92
Amherst, Charles   162
Andrews, Joan   216
Ansley, Warwickshire   155
Anstye, Alexander   194

Apprenticing poor children   98, 125, 166, 206, 210, 211
Arbury, Warwickshire   155, 162
Archbishop of Canterbury   17, 30, 41, 59, 67, 84, 120, 131, 165
Archbishop of York   41, 59, 173
Archer, Ian   174–7
Arkell, Tom   203
Ashby, William   108
Ashwell, Elizabeth   119
Ashwell, John   119, 120
Astley, Joyce   154
Aston, Birmingham   74, 75
Aston, Margaret   63
Aston Hall, Birmingham   74, 146
Atkins, Jude   229
Austin, Ann   123
Aylesford, Kent   93
Ayres, Widow   201

Bablake Boys' Hospital, Coventry   95
Badges and insignia worn by almspeople   97, 167–8
Baginton, Warwickshire   229
Bailey, Brian   9
Baker, Henry   106n
Baldock, Widow   123
Balsall, Warwickshire   102, 121
Banbury, Oxfordshire   190
Banks, Sir John   149
Banks's Almshouses, Maidstone   149, 151, 232
Barnard Castle, County Durham   39, 150
Basley, Thomas   152
Bath, Somerset   94
Battle, Thomas   108
Baylye, Ralph   180
Baynton, Sir Henry   66, 71
Beamsley Hospital, West Yorkshire   59, 148
Beaufort, Cardinal Henry   140
Beckenham, Kent   72
Bede House, Higham Ferrers   159
Bede House, Lyddington   98, 114, 116
Bedfordshire   47
Bedlam. See Bethlehem Hospital, London
Bedworth, Warwickshire   51, 59, 88, 100
Beggars, begging   20, 21, 22, 23, 24, 25, 28, 64, 182, 183, 186, 190
Begging by almspeople   160, 183, 184
Beier, A. L.   34, 152

Bellott, Thomas   94
Benson, John (Bourton-on-Dunsmore)   213
Benson, John   201, 207
Benson, Samuel   213
Benson, Thomas   202
Benson, Widow   207
Benson, William   202
Berkeley, Robert   144, 146
Berkeley's Hospital, Worcester   144, 146
Berkshire   49
Berkswell, Warwickshire   151, 154
Berry, Gabriel   154
Bethlehem Hospital, London   26, 91
Bettey, Joseph   152
Bexley, Kent   95
Biddle, Joan   216
Binckes, Rev. William   111n, 135, 209
Bird catcher   205, 222
Birdingbury, Warwickshire   217
Birkfield, John   106n
Bishop Auckland, Durham   59, 87, 161
Bishop of Durham   39, 59, 86, 87, 108, 111, 134, 158, 160
Bishop of Worcester   229
Bishops   22, 29
Bishops Itchington, Warwickshire   34
Bishopwearmouth, County Durham   59, 156
Black, John   130
Blacke, John   180
Blackfriars, Ipswich   24
Blackheath, London   132
Blackheath Hundred   98
Blaydon, Angela   126
Bleachfield Almshouses, Alcester   60, 225
Bliss, Alice   203n, 205
Bliss, Henry   181, 203n, 205
Blithe, Matthew   115
Blythe, Alice   202
Blythe, Thomas and Eleanor   203
Bodkins, John   124
Bodmin, Devon   24
Bolton, Mary   122
Bond, Thomas   78n
Bond's Hospital, Coventry   26, 28, 51, 95, 105, 131, 164
Boone's Almshouse, Lee   106, 183
Botelho, Lynn   105, 113, 152, 167, 172, 174–7
Boughton, Sir William   110

Boulton, Jeremy   14
Bow, London   83
Bowes, John   59
Bowes, Martin   82, 105
Bowes Almshouse, Woolwich   105, 113
Boys, Sir John   118, 128, 180, 183
Bredon, Thomas   110
Bridewell. *See* House of Correction
Bridewell Hospital, London   24, 26, 29,
    91, 175
Bridges   57, 79, 80
Bridges, Brooke   162
Bridges, John   60, 86, 162
Bristol   34, 44, 47, 99
Broad, John   6, 35, 188–9, 222, 235
Broadwell, Warwickshire   190, 200, 202,
    209, 211, 215, 221
Broke, Sir Thomas   63
Bromham, Wiltshire   66, 67
Bromley College, Kent   100, 134, 149, 151
Brooke, William, Lord Cobham   41, 73,
    79, 80, 83, 84
Brookes, William   229
Brougham Commission   54, 172
Browne's Hospital, Stamford   117, 140,
    147
Buckingham   163
Buckinghamshire   47, 162, 163, 164, 171
Burgesses   15, 36, 43, 71
Burghley, Lord. *See* Cecil, William
Burial costs for almshouses residents   122,
    148, 204
Butcher   77
Butler, George   92
Butler, Robert   169
Butler, Widow   154
Bynge, Robert   119

Caffrey, Helen   13, 144
Cambridge   60
Cambridge University   191, 193, 195
Canning, Isabella   202
Canterbury, Kent   39, 58, 78, 84, 88, 95,
    97, 100, 104, 109, 110, 118, 119, 120,
    125, 128, 164
Carpenter, Christine   57
Carte, Thomas   109
Carter, Mary   122
Cartwright, Thomas   81
Castle Eden, County Durham   154
Castle Rising, Norfolk   59, 73

Cathedral beadsmen   128, 161
Catholic recusants   85, 209
Cavallo, Sandra   198
Cawston, Norfolk   170
Cecil, Robert   79
Cecil, Thomas, Baron Burghley   90n, 98,
    114, 117
Cecil, William, Lord Burghley   41, 79, 83,
    90n, 94, 108, 226
Census of the Poor, Norwich   105
Census of the Poor, Warwick   107, 152,
    182
Chaderton, Laurence   81, 85
Chamberlaine, Rev. Nicholas   51, 58, 88,
    100
Chancery, Court of   121, 191, 195, 196,
    210
Chantries   11, 40, 62, 63, 64, 67, 82, 84,
    174
Chantry almshouses   11, 40, 62, 84, 103,
    127
Chapman, Richard   92
Charity   11, 15, 31, 41, 59, 72, 124, 183,
    229
    abuses of   54, 194, 195, 235
    and poor relief   2, 4, 7, 11, 41, 183,
        189, 213, 215, 226
    attitudes to   49, 54, 64, 65, 67, 81, 170,
        184
    benefactors   11, 29, 30, 36, 194
    casual, informal   11, 183–4, 205
    changes in charitable giving   57, 59,
        193
    charitable bequests   7, 30, 43, 183
    charitable funds   29, 49, 190, 191
    charitable trusts and trustees   30, 31,
        43, 121, 196–7, 208, 211, 212
    endowed charity   11, 18, 21, 43, 194
    local charities   10, 194
    medical charities   54
    medieval   59, 64
    motivation for   61
    religious motivation for   42, 56, 61, 66
    secularisation of   65
    separation from poor relief   235
    subscription charities   54
Charlecote Park, Warwickshire   75
Charles II   59n, 60, 160, 226
Charterhouse, London   70, 133, 139n
Chatham, Kent   41, 93, 99, 108, 124, 231
Chatham Chest   108

Chebsey, Mr 213
Chesham, Buckinghamshire 163
Cheshire 53
Chester 92
Chester-le-Street, County Durham 77, 100, 105, 122
Child, Widow 124
Children in almshouses 91, 94, 95, 97, 103, 136, 182, 225, 235
Chilvers Coton, Warwickshire 155
Chittam, John 203
Chittam, William 165, 200, 203, 205, 212, 222
Christ's Hospital, Abingdon 80, 130
Christ's Hospital, Buckingham 226n, 227n
Christ's Hospital, Ipswich 24, 93
Christ's Hospital, London 26, 28, 36, 77, 91
Christ's Hospital, Sherburn. See Sherburn Hospital, Durham
Chubb, Matthew 44
Church, the 5, 15, 40, 59, 60, 61, 64, 81, 82, 84, 85, 87, 88, 100, 209, 210. See also Parish church
Church ales 6, 60
Church attendance 127, 128, 199, 208, 209, 229
  by almspeople 127, 128, 129, 199
Church houses 6, 7, 22, 35, 60, 154
Church rates 7
Church seating for almspeople 67, 147n, 161, 189
Churchwardens 8, 27, 60, 61, 86, 92, 93, 95, 123, 124, 135, 155, 205, 208, 210, 221, 225
Churchyard 61, 183, 184
Civic humanism 64
Civil War, English 86, 100, 208
Clark, Alderman John 51, 102
Clark, John 1
Clarke, Dorothy 121, 204n
Clarke, Edmund 208, 209
Clarke, Mary 209
Clay, Rotha Mary 9, 37, 38
Cleaver, Samuel 208
Cleaver, Widow 202
Cleaver, William 208
Clerkenwell Workhouse 100

Clothing, gowns and livery in almshouses 62, 67, 94, 130, 132, 138, 158, 161, 166, 167, 169, 173, 189, 225, 230
Clun, Shropshire 59, 73
Coal trade, merchants 15, 86
Cobham, Kent 33, 130
Cobham, Lord. See Brooke, William
Cogan, John 88, 100
Coleshill, Warwickshire 92
Colfe, Abraham 59
College of Matrons, Salisbury 142, 144
Colleges 11, 74
Colston's Almshouses, Bristol 99
Colthurst, Edward 72
Commission for Charitable Uses 31, 189, 195–6, 215, 235
Commonwealth 34, 100, 208
Coningsby, Thomas 108
Coningsby Hospital, Hereford 159
Constable, Sir John 165
Constables 32, 33, 208, 209
Cooking in almshouses 148, 149, 158, 159, 168
Cooks, Widow 205
Cooper, Sarah 122
Cooper's Almshouse, Sedgefield 105
Cordell, Sir William 41, 82, 85
Cornwall 15, 47, 53, 93
Corporation of the Poor 34
Cosin, John, Bishop of Durham 59, 78, 86, 87, 88, 127, 160, 161, 227
Cost of founding an almshouse 30–1, 51, 57, 59, 72
Cost of living 170, 174, 177, 178
Costyn, John 175
Cottages 21, 22, 27, 31, 60, 72, 151, 154, 170, 219, 220, 229
  illegal 33, 202
  land attached to 32, 171, 221
  licensing of 21, 27, 33, 35
  prohibition of 21, 221
Coughton, Warwickshire 51, 85, 172
County almshouses 29
County gaol 28
Court of Augmentation 39
Coventry 26, 28, 35, 38, 40, 51, 53, 78, 91, 95, 102, 105, 106, 164
Cowden, Kent 168
Cox, Mary 213
Cranbrook, Kent 152
Cratfield, Suffolk 152, 167, 176

Croft, Pauline 85
Cromwell, Thomas, MP 24
Croydon, Surrey 41, 59, 97
Crust, Linda 9
Cullum, Patricia 61, 183
Cumberland 46, 49, 53
Cumberland, Countess of (Margaret Clifford) 59

Darowen, Montgomery 193
Davenport, Rev. George 59, 87
Davies, Humphrey. *See* Davis, Humphrey
Davis, Edmund 194, 195
Davis, Humphrey 1, 51, 60, 142, 164, 191, 194, 195, 197, 236
Davis, Thomas, Bishop of St Asaph's 193
Davis, Thomas (junior) 195, 196, 197, 201
Davis, Thomas and Katherine 194, 195
Davison, Ann 122–3
Davison, Dorothy 156
Dayrell, Dorothy 163
De la Pole, William and Alice, Earl and Countess of Suffolk 62, 160
Deale, Daniel 154
Delaval, Thomas 86, 106, 129
Deptford, Kent 7, 79, 99
Devon 15, 30, 47, 67
Disabled, disability 22, 25, 28, 71, 90, 103, 105, 108, 109, 110, 114, 123, 180, 204, 214
Disorderly behaviour in almshouses 81, 115, 129, 130, 131, 132, 133, 135
Dissenters, non-conformists 88, 100, 129, 208, 209, 210n
Dissolution of the monasteries, chantries, guilds and fraternities 11, 14, 22, 36, 37, 38, 39, 46, 82, 161, 174
Dollman, F. T. 10
Dorchester, Dorset 44
Dorchester on Thames, Oxfordshire 80
Dorset 44, 45, 53
Dover, Kent 92, 99, 134
Drake, Sir Francis 108
Drapers' Company 83
Drapers' Company Almshouses, Shrewsbury 120
Drapers' Homes, Margate 100
Drew, Goodwife 180
Duck, Sir John 77, 78, 104, 117, 161

Duck's Almshouse, Great Lumley 117, 122, 123
Dudley, Ambrose, Earl of Warwick 73
Dudley, Robert, Earl of Leicester 28, 29, 30, 31, 41, 59, 67, 73, 81, 83, 100, 101, 102, 108, 126, 127, 134, 160, 161, 168, 173, 226
Duke, Mary 100
Dun, Jane 88
Dunchurch, Warwickshire 51, 60
Dunck's Almshouse, Hawkhurst 123
Dunckley, Samuel 151
Dunk, Sir Thomas 95, 125
Dunne, Anne 122
Durham, City of 59, 77, 78, 86, 87, 92, 127, 128, 142, 155, 156, 161
Durham, County 15, 17, 39, 41, 43, 44, 45, 46, 47, 48, 53, 54, 58, 103, 104, 105, 107, 112, 113, 126, 129, 149, 150, 154, 171
Durham Cathedral 127, 128, 161
Dury, Ann 213
Dury, Widow 217
Dutch Republic, almshouses in 14, 113, 114
Dyer, Elizabeth 122

Eares, Edward 201
East Claydon, Buckinghamshire 154
East Farleigh, Kent 123
East Grinstead, Sussex 139n
East India Company 95
Eastbridge Hospital, Canterbury 84, 92, 104, 183
Ebbon, Thomas 60
Economic circumstances of almshouse residents prior to admission 117–26, 138, 181, 182, 201–2, 203, 204
Economy of makeshifts 3, 229
Eden, John 131
Edward VI 26
Edwards, Joyce 71
Elderly 28, 35, 90, 232, 235
Elderly poor 12, 18, 25, 71, 90, 183, 186
Elite, wealthier almshouses 9, 13, 33, 126, 132, 133, 134, 139, 140, 142, 143, 148, 160, 170, 172, 173, 181, 189, 225, 230
Elizabeth I 30, 31, 73, 160, 226
Eltham, Kent 151
Enclosure 168, 210n, 214, 223

Enclosure Agreement. *See under*
Leamington Hastings
Erlingham, Gloucestershire   102n
Essex   47, 177
Europe
almshouses in   14
poor relief in   14, 35, 64, 65
Evans, John   124
Evelyn, John   140
Ewelme, Oxfordshire   62, 83
Executors   30, 63, 78, 193, 194, 205
Exeter   47
Experience of almshouse life   13, 14, 18,
117, 132, 133, 136
Expulsion from almshouses   88, 97, 115,
128, 130, 131, 132, 135, 168, 181, 182,
186, 199, 229
Eyffler, Nicholas   42, 58, 78
Eyffler's Almshouse, Warwick   103, 114,
142, 143, 144, 147, 149, 153, 227

Falconer, Edward   116
Falconer, Nurse   116
Family and Community Historical
Research Society   13
Family support for almspeople   169,
181–2, 206
Faversham   80, 94, 95, 99, 154
Feckenham, John   94
Fennel, Griffin   214
Fillongley, Warwickshire   35
Fire. *See* Warwick, Great Fire of
Fishermen's Hospital, Great Yarmouth
99
Fishmongers' Company   99
Foad, John   80
Food, provided in almshouses   7, 62, 148,
158, 159, 169
Ford, William   78n, 116
Ford's Hospital, Coventry   40, 51, 106,
115, 116, 131, 151, 153, 164
Forebrace, Jane   115
Founders of almshouses   14, 17, 31, 41,
42, 43, 51, 55, 59, 73, 77, 91, 108, 133,
144, 225
Catholic   85
childless   58, 60
clergy   51, 59, 60, 87
gentry   44, 51, 59, 71, 74, 226
heirs of   60, 164, 191, 194, 196, 225

memorialisation of   10, 18, 42, 56,
144, 226
merchants   44, 58, 59, 160, 226
occupations of   56, 60
religious motivation of   56, 61–2, 64,
66, 81–6, 88
status enhancement of   51, 56, 73, 74,
75, 77, 78, 144, 146
women   58
Fowler, Elizabeth   153
Foxe's Book of Martyrs   81
Framlingham Poor House, Suffolk   232
Frampton, Lincolnshire   34
France   93, 200n
Frieston Hospital, Kirkthorpe   148
Frisbye, Richard   109
Frosterley, County Durham   169
Fulnetby, Thomas   99, 100
Furniture, provided in almshouses   147,
148, 158

Gainsborough, Yorkshire   83
Gardens in almshouses   13n, 156, 159,
169, 186
Garrett, Rev. John   212
Garrett, Thomas   201, 221
Gateshead, County Durham   39, 116, 124,
150, 152, 156
Geffrye, Robert   98
Geffrye Almshouses, Shoreditch   98, 133
Gender of almshouse occupants   111–17,
203, 231
Gentry   11, 15, 43, 57, 59, 60, 71, 73, 75,
77, 102, 194, 198, 210, 212, 222
Gibson, Jane   101, 156
Gift exchange, theory of   62
Gilbert Returns   49, 50
Gillham, Joseph   124
Gilpin, Bernard   83, 106, 129
Gisborne, Amy   201
Glazier   78
Gloucester   24, 28, 40, 173
God's House, Ewelme   62, 83, 90n, 127,
140, 160
Godfrey, W. H.   139
Godson, Richard   110
Goldsmith   82
Goodall, John   127, 132
Goose, Nigel   44, 53, 113
Governors and trustees of almshouses   58,
67, 78, 79, 80, 82, 86, 90, 91, 92, 100,

106, 114, 115, 121, 122, 128, 129, 130,
    131, 132, 133, 134, 136, 137, 138, 156,
    164, 165, 166, 168, 169, 186, 196, 198,
    199, 200, 201, 204, 206, 207, 208, 223,
    225, 227, 228, 231, 236
Gowns in almshouses. *See* Clothing
Gramer, James   72, 105, 151
Gratitude expected of poor   70, 129, 130,
    133, 215, 222
Gravesend, Kent   93n, 98
Great Linford, Milton Keynes   95
Great Lumley, County Durham   77, 161
Great Yarmouth, Norfolk   99
Greatham Hospital, Durham   39, 41, 107,
    108, 134, 147, 157, 158, 173
Green, Adrian   151
Greenwich   31, 41, 48n, 59, 72, 73, 82, 83,
    98, 102, 115, 118, 134, 168
Gregory, Dr David   153
Griffin, John and wife   131, 132
Griffin, Margery   114
Griffith, John   115
Grolliver, Foulke   201
Guild almshouses   7, 9, 11, 22, 40, 61, 62,
    94, 99, 119, 158, 173
Guild of the Holy Cross, Stratford upon
    Avon   40, 147, 173
Guild of the Holy Trinity and St George,
    Warwick   82
Guildford, Surrey   30, 59, 67, 165, 184
Guildhall   83, 140, 146, 147n
Guilds and fraternities   9, 11, 36, 40, 60,
    77, 79, 80, 82, 83, 147
Guilliams, Joan   205, 218
Guilliams, Margery   204–5, 218

Haarlem, the Netherlands   58n
Habitation orders   4, 6, 27, 35, 216, 217,
    219
Hackington, Kent   41, 70, 78, 134, 159
Hadleigh, Suffolk   123, 189, 222
Hall, Henry   201
Hall, Jeffrey   202
Halsham, Yorkshire   165
Harding, Dorothy   124
Hargrave, Richard   121, 148
Harrietsham, Kent   48n, 99
Harris, Thomas (almshouse founder)   125
Harris, Thomas (labourer)   121
Harrison, William   180, 181
Hawkhurst, Kent   95, 123, 124, 125

Hawkins, Sir John   41, 83, 108, 114, 128
Hawkins's Hospital, Chatham   41, 79, 82,
    83, 97, 99, 108, 114, 115, 117, 122, 128,
    130, 131, 134, 147, 180
Hawten, Thomas   216
Hawten, Widow (or Horton)   203n, 204,
    212
Hayselden, John   124
Hearth tax   47, 49, 52, 61, 118, 120, 123,
    150, 188, 203, 205, 206, 207n, 212
    exempt from   47, 48, 49, 51, 52, 118,
        123, 190, 203, 205, 207n, 212, 216,
        217, 218
    geographical differences   47, 48, 150
    number of hearths   47, 48, 203, 204, 208
Heath, Sidney   10, 139
Helmsley, North Yorkshire   59
Hemsworth, Yorkshire   173
Henley-in-Arden, Warwickshire   61
Henry, Prince of Wales   75
Henry VII   26, 59n, 147
Henry VIII   82, 161
Hereford   108, 159
Hesketh, Sir Thomas   165
Heslington, Yorkshire   165
Hetton-le-Hole, County Durham   86
Higham Ferrers Bede House,
    Northamptonshire   159
Hill, Sir Rowland   81
Hill, Warwickshire   190, 202
Hincks, Thomas   219
Holditch, Devon   63
Holgate, Robert, Archbishop of York   59,
    173
Holte, Sir Robert   75
Holte, Sir Thomas   74, 168
Holte Almshouses, Aston   146, 168
Holyhead, Wales   92
Honywood, Anthony   162
Hoo, Kent   93
Hôpital général   25
Horden, Peregrine   60, 61, 65
Horton. *See* Hawten, Widow
Hoskins, W. G.   140
Hospital. *See* Almshouse definition
Hospital of God, Greatham. *See* Greatham
    Hospital
Hospital of St Edmund King and Martyr.
    See King James' Hospital, Gateshead
Hospitals for children   7n, 91, 94, 95
Hosyer's Almshouse, Ludlow   62

Houghton-le-Spring, County Durham
    59, 83, 86, 87, 109, 161
House of Correction   24, 25, 26, 27, 28,
    29, 30, 70, 80, 95, 135, 154, 199, 228
House of Noble Poverty. *See* St Cross
    Hospital, Winchester
Housing, poor people's   3, 4, 6, 31, 151,
    152, 220
    building materials   219, 220, 221
    maintenance, repairs   156, 218
    regulation of   135, 220, 221
    sub-tenants, inmates   21, 27, 32, 33,
        34, 152, 202, 216
Housing policy   17, 18, 20, 23, 35
Housing provided for the poor   11, 18, 20,
    21, 25, 27, 33, 35, 36, 60, 61, 152, 153,
    154, 157, 216, 221
Howard, Henry, Earl of Northampton
    59, 73, 74, 85, 102, 115, 134
Howard, Lord, of Effingham   108
Howson, Brian   9, 10
Hughes, Anne   77
Hull, Yorkshire   47
Humphrey Davis Almshouse, Leamington
    Hastings   30, 51, 102, 113, 123, 125,
    135, 142, 148, 165, 167, 168, 169, 178,
    181, 182, 189–223, 227, 228, 235, 236
Hundred Hospitals   84, 236
Huntingdonshire   47
Hutchinson, Richard   128
Hutchinson, William   101, 127, 161, 169
Hutton, Matthew, Archbishop of York
    41, 59

Impotent. *See* Disabled
Independence of almshouse residents   91,
    117, 136, 142, 143, 155, 158, 159, 166,
    184, 186, 230, 231, 232, 236
Inflation   12, 18, 43, 163, 164, 166, 172,
    173, 174, 177
Ingram, George   60, 162
Inmates, lodgers in almshouses   34, 181,
    182, 186, 199
Inmates, sub-tenants in poor people's
    houses   21, 27, 32, 33, 34, 152, 202, 216
Ipsley, Warwickshire   124
Ipswich   24, 91, 93, 108
Ironmongers' Company   98, 133
Isaacson, Anne   209
Isaacson, Susannah   214
Isaacson, Thomas   203, 209

Jakenett, Thomas   60
James I   40, 73, 74, 226
Jelly, Catherine   206
Jelly, Nicholas   148, 206, 209, 212, 218
Jemmat, Samuel, Master of the Lord
    Leycester Hospital   110, 229
Jervyes, Elizabeth   135
Jesus Hospital, Canterbury   95, 110, 115,
    118, 120, 128, 130, 168, 180, 183
Johnson, Dr Samuel   146
Johnson, Widow   202
Jolles, Sir John   83
Jordan, W. K.   11, 12, 29, 30, 31, 39, 42,
    43, 44, 46, 47, 59, 60, 65, 71, 72, 79, 85,
    143, 162, 163, 164, 169, 171, 178, 194,
    226
Justices of the Peace   20, 22, 23, 27, 29,
    32, 35, 36, 71, 129, 166, 189, 215, 216,
    217, 219, 222, 229, 235

Keelmen of Newcastle upon Tyne   79, 136
Keelmen's Hospital, Newcastle upon Tyne
    79, 99, 136
Kenardington, Kent   153
Kendal, Cumbria   184
Kenilworth, Warwickshire   73, 102n, 110
Kent   15, 17, 42, 43, 44, 45, 46, 47, 48, 54,
    58, 64, 70, 88, 93, 103, 104, 105, 107,
    112, 119, 127, 149, 150, 151, 162, 171,
    178
Kepier Free Grammar School and
    Almshouse, Houghton-le-Spring   43,
    46, 83, 86, 87, 91, 95, 106, 129, 157
Kepier Hospital, Durham   37, 39
Kepier Priory, Durham   83
Killingworth, Oliver   193, 194
King, Steven   49, 170
King James' Hospital, Gateshead   39,
    116, 134, 150, 153, 226
Kingsborough, Rev.   200
Kirkthorpe, West Yorkshire   148
Kites Hardwick, Warwickshire   190, 205,
    220
Knatchbull's Act. *See* Acts of Parliament,
    1736 Act for Amending the Laws
    relating to the Settlement, Employment
    and Relief of the Poor
Knight, Margaret   115
Knollys, Sir Francis   24
Knowle, Thomas, Mayor of Faversham   80

Lady Hewley's Almshouse, York 106
Lady Leveson's Hospital, Temple Balsall
102, 107, 116, 130, 134, 144, 148, 153,
161, 167, 168, 170, 182, 204
Lamb, Magdalen 154
Lambarde, William 31, 41, 72, 79, 82, 83,
97, 98, 118, 126, 128, 168, 226
Lambe, William 42, 82, 173
Lambeth, London 60
Lancashire 46, 47, 53, 79
Langley, Anne 58
Lapworth, Warwickshire 153
Lasey, John's wife 132
Latimer, Sir Thomas and Lady Anne 63
Lawyers 60, 72, 75, 86, 100, 162, 195
Leamington Hastings, Warwickshire 1,
18, 30, 51, 60, 102, 111n, 123, 125, 135,
142, 164, 188–223, 236
Enclosure Agreement, 1665 208, 210,
218
Leamington Hastings Almshouse,
Warwickshire. See Humphrey Davis
Almshouse
Lee, London (formerly Kent) 106
Leech, Henry 131
Leicester, Earl of. See Dudley, Robert
Leigh, Dame Alice 58, 77, 81, 83, 144
Leigh, Kent 124
Leigh, Sir Thomas 58, 77, 81
Length of stay of almshouse occupants
108–9, 110
Lenham, Kent 162
Leonard, E. M. 25
Lepers 231
hospitals for 38, 39, 41, 70, 90, 103,
135, 143
Lepers' Hospital, Bath 94
Lever, Ralph 81
Lever, Thomas (Leamington Hastings)
211
Lever, Thomas, Master of Sherburn
Hospital 81
Leveson, Lady Katherine 73, 102, 121,
129, 161
Lewisham, London 59
Libraries 63, 87
Lichfield, dean of 209
Lichfield, diocese of 17, 40
Lichfield, Staffordshire 160
Lilburne, George 86, 87, 109, 161
Lilleshall, Shropshire 102

Lincoln Cathedral 209
Lincolnshire 9, 45
Linton Park Almshouses, Kent 162, 178
Livery companies 7, 36, 79, 80, 99, 177
Clothworkers' 173
Drapers' 83, 120
Fishmongers' 99
Ironmongers' 98, 133
Merchant Taylors' 175
Llanfyllin, Montgomery 191
Location of almshouses 51, 55, 61, 73,
75, 78, 135, 143, 184, 227
Lock, Mrs Samuel 117
Lodgers, inmates in almshouses 34, 181,
182, 186, 199
Lodgings 148, 152, 153, 214, 221
Lollardy 64, 84
London 17, 20, 21, 23, 25, 26, 28, 34, 35,
42, 47, 63, 77, 82, 92, 93, 94, 98, 101,
110, 174, 175, 176
City Corporation 26, 28
hospitals 24, 26, 28, 29, 36, 77, 82, 91,
92, 93, 175
livery companies 36, 79, 80, 99
Long Itchington, Warwickshire 102
Long Melford, Suffolk 41, 85
Longport, Canterbury 58, 144
Looijesteijn, Henk 113
Lord Leycester Hospital, Warwick 28, 29,
30, 31, 33, 41, 48n, 67, 81, 93, 104, 108,
109, 110, 116, 118, 126, 130, 131, 134,
140, 146, 149, 159, 167, 168, 169, 170,
171–2, 173, 181, 189, 225, 226, 229
Lowe, William 93
Lucy, Sir Francis 75
Lucy family 75, 77
Ludlow, Shropshire 62
Lunacy 90, 213, 231, 235
Lyddington Bede House, Rutland 90n,
98, 114, 116

MacFarquhar, Grace 191
Machin, John 88
Magistrates. See Justices of the Peace
Maidstone, guild almshouses 22, 61
Maidstone, Kent 62, 93, 94, 100, 124,
149, 232
Maisons Dieu 6, 61
Makepeace, Mary 220
Man, Jane 111n, 135, 182, 199, 213, 222
Man, John 194, 218, 220

Man, Thomas 182, 199, 202, 203, 206
Mancetter, Warwickshire 72, 105, 151
Mann, Widow 129
Manwood, Sir Roger 41, 70, 78, 83, 116, 134, 159, 164, 167, 226
Manwood's Hospital, Hackington 41, 115, 123, 134, 164
Margate, Kent 100
Markus, Thomas A. 146
Marlborough, Wiltshire 31
Marriage, wives in almshouses 114, 115, 116, 132, 153, 225
Marshall, Peter 67
Mary, Queen of Scots 24
Mary I 26
Mason, John 1
Masters, James 120
Masters, John 205
Masters, wardens in almshouses 38, 81, 88, 97, 110, 134, 137, 139, 144, 153, 158, 182, 189, 229, 230
Material benefits in almshouses 13, 17, 18, 91, 94, 138–71, 225, 229
Matthews, Elizabeth 204
Matthews, Faith 203, 204, 213
Matthews, John 204, 208, 219
Matthews, Thomas 203, 204, 213, 220
Maunt, Goodwife 153
Maunton, Thomas 97
Mauss, Marcel 62
Maynard and Cotton Almshouses, Canterbury 119, 120
Mayor of London 63, 64, 77, 81, 82
McIntosh, Marjorie Keniston 5, 7, 11, 12, 14, 24, 37, 38, 39, 40, 41, 42, 44, 46, 61, 62, 65, 71, 123, 189, 222
Medieval hospitals and almshouses 6, 8, 9, 10, 15, 38, 46, 57, 61, 70, 84, 90, 92, 103, 111, 119, 127, 133, 140, 143, 148, 157, 172, 226
  corrodians in 38, 119
  decay of 38
  for lepers 38, 39, 41, 70, 90, 103, 135, 143
  for pilgrims 39, 70, 92, 103
  loss of 11, 37, 38, 40
  monastic institutions 11, 40, 93, 157
  secular 11
  survival of 11, 17, 37, 38, 39, 40, 41, 46, 47, 84

Memorialisation 10, 18, 29, 63, 66, 67–71, 89, 198
Merchant Venturers' Almshouses, Bristol 99
Merchants 11, 43, 57, 59, 60, 63, 71, 77, 78, 79, 82, 99, 132, 136, 160, 194
Middlesex 47
Miller, George 120
Milton, Kent 93n, 98
Minimum subsistence budget for an almsperson 18, 174–9
Mixed economy of welfare 14, 19, 188, 197
Monasteries 11, 20, 38, 119
Monastic infirmaries 93
Monastic lands 74, 75, 77
Monks and nuns 174
Moory, Edward 106n
Morden, Sir John 132
Morden College, Blackheath 99, 132, 134, 144
Morgan's Almshouses, Frosterley 169
Mortmain 30
Muldrew, Craig 170
Municipal reform 235
Municipal Reform Act. See Acts of Parliament, 1835 The Municipal Corporations Act

Nantwich workhouse 30
Napleton, Thomas 99
Neale, Nicholas 108
Neglect and abuse of almshouses 54, 119, 131, 133, 137, 164, 195, 196
Netherlands, The 58, 113
New Cobham College, Kent 33, 41, 80, 82, 83, 84, 95, 97, 101, 103, 110, 118, 122, 130, 134, 143
New Poor Law 23
New Romney, Kent 95, 124
Newcastle upon Tyne 46, 79, 86, 99, 110, 136
Newcombe, Thomas 60
Newdigate, Sir Richard 155, 162
Nicholas Chamberlaine's Almshouse, Bedworth 51, 59, 88, 100
Nobles, nobility 15, 59, 73, 75, 102, 226
Non-conformists, dissenters 88, 100, 129, 208, 209, 210n
Norfolk 47, 102, 115, 162, 171
North, Rev. Oliver 59, 95

North America, almshouses in   232
Northallerton, North Yorkshire   39
Northampton, Earl of. *See* Howard, Henry
Northumberland   46
Norwich   24, 40, 47
Nottinghamshire   46n
Number of almshouses   17, 39, 44, 45, 47,
    53, 54, 57, 86
  increase in   30, 37, 42, 44, 46, 53
  regional difference in   40, 46, 47, 51,
    55, 79
Number of places in almshouses   44, 53, 72
  in relation to the over-60 population
    44, 47, 48, 53
Nuneaton, Warwickshire   61, 183
Nurses   51, 116, 119, 158, 159, 165, 180
Nursing care   97, 132, 136, 169, 181, 182,
    213, 221

Oakley, Adam   203, 219
Oakley, Jane   203
Occupants of almshouses   13, 17, 18, 89,
    90–125, 137, 200–7, 228
  age of   91, 103, 106, 107, 108, 111,
    116, 201, 231
  children   91, 94, 95, 97, 103, 136, 225,
    235
  family members   95, 97, 103, 122, 169,
    182
  founders' relatives   100, 101
  gender of   111–17, 203, 231
  length of stay of almshouse occupants
    108–9, 110
  lodgers, inmates   34, 181, 182, 186,
    199
  receiving poor relief   122, 182
Oken, Thomas   42, 58, 78, 79, 82, 129,
    160
Oken's almshouses, Warwick   107, 113,
    122, 143, 144, 151, 167, 182, 227
Oken's Charity, Warwick   58, 79
Old age   13, 22, 71, 103–11, 113, 114, 124,
    129, 180
Old Poor Law   4, 216
Oldcastle, Sir John   64, 73
Oliver, George   122
On-site supervision in almshouses   132,
    133, 134, 135, 136, 230
Orme, Nicholas, and Margaret Webster
    15, 38
Oudemannenhuis   14, 114

Oudevrouwenhuis   14
Out-pensioners of almshouses   38, 107,
    109, 113, 157, 206, 207, 214
Over, Elizabeth (widow)   220
Over, John (Carpenter)   209
Over, John (Papist)   209
Over, John (various)   193, 196, 215, 221,
    222
Over, Matthew (or Richard)   203n, 207
Over, Matthew   1, 195, 196, 236
Over, Richard   169, 200
Over, Widow (various)   169, 203n, 212
Overseers' accounts   6, 122, 123, 155, 166,
    167, 176, 188, 202, 203, 204, 205, 212,
    216, 219, 220, 222
Overseers of the poor   8, 14, 27, 33, 35,
    95, 124, 156, 175, 177, 195, 205, 208,
    210, 211, 212, 213, 214, 216, 217, 218,
    220, 222, 229
Oxford   24

Pain, Elizabeth   122
Palace Green Almshouses, Durham   87,
    127, 142, 143, 161, 169, 170
Palmer, Thomas   109
Pardy, Agnes   182
Parish almshouses   8, 9, 60
Parish church   22, 60, 67, 75, 83, 135, 143,
    155, 184, 190, 191, 193, 198, 210, 212
Parish clergy   95, 134, 135, 209, 210, 211,
    212, 225
Parish housing   6, 7, 9, 11, 21, 27, 32, 33,
    35, 57, 61, 72, 190, 216–21, 229
Parish officials   27, 32, 72, 93, 122, 124,
    125, 134, 135, 166, 196, 214, 225, 227,
    235
Parish paupers admitted to almshouses
    33, 118, 122, 123, 125, 167, 204, 206
Parish paupers excluded from almshouses
    125, 231
Parish poor box   7, 193
Parish stock   72, 197, 210
Parker, Matthew, Archbishop of
    Canterbury   39, 81, 82, 84, 92
Parliament   23, 24, 25, 31, 82, 84, 86
Parliament, Member of   75, 86, 197n
Paston family   63
Patrick, Joan   120, 149
Patrick, Thomas   120

Patronage, exercise of   80, 89, 102, 103, 109, 118, 133, 137, 196, 198, 207, 222, 228

Patrons of almshouses   29, 102, 103, 110, 118, 186, 198, 207

Pearce, Raphael   88

Pedley, Alice   219

Pedley, Nathaniel   219

Pedley, Richard   201

Pedley, William   219

Pelling, Margaret   105

Pembroke, Countess of (Lady Anne Clifford)   59

Pembury, Kent   162

Perkins, George   193

Pestell, William and Mary   122

Phelps, Brown and Hopkins   172

Philipot's almshouse, Eltham   151

Phipps, Bridget   121, 204n

Phipps, Dr William   121

Phipps, William (Canterbury)   120

Pickering, Alice   116

Pigeon, Roger   144

Pike, John   194

Pilgrims   39, 92

Pillay, Mary   154

Pinnock, Henry   98

Pisford, Wiliam   78n, 116

Pittington, County Durham   156

Plague   21, 94

Poor, the   37, 38, 57, 66, 210, 212, 223, 235
    attitudes to   14, 20, 22, 34, 49, 64, 183, 215–16, 222, 223, 231–2, 236
    deserving and undeserving   2, 5, 13, 70, 71, 183, 184, 215–16, 222, 228
    material lives, living conditions, experience of   3, 14, 21, 151–2, 175, 180, 184, 186, 219, 229

Poor relief   2, 4, 5, 11, 17, 22, 41, 46, 57, 61, 63, 80, 118, 122, 123, 166, 178, 212, 213, 214, 216, 217, 221
    amounts paid out in   5, 175, 176, 177, 218
    badges for recipients of   34, 168
    boarding out poor people   33, 124, 152, 204, 205, 214, 217
    burial costs   124, 206
    clothing   176, 206, 214
    collectors for   22
    expenditure on   5, 34, 49, 197, 214, 215

fuel   80, 123, 175, 176
    house repairs   205, 206, 217, 218, 220
    housing, rent payments   6, 27, 123, 155, 156, 218, 220
    in Europe   14, 35, 64, 65
    late medieval   5, 12, 61, 65
    parish poor rates   11, 30, 32, 49, 63, 215, 223, 235
    rate-based system   27, 36, 65, 189, 231
    recipients of   33, 35, 118, 122, 123, 124, 166, 167, 182, 201, 228, 229
    regional differences in   49, 170

Poor Travellers' Rest, Rochester   92

Poors Plot Charity, Leamington Hastings   188, 205, 208, 209, 210–16, 217, 221, 222, 223

Popularity of almshouses   28, 45, 46, 55, 57, 225

Porter, Mary   152

Porter, Stephen   133

Poslingford, Suffolk   152, 176

Possessions of almshouse occupants   121, 122, 148, 149

Pots, John   117

Poverty   29
    concern about   5, 55
    life-cycle   12, 105
    nature and scale of   3, 4, 5
    regional differences   49, 51
    response to   5, 11, 22, 30, 40, 41, 53, 56, 70, 226, 236

Prayers
    for the dead   62, 63, 67, 82, 127, 129
    in almshouses   62, 82–3, 117, 127, 128, 129, 144, 160, 165, 181

Prescott, Elizabeth   10, 37, 42, 44, 46, 64, 86, 139, 140, 151, 159

Previous occupations of almshouse residents   98, 118, 119, 120, 153

Priory Almshouses, Alcester   60, 225

Prisons, prisoners   63, 77, 228

Privilege, almshouses as places of   28, 117, 173, 187, 224, 225, 228

Privy Council   23, 28, 41, 75

Public lavatory   63

Puckering, Sir John   75

Puckering, Sir Thomas   75, 77, 98

Purgatory   62, 63, 64

Purpose of almshouses   1, 91, 125, 127, 129, 199, 226

as a response to social need   12, 18,
    37, 41, 42, 43, 49, 51, 54, 55, 88, 224,
    226, 227
as chantries   11, 40, 62, 84, 103, 127
enhance status of founder   51, 56, 73,
    74, 75, 77, 78, 144, 146
memorialisation   10, 18, 63, 66, 67–71,
    89
Purt, Thomas   109
Pynder, Franciscus   97

Quarter sessions   6, 27, 29, 33, 126, 135,
    154, 188, 199, 204, 209, 216, 217, 219,
    221, 222, 230
Queen Elizabeth Hospital, Greenwich   31,
    41, 72, 82, 83, 98, 118, 134, 168
Queens' College, Cambridge   191, 193,
    195
Quested, Mark   99
Quested's Almshouse, Harrietsham   48n

Rachell, Ralph   180
Radway, Elizabeth and Ann   154
Ragdale, Owen   42
Rawlins, Anthony   72
Reading   25
Reformation   28, 51, 65, 66
    effects of   11, 39, 57, 62
Refuge for unmarried mothers   63
Religious observance in almshouses   62,
    65, 82–3, 85, 89, 117, 127, 129, 161, 199
Responsibility
    civic   56, 75, 78
    of land ownership   56, 74, 76, 102
Restoration of the Monarchy   59, 87, 88,
    160, 209
Rexroth, Frank   158
Reynolds, John   124, 125
Richmond, Colin   63
Robinson, Barbara   123
Robinson, Isabel   154
Rochester   92, 94, 95, 128
Rochester Bridge Wardens   80
Romaldkirk, County Durham   101, 105,
    127, 161, 169
Rosenthal, Joel   61
Rothwell, Northamptonshire   42
Royal Hospital, Chelsea   59n, 227
Royal Hospital for Seamen at Greenwich.
    See Royal Naval Hospital

Royal hospitals and almshouses   26, 48n,
    59n, 99, 146, 147, 227, 239n
Royal Naval Hospital, Greenwich   48n,
    99, 146, 227
Rubin, Miri   60, 64
Rugby, Warwickshire   42, 51, 70, 81, 110,
    134, 135, 160, 172, 190
Rugby School, Warwickshire   81, 95, 134,
    142
Rules in almshouses   9, 34, 82, 91, 93, 118,
    126–35, 157, 158, 168, 180, 182, 183,
    186, 199, 200, 225, 229, 230
Rules, penalties for breach of
    expulsion   88, 97, 115, 128, 130, 131,
        132, 135, 168, 181, 182, 186, 199, 229
    fines, loss of allowance   97, 98, 115,
        128, 129, 130, 131, 135, 165, 182,
        186, 229
Rushall, Mary (Goody)   205, 213
Rushall, William   222
Russell, Richard   209
Russell, Widow   203n
Ryland, David and Mary   209

Sackville College, East Grinstead   139n
Sailors   7, 79, 93, 99, 108, 114, 128, 146,
    161, 227
St Asaph's, diocese of, Wales   193
St Bartholomew's Hospital, Chatham   91
St Bartholomew's Hospital, Gloucester
    28, 40, 173
St Bartholomew's Hospital, London   26,
    77, 91, 93
St Bartholomew's Hospital, Oxford   157
St Bartholomew's Hospital, Sandwich
    119
St Cross Hospital, Winchester   140, 158
St Edmund's Hospital, Gateshead. See
    King James' Hospital
St Giles' (Great) Hospital, Norwich   40
St Giles' Hospital, Durham. See Kepier
    Hospital
St John, Nicholas, MP   31
St John's Hospital, Barnard Castle   39,
    150
St John's Hospital, Canterbury   39, 84,
    88, 97, 109, 120, 157
St John's Hospital, Coventry   38
St John's Hospital, Lichfield   160
St John's Hospital, Sandwich   117, 180

St John the Baptist's Hospital, Warwick 38
St John the Baptist and Thomas the Martyr Hospital, Stamford 84
St Martin-in-the-Fields parish almshouses, London 8
St Mary Magdalene Hospital, Newcastle upon Tyne 91
St Mary's Hospital, Chichester 140–1
St Michael's Hospital, Warwick 38, 77
St Nicholas Harbledown, Canterbury 39, 97, 109, 113, 135, 157
St Sepulchre's Priory, Warwick 38, 75
St Stephen's Hospital, Hackington. *See* Manwood's Hospital
St Thomas's Hospital, Canterbury 39
St Thomas's Hospital, London 26, 77, 91
Salisbury, Wiltshire 24
Sancroft, William, Archbishop of Canterbury 87
Sandes Hospital, Kendal 184
Sandwich, Kent 70, 99, 100, 106, 117, 119
Savoy Hospital, London 26, 59n, 91, 92
Schoolmasters 73, 79, 80, 95, 124, 134, 181, 191, 193, 194, 205, 210, 228
Schools 29, 42, 57, 70, 80, 87, 95, 110, 134, 194
Scotland 93
Scotten, Mary (Widow) 169, 203n, 204, 205
Seamen's Hospital, Dover 99, 134
Seckerston, Ralph, MP 26
Sedgefield, County Durham 105
Sedgely, Thomas 193
Serlys, Robert 72
Servants 89, 95, 100, 101, 102, 114, 121, 122, 153
Servants in almshouses 95, 114, 132, 149, 158, 225
Settlement 20, 21, 32, 33, 34, 217, 228
  disputes 4, 217, 221
Sevenoaks, Kent 70, 95
Shakespeare, William 73, 84
Shamwell Hundred 98
Sharp, Buchanan 214
Sharpe, Margaret 123
Shenley, Buckinghamshire 165
Sherburn Hospital, Durham 39, 41, 81, 88, 93, 106, 107, 108, 111, 114, 134, 135, 147, 149, 153, 157, 158, 173, 226
Sheriff, Lawrence 42, 81, 142, 160, 172

Shoemaker 98, 124
Shotesham, Norfolk 102, 115
Shrewsbury, Shropshire 120
Shropshire 46n
Shustoke, Warwickshire 51
Sidney, John Shelley 103
Size of almshouses 71–2, 139, 227
Slack, Paul 5, 12, 13, 24, 35, 90, 231
Slaymaker 216
Smith, Henry 209
Smith, John and Ann 58
Smith, Richard 108, 115
Social need, almshouses as a response to 12, 18, 37, 41, 42, 43, 49, 51, 54, 55, 88, 224, 226, 227
Soldiers 29, 39, 101
  disabled 28, 103, 108, 126, 161, 226, 227
  discharged 20, 108
Somerset 44, 47
Southam, Warwickshire 152, 190
Southlands Hospital, New Romney 95
Spencer, Earl 102
Spillman, Edmund 108
Squatters 31, 32
Squire, Ralph 92
Squire, Thomas 193, 194, 195, 210
Stafford, Thomas 165
Stafford family 198
Staffordshire 73
Stamford, Lincolnshire 41, 84, 90n
Standard of living 150
  in almshouses 150, 160, 162, 163, 171–87, 225
  of the poor 151
Stanley, Joseph 133
Stipends in almshouses 18, 33, 62, 72, 86, 115, 117, 118, 122, 132, 138, 158–74, 177, 178, 214, 225
  additional payments to almspeople 134, 165, 181
  changes in 164, 165, 171, 173, 178, 200
  differences between men and women 165, 170, 231
  geographical differences 170
  insufficient 178, 181, 186, 229
  lack of 160, 162, 178, 186, 217, 225, 229
  late medieval 62, 158, 160, 172, 173
  loss of stipend, fines 97, 98, 115, 128, 129, 130, 131, 135, 165, 182, 186, 229

Stone, Robert 80

Stoneleigh, Warwickshire 51, 58, 81, 144,
    151, 204

Stoneleigh Abbey, Warwickshire 77

Stowe, John 102, 181

Stratford-upon-Avon almshouses 22, 40,
    51, 97, 102n, 109, 119, 120, 147, 149,
    173, 182, 204

Stromble, Oliver 119

Strype's *Life of Archbishop Parker* 81

Stunt, Elizabeth 123

Styleman, John 95

Styles, John 167, 168, 175

Suffolk 47, 152, 174, 175, 177

Suffolk, Earl and Countess of. *See* De la
    Pole, William and Alice

Sunderland 86, 100

Surrey 126

Sutton-at-Hone, Kent 156

Sutton Valence, Kent 42, 82, 173

Symson, Mary 109

Tailor 98

Tamworth, Staffordshire (part formerly
    Warwickshire) 51

Tangiers 93

Tarsey, Ann 218

Tasburgh, John 63

Tayler, Widow 155

Taylor, Ann 152

Temple Balsall, Warwickshire 51, 73, 102,
    107, 116

Terling, Essex 155, 162, 174, 175, 176

Tewart, Elizabeth 101

Thane, Pat 181

Thomas Iddenden's Charity, Hawkhurst
    124

Thompson, Ann 152

Thompson, Eleanor 216, 217

Thompson, William 217

Thomson, J. A. F. 43, 65

Throckmorton, Sir Robert 85, 172

Thurrock, Essex 110

Tilden, John and Ann 103

Tiverton, Devon 42, 144

Tomkins, Alannah 13, 14, 15, 136, 184,
    186, 224

Tomlinson, Widow 155

Tonbridge, Kent 176

Tooley, Henry 108

Tooley's Almshouse, Ipswich 93, 108

Town corporations 11, 23, 24–5, 29, 39,
    40, 51, 56, 60, 61, 75, 78, 80, 83, 95, 99,
    102, 119, 120, 124, 131, 133, 134, 164,
    173, 180, 182, 225

Travellers 29, 92, 93, 231
    almshouses for 29, 38, 61, 70, 90, 91,
    92

Travellers' Rest, Coleshill 92

Travellers' Rest, Rochester 92

Trentham, Staffordshire 102

Trevor, Sir Thomas, Baron of the
    Exchequer 1, 30, 191, 195, 196, 197,
    198, 202, 204, 236

Trevor, Sir Thomas II 196n, 198, 210, 220

Trinity Hospital, Aylesford 134

Trinity Hospital, Greenwich 48n, 59, 102,
    114, 115, 134, 139n, 149, 158, 225

Trinity House Almshouses, Deptford 7,
    79, 99

Trollope, Anthony 13, 111, 189

Trustees of almshouses. *See* Governors and
    trustees

Tue, Ann 167, 204, 205, 217

Turley, William 125

Turner, Joseph 212, 213, 217, 218

Turner, Widow (Durham) 155

Turner, Widow (Leamington Hastings)
    203n, 217

Twiggar, Jane 203, 206, 222

Twiggar, Nicholas 212

Twiggar, Richard 203

Twycrosse, Agnes 182

Urchfont, Wiltshire 152

Vagabonds, rogues 25, 28, 29, 135

Vagrants, vagrancy 20, 21, 22, 23, 24, 25,
    26, 28, 29, 32, 70, 91, 93, 108, 226, 228,
    236

Van Leeuwen, Marco 198

Vaughn, John 130

Verney, Edmund 154

Virgin Mary Hospital, Newcastle upon
    Tyne 110

Visitations of almshouses 29, 164, 229

Vives, Juan Louis 64

Wakeley, Daniell 120

Waldron, John 42, 67, 144

Wales, Tim 5, 170

Walford, Thomas 194

Walker, Margaret 109
Wallett, Elizabeth 120
Walpole St Peters, Norfolk 169
Walsham, Alexandra 84
Walton, Richard 1
Walton, Timothy 152
Ward, Widow 124
Wardell, John 122
Wardens, masters in almshouses 38, 81,
    88, 97, 110, 134, 137, 139, 144, 153, 158,
    182, 189, 229, 230
Warner, John, Bishop of Rochester 100
Warton, Lancashire 41, 59
Warwick 22, 28, 29, 31, 34, 38, 41, 42,
    51, 53, 58, 59, 60, 73, 75, 77, 78, 79, 82,
    83, 98, 102, 103, 107, 108, 122, 127, 129,
    135, 142, 143, 144, 152, 160, 182
    Earl of 73, 103
    Great Fire of, 1694 53, 113, 122, 143
Warwickshire 1, 15, 17, 40, 42, 43, 44,
    45, 46, 47, 48, 49, 51, 53, 58, 60, 71, 74,
    103, 104, 105, 107, 112, 113, 126, 144,
    149, 150, 151, 154, 161, 171, 190, 191,
    198, 204
Watson, Thomas 208
Watts, Margery 34, 182
Watts, Richard 92, 94
Wealth
    availability of 51, 57, 89
    disparities in 49, 53
Wealthier, elite almshouses 9, 13, 33, 126,
    132, 133, 134, 139, 140, 142, 143, 148,
    160, 170, 172, 173, 181, 189, 225, 230
Weaver 98
Webb, Beatrice and Sidney 35
Wedon, Thomas 163
Welfare 14, 35, 224
    local economy of 14, 18, 188, 189,
        197, 200, 214, 222, 227, 228
    system 14, 20, 29, 35, 226
Welfare policy 41, 43, 70, 226. See also
    Housing policy
West, Robert 58
West Farleigh, Kent 59, 95
West Malling, Kent 124
West Orchard, Coventry 51, 102
Weste, Mary 93
Westerham, Kent 72
Westgate Almshouses, Warwick 34, 77,
    182
Westminster 147, 175

Westmorland 40, 46
Wheatley, Thomas 95
Wheeler, Mary 119
Wheeler, Richard and wife 203n
Wheler, Dame Dorothy 200, 207
Wheler, Sir William 200, 221
Whetstone, Francis 110
Whitehead, Mr 124
Whitehead, Widow 212
Whitgift, John, Archbishop of Canterbury
    39, 41, 59, 79, 84, 97, 104, 182, 183
Whittington, Richard 63, 64, 78
Whyte, William 146
Wigston, Leicestershire 87
Wigston, William 78n, 116
Wilcox, Jeffrey (Nicholas) 202
Wilcox, John 201
William III 110
William and Mary 146, 227
Willingham by Stow, Lincs 9
Willoughby, Warwickshire 154
Willoughby, William 61, 183
Wills and inventories 31, 58, 63, 70, 164,
    171, 172, 183, 188, 191, 193, 194, 195,
    204, 209
    of almshouse residents 119, 120, 121,
        148, 149, 204
Wilson, James 135
Wilson, Robert 131
Wiltshire 31, 152
Winchester 31
Winston, County Durham 156
Women in almshouses, position of 113,
    114, 116, 117, 136, 153, 230, 231
Woodburne, Widow 152
Woolwich, London 82, 105
Worcester 144
Worcester, diocese of 17, 40
Work 20, 25
    employment of almspeople 61, 62, 95,
        97, 98, 110, 111, 116, 117, 180, 181,
        182, 225, 235
    importance of 20, 21, 70, 98
    provision of, for the poor 24, 25, 30,
        70, 80, 94, 211
Work schemes 29, 34, 98
Workhouse Test Act. See Acts of
    Parliament, 1723 Act for Amending
    the Laws relating to the Settlement,
    Employment and Relief of the Poor

Workhouses   6, 14, 23, 24, 29, 30, 34, 35,
    36, 54, 70, 114, 125, 154, 158, 232, 235,
    236
Worme, John   107
Wotton-under-Edge, Gloucestershire   102n
Wren, Sir Christopher   132, 146
Wrightson, Keith and Levine, David   155,
    162, 174–7

Wrott, Katherine   156
Wycliffe, John   64
Wye, Kent   72, 103

Yoakley, Michael   100
York   47, 106
Yorkshire   45, 46n, 47, 54, 59, 144, 148,
    162, 171, 183

PEOPLE, MARKETS, GOODS:
ECONOMIES AND SOCIETIES IN HISTORY

ISSN: 2051-7467

PREVIOUS TITLES

1. *Landlords and Tenants in Britain, 1440–1660:*
Tawney's Agrarian Problem *Revisited*
edited by Jane Whittle, 2013

2. *Child Workers and Industrial Health in Britain, 1780–1850*
Peter Kirby, 2013

3. *Publishing Business in Eighteenth-Century England*
James Raven, 2014

4. *The First Century of Welfare:*
Poverty and Poor Relief in Lancashire, 1620–1730
Jonathan Healey, 2014

5. *Population, Welfare and Economic Change in Britain 1290–1834*
edited by Chris Briggs, P. M. Kitson and S. J. Thompson, 2014

6. *Crises in Economic and Social History: A Comparative Perspective*
edited by A. T. Brown, Andy Burn and Rob Doherty, 2015

7. *Slavery Hinterland: Transatlantic Slavery and*
Continental Europe, 1680–1850
edited by Felix Brahm and Eve Rosenhaft, 2016

Lightning Source UK Ltd.
Milton Keynes UK
UKHW022146290120
357834UK00004B/220

WARD RIVER PRESS

Cover: www.headdesign.co.uk

 eBook available

Inside those walls was a man, as young as I was, learning how to become a man of God. He owns my heart to this day.

Levi's Gift tells the story of Lena and her daughter Mattie who has just given birth to a stillborn son. Following Mattie's spiral into depression, Lena takes her from their home in America to Italy in an attempt to rescue her and rekindle in her the sense of family and identity she lost after the death of her child.

But this requires Lena to reveal what she experienced as a young woman in Italy – the love she has secretly treasured all her life.

She hopes that by encountering the past together, they can find hope for the future.

Praise for *The Secret Son*

'With its many twists and turns this unusual and absorbing book takes a reader on a touching journey to an unpredictable ending' – *Woman's Way*

'A heartfelt debut' – *Irish Examiner*

'Phenomenal' – *writing.ie*

JENNIFER BURKE won Poolbeg Press and TV3's Write a Bestseller competition in 2013 with her first novel, *The Secret Son*. She has also contributed a short story to the book *If I Was a Child Again*, a collection of short stories from Irish writers published in 2013 in aid of Barnardos. In 2012 she had a short story published in the *From the Well* anthology.

Jennifer is an active member of the Irish Writers' Centre and was shortlisted in 2012, 2013 and 2014 in the Fish Publishing Flash Fiction competition.

www.wardriverpress.com

ISBN 978-1842236291

9 781842 236291